Struggling for Leadership: Antwerp-Rotterdam Port Competition between 1870–2000

Contributions to Economics

http://www.springer.de/cgi-bin/search_book.pl?series=1262

Georg Bol/Gholamreza Nakhaeizadeh/
Karl-Heinz Vollmer (Eds.)
Risk Measurements, Econometrics and Neural Networks
1998. ISBN 3-7908-1152-1

Joachim Winter
Investment and Exit Decisions at the Plant Level
1998. ISBN 3-7908-1154-8

Bernd Meyer
Intertemporal Asset Pricing
1999. ISBN 3-7908-1159-9

Uwe Walz
Dynamics of Regional Integration
1999. ISBN 3-7908-1185-8

Michael Carlberg
European Monetary Union
1999. ISBN 3-7908-1191-2

Giovanni Galizzi/
Luciano Venturini (Eds.)
Vertical Relationships and Coordination in the Food System
1999. ISBN 3-7908-1192-0

Gustav A. Horn/Wolfgang Scheremet/
Rudolf Zwiener
Wages and the Euro
1999. ISBN 3-7908-1199-8

Dirk Willer
The Development of Equity Capital Markets in Transition Economies
1999. ISBN 3-7908-1198-X

Karl Matthias Weber
Innovation Diffusion and Political Control of Energy Technologies
1999. ISBN 3-7908-1205-6

Heike Link et al.
The Costs of Road Infrastructure and Congestion in Europe
1999. ISBN 3-7908-1201-3

Simon Duindam
Military Conscription
1999. ISBN 3-7908-1203-X

Bruno Jeitziner
Political Economy of the Swiss National Bank
1999. ISBN 3-7908-1209-9

Irene Ring et al. (Eds.)
Regional Sustainability
1999. ISBN 3-7908-1233-1

Katharina Müller/Andreas Ryll/
Hans-Jürgen Wagener (Eds.)
Transformation of Social Security: Pensions in Central-Eastern Europe
1999. ISBN 3-7908-1210-2

Stefan Traub
Framing Effects in Taxation
1999. ISBN 3-7908-1240-4

Pablo Coto-Millán
Utility and Production
1999. ISBN 3-7908-1153-X

Frank Riedel
Imperfect Information and Investor Heterogeneity in the Bond Market
2000. ISBN 3-7908-1247-1

Kirsten Ralf
Business Cycles
2000. ISBN 3-7908-1245-5

Michele Bagella/Leonardo Becchetti (Eds.)
The Competitive Advantage of Industrial Districts
2000. ISBN 3-7908-1254-4

Frank Bohn
Monetary Union and Fiscal Stability
2000. ISBN 3-7908-1266-8

Jaime Behar
Cooperation and Competition in a Common Market
2000. ISBN 3-7908-1280-3

Michael Malakellis
Integrated Macro-Micro-Modelling Under Rational Expectations
2000. ISBN 3-7908-1274-9

Stefan Baumgärtner
Ambivalent Joint Production and the Natural Environment
2000. ISBN 3-7908-1290-0

Henri Capron, Wim Meeusen (Eds.)
The National Innovation System of Belgium
2000. ISBN 3-7908-1308-7

Tobias Miarka
Financial Intermediation and Deregulation
2000. ISBN 3-7908-1307-9

Chisato Yoshida
Illegal Immigration and Economic Welfare
2000. ISBN 3-7908-1315-X

continued on page 335

Reginald Loyen · Erik Buyst
Greta Devos (Eds.)

Struggling for Leadership: Antwerp-Rotterdam Port Competition between 1870–2000

With 44 Figures and 40 Tables

Physica-Verlag
A Springer-Verlag Company

Series Editors
Werner A. Müller
Martina Bihn

Editors
Reginald Loyen
Professor Dr. Erik Buyst
University of Leuven
Center for Economic Studies
Naamsestraat 69
3000 Leuven
Belgium
reginald.loyen@econ.kuleuven.ac.be
erik.buyst@econ.kuleuven.ac.be

Professor Dr. Greta Devos
University of Antwerp
Center for Business History
Prinsstraat 13
2000 Antwerp
Belgium
greta.devos@ufsia.ac.be

ISSN 1431-1933
ISBN 3-7908-1524-1 Physica-Verlag Heidelberg New York

Cataloging-in-Publication Data applied for
Die Deutsche Bibliothek – CIP-Einheitsaufnahme
Struggling for leadership: Antwerp-Rotterdam port competition between 1870–2000; proceedings of the International Conference on Comparative Antwerp-Rotterdam Port History, held at Antwerp, 10–11 May, 2001 / ed.: Reginald Loyen ... – Heidelberg: Physica-Verl., 2003
(Contributions to economics)
ISBN 3-7908-1524-1

Physica-Verlag Heidelberg New York
a member of BertelsmannSpringer Science+Business Media GmbH

Softcover Design: Erich Kirchner, Heidelberg

SPIN 10888222 88/2202-5 4 3 2 1 0 – Printed on acid-free and non-aging paper

Preface

The present volume contains the proceedings of an international conference on the economic history of the seaports of Antwerp and Rotterdam (1870-2000). This venue was held at Antwerp on 10-11 May 2001 and was hosted by the Antwerp Port Authority.

This international conference aimed at confronting the development of both ports. In the course of the last century and a half, economic growth in the ports of Antwerp and Rotterdam has been staggering. Maritime economic historians, economists and geographers alike have investigated the development of both ports extensively, but separately. So far, only a limited number of attempts have been made to analyse Rotterdam-Antwerp port history from a comparative perspective. The papers presented at the conference provide a challenging starting point to ascertain how and why both ports reacted differently to virtually the same economic and political stimuli. By bringing together both historians, economists and lawyers with different fields of interest, we have attempted to put the history of the ports of Antwerp and Rotterdam in a broader international and comparative perspective.

The conference's "secondary" aim was to present the final results of a four-year research project into the twentieth century history of the port of Antwerp. After four years, all participating researchers agreed that the need for a thorough, comparative and up to date scientific survey of the development of the port of Antwerp was very high. Simultaneously the conference introduced a new, two-year comparative research project on the history of the ports of Antwerp and Rotterdam.

- The four-year project actually started in 1997. The Fund for Scientific Research - Flanders (FWO) funded three full-time researchers, while the Antwerp Port Authority paid for another extra researcher. The project's official title read: "functional shifts in the port of Antwerp 1900-1994 with attention to macro-economic, micro-economic, political-institutional and social aspects" (hence "functional shift project"). In short, the project aimed at providing an historical understanding of how the port of Antwerp managed to develop from a mono-functional port at the dawn of the twentieth century to a multifunctional port today. In order to meet this objective, a multidisciplinary approach was deemed most suited and facilitated a division of the workload into four more or less equal determinants of port development: macro-economic aspects (i.e. cargo flows; University of Leuven), micro-economic aspects (i.e. land policy; University of Antwerp), political-institutional aspects (University of Gent) and employment (University of Gent). Additionally, two researchers (University of Antwerp) worked on company networks and on an econometric analysis of throughput. Each researcher's final results have been reproduced in the present volume.
- From its conception, the functional shift project concentrated on Antwerp only. This also turned out to be its main weakness. Therefore this conference had a marked comparative dimension. Firstly, this allowed researchers to better assess Antwerp's historical development. Secondly, it introduced the two-year Antwerp-Rotterdam research project, which started in 2001. This endeavour in-

volved the universities of Leuven and Rotterdam and received funds of the Flemish Dutch Research Committee (VNC). Officially known as the "Rotterdam and Antwerp: a century and a half of port competition in the Rhine-Scheldt-Meuse delta"-project, it aimed more specifically at comparing the development of the port of Rotterdam and the port of Antwerp (1860-2000). Attempting to ascertain why certain cargo flows choose Antwerp and not Rotterdam (or vice versa), the Rotterdam-Antwerp project has - in a nutshell - been focusing on cargo-flows, port dues, handling charges, freight rates and value added creation.

We would like to thank Dr. Jan Blomme of the Antwerp Port Authority for kindly hosting the conference and for his continuous enthusiastic support. Additionally, we kindly acknowledge the generous support of our sponsors: the Fund for Scientific Research - Flanders (FWO), the Flemish Dutch Research Committee (VNC) and the Antwerp Port Authority. We are grateful to Professor Lars Scholl, Professor Jaap Bruijn and Professor David M. Williams who have supported our research efforts from the very beginning. A special word of thanks to the members of the scientific committee, presiding over the conference: Dr. Ferry de Goey, Professor Hilde Meersman, Professor Paul van de Laar, Professor Eddy Van de Voorde and Professor Eric Van Haute. The conference was also well served by commentators on the individual papers. Therefore a sincere thank you to the many referees: Professor David Starkey, Dr. Honoré Paelinck, Professor Hugo Roos, Dr. Adrian Jarvis, Professor Sarah Palmer, Professor Fernand Suykens, Dr. John Barzman, Professor Gordon Jackson and Professor Lewis Fischer. A number of people helped out at more than one occasion. Thanks to Jean Pierre Verschueren and Ilse Stalmans of the Antwerp Port Authority's public relations team for smoothly solving the many practical and organizational problems. Filip Heremans of the University of Leuven deserves every credit for maintaining the conference website. Bart Sas and Sabine Janssens of the University of Antwerp, who helped out with technical or practical matters at a number of occasions, should also be mentioned here. Last but not least we thank Francine Olenaed (University of Leuven) for her technical assistance with the volume's layout.

Leuven, May 2002

The editors,

Reginald LOYEN
Erik BUYST
Greta DEVOS

Table of Contents

Port authority cluster

Port user cluster

Research agenda

Annex

Introduction

Reginald Loyen, Erik Buyst, Greta Devos and Jan Blomme

University of Leuven, University of Leuven, Antwerp Port Authority, University of Antwerp, Belgium

Over the last couple of decades the face of the maritime sector has changed rapidly and fundamentally. Although the final implications of this development process cannot be fully assessed yet, prominent scholars already speak enthusiastically of a new "logistical revolution" (Andersson 1986) or of a fifth Kondratieff cycle (Rodrigue, Comtois and Slack 1997). The main driving force behind the whole process is often summarized as the "globalization of the world economy". Many factors push globalization forward, but a key element is undoubtedly the advance of communication and transport technologies (Kenwood and Lougheed 1999, 247-265). The breakthrough of new information and communication equipment resulted in the realisation of a worldwide logistic network (Harlaftis and Starkey 1998). Accompanied with the introduction of the container, it revolutionized the shipping business during the final quarter of the twentieth century (Broeze 1998).

One of the most visible symptoms of this "revolution" has been the continuous increase in (container)vessel size (McLellan 1997). The particularly high operational costs of these ships made many seaports redundant. Those ports that remained in service, turned into hub ports and created a system of smaller "feeder ports" in order to generate sufficient cargo. In the ports, an extraordinary logistics machinery, necessary to keep pace with this scaling up practice, came into existence. Shipping agents, forwarders, stevedores, distribution companies, cargo handlers and numerous other transport service providers, which used to work relatively independently, now started to integrate their activities.

Ship-owning companies integrated horizontally by means of shipping conferences, alliances or take-overs (Lim 1998). The resulting economies of scale, gained at sea, obviously demanded changes in land operations. Here, vertical integration led to a better grip on the logistic chain. After acquiring e.g. a cargo handler and a road hauler, a shipowner could offer a door-to-door service to his customers (Ojala 1995, CEMT 1987). As both types of integration were mutually linked, this resulted in a remarkable number of amalgamations and coalitions. In Rotterdam and Antwerp for example, non-European stevedores like Hutchison and Port of Singapore Authority recently assumed control over several "local" companies (respectively European Container Terminus and Hesse Noord Natie). These take-overs drastically changed the familiar container handling landscape in both seaports. For the ports of Antwerp and Rotterdam, located within a stone's throw, this trend - paradoxically - led to increased competition as well as integration. New strategic choices and policies forced themselves upon the port sector.

This pronounced tendency for concentration put (e.g.) port authorities in a somewhat uncomfortable position. In landlord ports - like Antwerp and Rotterdam- port authorities have had to re-think their market strategy in order to maintain competition amongst their cargo handlers. Should they warrant competition within the port or should they tolerate one dominant player? Should they assume or abstain from commercial responsibilities? Should they concentrate their efforts to assure maritime access or should they build and fully equip docks and terminals?

In order to answer these and other strategic questions, a sound historical awareness is mandatory. This volume does not only present a historical framework, but also offers an ideal opportunity for reflection. The speed as well as the sheer complexity of the developments in the maritime and ports industry implies that many choices - even strategic ones - often have to be taken at short notice. It is therefore in the interest of everyone in the port business to stop from time to time, step aside and reflect about the trends of the past and the future. The exchange of ideas and opinions between policy makers and scholars undoubtedly enriches this process. History may perhaps not directly provide an answer to today's problems, since curiosity is the driving force behind historical research and because present situations are never identical to past circumstances (the general context is always different). A better understanding of historical developments might however grant a general framework or point of reference, enabling today's decision-makers to draw more balanced conclusions. Because of the many similarities between past and present trends affecting ports and their environment, a historical understanding quite often turns out to be the secret of success[1].

Apart from offering a historical framework for reflection, this volume also presents an academic state of the art in the field of Antwerp-Rotterdam economic port research. It actually aims at confronting the expansion of both seaports in all their aspects and thus studies the competition that marked the evolution of both North Sea ports. The volume's approach therefore is invariably of a comparative and multi-disciplinary nature. The staggering spatial and economic growth of Antwerp and Rotterdam has already been extensively studied in the past, but rarely from a comparative and multidisciplinary perspective. By confronting the growth of both ports in this way, the volume ascertains why and how the two ports reacted so differently to virtually the same economic and political trends. Next to providing a framework and a comparative standpoint, this book also intends to put the history of the ports of Antwerp and Rotterdam in a broader, more international context, by

[1] One well-known example of past/present similarities is the often-quoted comparison of containerization with steam shipping. Indeed, in many ways the advent of the container during the final quarter of the twentieth century could be considered analogous to the transition from canvas to coal in the final quarter of the nineteenth century. Like steam shipping, containerization drastically altered cargo handling in seaports and revolutionized the whole concept of transport. Remarkable increases in productivity have been obtained in both cases. Each innovation also required a considerably level of investment (De Leeuw 1989, 260-261). Notorious is also the debate on the similarities between the globalization of the economy in the nineteenth and the twentieth centuries (O'Rourke and Williamson 2000).

offering comparisons with other ports. Finally, this collection of scholarly studies proposes to redefine the research agenda of port history.

In order to achieve these goals the volume has been composed as follows. First a historiographical chapter places the present volume in the international literature. Then, the individual contributions have been grouped in three clusters. Each cluster contains a number of chapters dealing with the same theme and is identically organized: The opening chapter deals with Antwerp; the second with Rotterdam and the third section includes comments and generalizations. Finally, to round off the volume, a view on new opportunities in port history follows.

The first cluster treats of the physical context: port throughput and spatial expansion throughout time. These aspects of port operations have been studied from a historic, as well as from an economic point of view. In many ways this is however the heart of the matter because it deals with the four W-questions: What kind of commodities are handled in the ports? Where have they come from and where are they going (i.e. what is the fore- and the hinterland)? When did new trends emerge? Why are those commodities put through these specific maritime centres? In order to answer the latter W-question, the second and third cluster elaborate on two major "local" players, respectively on port authorities and port users. They have after all, shaped each seaport's response to the international economic and political climate. To a large extent, the interaction between those two players has determined the fate of the ports of Rotterdam and Antwerp. In this volume both clusters help to explain the functional and spatial shifts observed in the throughput cluster. The importance of port authorities is the subject of the second cluster. It concentrates on the political-institutional frameworks as well as on land policy in the Antwerp and Rotterdam seaports. The third and final cluster focuses on those who are actually doing the job: the dockers and the entrepreneurs. These port users obviously fulfilled a crucial part in keeping Rotterdam and Antwerp on their toes.

After having established the ratio behind the volume's composition, each cluster will now be presented in detail.

Preceding the three clusters stands David Williams' (University of Leicester) introductory historiographical chapter. In describing the recent trends in maritime and port history, Williams provides the wider context and sets the scene for this volume. After analysing the advent of maritime history, he turns to port history. Williams notices a shift of emphasis in analysis towards assessing economic rationale. As early port studies deal with typology, port size, modelling, dock construction etc, recent work focuses on the economics of, and the justification for port development. He also points out that competition might be an inevitable feature of port studies, but that it has not tended to be directly examined, but rather as an element of the experience of individual ports. Finally he elaborates on the growth of interest in port policy of governments and on the huge expansion of work on seafaring and port labour.

The first cluster deals with the port's core-business: throughput. Reginald Loyen (University of Leuven) and Paul van de Laar (University of Rotterdam) respectively discuss the evolution of throughput in the ports of Antwerp and Rotterdam. Loyen surveys the shifts in Antwerp throughput during the twentieth century. He approaches the subject by looking at the evolution of port functions and by considering maritime as well as hinterland traffic. Using well-known theories he ultimately designs a port transition model in order to describe and explain the evolution of throughput in the port of Antwerp. Van de Laar's approach is much more straightforward and also treats of a smaller time span (1880-1914). After solving a large number of methodological problems regarding Rotterdam throughput, he discusses the development of individual trades. Van de Laar confirms Rotterdam's importance as a Rhine and as an intermediary transit port. Finally he dwells on Rotterdam's increasing dependence on Germany. David J. Starkey (University of Hull) scrutinized the papers by Loyen and van de Laar.

Using Loyen's dataset Sabine Janssens, Hilde Meersman and Eddy Van de Voorde (University of Antwerp) estimated a number of econometric specifications in order to measure the impact of port authorities on throughput. Confronted with the obvious link between international trade and throughput, they investigated if (and to which extent) port authorities may influence port traffic. They concentrated their effort on the post-war period and tried to quantify the relationship between throughput and international trade using modern econometric techniques. Next, Honoré Paelinck (Port & Transport Consulting) discusses their conclusion that port authorities exert considerable influence and have to become important players in the field of national and international logistics.

With the vertical and horizontal integration of the logistics sector in mind, this is not an inconsequential conclusion. In his comparative chapter on the containerization in Antwerp and Rotterdam, Theo Notteboom (University of Antwerp) looks at the details of this integration trend. After describing the advent of the container, Notteboom focuses on the evolution of container throughput and on the spatial development of container handling facilities in the Antwerp and Rotterdam ports. Next he discusses (dis)similarities between both ports and concludes that containerization allowed Antwerp and Rotterdam to enlarge their distribution functions and to become important logistics centres. Notteboom adds that the functional interactions between Antwerp, Rotterdam and logistic zones in the hinterland intensified dealings between the ports. These spatial-economic spillovers and the process of spatial deconcentration of both seaports is also the thesis of Arjen van Klink's (Rabobank) contribution. First he situates both ports in the same port transition model. In the final phase of his model, like Notteboom, he argues that Antwerp and Rotterdam slowly integrate spatially. He points to the location pattern of European Distribution Centres, to rising inter-port traffic and to multimodal transport. Along the lines of Van Klink's contribution, Jan Blomme (Antwerp Port Authority) considers the post-war spatial development and planning of the port of Antwerp *in se*. Blomme approaches this problem as a port strategist and uses historical data to conclude that newly built infrastructure is now used much more efficiently. This remarkable increase of infrastructure productivity is – according to Blomme - largely explained by containerization.

The second cluster is entirely devoted to the role and importance of the port authority in the ports of Rotterdam and Antwerp. As shown in the previous cluster, this local player has quite some bearing on a port's evolution. First of all, Frank Seberechts (University of Gent) and Henk Molenaar (University of Rotterdam) debate municipal port politics. Seberechts advocates "a prudent approach".

He reconstructs ties and relationships between several crucial players and manages to determine the exact role of port firm managers in the catholic and liberal (and not the socialist) parties. Thanks to his network analysis Seberechts establishes a number of links and probable contacts between people. He concludes that, through these channels, liberal and catholic business circles had considerable influence on the scope of port expansion. Molenaar's chapter on Rotterdam port policy is of a slightly different, more analytical nature. Molenaar consecutively discusses the port policy arena and the historic development of port policy from various perspectives. He also looks at different types of steering-mechanisms in port strategy. The author concludes that policy makers have reached what he calls "the end of the sea" and should better look at individual customers and relations. Along the same line Molenaar finally adds eight "pitfalls" for historians, active in the field of port research. Adrian Jarvis (Merseyside Maritime Museum) criticized Seberechts' and Molenaar's diverse contributions.

Because of its specific significance and susceptibility for municipal port strategy, Greta Devos (University of Antwerp) and Ferry de Goey (University of Rotterdam) wrote additional chapters devoted exclusively to land policy. Devos starts out by sketching the specific situation in the port of Antwerp. Next, Devos chronologically discusses trends in land-use policy in Antwerp up to 1994. She finds that the focus in land-use policy in Antwerp shifted from shipping (companies and agents) to (petrochemical) industry and cargo handlers. Devos not only concludes that the port authority's land allocation policy has become more transparent, she also points to a shift in land granting criteria (from potential investment or traffic to value added creation). In his discussion of land-use policy in the port of Rotterdam, de Goey argues that there was a close causal link between land-use policy and the increase in throughput. He discerns two periods, separated by World War II: Prior to 1940 the port authority took care of infrastructure while the enterprises developed superstructure. After the war, the Rotterdam port authority only rented out land and - because demand exceeded supply - employed a land allocation system based on the cargo generating effect of the applicant. De Goey proves to which extent the positive causal link between phenomenal changes in throughput levels as well as composition on one hand and land-use policy on the other hand actually took place. Sarah Palmer (University of Greenwich) examined both papers closely and drew a closer comparison.

From the papers on municipal politics as well as on land-use policy it has become clear that a study of the institutional position of port authorities in the Low Countries supplies the deficiency. The contribution of Henrik Stevens (Zeeland Seaports) adequately fills this gap. After making a number of fairly general remarks on port comparisons, Stevens discusses the evolution of the port authority's position. He deals with legal, political as well as economic and societal aspects. In analysing the Rotterdam port authority's current repositioning, he looks at a recent corporate plan. Stevens describes the evolution of a port authority that occupied a supreme position as the implementer of (inter)national ambitions and plans to an authority which now has to take account of other layers of government and business.

The third and final cluster groups a number of papers on port users. Stephan Vanfraechem (University of Gent) and Erik Nijhof (University of Utrecht) compare the evolution of dock-labour in the ports of Antwerp and Rotterdam. The authors however exclusively survey the decasualization process of port-labour in both ports. Decasualization took place in the 1950s and 1960s and can be described as the shift from a casual to a more permanent form of employment in cargo handling. Vanfraechem sets out by situating decasualization in the port of Antwerp against a background of unemployment, work refusal and job insecurity. Next he describes in great detail how trade unions and employers tried to reach an agreement on an intermediate form of decasualization and on the reformation of the hiring system. Vanfraechem concludes however that the balance of the talks was poor - if not insufficient - and queries: "much ado about nothing"? He finally argues that the employers not only acted on financial but also on mental considerations. Faced with a completely different supply (a lack) of labour in Rotterdam, Nijhof looks at decasualization in the Dutch seaport. His chapter treats of a wider time span and also discusses labour productivity versus technological innovations as well as upgrading the social status of the docker. In so doing Nijhof identifies several stages between the extremes of an exclusively casual labour force and regular labour contracts. He concludes that decasualization was primarily caused by the post-war government wage policy combined with the unique position of the dockers on the Rotterdam labour market. In his critique John Barzman (University of Le Havre) compared the developments in the Low Countries with those in the French seaport of Le Havre and discussed a number of issues regarding methodology as well as content.

Hugo van Driel (University of Rotterdam) studied port users from a different point of view, namely that of technological evolution. Van Driel focuses on the first wave of mechanization in two major dry bulk trades (ores and coal). The mechanization occurred between 1885 and 1920 and consisted of the introduction of floating and shore-based grab cranes. The author embarks by describing the characteristics of the innovations as well as the bottlenecks and prospects they presented. Van Driel furthermore focuses on the political and commercial context of the innovations (structure of industry, identity of innovators etc). He puts the finishing touches to his chapter by including several comparative hypotheses. As Antwerp originally lagged behind in the mechanization of the ore and coal trades, this comparison provides an interesting, though speculative case. Gordon Jackson (University of Strathclyde) referees this chapter and puts it in a British context.

By way of conclusion, Erik Buyst and Reginald Loyen (University of Leuven) put forward their vision on new directions in port history.

The research agenda concerns the specific Antwerp-Rotterdam situation as well as port history in general (see also Williams 1993, Hattendorf 1994, Broeze 1995, etc.). This collections of essays not only contributes to the historical understanding of Antwerp and Rotterdam, but also generates three major research opportunities: comparative research, "integrated" investigations and the human factor.

A. The multidisciplinary and comparative nature of this volume undoubtedly provides excess value. Indeed, it is often said, "good historiography is comparative history". No historian can possibly disagree: it is next to impossible to fully understand or explain a proposition if it is examined in a situation of "splendid isolation". Putting an analysis in a proper context always boosts its explanatory power. Notwithstanding this noble starting point, most maritime economic historians have kept well clear of a truly comparative endeavour. As a rule, research in the field of port history apparently tends to result in single-port studies. As such, even this volume may not be considered as comparative research in the true sense of the word, as mostly two authors combined their knowledge in a relatively independent way. But already this collection of papers opens new research possibilities and perspectives. As for instance Jackson's comments showed, further international comparative research and exchange helps us to gain a clearer understanding of port development. From an Antwerp and Rotterdam perspective, co-operation in the Hamburg-Le Havre seaport range would certainly generate new insights.

Conversely, in order to reach a more appealing level of comparison, two essential prerequisites have to be in place.

1. Obviously a general framework for port history has to be (further) established. This is an absolute necessity for it will allow a swift elimination of the current shortcomings. The introduction of such paradigms would permit maritime economic historians to raise the right questions. In so doing scholars would also avoid reducing port history to story telling (Jarvis 1999, 21-23 and 29). On top of that, port transition models would allow scholars to better attribute weights to the various determinants of throughput and exceed truisms like simply linking throughput to international trade or land-use policy. Consequently the need for a broad survey of seaport development has to be recognized.
2. The second precondition regards extensive time-series on shipping movements, throughput, infrastructure, investment etc. A quantitative frame of reference would tremendously facilitate comparative port research and simultaneously improve qualitative analyses. When taking port history out of its "pigeon hole" (Jarvis 1999, 34) historians should not boggle at "new" types of measurement like value added. In the present volume Molenaar reminded us in no uncertain terms that a scholar's concepts and methodology should be enhanced and kept up to date.

B. The second major deficiency of current investigations in port history is twofold: a curious tendency towards the "long nineteenth century" as well as "navel-gazing". This orientation towards the nineteenth century affects maritime economic history in general. Apart from this preoccupancy, time and again the focus lies on the evolution of the port as such ("navel-gazing"). Ports do not stand or act alone: Ports are intermediaries between fore- and hinterland or between a city and "the rest of the world". Therefore they should not be approached as isolated entities. This implies that studies of for instance port dues or other ship handling costs should rather take general transport costs into account. This kind of quantitative research also holds promises of new explanations and insights into the mechanism of port choice and development. In the case of landlord ports (like Antwerp and Rotterdam), the urban dimension should be included as well. All too often research into cargo-handling technology or port investment in general ignores the crucial and diverse role of the municipality. Rotterdam as well as Antwerp are port cities in the broadest sense of the word. Therefore this urban element should be taken into account. This has partly been performed (for Rotterdam); Antwerp trails however. Spatial dynamics (cfr economic geography) could be included (waterfront redevelopment e.g.). The specificities of landlord ports include that for Antwerp and Rotterdam a lot remains to be done in the field of port investments. Notwithstanding a recent upsurge in international attention for this subject, Antwerp and Rotterdam historians have hardly studied this theme. Additionally, Antwerp is well behind researching technological innovations in cargo-handling.

C. Arguing in favour of port modelling is not equal to ignoring the "human factor", on the contrary! In this volume, Gordon Jackson correctly pointed to the fact that *it was the inter-play of people that got things done.* After all, successes or failures can - to a certain extent - be assigned to the role of personalities in government or in business. Perhaps with the notable exceptions of politicians, the impact of individual port authority directors, port aldermen, company managers (etc) on port expansion has - at least in the Low Countries - barely been the subject of scientific studies. Apart from some exceptions port historians do apparently not share the recent international surge in interest in networks instigated by Boyce's seminal dissertation (Boyce 1995). Another popular line of research, conceptualization, has also barely concerned port historians (see Williams in this volume). A number of studies in the field of business history (cargo-handlers, stevedores, merchant houses, ...) and individual port lobbies (chambers of commerce, ship owners organisations, trade unions...) do partially cover these lacunae though.

References

Andersson AE (1986) The four logistical revolutions. Papers of the regional science association LIX: 1-12

Boyce G (1995) Information, mediation and institutional development: the rise of large scale enterprise in British shipping, 1870-1919. Manchester

Broeze F (1995) (ed) Maritime history at the cross-roads: a critical review of recent historiography. St. John's (Research in maritime history IX)

Broeze F (1998) Containerization and the globalization of liner shipping. In: Starkey DJ, Harlaftis G (eds) Global markets: the internationalization of the sea transport industries since 1850. St. John's, pp 385-423

CEMT (1987) The role of shippers and transport operators in the logistic chain. Round table 76. Paris

De Leeuw PAH (1991) Technological innovations and the liner conference system. The case of the North Atlantic (1850-1984). In: Koninckx C (ed) Proceedings of the international colloquium "Industrial Revolutions and the sea". Brussels, pp 255-265

Harlaftis G, Starkey DJ (1998) Global markets: the internationalization of the sea transport industries since 1850. Sevilla

Hattendorf JB (1994) (ed) Ubi sumus. The state of naval and maritime history. Newport

Jarvis A (1999) Port history: some thoughts on where it came from and where it might be going. In: Fischer LR, Jarvis, A (eds) Harbours and havens: essays in port history in honour of Gordon Jackson. St. John's, pp 13-34 (Research in maritime history XVI)

Kenwood AG, Lougheed, AL (1999) The growth of the international economy (1820-2000). An introductory text. London/New York

Lim S (1998) Economies of scale in container shipping. Maritime policy and management XV-4: 361-373

McLellan (1997) Bigger vessels: how big is too big? Maritime policy and management XXIV: 193-211

O'Rourke KH, Williamson JG (2000) When did globalization begin? Cambridge. NBER Working paper 7632

Ojala L (1995) Eastern/Western European shipping companies and multimodal transport organisations. Maritime policy and management XXII-4: 331-344

Rodrigue JP, Comtois C and Slack B (1997) Transportation and spatial cycles: evidence from maritime systems. Journal of transport geography V-2: 87-98

Williams DM (1993) The progress of maritime history (1953-1993). Journal of transport history XIV-2: 126-141

Recent trends in maritime and port history

David M. Williams

University of Leicester, United Kingdom

The publication of this volume is a reflection of two trends. One is the ongoing great changes and challenges facing ports today; the other is the recent upsurge of interest and research in maritime and port historical studies. The first impetus, how challenges have and are being met by ports is at the heart of this volume and we have a host of fascinating papers to consider. In commenting on recent trends in maritime and port history, the aim of this introduction is to provide a wide context for the chapters and discussions that are to follow.

Any survey of past research must embody historiography and bibliography[1]. Instructive and useful these may be, it must be admitted that historiography and bibliography rank high in the league table of boring conference presentations. With this in mind my comments on recent trends in maritime and port history while discussing past books, papers and research projects also include some general observations on patterns of development in shipping and ports. In addition besides commenting on research undertaken, there are reflections on what has not been done.

The first observation to be made must relate to terminology. Twenty-five years ago scholars might well have met to discuss the history of shipping and ports, but not maritime and port history. "Maritime history" and even more so "Port history" are relatively new terms. While the history of men in boats or ships has always been a popular subject, the development of maritime history as a specialized thematic area of study is of recent origin. Its appearance is in part due to the general trend towards the fragmentation of history into specialist fields of study or subdisciplines that has taken place in the past half century. This in turn was associated with the enormous expansion of the social sciences that promoted new themes and

[1] The footnotes to this paper in no way comprise a full, complete reflection of the volume of recent research in maritime and port history. Rather, the notes provide references to some, but by no means all, important studies. Inevitably, there is a subjective dimension. For an impression of the sheer volume of study and the range of maritime and port themes being researched see the ongoing bibliography in *Tijdschrift voor Zeegeschiedenis*. This, ongoing for two decades, had reached 30883 items by the end of 2000! Useful bibliographical guides arranged on a country basis are to be found in Broeze 1995, Hattendorf 1994. Perhaps the best way to gain an appreciation of the character and variety of recent research is through a review of the publications of the International Maritime Economic History Association – the *International Journal of Maritime History* and companion series, *Research in Maritime History*. These, launched in 1989 and 1991 respectively, and both throughout under the editorship of Lewis R. Fischer, comprise well over forty issues.

the application of analytical approaches little used in previous historical study. From such developments emerged maritime history along with urban, rural, financial, labour, business, feminist and many more histories. An important stimulus to the growth of these new specialisms was that the process that promoted them was international, moreover they came at a time when advances in communications and personal travel enabled the rapid dissemination of research ideas and the more frequent joining together of scholars with common interests at workshops and conferences.

The emergence of maritime history as a specialist field of study can be dated from the 1960s. In 1960, the *Commission Internationale d'Histoire Maritime* was created under the auspices of the International Congress of Historical Sciences. The International Commission stimulated the formation of national commissions. Amongst the earliest were the Dutch and Belgian Commissions. A much-quoted benchmark is that of the appearance in 1971 of a new journal entitled *Maritime History*[2]. This brave venture was plagued with publisher problems and had a relatively brief existence. Its importance lies in that its focus was exclusively on the mercantile marine and marked a growing stress on the mercantile as opposed to the naval. Other significant developments in the 1970s were the publication of the seminal four volume maritime history of the Low Countries, *Maritieme Geschiedenis der Nederlanden* (1976-78)[3] and, in 1979, the establishment within the Royal Belgian Academy of Sciences of a scientific committee to undertake a systematic study of the maritime history of Belgium. Outside Europe, the birth of the Australian journal of maritime history, *The Great Circle* in 1979 demonstrated the international character of the new growth of interest. Nevertheless, the great leap forward came in the 1980s when at the Berne congress of the International Economic History Association a Maritime Economic History Group was formed[4]. This in turn became the International Maritime Economic History Association whose Journal, *The International Journal of Maritime History*, launched in 1989, immediately became the pace setter and principal vehicle for the study of maritime history. More so, the founder editors, Fischer and Nordvik, established a context for maritime history. Within that context they stressed three criteria for maritime history: an international dimension, a focus on economic and social history and the integration of maritime history into the larger discipline (Editorial 1989). Such criteria continue to be a pertinent yardstick for assessing research.

The development of port history as a new historical speciality is more recent. The study of ports, either individually or collectively, is hardly a new phenomenon but traditionally it was the province of geographers rather than historians. The origins of the concept of port history lie in the same trends that generated maritime history, namely, the great expansion of the social sciences. More specifically, port

---

2 Edited by Robin Craig, four volumes were produced between 1971 and 1974. A fifth volume, which appeared under this title in 1977, was not directly connected with the earlier series.

3 *Maritieme Geschiedenis der Nederlanden* 4 volumes, Bussum, 1976-78. A total of 37 authors contributed to the work.

4 On the origins and early development of maritime history see Davis 1978, Bruijn 1998, Williams 1993 and Hattendorf 1994.

history emerged from the development of two new specialisms, maritime history and urban history. The stimulus from maritime history is obvious enough, so too that of urban history where the very different economic structure and cosmopolitan society of ports as opposed to other cities soon became a recognized aspect of study (Proudfoot 1996). In the new approach to the history of ports, two pioneering studies were those of Gordon Jackson, *History and Archeology of Ports* published in 1983 (Jackson 1983) and Frank Broeze's edited volume, *Brides of the Sea: Port Cities of Asia* which appeared in 1989 (Broeze 1989 and 1997). Both advanced important ideas and approaches and stimulated a wave of research and conferences. An early, significant international conference was that organized in the Netherlands in 1987 on "Shipping Companies and Port Authorities in the nineteenth and twentieth centuries" (Akveld and Bruijn 1989). A further stimulus to port history was the container revolution that impacted on old and new ports and gave rise to much public discussion of issues such as the collapse of dock labour forces and dockland re-development.

Thus recent decades have witnessed an enormous and worldwide growth of interest and activity in maritime history and port history. The volume of publications has been immense, not least because of the increasingly broad definition of maritime history (Williams and White 1991, iii-xi, Broeze 1998, 195-208). Also contributing to the flood of publications has been the pressure on academics to publish, the revolution in printing and, because of these, the ease and enthusiasm with which conference proceedings soon appear in print. These are interesting aspects of historiography but beyond our current context. This paper confines itself to reviewing work on post-1850 shipping and port history produced in the last twenty years or so.

The history of shipping and ports since 1850 is complex. However, in essence it can be summarized in three words: coal, oil and boxes! This may appear a trite and superficial comment but it serves to emphasize the key feature facing shipping and ports, that of accommodating and adapting to technological change. Coal in the form of steam power had a true revolutionary impact in freeing shipping from its traditional subservience to wind and tide and permitting the development of scheduled services. All sorts of implications flowed from this not least those for ports that had to accommodate these new requirements. That process of accommodation was ongoing for the shift to iron hulls saw regular increases in vessel size. Just as steam transformed the seaward size of port activity so too it did on land through the railway. Hinterlands expanded and often came to overlap. The impact of oil for shipping was not so much in terms of a means of ship propulsion but rather as a new, rapidly growing, bulk trade demanding specialized vessels. For ports, oil gave rise to huge new port terminal industries. Profound too was the effect of oil in the form of petrol engine and road and air transport. For ports, motor transport created new forms of distribution and a huge new trade in ferry transport. Shipping benefited from the latter but aviation was to wipe out long distance passenger traffic almost entirely. Boxes - containerization, represent the third great technological change. Together with bulk carriers their impact on shipping and ports requires no elaboration.

If new technologies can be said to be the chief feature of nineteenth and twentieth century shipping and port history, a second strand is that of a larger scale of business in terms of both operation and management. This followed from the new levels of technology. The greater utilization of capital with its enormous financial implications increasingly led to larger corporate structures in both shipping and port enterprise. In shipping, these relatively soon assumed an international dimension, indeed the world of shipping represents one of the earliest trends towards globalization. For ports, especially in the long run, size became crucial.

Developments in technology and the resulting greater scale of business impacted no less on labour than they did on management. The experience of seafaring and dock labour represents a third strand of maritime and port history. Seafaring labour, both in the sense of the nature of work and those who perform it, has it own special character; dock work too, has its peculiar features. Steam transformed labour at sea and affected work in ports; containers had a profounder consequence for labour than on any other factor of production in the port sector.

Such then are the key features of the past two centuries of shipping and port history. How has recent research illuminated these trends? On the technological aspect the focus in the 1970s and 1980s was very much on transfer of technology, the shift from sail to steam. This shift was examined at various levels. The first was that of the operational and management problems associated with a new technology (Palmer 1978, Jackson 1992). A second area of study was that of the uneven diffusion of steam on different routes and in different trades (Harley 1971, 1985 and 1988, Kaukiainen 1992). Here discussion focused on the relative economics of steam and sail. The third area of study was that of the transfer of technology and the experience of national fleets in moving from sail to steam[5]. Here there was scope for considerable international comparison and accounting for the speed or tardiness of transition. The issue of state support was a matter that gave rise to considerable debate not least on the interpretation of mail contacts as commercial practice or subsidy (Harcourt 1988).

A feature of the shift to steam was that of the emergence of liner and tramp shipping – although there is scope for considering how far this distinction was entirely new. The experience of large liner companies was a theme taken up by business historians as early as the 1960s. Of course there was nothing new about company histories; anniversaries were traditionally celebrated with commissioned volumes. But the new business histories took a more objective and much more analytical approach. Many such studies were undertaken in the 1960s, 70s and 80s. Fewer have appeared since then, but the work of Wray on the Japanese company NYK and Valdaliso on Spanish shipping are especially important (Wray 1984, Valdaliso 1991 and 2000). In the context of this volume the major survey of CMB by Devos and Elewaut has a special relevance (Devos and Elewaut 1995); so too Flayhart's recent book on the American Line with its Red Star association (Flayhart 2000).

Perhaps the most significant recent work on shipping companies to emerge is that of Gordon Boyce, *Information, mediation and institutional development: the*

[5] An examination of the experience of the USA (by Safford), Britain (Palmer), Canada (Sager and Panting), Scandinavia (Nordvik) and Germany (Kresse) appears in Fischer and Panting, *Change and Adaptation.* See also Kaukiainen 1992 and 1993. Wray 1986, Chida and Davies 1990.

rise of large scale enterprise in British shipping, 1870-1919 (Boyce 1995). This breaks new ground by analyzing the growth and success of large companies. Boyce shifted the focus away from Chandler's theory of growth through internal efficiencies. He stresses the contribution to success of external efficiencies, networking and external information flows gained through contracts with brokers, agents and conference organization. In so doing Boyce provides an alternative theoretical frame to evaluate the process of change.

Networks and organizational structures heavily based on family and local ties is a strong theme in another important recent study, that of Gelina Harlaftis in her *History of Greek-owned Shipping* (Harlaftis 1996). Her work's subtitle, "The making of an international tramp fleet" embraces a significant force in twentieth century international shipping but at the same time it points up one of the great gaps in research. This is the relative lack of significant studies of the tramp sector and tramp shipping companies. Of course the archival records for smaller tramp companies may be fewer and less accessible yet one feels that historians have been seduced by the glamour of liners. The outcome is a somewhat distorted understanding of the business and structure of shipping.

The research of Harlaftis, Wray and Valdaliso which is largely set in the twentieth century points to a further area of omission. It has to be said that the emphasis of historical study on shipping has been on the pre-1914 era. Of course this is a broad generalization, nevertheless a review of the literature throws up this bias. This might occasion some surprise for the post World War I era was one which besides seeing the highly significant growth of motor shipping and the oil trade was one when shipping internationally underwent its most traumatic era. Perhaps because the impact of the great slump is so well known there has been almost a tendency to assume that there is little new to add. It is remarkable that if one searches for material on British shipping in the 1930s - and the British mercantile marine was still by far the largest in the world at that time - recourse has to be made to contemporary surveys or to the study of Sturmey, *British Shipping and World Competition* (Sturmey 1962). Sturmey's analysis, without doubt, was seminal, but it appeared in 1962. Interestingly, the most noticeable studies of interwar shipping tend to be of fleets that did make the transition to oil or which fared relatively well in the troubled times – the shipping of Norway, Greece, Japan and the USA.

The surprising relative neglect of the interwar years bears out Professor Palmer's observation that in the economic history of shipping "there is still a great way to go before the twentieth century is as well served as the nineteenth" (Palmer 2000, 5). That reflection is borne out still further when one reviews the third quarter of the twentieth century. Such major developments as the impact of air transport on passenger liner shipping, while gaining coverage in the final chapters of company histories, has not been explored in any general sense at the academic level. Nor has the expansion of the cruise industry which was stimulated in part by the entry of redundant liners. The implications for ports of the end of passenger liners and the huge growth of cruising, again awaits full investigation. So too, in great measure, the huge rise of the car ferry trade.

In contrast, however, two post 1960s features of shipping have excited historians. The rise of huge bulk carriers and containerization although "newish" developments have generated a considerable number of studies and two separate monographs on containerization are soon to appear (Broeze 1998). Perhaps this is because like steam, a century earlier, these advances have been truly revolutionary in their effect. Again, they have promoted global organization and, as suggested earlier, they have given a new impetus to port study and port history.

Let us turn more exclusively to port history. The features of the last quarter century or so are two fold: first the enormous expansion of study and second a shift in approach and focus. The expansion has been quite remarkable and has resulted in an array of impressive studies of individual ports: these include Suykens et al. and Veraghtert on Antwerp; Maass and Prange on Hamburg, Scholl on Bremerhaven, Jarvis on Liverpool, de la Puerta Rueda on Bilbao, Dharmesena on Colombo, Tull on Freemantle, Broeze on Dubai and this list could be long extended (Suykens 1986, Veraghtert 1989, Maas 1990, Prange 1989, de la Puerta Rueda 1994, Dharmasena 1998, Tull, 1997, Broeze 1999, Scholl 1999). Again there have been studies of groups of ports for example of Britain, Norway, Spain, Japan, Australia and the ASEAN region to name but a few surveys (de la Puerta Rueda 1997, Tull 1999, Fischer and Nordvik 1996, Trace 1997, Rimmer and Taniuch 1997). In addition a range of facets of port history, economic, technological, administrative and social have commanded attention.

How has this new wave of study differed from the past. Traditionally, studies of the history of ports focussed on such aspects such as the typology of ports, criteria for assessing size, dock construction, port operation and governance. Early studies of typology offered a wide variety of classifications including form of ownership, form of traffic and the size of vessels using ports. More imaginative were classifications based on type of inland connections, rail or water or the two combined. (Interestingly, down until 1945, roads were seldom included in the inland connections). A further distinction was made between ports that were purely gateways and those that also had industrial bases (Sargent 1938). A further way of classifying ports was by size with a variety of measures such as berthing accommodation, capacity for cargo handling, volume or value of cargoes landed and tonnage entering giving much scope for ingenuity and debate.

Studies of the typology of ports are less prominent now, partly because it is recognized that the complexity of possible categories is so great and because many ports would straddle a variety of categories. Jarvis, in a recent consideration dismisses the exercise of typology, but nevertheless advances new criteria. One is the demographic although in his suggestion of capital, metropolitan, lesser and "wilderness" ports, the scope for further debate is evident. More provocatively he suggests "the physical difficulties of constructing a port in the first place, for this determines the extent of its debt charges; the amount of capital per yard of quay is an infrequently calculated but very useful index" (Jarvis 1999, 13-34). This observation is very pertinent because the high and lumpy cost of dock construction had, and perhaps even more so in a modern age, very long term implications. So, there still may be value in considering criteria for the typology of ports and recognising that the criteria will change over time. Likewise in recognising that new types of ports will emerge. Here, principal and satellite container ports, road transport ferry ports, cruise ports and even leisure, yachting marinas (new or based on redundant old port facilities) are obvious additions to any listings.

A further aspect of research undertaken before the threshold of this study's definition of "recent", was that of attempts to theorize the process of the growth and shifting location of individual ports. A seminal attempt to provide a general thesis was the "Anyport" model advanced by Bird (Bird 1963 and 1971, 66-76). This has been widely referred to. Despite its vintage, which means no account is taken of the revolutionary changes of the last forty years, this study represents a pioneering tool and one still useful for examining development before the 1970s. Bird's model, nevertheless, has been criticized. Many ports do not conform; more so, Bird suggested that ports evolve over time, upgrading facilities in response to economic or technical stimuli. Implicit in this was that bigger and better docks were crucial in determining a port's success. Jackson has queried this emphasis, arguing that while good docks were clearly of great significance, they should be viewed as but one of many variable economic and political factors which influenced a port's long or short term success. Jackson stresses that, "trade does not automatically follow docks". He observes that in determining success, "Much is made of the importance of port facilities, but historical evidence would seem to show that these are less important than total transport networks and mercantile connections which constantly change" (Jackson 1992). This view is an important corrective, nevertheless one might reflect that post-1960, the huge increase in vessel size and new freight technologies - although these were related to shifts in trade and politics - have meant that dock facilities have come to be crucial.

Even so, there may be a case for placing a special emphasis on mercantile connections in the success of port development. Such connections are to be viewed partly in the sense of networking and access to the external information flows as stressed by Boyce but also in the sense of the ease of urban transport and communication and the efficiency and cost of transmitting mercantile information. Jarvis lays stress on the latter and also speculates on the formulation of a new model for port development that like Bird's utilizes temporal divisions but is based not on dock construction but on communications technology (Jarvis 1999, 32-34).

Besides typology, port size and modelling, early studies were concerned with dock construction, governance and efficiency. In each of these areas, recent research embodies new approaches and new questions. Studies of the development of infrastructure, in particular the construction of docks and cargo handling facilities tended to focus on the technical aspects of construction and almost implicitly assumed that such investment was logical and to sound purpose. Recent studies focus far more on the economics of, and the justification for, building and installing handling facilities (Jarvis 1996 and 1998). How and when ports respond to the challenge of growing ship size and the increasing pace of technological change is an important aspect. The rush, at the end of the nineteenth century, by a number of ports to build deep docks was hardly justified in terms of potential traffic. Likewise, there is a recognition that, ay any time, the latest, most efficient facilities because of their higher cost may not necessarily be the most economic investment. The pursuit of the newest, biggest and best may not always be the wisest policy and investment decisions have to be judged in the context of individual ports.

The shift of emphasis in analysis towards assessing economic rationale is also to be seen in approaches to assessing the success of ports. Besides measures evaluating cargo handled, dock space and port revenues, recent work has been concerned with measures of efficiency in cargo handling, throughput and turn around times (Loyen 2000). On the ratios of time in port and time at sea of cargo vessels since the mid-nineteenth century, there is still much to be done. Improvements often came relatively late, Blue Funnel Line ships in the Australian trade were spending as much as 60 percent of their time in port in the 1950s (Falkus, 1999, 358). It might also be added that the recent huge advances in turn around times and the consequent lack of a seafarers presence in port has profoundly changed the social life and fabric of port cities.

On the governance of ports, interest has shifted away from administrative practice (although revealing studies have been undertaken of Liverpool in the nineteenth century, (Jarvis 1994)) and more towards considering the relationships of the users of ports, particularly ship owners with port management. Here the definition of ports as "communities of merchants" and the theme of that important conference held in the Netherlands in 1988, "Shipping Companies and Authorities in the nineteenth and twentieth Centuries": their common interest in the development of port facilities" is called into question! More and more research emphasizes disparate interests and conflict rather than community and common interest. The very different needs of sail and steam ship owners, of liner and tramp companies, and the demands of oil companies gave rise to significant clashes of sectoral interests. So too, were the pressures which liner companies were to exert over their choice of terminal ports (Broeze 1991a). There is considerable debate over the relative strength of companies and port authorities and shifts in such relationships over time. Docks do not make trade, in theory vessels can often go elsewhere but owners are drawn to efficient facilities (Olukoju 1994). The current requirement of global container companies for huge, dedicated terminals and ports has ensured that research on the relationship between users and providers is ongoing.

The relationship is, of course, crucial to the business of individual ports. That business is viewed and measured absolutely and relatively because of the competitive dimension. Growing competition between ports is a feature of the past century and a half arising from the increasing scale of operation, the development of an international, world and global economy and the expansion of hinterlands through advances in inland transport. Thus competition between ports is an inevitable feature of port studies yet it has tended to be examined as an element of the experience of individual ports rather than directly. Specific studies of competition and rivalry are relatively rare. Competition between ports is very much a matter of dock facilities and hinterland networks. Discussion has focused on these, but a feature yet to be explored is that of how ports promoted themselves through advertising, publicity and public relations.

One further trend of research has been the growth of interest in the port policy of governments. This has thrown up some interesting international contrasts in attitudes and experience. Where countries have relatively small coastlines and few ports, government has long accepted a responsibility and made positive, planning policy decisions. Pre-1914, the building of the port of Hamburg with state loans, the linking of Rotterdam and Amsterdam to the sea with state financed waterways and the development of Antwerp as a modern port with docks built by city and state, all embodied national planning, a national port policy. In contrast, in most other North Atlantic countries with extended coastlines and many ports, the concept of a national ports policy was given little or no consideration and not acted on (Jackson 1998, Fischer 1999, de la Puerta Rueda 1997). Further aspects of policy at government and city level are the new forces of greater democracy and accountability and the environmental issue. The latter has served to check ambitions to extend port terminal industry.

As yet this review of maritime and port history research has been orientated to capital. The past twenty years or so has seen also seen the huge expansion of work on seafaring and port labour. Here the influence of the social sciences has been most apparent for this field has attracted the attention of not only economists and economic historians but also those of sociologists and political scientists. As with shipping and port studies, research has been uneven in its coverage. A review throws up some interesting anomalies. On labour in merchant shipping, the criticism that the twentieth century is less well served than the nineteenth again has relevance. This may be because the most dramatic change in the nature of labour at sea was that resulting from the shift to steam. Yet having said this, it is probably true that for the period from 1850-1914 studies of labour in sail rather than steam are more prominent[6]. Looking first at the seafarer's life and experience, a series of studies which had their roots in the Atlantic Canada Shipping project embraced not merely the nature of conditions and work aboard ship but also the profile of the labour force in terms of the age, length of sea experience and literacy of seamen (Ommer and Panting 1980, Sager 1990). Also addressed was the issue of manning - size of crews - and the frequency of changes of crew during voyages including the study of desertion. A range of other studies have considered welfare - afloat and ashore - and the increasing concern of governments' over the supply, quality, training and contracts of seamen (Schuman 1996). Fischer has undertaken a detailed examination of the market for seamen through the analysis of international wage rate patterns (Fischer 1992, Fischer and Nordvik 1987). He suggests that a less than perfect market prevailed both in national and international terms. His work on the market has encouraged others including the distinguished Charles Kindleberger (Fischer 1994, Kindleberger 1992, Balachandran 1997).

Of course the most dramatic change in the nature of seafaring labour was that associated with the shift to steam which shifted the balance of labour from on deck to below deck. This perhaps has not received the weight of study that might be expected. Analyses of the new make up of the seafaring labour force are quite common and there is work on the position of ship's engineers (McMurray 1980, Dixon 1996) yet the subdivisions within the steam ship labour force and the changing nature of labour - in the sense of work - await fuller study. Some debate has ensued over whether the shift to steam together with the tighter regulation of seamen's contracts changed the status of seafarers for the worse (Gerstenberger 1996). Whatever, the changing nature of the work force, the much greater size of crew on large steam vessels and the concentration of ownership combined with general trends in society towards organization led to the beginning of unionization

[6] In part this arises because one of the great stimuli to research in maritime labour (and for maritime history, generally) was the Atlantic Canada Shipping project whose focus was more on sail than steam.

within seagoing labour[7]. The inherent weaknesses of an internationally dispersed and transient labour force promoted a tendency to militant action but also limited success.

As stated the emphasis of studies on seamen has tended to be pre- rather than post-1914. This is not to suggest that seafarers have been neglected thereafter. Far from it, there are some important studies, but these are more in the field of applied sociology rather than history (Lane 1986). In the last forty years of the twentieth century, the tendency towards flagged out ships and third world crews is one that has gravely intensified the problems of labour organization. It has also deterred scholars who traditionally have favoured studies within a national context. Yet the ITF has achieved limited success in establishing a system of multinational industrial relations and collective bargaining and a few academics have braved the new, global world of seafaring labour (Koch-Baumgarten 1998, Northrup and Rowan 1986, Lane 1996).

Material on dock labour is remarkable in its extent, indeed dock workers rank amongst the most studied of all urban workers. Their numbers and world wide distribution partially account for this. Perhaps, more so, the special features of dock labour, - the emphasis on casual work, the tendency towards radical views and militancy and the concentration of workers in particular urban locations - have exerted a fascination for historians. More recently, the speed with which such a numerous and powerful body of labour was decimated by technological change has added both a poignancy and relevance to study.

Recent research has ranged widely with important studies covering many European Countries, North America and Australia and New Zealand. Many national experiences and some aspects of the international dimension featured in the important conference held in Amsterdam in 1997 entitled the Comparative International History of Dock Labour (Davies 2000). Viewing studies undertaken in the last twenty years or so, a number of themes have been prominent. Of major interest has been the issue of casualization; its nature, extent and implications (Phillips and Whiteside 1985). Research has tended to qualify previously held generalizations: without doubt ports relied very heavily on casual labour but not exclusively for almost all port labour forces had a section of labour which enjoyed permanent employment. Moreover, within the casual element, there were degrees of casuality albeit often based on favouritism, cliques or kickbacks. The extent of structure and organization within this labour market, both from the standpoint of employers and workers, has been much reviewed. So too, has the unionization of labour. Besides the inherent difficulties of organization, an issue to emerge in this specific context has been that of division and antagonism between rank and file and official leadership which often led to unofficial, spontaneous action and sometimes break-away moves (Lovell 1969). This division emerged relatively early within organized dock labour and at one and the same time was a cause of weakness and source of radical vitality. Its overall, persistent effect was to ensure that port labour relations

[7] Work on maritime trades unions has been described as an "exotic sector for labour studies". Nevertheless, for an impressive international perspective see the seminal study, Broeze 1991b. An examination of unionisation in a national context see Marsh and Ryan 1989. A major study of labour in Hamburg is Rath 1988.

generally were bitter and violent (Bergholm 1996, Barzman 1997 and Vanfraechem 2000). Dockers' unions also have considerable significance in the wider context of labour history. Because of their high public profile, dockers' unions were prominent within national labour contexts often seeking alliances with other unions. Syndicalism was an important influence in this trend. More unusually, dockers' unions also sought alliances overseas. Perhaps this should not come as a surprise as shipping and port business was international and just as cosmopolitan society in port towns looked inwards and outwards, so too did organized labour.

Dockers often, although not invariably lived in certain parts of port cities and conferred on those areas special aspects of class, subcultures and social structure. Insufficient work has been done on these features although studies of London, Rotterdam, Hamburg and Scandinavian ports have been made (Hill 1976, Gruttner 1984, Nijhof and Schrage 1988, Andersen 1992). The destruction or redevelopment of dockland areas and simultaneously the ending of traditional dockers' communities and subcultures are all part of the enormous changes wrought by the revolution in port technology. The ultimate impact of containerization on labour can only now begin to be put into a true historical perspective although it has attracted much contemporary commentary. Now, after the dust of bitter dispute, social trauma and the great shifts of economic and social fabric a more objective and longer-term analysis is underway.

A final comment before leaving maritime labour. Shipping and port business are service trades whose labour force comprises seafarers and dockers. But a further group within the maritime labour force are those engaged in the repair and maintenance of shipping. These workers who keep vessels moving are operatives in the service sector rather than industrial shipbuilding workers. Their work and their sector await research.

In the last half-hour or so, we have reviewed the progress of maritime and port history and some features of the body of published work that has appeared in the last quarter century. That work has been extensive and wide-ranging and by any standards its practitioners are entitled to a measure of self-congratulation. But, not without qualification; coverage has been uneven, some research has been too narrowly contained and most has sought the womb-like comfort of the national or even single company or port dimension. Genuine, international comparative studies are rare.

In the context of maritime and port history, this volume represents a great and significant opportunity. In compiling this introduction, my endeavour has been to convey the main features of recent research. Those features, closely in the port history context and in the wider shipping dimension too, are borne out by the contents of this volume. Traffic, technological change, policy and labour are key themes. Any fuller understanding of the experience of Antwerp and Rotterdam, two of the world's great ports, must represent a significant contribution to maritime and port history. But that contribution is enormously enhanced by the comparative dimension. I have just observed that genuine comparative studies are rare, how much more so comparative projects. May I applaud the initiative that brought this project into being and the occasion of this volume that promises to add much to our understanding. Earlier this morning I noted the criteria by which maritime and port history have sought to be judged – those of an international dimension, a focus on economic and social history and the integration of maritime history into the larger discipline. This volume sets fair to fulfil these obligations.

References

Akveld LM, Bruijn JR (eds) (1989) Shipping companies and authorities in the 19th and 20th centuries: their common interest in the development of port facilities. Den Haag

Andersen SA (1992) Dockers culture in three North European port cities: Hamburg, Gothenburg and Aarhus (1880-1960). A study of subcultures and their social contexts. In: Holm P, Edwards J (eds.) North sea ports and harbours – Adaptations to change. Esbjerg, pp 133-158

Balachandran G (1997) Recruitment and control of Indian seamen: Calcutta, 1880-1935. International journal of maritime history, IX: 1-18

Barzman J (1997) Port labour relations in Le Havre 1928-1947. International journal of maritime history, IX: 83-106

Bergholm T (1996) Masculinity, violence and disunity: waterfront strikers and strikebreakers in Finnish ports in the 1920s and 1930s. International journal of maritime history VIII: 23-42.

Bird J (1963) The major seaports of the United Kingdom. London

Bird J (1971) Seaports and seaport terminals. London

Boyce G (1995) Information, mediation and institutional development: the rise of large scale enterprise in British shipping, 1870-1919. Manchester

Broeze F (ed.) (1989) Brides of the sea. Port cities of Asia from the 16th –20th centuries. Sydney/Honolulu

Broeze F (1991a) Albert Ballin. The Hamburg-Bremen rivalry and the dynamics of the conference system. International journal of maritime history, III: 1-32

Broeze (1991b) Militancy and pragmatism. An international perspective on maritime labour (1870-1917). International review of social history XXXVI: 165-200

Broeze F (1995) (ed) Maritime history at the crossroads: a critical review of recent historiography, St. John's

Broeze F (ed) (1997) Gateways of Asia. Port cities of Asia in the 13th-20th centuries. London/New York

Broeze FJA (1998a) Riding the wave: the state of maritime history, opportunities and challenges. In: Van Royen PC, Fischer LR and Williams DM (eds.) Frutta de mare: evolution and revolution in the maritime world in the 19th and 20th centuries. Amsterdam, pp 195-208

Broeze F (1998b) Containerization: the globalization of liner shipping. In: Starkey DJ, Harlaftis G (eds) Global markets: the internationalization of the sea transport industries since 1850. St John's

Broeze (1999) Dubai: from creek to global port city. In: Fischer LR, Jarvis A (eds) Harbours and havens: essays in port history in honour of Gordon Jackson. St. John's, pp. 159-190

Bruijn JR (1998) Reflections on the recent past of maritime history in the Netherlands and abroad. In: Van Royen PC, Fischer LR and Williams DM (eds.) Frutta de mare: evolution and revolution in the maritime world in the 19th and 20th centuries. Amsterdam, pp 9-17

Chida T, Davies PN (1990) The Japanese shipping and shipbuilding industries. London
Davies S (ed.) (2000) Dock workers: international explorations in comparative labour history, 1790-1970. Ashford
Davis R (1978) Maritime history: progress and problems. In: Marriner S (ed) Business and businessmen. Studies in business, economic and accounting history. Liverpool
De la Puerta Rueda N (1994) El puerto de Bilbao como reflejo del desarrollo industrial de Vizcaya (1857-1913). Bilbao
De la Puerta Rueda N (1997) Management and finance in nineteenth century Spanish ports. The Northern Mariner, VII: 41-49
Devos G, Elewaut G (1995) CMB 100: a century of commitment to shipping 1895-1995. Antwerp
Dharmasena (1998) The port of Colombo. Tokyo
Dixon C (1996) The rise of the engineer in the nineteenth century. In: Jackson G, Williams DM (eds), Shipping, technology and imperialism. Aldershot, pp 243-261
Editorial (1995) Editioral. International journal of maritime history I:1
Falkus M (1999) The Blue Funnel legend. A history of the ocean steam ship company, 1865-1973. Houndsmill
Fischer LR (1992) Around the rim: seamen's wages in North Sea ports 1863-1900. In: Fischer LR (et al) North Sea. Twelve essays on the social history of maritime labour. Stavanger
Fischer LR (ed.) (1994) The market for seamen in the age of sail. St John's
Fischer LR (1999) Port policies: seaport planning around the North Atlantic, 1850-1939. In: Fischer LR, Jarvis A (eds) Harbours and havens: essays in port history in honour of Gordon Jackson. St. John's, pp 229-244
Fischer LR, Panting GE (1985) Change and adaptation in maritime history: The North Atlantic fleets in the nineteenth century, St John's
Fischer LR, Nordvik HW (1987) From Namsos to Halden: myths and realities in the history of Norwegian seamen's wages, 1850-1914. Scandinavian economic history review XXXV-1: 41-66
Fischer LR, Nordvik HW (1996) The evolution of Norwegian ports. In: Scholl LU and Edwards J (eds.) The North Sea: resources and seaway. Aberdeen pp 11-55
Flayhart WH III (2000) The American Line 1871-1902. New York
Gerstenberger H (1996) Men apart: the concept of total institution and the analysis of seafaring. International journal of maritime history, VIII: 173-183
Gruttner M (1984) Arbeitswelt an der Wasserkant. Göttingen
Harcourt F (1988) British oceanic mail contracts in the age of steam 1833-1914. Journal of transport history, IX: 1-18
Harlaftis G (1996) A history of Greek-owned shipping: the making of an international tramp fleet, 1830 to the present day. London/New York
Harley CK (1971) The shift from sailing ships to steamships, 1850-1890: a study in technological change and its diffusion. In: McCloskey DN (ed) Essays on a mature economy: Britain after 1840. London, pp 215-237
Harley CK (1985) Aspects of the economics of shipping, 1850-1913. In Fischer LR, Panting GE (eds.), Change and adaptation in maritime history: The North Atlantic fleets in the nineteenth century, St John's, pp 167-186
Harley CK (1988) Ocean freight rates and productivity, 1740-1913: the primacy of mechanical invention reaffirmed. Journal of economic history IIL: 851-76

Hattendorf JD (1994) Ubi sumus? The state of naval and maritime history, Newport/Rhode Island
Hill S (1976) The docker: class and tradition in London. London
Jackson G (19) Ports, ships and government in the nineteenth and twentieth centuries. In: Van Royen PC, Fischer LR and Williams DM (eds.) Frutta de mare: evolution and revolution in the maritime world in the 19th and 20th centuries. Amsterdam, pp 161-176.
Jackson G (1983) The history and archaeology of ports. Tadworth
Jackson G (1992a) Do docks make trade?: the case of the port of Great Grimsby. In: Fischer LR (ed) From wheel house to counting House: essays in maritime business history in honour of Professor Peter Neville Davies. St John's, pp 17-41
Jackson G (1992b) Operational problems of the transfer to steam: Dundee, Perth and London Shipping Company (1820-1845). In: Smout TC (ed.) Scotland and the Sea. Edinburgh, pp 154-181.
Jackson G (1998) Ports, ships and government in the nineteenth and twentieth centuries. In: Van Royen PC, Fischer LR, Williams DM (eds.) Frutta de mare: evolution and revolution in the maritime world in the nineteenth and twentieth centuries. Amsterdam, pp. 161-176
Jarvis A (1994) The members of the Mersey Docks and Harbour Board and their way of doing business. International journal of maritime history VI: 123-139
Jarvis A (1996) The Liverpool dock engineers. Stroud
Jarvis A (1998) Port and harbour engineering. Aldershot
Jarvis A (1999) Port history: thoughts on where it has come from and where it might be going. In: Fischer LR, Jarvis A (eds) Harbours and havens: essays in port history in honour of Gordon Jackson. St. John's, pp 13-34
Kaukiainen Y (ed.) (1990) The Baltic as a trade route: competition between steam and sail. Kotka.
Kaukiainen Y (1992a) Coal and canvas: aspects of the competition between steam and sail c1870-1914. International journal of maritime history IV: 175-192
Kaukiainen Y (1992b) The Baltic as a trade route: competition between steam and sail. Kotka
Kaukiainen Y (1993) A history of Finnish shipping. London
Kindleberger CP (1992) Mariners and Markets. Hemel Hempstead
Koch-Baumgarten S (1998) Trade union regime formation under the conditions of globalization in the transport sector: Attempts at transnational trade union regulation of flag of convenience shipping. International review of social history, VIIL: 370-402
Lane T (1986) Grey dawn breaking: British merchant seafarers in the late twentieth Century. Manchester
Lane T (1996) Flags of convenience and the globalization of the seafaring labour market. In: Scholl LU, Edwards J (eds) The North Sea: resources and seaway. Aberdeen, pp. 56-90
Lovell J (1969) Stevedores and dockers: A study of trade unionism in the port of London, 1870-1914. New York
Loyen R (2000) Structural breaks and functional shifts in the port of Antwerp: a model for transhipment. Paper presented at the 3rd international congress of maritime history, Esbjerg.
Maass D (1990) Der Ausbau des Hamburger Hafens (1840 bis 1910). Hamburg
Marsh A, Ryan V (1989) The seamen: a history of the national union of seamen. Oxford

McMurray HC (1980) Technology and social change at sea: the status and position on board of the ship's engineer, circa 1830-1860. In: Ommer R, Panting G (eds) Working men who got wet. St John's

Nijhof E, Schrage P (1988) Behind the picketline. The home front of Rotterdam workers in times of social welfare. In: Heerma van Voss, L and Diederiks H (eds.) Papers presented to the fourth British conference on labour history. Amsterdam

Northup HR, Rowan RL (1983), The international transport workers' federation and flag of convenience shipping. Philadelphia

Olukoju A (1994) The making of an "expensive port": shipping lines, government and port tariffs in Lagos, 1917-1949. International journal of maritime history, VI: 141-159

Ommer R, Panting G (eds.) (1980) Working men who got wet. St John's

Palmer S (1978) Experience, experiment and economics: factors in the construction of early merchant steamships. In Matthews K, Panting G (eds.), Ships and shipbuilding in the North Atlantic region. St John's, pp 231-247

Palmer S (2000) Seeing the sea: The maritime dimension in history. Greenwich

Phillips G, Whiteside N (1985) Casual labour: the unemployment question in the port transport industry, 1880-1970. Oxford

Prange C (1989) The development of the port of Hamburg in the 19th and 20th century. In: Akveld LM, Bruijn JR (eds) Shipping companies and authorities in the 19th and 20th centuries: their common interest in the development of port facilities. Den Haag

Proudfoot PR (1996) Seaport Sydney: the making of the city landscape. Sydney

Rath J (1988) Arbeiter im Hamburger Hafen. Hamburg

Rimmer P, Taniuch T (1997) Japan's seaports and regional developments during the era of hispeed growth (1960-1975). In: Broeze F (ed) Gateways of Asia. Port cities of Asia in the 13th-20th centuries. London/New York, pp 336-366.

Sager EW (1990) Seafaring labour: the merchant marine of Atlantic Canada, 1820-1914. Montreal

Sargent AJ (1938) Seaports and hinterlands. London

Scholl LU (1999) The port of Bremerhaven (1827-1918). In: Fischer LR, Jarvis A (eds) Harbours and havens: essays in port history in honour of Gordon Jackson. St. John's pp 191-212

Schuman P (1996) The social position of seafarers: some basic principles of changes in Dutch merchant-shipping law, 1840-1914. In: Jackson G, Williams DM (eds), Shipping, technology and imperialism. Aldershot, pp 243-261

Sturmey SG (1962) British shipping and world competition. London

Suykens F (1986) Antwerp, port for all seasons. Antwerp

Trace, K (1997) ASEAN ports since 1945: maritime change and rivalry. In: Broeze F (ed) Gateways of Asia. Port cities of Asia in the 13th-20th centuries. London/New York, pp. 313-338

Tull M (1997) A community enterprise: the history of the port of Fremantle, St. John's

Tull M (1999) Australian ports since 1945. In: Fischer LR, Jarvis A (eds) Harbours and havens: essays in port history in honour of Gordon Jackson. St. John's, pp 111-138

Valdaliso JM (1991) Growth and modernization of the Spanish merchant marine, 1860-1935. International journal of maritime history, III: 10-20

Valdaliso JM (2000) The rise of specialist firms in Spanish shipping and their strategies of growth, 1860-1930. Business history review, LXXIV: 267-300

Vanfraechem S (2000) Dockers' militantism: sign of the times? The struggle of Antwerp dockers for better labour conditions, 1900-1972. Paper presented at the 3rd International congress of maritime history, Esbjerg.

Veraghtert (1989) The expansion of the port of Antwerp. In: Akveld LM, Bruijn JR (eds) (1989) Shipping companies and authorities in the 19th and 20th centuries: their common interest in the development of port facilities. Den Haag

Williams DM (1993) The progress of maritime history. Journal of transport history XIV: 126-141

Williams DM, White AP (1991) A select bibliography of British and Irish university theses about maritime history. St John's

Wray WD (1984) Mitsubishi and the NYK, 1870-1914. Cambridge

Wray WD (1986) Shipping: from sail to steam. In: Jansen M, Rozman G (eds.) Japan in transition: from Tokugawa to Meiji. Princeton, pp 248-270

Throughput cluster

Throughput in the port of Antwerp (1901-2000): an integrated functional approach

Reginald Loyen

University of Leuven, Belgium

Introduction

This paper deals with the issue of throughput in the port of Antwerp. What do we gain by establishing the growth of a port's throughput? The cargo passing through the port tells us a lot about the domestic and the international economic state of affairs. The port is after all, the junction where cargo-flows from the hinterland to the foreland and vice versa converge, group and split up again. Since throughput is an indication of a nation's or a region's prosperity, seaports should be the obvious foci of attention for any economic historian, not just for those interested in the "maritime dimension". Although seaports clearly epitomise the proverbial navel string of a country's economic, commercial and social life, little quantitative as well as methodological work has been done in this field (Jackson 1983). This unenthusiastic attitude is surprising. Luckily we do have a large number of excellent, but often "introvert" detailed studies into ports in all their aspects at our disposal. Frankly, a macro-economic and generalising approach, which recognizes the wider perspective and which is so typical for maritime economic history, would most likely fail without this research (Williams 1993, Jarvis 1999).

The aim of this paper is therefore twofold: to make a methodological point regarding port historiography and - secondly - to describe, analyse and explain in greater detail the structural changes in the cargo-flow patterns of the port of Antwerp. After all, the past one hundred years have brought great change in the field of throughput, not only in terms of tons but also in the field of cargo-handling. We intend to provide insight in and understanding of the determinants of changes, which took place in the port in the course of the twentieth century. Our discussion will concentrate on throughput. Ideally speaking, other aspects should also be taken into account.

The paper hence starts out by questioning whether a functional approach is appropriate or not. Next, it discusses a range of alternative ways of studying port throughput. Consequently the paper argues that maritime economic historians have to tackle port history in a more paradigmatic way. After this methodological chapter it turns to the sources that should make the integrated functional approach feasible. Finally it chapter on the cargo-flows themselves and tries to apply this approach to port development. As far as possible within the limited scope of this paper, a comprehensive descriptive analysis of both maritime as well as continental throughput is given.

1. Conceptual and methodological framework

A seaport can best be described as a logistic and industrial junction in the global transport network with a strong maritime character, where a functional and spatial combination of activities takes place (Kuiler and Verhoeff 1973, 110-111, Notteboom 2000, 19-22). Some seaports also have an apparent urban aspect. These so-called port cities are urban settlements with specific characteristics, derived from their maritime functions (Murphey 1989, 227). In some ports, like Antwerp and Rotterdam, there even exists an institutional link between city council and port authority. The port authority is the organization responsible for providing various maritime services required to bring ships alongside land. In these ports the port authority is in some way or other always politically controlled by the municipality. It will manage the port's basic infrastructure (quays, locks, land policy, ...), exert policing duties and collect port dues. Contrary to other kinds of port authorities, it will not engage in the actual loading and unloading of ships, nor in storing and transporting commodities. This task is left to the private sector. These companies can be summarized under the heading "port users". The real consumers of port services are however the original producer and the final consignees of the shipped goods. The consumers of port services shouldn't be confused with port users like shipping agents, mercantile houses, stevedores, shipowners, pilots, tugs, inland carriers, industrial plants, ... Those companies handle the cargo, which moves in and out of the port on a day-to-day basis.

These in- and outward bound cargo-flows (also called "throughput") make up the core-business of the port's economic activities. Various types of cargo-flows can be discerned: inward (import) versus outward (export), domestic versus international traffic. Some of the international traffic may be in transit as well. Meaning that it will only cross the port's home country en route to a foreign destination.

How can we best study port throughput? We strongly argue in favour of a functional as well as a paradigmatic approach.

1.1. The functional approach

When speaking of port functions, this can be interpreted in two respects: economic importance and assignment[1]. The "functional approach" we advocate in the present paper is exclusively interested in the latter. Emphasis not so much lies on eco-

[1] There exists a sizeable literature regarding the function or the economic importance of a port for the regional and national economy. In the scope of this paper we will only mention the annual reports of the Central Bank of Belgium titled *Economic importance of the port of Antwerp* (since 1985) and the much debated Economic Impact Studies. Also see: Waters 1977, Chang 1978, Winkelmans 1993, Peeters 1995.

nomic importance in quantitative terms, but rather on a port's assignment and operation. Since the turn of the century the notion of port function has regularly appeared in authoritative literature which aimed at determining a port's task, duty or goal (Baudez 1965, 67, Jolmes 1966, 387 and 390, Frankel 1987, 8).

The French economist P. de Rousiers was probably the first to refer systematically and coherently to a port in terms of its functions (De Rousiers 1909, XV-XLVI). He did so in trying to explain the cargo-flows of certain ports. Writing in 1909, De Rousiers asserts that modern ports achieved a multifunctional character by definition on account of the rise in modern means of transport. That is how they distinguished themselves from ports of the pre-industrial age. De Rousiers basically discerned three functions: a regional, an industrial and a commercial function and quickly added that "il ne faut pas perdre de vue que les différentes fonctions des ports se prêtent forcément une aide mutuelle" (De Rousiers 1909, 822). The regional function mainly concerns goods being loaded and unloaded in the port. The port is simply the most favourable point of transhipment between maritime and continental transport. It equals in other words cargo-handling and accessories. The industrial function covers those commodities that come to the port not because it is a place of transhipment, but because of the presence of certain industries in the port area. The industrial function only appeared in the course of the nineteenth century and included oil mills, sugar refineries, textile industry, wood and paper mills, petroleum refineries, chemical plants, flour mills, steel industry, shipbuilding.... The commercial function includes goods that pass through the port neither because of the transhipment possibilities, nor because of the industry, but for commercial reasons. The port attracts these commodities because they can be sold, distributed or stored and re-exported. The commercial function encompasses the activities of distribution firms, forwarders, shipping agents, storage companies, but also insurance companies, banks and exchanges concerned with the maritime dimension. Mercantile houses will also attract cargo-flows whose original destination might have been another port. The commercial function is probably the oldest port function, but had lost much of its momentum since the First World War.

Since its publication, De Rousiers' scheme has constantly been a source of inspiration as well as of annoyance. At a number of occasions researchers cursed its inaccuracy, rigidity or obsoleteness (Romus 1944, 164-168, Vigarié 1979, 116-119). Kuiler and Verhoeff published a workable and consistent revision, which found a ready reception with many transport economists (Kuiler and Verhoeff 1973, 110-140). They distinguished four port functions: primary or transport functions, commercial, industrial and residential function.

But even Kuiler and Verhoeff, writing in the 1970s, did not anticipate the advent of a new function. The distribution function came into existence in the late 1960s and was the result of the strong expansion of international trade in semi manufactures. The scaling up that took place in the scope of the "container revolution" led to rationalization of existing shipping lines and a reduction in the number of ports of call. Hence the remaining mainports started to function as hubs, redistributing traffic to hierarchically speaking lower ports. The technical discontinuity between huge maritime shipments and relatively small inland traffic could henceforth be neutralized in the ports. Physical distribution also was the last possibility of introducing cost-cutting measures (Suykens 1986b, 97-108, Vigarié 1979, 130-145).

In a nutshell, we distinguish four port functions, namely the primary, the industrial, the commercial and the distribution function. Because the lack of a rigorous scientific demarcation of a port function, we cannot determine when exactly a shift in port functions occurs. A functional shift cannot be detected (or predicted) with mathematical precision. This also implies that functional shifts do not necessarily signify the loss of other port functions. It is merely a shift in emphasis. Over time there will be a deepening of existing functions and a widening towards new functions. In this paper, port functions are not a goal as such, as with De Rousiers, but merely a beginning. The port functions make up a frame of reference thanks to which we can modulate the development of the cargo-flows. Contrary to De Rousiers we do not explain a port's throughput by means of port functions. Functions and throughput attend each other. Structural shifts in port functions and cargo-flows can be explained by looking at the determinants of the (derived) demand for port services. The functional approach has in itself, little explanatory value. This was first put forward by Vigarié and summarized in his famous "triptyque portuaire".

A clear, but balanced mechanism is without any doubt one of the amenities of a concept like the triptyque portuaire, which encompasses fore- and hinterland as well as the port itself. "La notion de triptyque (...) regroupent obligatoirement l'intégralité des facteurs de détermination qui modèlent les trafics, et toutes les explications qu'on peut rechercher"[2]. Defining hinterland and foreland does remain problematic however. Recently both concepts have been under fire from economists (eg Blumenhagen 1981, Hayuth 1982, 14). Writing in 1938, Sargent noted that "the term hinterland expresses something real, but far from simple or easy to describe" (Sargent 1938, 15). Generally speaking the concept of hinterland refers to the area from which the loaded commodities in the seaport originate and to which the unloaded commodities in the seaport are sent (Bird 1971, 125). Rather less well known is the notion of "foreland". "Forelands are the land areas, which lie on the seaward side of a port beyond maritime space and with which the port is connected by ocean carriers" (Weigend 1956, 2-3). Building on Vigarié's ideas Robinson introduced the concept of the foreland-hinterland continuum. "The separation of foreland and hinterland relationships of a port into two neatly labelled packages represents a false dichotomy. The flows from foreland to hinterland might be better viewed as a continuum. (...) The spatial analysis of port-linked flows must regard the landward segment of the flow as a portion of a flow continuum rather than as a flow between port and hinterland, as in the traditional hinterland model" (Robinson 1960, 307, Notteboom 2000, 31-40). In this paper we will maintain Robinson's "integrated" approach and take factors from hinterland as well as foreland into account when discussing the determinants of throughput.

---

[2] Vigarié 1979, 70. First published in 1964. For an elaborate discussion of the triptyque portuaire: Charlier 1981, 29-138.

1.2. A paradigmatic approach?

The origin, current situation and future development of a seaport depends on various economical, political, financial, geo-physical, technological, organizational, social and cultural factors home and abroad. All of these elements have been summarized in comprehensive paradigms.

In the 1980s and 1990s a number of problems arose regarding the generalizations in the existing port transition models. The complex character of port operations can partially account for the lack of generalization. Not only have the generalizations come under fire, also the lack of explanation has been criticised on various occasions (e.g. Jarvis 1999, 13-34). Some authors have even argued that the current surfeit actually mars the unique advantages of a model (e.g. Layton 1981, 23-31).

Generally speaking, two kinds of port transition models can be distinguished: regarding port systems and regarding individual ports. In this paper we are only interested in the latter, as the former kind describes and explains especially the interactions between ports (e.g. establishment of a port hierarchy). Quite well known in that respect is the model by (Taaffe, Morril and Gould, 1963). From literature four influential and useful examples of single port transition models can be identified: the Anyport model (Bird 1971, 66-75), the organizational model (UNCTAD 1992, 47-50), the interface model (Hoyle 1988, 3-17) and the Rotterdam model (Van Klink 1995, 17-23). We have used these models in order to establish a new paradigm.

1.3. The Hanseatic paradigm

Unlike some foreign ports, the port of Antwerp has not yet been the object of such modelling. It is clear from what precedes that an integrated functional and paradigmatic approach is generally accepted as well as criticised for hardly generalising and/or explaining. Bearing this in mind, a new transition model should treat throughput, spatial and functional shifts in a diachronic and general way. This can only be warranted when designing a model valid for all the large seaports in the Hamburg-Le Havre range, and by extension any comparable port world wide.

The model's name was chosen in accordance to the "Hanseatic" tradition - a set of common features which many maritime economists and lawyers have identified (Suykens 1982, 78, Suykens 1986a, 105-126, Van Hooydonk 1996). In so doing they distinguish seaports managed by the city council from seaports ran as total organisations, where maritime access and cargo-handling are the responsibility of one single organisation. The port of Antwerp has however always been managed by the city council (Kinart and Bollengier 1931, 1-24, Suykens 1985). Notwithstanding recent port privatization and Europeanization, the Hanseatic tradition still is very much alive.

Seaport development can be summarized in four stages. With every new functional shift a new stage dawns. The timing of these shifts shouldn't be strictly interpreted: the dates are symbolic landmarks rather than accurate points in time.

First functional shift: from primary function to commercial function (1860-1900-1945)

The primary function encompasses sea transport, overland transport and cargo-handling. It dominated port activities until the middle of the nineteenth century. Approximately from the 1860s onwards, the commercial function prevailed. It includes all service industries in the seaport: not only cargo-handlers and shipping agents, but also mercantile houses and banks. The port's commercial function attracted goods that otherwise wouldn't have passed through the port. Excellent transport connections were however a prerequisite.

This functional shifts was also attended by radical changes in the seaport's throughput. The composition of the incoming cargo-flow shifted from relatively expensive colonial general cargo to cheap bulk commodities (ores and agricultural produce). From the 1860s onwards, those bulk goods were also transported on large-scale basis to industrial centres deep in the hinterland. These industries on their turn produced (semi) manufactures, which were again exported via the seaport. New overland transport links also facilitated the export of ores from mines in the hinterland. In other words: also the outward traffic flow experienced a structural break: ballast (sand, stones, water) was substituted by ores (especially coal) plus iron and steel manufactures.

The new commercial function and the shifts in throughput required radical spatial changes. Seaport and city slowly started to grow apart as the port expanded downstream. Characterising for this expansion is the enlargement of mooring length and the attention devoted to the removal of goods from the quays by rail, barge or cart. The quays themselves drastically increased in surface and often included transit sheds etc. At the turn of the century this demand for more backup land resulted in a new expansion of the port area. Moreover, demand for larger water surfaces increased, which facilitated direct transhipment.

Second functional shift: from commercial towards industrial function (1945-70)

The commercial function fell victim to the fast progress in transport and telecommunication. Since the number of intermediaries consequently decreased, the mediatory role of seaports declined as well. Additionally, government interference in international trade and several wars ruptured traditional commercial contacts. The industrial function only really broke through after World War II, especially in the field of oil refining. For the port, the industrial function guaranteed a steady flow of commodities and therefore lessened port competition.

After 1945 throughput in seaports underwent radical changes. Especially the imports rose spectacularly on account of the import of crude petroleum. The newly-build refineries also generated the raw material of other chemical plants, which also settled in the port area. Next to petroleum, ores represented an important share of imports. Compared to oil and ores, the transhipment of agricultural produce dwindled. Total exports also rose. The position of (semi) manufactures improved. Exports of coal exacerbated seemingly undisturbed and virtually disappeared. This was largely compensated by an increasing export of petroleum derivatives and chemicals. The increase (especially in chemicals) mostly supported on transit. Compared to the interwar period transit constantly rose.

The industrial take-over necessitated a gigantic expansion of the port complex. The downstream enlargement implied that city and port definitively went separate ways. The new sites offered possibilities for refineries, chemical plants and other factories. Besides the continuous attention over the years for surface and length of quays, depth of docks was also considered important.

Third functional shift: from industrial function to distribution function (1970-)

The industrial function lost momentum in the course of the 1960s. Although the presence of the industrial function remained important to the port's prosperity, a new functional shift was heralded in the 1970s. The new distribution function solved the discontinuity between maritime and continental shipments in the foreland-hinterland continuum. The distribution function not only included intermediary storage in the seaport, it also encompassed industrial distribution centres. Typical for the distribution function is however control over the logistic chain. The distribution function further affected port competition radically since ever more cargo-flows became ever less embedded. In the near future this will lead to port networks.

Regarding throughput, the aggressive advent of the container and the materialization of a relatively heterogeneous cargo-flow attended the distribution take-over. Remarkable in this regard is the status quo of classic imports like ores. After a rather modest post-war presence, we again notice a steady increase in the discharging of coal. Chemicals and finished commodities are the front-runners, but they do not dominate imports. For two exceptions, basically the same trends can be observed for the exports as well. The export of petroleum derivatives, and with it chemicals and finished products, continued to grow after 1970. Remarkable is the catch-up of foodstuffs and fodder from the 1980s onwards. Not surprisingly the port once again exports ores (namely scrap iron). Contrary to the previous stage, the heterogeneity and the amount of transit of both in - and outgoing cargo - flows has been dramatically amplified.

The shift towards distribution made a new enlargement of the port inevitable, albeit in a more modest way than before 1970. Separate docks, with great draught, special cranes and a lot of backup land were taken into service. Most of these docks were build downstream and exclusively for container handling. Because of the port's downstream development, some of the older docks, in the immediate vicinity of the city had been neglected. These obsolete installations are now radically renovated and returned to the urban cause. In this way port and city once again co-operate.

Determinants

Consequently the question arises as to which factors determined the shifts in port functions, throughput and spatial behaviour. Although studies assessing the various factors influencing port performance are scant, the most important determinants of throughput can be excerpted from international literature (Tongzon 1995, Seidenfus 1987, Slack 1985, Van Klink 1995, 17-32).

Probably the most important factor in the development of a seaport is the international economy or world trade. Since the Industrial Revolution the volume of transport has been continuously accruing. This growth is obviously connected with the globalization of the economy and the international division of labour. In other words, industrial production, business cycles, trade elasticity and politics have to be analysed.

Technological innovation is in three respects a major element in explaining port development: firstly, the introduction of new ship types and the advent of unit load; secondly: organizational renewal and thirdly, productivity improvements in key economic sectors (like steel).

A country's transport policy is also crucial to a port's evolution. In one respect the construction of bridges, roads, canals etc. plays a prominent part. On the other hand port policy obviously might be primordial as well. A port may be proclaimed the national seaport in the scope of trade policy, regional development policy or colonization. This determinant also includes a social component, namely the role of the consumers of port services. The favourable economic conditions after World War II has led to an enormous increase in welfare and consequently to a bigger demand for consumer goods. It also caused environmental awareness.

The interaction between these three factors determines the volume and composition of the cargo-flows in the port. As the influence of the seaport on these elements seems negligible, we can name these factors the "exogenous determinants". They cause a proverbial cargo-flow in the foreland-hinterland continuum of a port range. This implies that geographical location has an impact on cargo size. Here the element of port competition also comes into play.

Which of those commodities actually flow through the seaport in question, will be determined on the local level. In the end it is this local level that determines to what extent a port can anticipate and take advantage of new opportunities, which present themselves in the foreland-hinterland continuum. On this "endogenous" level the demand for port service must be matched with an offer. So the power of local players remains great and is in no way limited to a bit of tinkering and readjusting. These endogenous elements form a "filter" on the cargo-flows; we discern the port authority and the port user as the two most important players.

The port authority plays a significant part on four levels. Firstly, the port authority determines to a large extent port capacity. Secondly, land policy also determines cargo-flows: embedding larger shippers in the port is after all, crucial. Land policy not only includes developing new sites, it also implies the creation of favourable location factors. Thirdly, we must also point to pricing and port charges (notwithstanding the fact that shippers are more concerned with costs associated with delays, loss of market or customer confidence). Fourthly, an appropriate marketing strategy will attract new cargo-flows and industrial plants. The image of the port is not only important for new customers, but also in selling the next port enlargement to the populace.

Port users play an important role on the local level because they also shape the port and determine to which degree the port will be able to answer to new opportunities. They mainly contribute to port capacity and efficiency. Shipowners, road haulers and inland shippers determine the all-important frequency, reliability and quality of the services. The work practices and creativity of forwarders and other logistical agents guarantee a punctual delivery at the lowest possible price. Terminal operators, who organize the cargo-handling process, and (petro)chemical industries must also be mentioned here.

2. Sources

An integrated functional approach might facilitate the study of throughput, but is it a viable, feasible method of investigation? After all, the average port statistics are not exactly drawn up to alleviate such a modus operandi. Obviously a comprehensive database on maritime as well as continental cargo-flows to-and-fro the port of Antwerp is indispensable for this approach[3]. In order to make the integrated functional approach work, the database should include continuous time-series, using a single universally accepted system of classification. We have opted for the *Nomenclature des Statistiques de Transport revisé* (NSTr). Since Veraghtert focused on the nineteenth century, we have limited our research to the twentieth century[4].

Regarding maritime cargo-flows, we have consulted the following sources. The trade statistics (*Tableau général du commerce de la Belgique avec les pays étrangers*) offer information on loading and unloading in the port, in terms of tons, for the period 1900-1939. Figures on transit were not included and are therefore not known. For the latter part of the twentieth century we have used statistics published by the Belgian National Institute for Statistics (NIS). For the time span 1947/1952-1983 we have relied upon the *Yearly statistics on the international traffic of ports* and for the period 1984-1989/94 we have used the *Statistics of the international traffic of the ports of the Belgian-Luxembourg Economic Union*. These time-series contain data on imports and exports of commodities (in ton), but also on transit. For a variety of reasons, from 1989 onwards, the NIS-series are incomplete. After careful consideration and consultation, we have opted to extend the NIS-series by forecasting it up to 2000 using the data published by the Port Authority in the *Statistical yearbook*. Although the forecasts yielded quite good results, these time-series should be handled carefully.

Regarding continental throughput, we have relied on publications of the Antwerp Port Authority and the Belgian National Railway Company (NMBS-SNCB) in combination with the aforementioned "classical" port statistics of the NIS. For continental traffic it is important to note that the latter source only covers international traffic. The *Statistics of sea and inland navigation* (1900-1969), the *Report of the harbourmaster* (1970-1985) and the *Statistical yearbook* (1986-2000), all

[3] The database contains data on in- and outward international and domestic shipments in terms of tons. Additionally continuous time-series on the origin and destination of the maritime and continental cargo-flows have been constructed. Although we will not dwell on this here, ship movements have also been included in the database.

[4] In his seminal dissertation on the cargo-flows of nineteenth-century Antwerp, Veraghtert used records of the local Chamber of Commerce. From 1901 onwards they gathered their information from the trade statistics. See also: Veraghtert 1976.

published by the Port Authority, have allowed us to construct a database on inland shipping. We have created time-series on railway traffic by means of the *Statistical survey* (1958-1962) published by the Port Authority and the *Mouvement commercial, industriel et maritime de la place d'Anvers* (1882-1912 and 1921-23) published by the Chamber of Commerce. Additional monthly reports from the NMBS informed us about railway throughput after World War II. Road haulage was yet another matter due to the paucity of data. A partial reconstruction becomes possible though, via the *Statistical survey* published by the Port Authority in 1959. Alternative sources, especially dealing with the first half of the twentieth century, were rather scant and we have therefore reconstructed domestic haulage as a residual.

How trustworthy are these sources? As a full-fledged analysis would lead us too far, this discussion will be limited to some general remarks and refer to literature. The problems with trade statistics are widely known (Federico and Tena 1989, Degrève 1982, Horlings 1996). Luckily they have hardly affected our data. The time-series gathered from the publications by the NIS are another matter however. It is important to know that they are based on custom documents. Hence they only take net weight into account and also consider outgoing bunker fuel. Another problem linked to this type of source is that of delayed registration (especially regarding transiting goods). That is one of the reasons why the official government statistics (NIS) differ so much from the statistics published by the local Port Authority (De Lombaerde 1994, Coeck et al. 1995). On the other hand, the Port Authority has installed a network of quay supervisors, regularly sending information on the cargo handled at their quay to a central office. The supervisors will however only register commodities that have been (un)loaded via the quay (refuelling of ships is thus not included). They will also consider the gross weight of the handled goods. This also explains why both series cannot simply be linked.

3. Cargo-flows

In this third and final chapter we turn to the evolution of the port's cargo-flows or throughput. This chapter attempts to apply the model, specified above, to the port's historic development.

In the course of the twentieth century throughput in the port of Antwerp rose from 10 million tons to 120 million tons (Fig. 3.1.). This did not come about in a linear way, but with small positive and negative shocks. Average growth amounted to 3,8 % per annum. A glance at Fig. 3.2. and Fig. 3.3. makes clear that the composition of the maritime cargo flows in the twentieth century underwent radical changes after World War II and after the Oil Crises. With respect to the functional approach, these charts confirm the phasing proposed in the model. We will now look at these changes in detail and also elaborate on the factors behind these developments.

Fig. 3.1. Total in- and outward bound maritime cargo flows in the port of Antwerp (1901-2000)

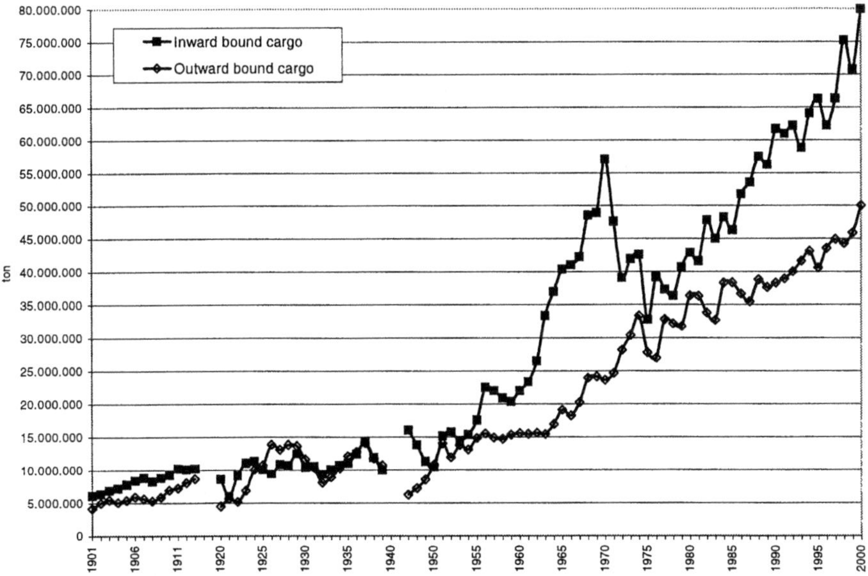

Sources: Tableau général du commerce de la Belgique avec les pays étrangers. Ports Maritimes (1901-1939). NIS, Jaarstatistieken over de internationale trafiek der havens (1947/52-1983). NIS, Statistiek over de internationale trafiek in de havens van de BLEU (1984-1989/94) and own calculations.

Between 1901 and 1913 total throughput almost doubled to 19 million tons, mostly due to a doubling of exports (especially 1911-1913). The composition of throughput between 1900 and 1913, and by extension between 1900 and 1945, can be traced back to the nineteenth century. In his influential work pertaining to the port of Antwerp in the nineteenth century, Veraghtert established a shift from traditional "colonial" imports (cotton, hides, sugar, coffee,...) to less expensive bulk goods (cereals, coal, petroleum and ores) in the 1860s. Although we will not dwell extensively upon the development of throughput in the nineteenth century, it is essential that we embark on a short excursion to the 1860s (Veraghtert 1986, Suykens 1986).

The 1860s are generally recognized as an era of unlimited free trade (Kenwood and Lougheed 1999, 64-70). The removal of free trade impediments was so far-reaching that economists often refer to this period as the first wave of globalization (Baldwin and Martin 1999). The Belgian economy, the first Continental economy to industrialize, benefited from this trend and international trade gradually increased between 1840 and 1873 (Veraghtert 1983, 49). This process of industrialization crystallized in the Walloon iron, steel- and coal industry, situated in South Belgium. Industrialization also transformed the newly unified German economy from an agricultural to an industrial society. Confronted with the depletion of local high-grade iron ore, heavy industry in the Ruhr as well as in South Belgium turned to large-scale imports. Because of the shift in labour forces from agricultural to industrial activities, the industrialization entailed a strongly rising demand for imports of agricultural produce. Plummeting transport prices made a steady flow of ores and grain via the ports of Holland and Belgium possible. Triggered by low transport costs, the first wave of globalization generated a stark process of specialization, which itself promoted trade. Industrial production in Belgium soon exceeded domestic needs and therefore exports were vital. Belgium's geographical location and low transport costs much aided this situation.

These fundamental shifts in the structure of the European economy commensurably altered the character of international trade and thus the structure of the port's throughput. Veraghtert, found that in the 1870s and 1880s nearly half of transhipment consisted of grain (Veraghtert 1994, Loyen 2001). This shows how cardinally this port was in facilitating the Industrial Revolution and the Agricultural Invasion in Belgium. Because of Belgium's heavy commitment to trade it developed an open economy, which made the country particularly sensitive to external shocks and international competition. By 1873 Belgian international trade stagnated, in line with the international return to protectionism. Paradoxically the reversion to old policies was necessary to allow for further industrialization, which only seemed possible in a protected environment. Industry faced growing difficulties in striking new markets for their products. Protectionism and nationalism however did not mute world trade, which rose until 1914 (Kenwood and Lougheed 1999, 70-73). Also in Belgium, international trade doubled between 1874 and 1895 and was highly correlated with industrial production (Veraghtert 1983, 30). Belgium was one of only a handful of countries, led by Great Britain, which adhered to the principles of free trade. Consequently Belgium continued importing ores and agricultural produce and exporting manufactures. Furthermore, proportionally speaking more and more of this trade entered/left the country via Antwerp. Veraghtert already demonstrated that the increase of ore imports via Antwerp and the Belgian iron- and steel production developed parallel.

The picture sketched by Veraghtert, is still very much accurate for the first half of the twentieth century. Fig. 3.2. shows e.g. that agricultural produce remained dominant until World War II dawned. Raw materials like ores and coal, which rose fast in the 1860-70s, still represented respectively 17 % and 12 % of average imports during the interwar period. The same goes for the exports. The strong position of half-finished iron and steel products had its roots in the last quarter of the nineteenth century. The frontrunners of the time were clearly coal, sugar and steel. Export of iron - and later - steel kept growing and started to dominate the outgoing cargo-flows, while traditional commodities like glass and zinc faltered. This throughput structure basically prevailed until World War II, thanks to a major expansion of the infrastructure of the port. Especially the 1880s saw a doubling of quayage and water surface. Between 1890 and 1906 not a single meter of quay was build on account of tensions between local and national political groups. The debate about the so-called "Grande Coupure" impeded every expansion of the port until 1907. Two decennia of infrastructural standstill perniciously impinged on throughput. The new development project of 1907 was executed in three stages: 1907, 1914 and finished in 1928. The Great War further slowed down expansion, while Rotterdam stayed unaffected. In 1928 however thirty-six kilometres of new quays was added (+1/4) and the water surface behind the locks virtually quadrupled (Himler 1993, De Kesel 1964).

Fig. 3.2. Composition of the inward bound maritime cargo flow of the port of Antwerp (1900-2000; NSTr classification)

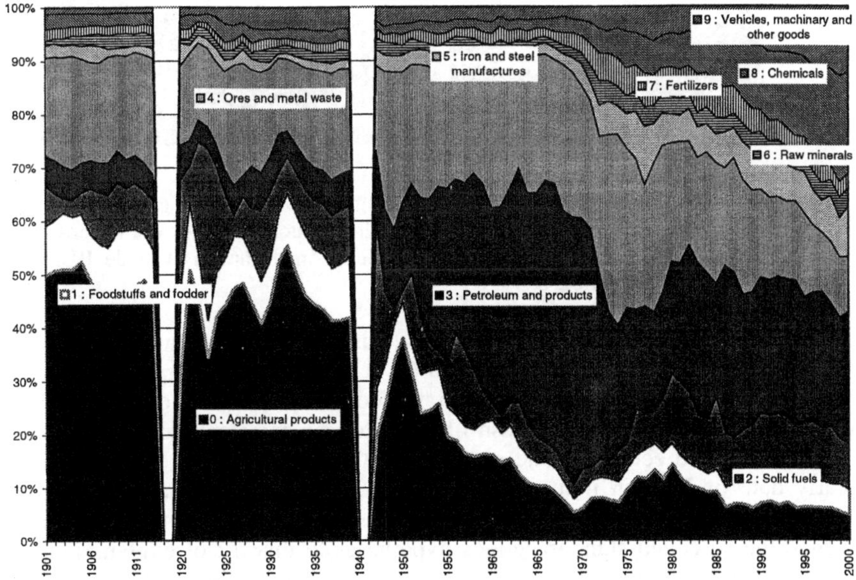

Sources: Tableau général du commerce de la Belgique avec les pays étrangers. Ports Maritimes (1900-1939). NIS, Jaarstatistieken over de internationale trafiek der havens (1947/52-1983). NIS, Statistiek over de internationale trafiek in de havens van de BLEU (1984-1989/94) and own calculations.

In light of the Industrial Revolution, the supremacy of half-finished iron and steel manufactures in the outgoing cargo-flows may seem acceptable enough for the nineteenth century. Fig 3.3. however makes clear that these steel uninterruptedly dominated exports for over a century. This is especially remarkable because steel hardly featured in the throughput of Antwerp's main rival, Rotterdam. The privileged position of steel in Antwerp ("the mother of all cargo-flows") must therefore be elucidated.

Fig. 3.3. Composition of outward bound maritime cargo flow of the port of Antwerp (1900-2000, NSTr-classification)

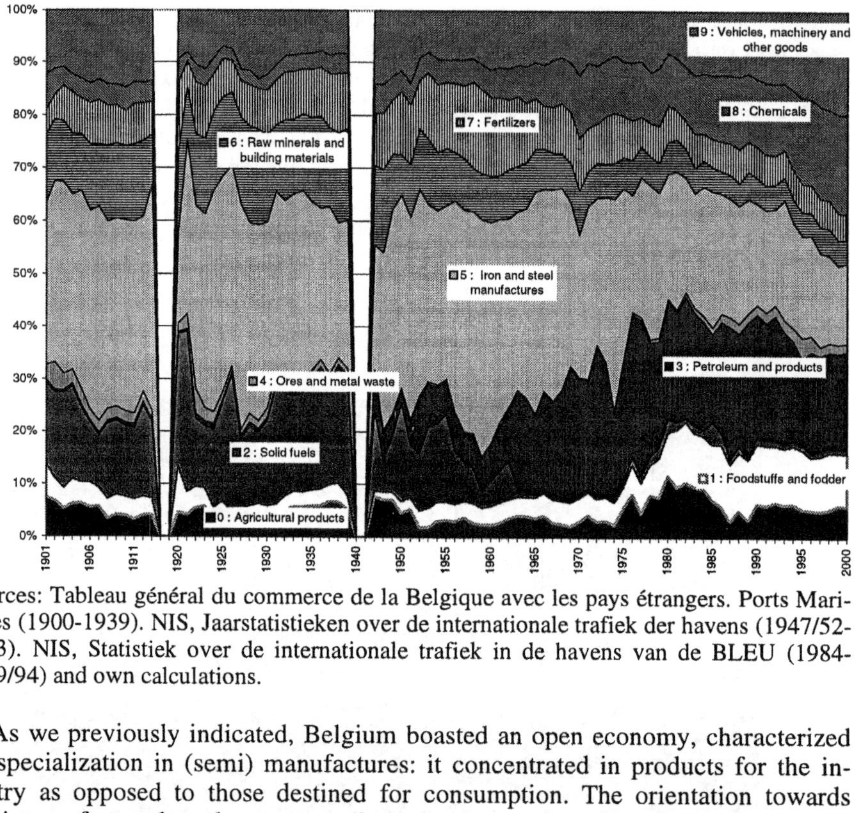

Sources: Tableau général du commerce de la Belgique avec les pays étrangers. Ports Maritimes (1900-1939). NIS, Jaarstatistieken over de internationale trafiek der havens (1947/52-1983). NIS, Statistiek over de internationale trafiek in de havens van de BLEU (1984-1989/94) and own calculations.

As we previously indicated, Belgium boasted an open economy, characterized by specialization in (semi) manufactures: it concentrated in products for the industry as opposed to those destined for consumption. The orientation towards semi-manufactured products wasn't limited to iron and steel industry, also in other branches of the economy one could finds the same level of specialization. The early date of Belgian industrialization, its dependence on coal, its geographical disposition and its lack of dynamic entrepreneurs can explain this. In 1960 Drèze added the so-called standard goods hypotheses to this list of explanations (Drèze 1961). Drèze maintained that if products are nationally differentiated and if there are economies of scale in production, small countries should specialize in production of goods for which the international demand is standardized. Because of their limited market size, small countries would be at a disadvantage in the production of more differentiated goods. In the production of standardized commodities, Belgium was rationally exploiting its comparative advantages.

Besides the widely held standard goods hypotheses, we should also consider the dubious role of the so-called mixed banks. The mixed banks or holdings triggered technological as well as organizational innovations and were also the driving force behind Belgium's foreign direct investments (especially constructing railways and tramlines all over the world). In their organizational sublimity and aided by others, the mixed banks created new overseas markets at the turn of the century. The impact of this re-orientation was especially felt in the port of Antwerp (Van der Wee and Veraghtert 1978). This of course had a bearing on the export of Belgian industrial commodities, but also led to the creation of shipping yards, non-ferrous metal companies, chemical companies and metal works in the province of Antwerp itself.

On the other hand, the mixed banks and their specialized holdings overconcentrated on technological progress directly linked to heavy industry by means of "defensive" investments. A system of "interlocking" clusters of companies, brought about by mixed banks, mitigated competition as many companies merely functioned as subcontractors. Because the organizational structure of the mixed banks focused on technological innovations in limited segments of the economy, from 1900 onwards, Belgium started to lag behind in the international race for technological innovation. New opportunities in sectors like textiles, chemicals or electricity didn't excite the mixed banks, which conveniently continued to develop heavy industry. Belgium obstinately clung to the heavy industry also because the market for non-durables and consumer durables remained limited in Belgium until the 1960s and the creation of the European Community. The foreign market was also a source of inertia since Belgium's colonial endeavours offered heavy industry a market in Africa (Van der Wee 1997).

The port of Antwerp thus played an important part in the strategy of the mixed banks. Antwerp was soon labelled as Europe's steel port and by extension as a typical general cargo port. The mixed banks and their steel factories, especially from 1900 onwards, had to rely on an extensive network of regular shipping lines distributing their manufactures all over the world (Drèze 1961, Oboussier 1917, 15-23, 51-53). Initially the government tried to create a Belgian merchant fleet (De Baets et al, 1995). For a variety of reasons, the government soon abandoned this scheme and established a network of regular steamship lines via mail subsidies (Devos 1991). This policy turned out to be extremely successful. It is widely held that industrial top brass aided by powerful German immigrants instigated this policy. Also the construction of a railway connecting Antwerp with the Ruhr (1843) strengthened Belgian-German relations at the expense of Rotterdam (Stengers 1968).

Table 3.1. Origin and destination of the continental cargo-flow of the port of Antwerp, modal split included (1900-2000)

	Domestic				International			
Year	Inland shipping	Railroad	Road haulage	Total	Inland shipping	Railroad	Road haulage	Total
1900	28%	45%	1%	73%	17%	10%	0%	27%
1910	25%	37%	2%	65%	26%	9%	0%	35%
1920	27%	33%	2%	62%	30%	8%	0%	38%
1938	24%	27%	9%	61%	31%	8%	0%	39%
1951	35%	25%	5%	65%	28%	7%	0%	35%
1960	32%	19%	13%	65%	29%	4%	3%	35%
1970	25%	18%	27%	71%	21%	4%	4%	29%
1980	19%	16%	20%	55%	29%	6%	10%	45%
1990	17%	14%	21%	52%	25%	8%	15%	48%
2000	19%	9%	22%	49%	27%	7%	16%	51%

Sources: NIS, Jaarstatistieken over de internationale trafiek der havens (1947/52-1983); NIS, Statistiek over de internationale trafiek in de havens van de BLEU (1984-1989/94); GHA, Statistieken over de zee- en binnenvaart (1911-1968); GHA, Statistisch jaarboek (1990-2000); NMBS, Spoorwegvervoer in de haven van Antwerpen, (1950-2000) and own calculations

Note that “domestic” includes the Grand Duchy of Luxemburg from 1922 onwards, which then joined Belgium in economic union).

Hence German manufactures joined Belgian products. Often they embarked on German ships stopping at Antwerp, before standing out to sea (Ehlers and Bultman 1915, 4). The picture presented in Table 3.1., regarding continental traffic, indicates however that at the turn of the century only one ton in three had a destination/origin in Antwerp's foreign hinterland. So the presence of the German semi manufactures should be put in the correct proportions. Table 3.2. shows the origin and destination of the maritime cargo flows of the port of Antwerp. It shows that half of Antwerp's throughput had a European origin or destination.

On the incoming side, the large European share can be explained by referring to the voluminous import of grain from countries like Russia and Rumania (Veraghtert 1988a). Furthermore, until 1945 approximately every third unloaded ton originated in and every second loaded ton was destined for Great Britain. The structure of Belgian international trade is not only reflected in the European dominance, but also in the strong presence of North America (15 % of in- and 12 % of outward bound commodities) and South America (14 % of both in- and outward goods (Baetens 1991, Veraghtert 1988b). Moreover the rather weak turnout of other continents corresponds with Belgian international trade. African and Asian regions initially stayed outside the reach of Antwerp, since they remained in a colonial grip (Veraghtert 1983 and 1986).

The Great War dramatically altered the economic structure of sea-borne trade. Immediately after the war throughput took a flying start as a consequence of the miserable state the country was in. In order to get the economy going again, invariably everything had to be imported (with disastrous financial consequences). This peak (of imports) was however short-lived. Although the 1920s meant new growth, cargo-flows barely changed. Like before World War I, half of unloaded goods were agricultural produce, followed by ores and mineral fuel (Fig. 3.2.) (Deprez 1939, 33-106). After the Great War initial exports were extremely small. Exports only started to grow spectacularly between 1920 and 1926 and contributed to the post-war revival of total throughput. Exports doubled in four years time thanks to a multiplication of coal exports with a factor seven in five years time. The French-Belgian occupation of the Ruhr (1923) and the British miners' strikes of 1921 and 1925 influenced coal exports. The post-war reparations and general chaos that immobilized the German economy, naturally impinged on Antwerp as well. German coal was also imported in large quantities in the framework of the economic restitutions and the Belgian-German trade agreement of 1925. Some of this coal was re-exported via Antwerp. Quotas on coal import were only introduced during the 1930s (Henau 1985). An increase in exports of iron and steel and an equally large increase of the export of building materials like cement, sand and bricks mainly stimulated growth in the 1920s. This is - by the way - almost the only occasion where exports exceeded imports[5]. By-products of the steel industry also caused a rise of chemical loadings, combined with the export of fertilisers. Notwithstanding the diversification into building materials, half-finished iron and steel products still dominated the outgoing cargo-flows (Fig. 3.3.). Exports of semi manufactures tripled between 1922 and 1927. By 1926 export had reached its

[5] Between 1925 and 1931 imports accounted for less than half of total throughput, normally it would invariably guarantee 60 %.

maximum. Only a sudden rise of imports lead to a continued over-all increase (Fig. 3.1.).

After World War I, the specialization in manufactures thus further affected Belgium's competitiveness and Belgian industry consequently had a hard time reconquering its long-established markets. During the Great War a number of traditional overseas markets had created their own heavy industry, which was also capable of producing the crude semi manufactures Belgium specialized in ("import substitution"). An improvement was only visible from 1924 onwards. Exactly how vulnerable the country was to sudden changes in the world economy became clear in 1921. The economy suffered a first blow due to diminished demand abroad and a collapse of prices, mainly caused by the conversion of the American economy to peacetime levels. The hinterland adjusted to the new post-war situation: in the early 1920s Antwerp gained the Grand-Duchy of Luxemburg as a potential hinterland (economic union), but simultaneously lost the economically important Duchy of Elzas, which was handed over to France as war booty. After a brief economic stagnation (1924-1925), the drastic devaluation of 1926 boosted exports and marked a new era of growth, which lasted till 1929. Unfortunately, the stabilization allowed Belgian industry to prosper without adapting its structure. The government too was tempted into expensive programmes like the construction of the Albert Canal, linking the port with the steel plants in South Belgium (Veraghtert 1983).

As could be expected after a successful economic stabilization, the port achieved a new record in 1929 with total throughput of 26 million tons. Safe for 1937, this peak wouldn't be repeated before the outbreak of World War II (Fig. 3.1.). By 1928-1929 the Belgian economy clearly overheated. Like the rest of the world, Belgian steel industry had increased heavily its production capacity throughout the 1920s. Furthermore the economic expansion had continued overconcentrating on the exportation of crude semi manufactures. The considerable ensuing interest cost, combined with high wages and large speculative stocks of raw materials made the thirties catastrophic for the steel industry in particular and for the Belgian economy in general (Hogg 1986).

In the United States, an important trading partner for the port (Table 3.2.), the agricultural sector was first affected in 1928. A year later followed the notorious stock exchange crash. Since most countries consequently resorted to protectionism and devaluation, the Belgian export-oriented economy was hit hard. Throughput in Antwerp dwindled from 26 million tons (1929) to 17 million tons (1932) at the nadir of the crisis. Compared to Rotterdam and Hamburg, Antwerp was least affected during the Great Depression though (Sohr 1919, 11). When British and American governments abandoned the gold standard, several countries, including Belgium, formed the Gold Block. This caused a sharp rise of the franc against the pound and the dollar, which naturally exacerbated exports. To neutralize the

Table 3.2. Origin and destination of the maritime cargo-flows of the port of Antwerp (average percentage of total in/outward flow, 1901-1987)

(Sub)continent	Origin				Destination			
	1901-13	1920-39	1947-70	1971-87	1901-13	1920-39	1947-70	1971-87
Europe	53%	42%	30%	38%	49%	46%	40%	41%
Asia	8%	7%	25%	10%	11%	10%	13%	17%
Middle East	0%	1%	22%	5%	0%	0%	4%	9%
South Asia	6%	5%	1%	1%	5%	5%	3%	2%
South East Asia	0%	0%	1%	1%	0%	0%	2%	2%
East Asia	1%	0%	1%	3%	6%	4%	4%	3%
Africa	1%	5%	13%	19%	5%	7%	11%	13%
North America	15%	19%	21%	21%	12%	11%	16%	17%
Central America	0%	2%	6%	4%	2%	1%	5%	3%
South America	14%	19%	5%	5%	14%	8%	6%	3%
Atlantic South America	12%	18%	4%	4%	12%	7%	5%	2%
Pacific South America	2%	2%	1%	1%	2%	1%	1%	1%
Australia	3%	2%	1%	3%	3%	1%	2%	0%
Remainder	6%	5%	0%	0%	4%	17%	7%	7%
Total	100%	100%	100%	100%	100%	100%	100%	100%

Sources: Tableau général du commerce de la Belgique avec les pays étrangers. Ports Maritimes (1901-1939), NIS, Jaarstatistieken over de internationale trafiek der havens (1947/52-1983), NIS, Statistiek over de internationale trafiek in de havens van de BLEU (1984-1987) and own calculations. Note: 1987-1994: these time-series are no longer reliable: a large group of unknown origins and destinations appears in the publications. The basic composition does not change however.

decline in exports the government adopted a deflationary policy and by 1932 even amended the long-established free trade policy with the introduction of custom tariffs. This policy was little successful and indirectly impeded exports further. Since unemployment was high, the deflationary measures provoked grave strikes in 1932 (Baudhuin 1946, Van der Wee and Veraghert 1978).

Consequently Belgium's exports to its major trading partners decreased. As we have already indicated, Britain was a key market for Belgian goods, especially in the fields of steel and textiles. Until 1931, with the sterling devaluation and the erection of tariff barriers, Britain had been Belgium's primary export market. Antwerp's transit trade was hit further by the re-introduction of the French "surtaxe d'origine", a special tax levied on goods imported into France via non-French ports (1934). Trade with Germany never regained normality on account of the reparations, the marks issue and the German experiments in exchange control. Germany nonetheless remained a vital supplier of coal and of highly developed metal and mechanical commodities, dear to the port of Antwerp (the ratio's in Table 3.1. hardly change). Increasing exports to more distant countries like Argentina, Brazil, China and Japan counterbalanced this decrease (Table 3.2.). Rather than changing its export structure, Belgium had found new markets for old goods (Hogg 1986). Already in the nineteenth century Latin America received special attention in the Belgian economy. Beside Russia, it was the most important foreign destination of Belgian capital at the turn of the century (Dumoulin 1993, Stols 1978). South America wasn't only a good market for the Belgian steel industry, it possessed important raw material deposits (wool, hides, nitrates, grain, bananas, rubber and coffee). Here the port of Antwerp and its merchant houses stepped in (Possemiers 1993).

By 1935 the Van Zeeland government put a radical new economic policy to work with a devaluation of the franc (28 %). It also decided that the immediate advantages of the devaluation would not be fully exploited in order to avoid antagonising other countries. In the port's throughput, a new upward trend can be identified (from 1933 onwards) with an annual growth of 10 %. Not surprisingly, outgoing cargo-flows increased stronger than ingoing (Fig. 3.1.). However favourable the initial results, foreign and domestic political turmoil prevented an all-out expansion of the economy. In 1937-1938 a new recession once again provoked protectionism and again a new fallback in throughput took effect: from 28 million tons in 1937 to 21 million tons in 1939.

The Second World War drastically altered the structure of the world economy. In a matter of years, oil substituted coal. New sea-borne trades came into existence. De-colonization offered new opportunities. Industry was attracted towards the sea and re-thought its location strategy. Subject to these and other international trends, the port of Antwerp experienced its largest spatial expansion ever. Throughput was naturally also affected by the take-over of the industrial port function.

Table 3.3. Most important international origins and destinations of the continental cargo-flow of the port of Antwerp, modal split included (1947-1992 in %)

	Inland shipping	Railroad	Road haulage	Share in hinterland
		Germany		
1947	83%	16%	0,9%	11%
1952	95%	4%	1,2%	35%
1960	91%	5%	4,3%	34%
1970	80%	8%	12%	39%
1980	75%	6%	18%	49%
1987	64%	8%	27%	52%
1992	58%	5%	36%	41%
		France		
1947	46%	53%	0,5%	45%
1952	70%	28%	2,2%	30%
1960	67%	25%	7,8%	29%
1970	55%	28%	18%	28%
1980	34%	33%	33%	25%
1987	23%	28%	48%	29%
1992	27%	11%	62%	24%
		The Netherlands		
1947	94%	5%	1,4%	17%
1952	93%	3%	4,4%	22%
1960	87%	2%	10,4%	28%
1970	81%	2%	17%	28%
1980	69%	8%	22 %	18%
1987	37%	12%	51%	8%
1992	50%	2%	48%	10%
		Switzerland		
1947	54%	46%	0,0%	26%
1952	90%	10%	0,4%	13%
1960	92%	7%	0,9%	9%
1970	76%	19%	5%	4%
1980	61%	32%	7%	6%
1987	64%	30%	6%	9%
1992	40%	45%	15%	4%

Sources: NIS, Jaarstatistieken over de internationale trafiek der havens (1947/52-1983). NIS, Statistiek over de internationale trafiek in de havens van de BLEU (1984-1989/94) and own calculations. Note: This table should be interpreted as follows: in 1947 the cargo-flow from/to Germany amounted to 11 % of the total cargo-flow from/to the hinterland of the port. This 11 % cargo flow was split up: 16 % travelled via railroad, 0,9 % via road and 83 % via canals. Note that from 1971 only a fraction of the Dutch traffic was recorded.

After World War II maritime cargo flows in the port of Antwerp took a false start. Since the port fell into Allied hands virtually unharmed, it was immediately employed in supplying the Allied armies and the freed people of Western Europe. The dollars earned in provisioning the Allied armies in Germany via the port of Antwerp and in making available African ores to the US, allowed a smooth transition to a peacetime economy. Safe for a slight stagnation in 1956, maritime throughput only really got going in 1951: it shot up almost unstoppable until it reached 80 million tons in 1970. This fourfold increase in two decades was largely driven by imports. The impact of petroleum and chemical industries on port traffic was enormous. In the 1950s inward bound cargo-flows tripled to 60 million tons in a decade's time: half of this increase can be attributed to the expansion of domestic petroleum imports, another quarter to ores for domestic use (Table 3.4.). Remarkably, after almost ¾ of a century, agricultural produce was quickly overtaken by crude petroleum. The average share of agricultural produce decreased from 50 % in 1948 to 17 % in 1972, while petroleum grew at an average rate of 9% per annum to a share of 35 % (Fig. 3.2.).

The gradual trend towards diversification of maritime destinations, instigated by the traditional Belgian industry, continued after World War II. Especially the Asian and American markets expanded. The phenomenal growth rate of imported crude petroleum caused a major shift in the origin and destination of the maritime cargo-flows (Table 3.2.). The share of Middle Eastern imports dramatically rose to 22 %. Before World War II, Asian cargo-flows mainly originated in South Asia and had a rather "colonial" character. The stagnation of agricultural imports accounts for a second import shift in the origins of throughput. The share of Latin-American countries dropped from averagely 18 % during the interwar years to 5% (1947-1970). The South American market, Argentina and Brazil in particular, collapsed since most Latin-American countries had launched a policy of import substitution during the Great Depression (Baer 1972). Protectionism, import substitution, an ensuing debt crisis and a flight of capital worsened the international position of the Latin-American economies (Cardoso and Helwege 1992, 109-137). This implied that Latin America was no longer an interesting market for traditional Belgian manufactures. On the European level, the dominance of Great Britain in imports as well as exports ceased to exist and was diversified with e.g. the Scandinavian countries. A final shift concerns the African countries, which increased their share in total imports from 5 % to 13 % (ores).

The unenthusiastic performance of exports is in stark contrast to the unparalleled performance of imports. Maritime exports remained stationary and only increased in the latter half of the 1960s. Outward going cargo-flows had initially grown fast and doubled to 10 million tons by 1950. This is consistent with the performance of the Belgian economy. A period of rapid development (1944-1948) was followed by a slower rate of growth until 1961 and then very high growth per annum until 1974. Notwithstanding the dynamic energy policy and the far-reaching monetary reforms introduced by the Van Acker government, a first limited recession took place in 1949. In 1949 sterling and a number of other currencies, including the franc, devalued. This stimulated exports and helped to somewhat poise the trade balance. Heavy industry remained successful nonetheless, because of the large demand for steel in the rebuilding of Europe, financed by the Marshall Plan. In the port itself a new dock was build with funds from the Marshall Plan. After the increase in demand for steel on account of the war in Korea (1950-1953), outgoing cargo-flows once again stagnated until the second half of the 1960s (Fig. 3.1.) (Baudhuin 1961, van Rompuy 1978, 213-232).

Steel manufactures nevertheless continued to dominate the outgoing maritime cargo-flows with a massive 37 %. This is very significant as it is a major explanation for the poor performance of the country's economy in the 1950s. Initially, due to the limited war damage, it was easy for the Belgian (steel) industry to regain a strong position. The aforementioned structural rigidity of Belgian industry implied that expansion focused on the traditional heavy industry. In some neighbouring countries post-war investments not only concentrated on re-establishing former factories, but also on new economic sectors like chemistry. The "old" Belgian industry consequently lost its comfortable position. Once the Korea Boom was over and the financial aid of the Marshal Plan had dried up (1952), industrial production stagnated and a new recession gradually took effect (until 1955). At last Belgium went along with the general upward trend after the recession of 1958-1959. Safe for 1964 and 1968, the economy boomed until 1974 when the oil producing and exporting countries decided to dramatically raise the oil price. In explaining the weakness of the Belgian economy in the 1950s, we should, for completeness' sake, also consider the impact of a number of pervasive political crises (and strikes) on the country's economic performance.

Regarding throughput it is remarkable that manufactures started experiencing fierce competition, especially from newcomers like fertilisers and finished goods. Thanks to the new industrial presence in the port, exports of chemical products, building materials and fertilisers strongly rose. The port's industry also generated cargo to compensate for the loss of coal. As coal had quietly been substituted by petroleum in most Western-European economies, demand for coal handling had also decreased. From the 1960s onwards, specialised petroleum derivatives eagerly took their place in the outgoing cargo flows (Fig 3.3.).

These "new" petroleum and chemical plants did not come about automatically. They are in stark contrast with the theory of the structurally rigid and export minded heavy industry, if it wasn't for two reasons. The establishment of the Benelux (1948), the European Community for Coal and Steel (1951) and the European Economic Community (1957) entailed the abolishment of tariffs and offered new trading possibilities. Industry was however still concentrated on producing iron, steel, non-ferrous metals, building materials and textiles. Unfortunately extremely favourable international economic circumstances as well as the ensuing integration of Belgium into the world economy and the European market provided new opportunities for the traditional sectors of the economy. Nonetheless, the establishment of the EC combined with a favourable geographic location, a peaceful social climate and relatively low wages, turned Flanders into an advantageous location for multinationals. Furthermore these foreign investments, encouraged by the expansionist legislature of the late 1950s, were mostly directed to new growth sectors. This brings us to the second reason. Belgian economic policy during the 1950s had been directed at creating a mixed economy. The concept of mixed economy assigned a pivotal role to the government in guiding the market. This policy was executed along four paths. Firstly, industrial renewal and, secondly, the social. Thirdly, fiscal policy was rationalized in terms of new taxes and cuts in public expenditure in order to balance the budget. Prime Minister Eyskens' so-called "Eenheidswet" provoked large parts of the economy to strike, including the port (1960-1961). Fourthly, modernization of infrastructure crystallized in the building of freeways and the expansion of the port of Antwerp.

By 1956 Parliament had unanimously agreed to a new expansion programme for the port. This "Ten Year Plan" was supposed to end unstructured and slow extension of the infrastructure. Once fully implemented, the Plan resulted in an increase of quay length by 1/3 and, more importantly, of water surface by ¾. Much like the plan of 1906, a new canal was dug in a seaward direction including a new lock (Himler 1986, de Kesel 1964). Most of the land surrounding this "Canal Dock" accommodated new petrochemical plants (Winkelmans 1972, Mingret 1976). The construction of freeways was largely a catch-up operation. In particular the missing freeway from the port towards Germany handicapped Antwerp, much to the advantage of Rotterdam. Not surprisingly Table 3.3. shows that the truck first penetrated Dutch and then French roads, this in strong contrast with the privileged relationship with Germany. Table 3.1. indicates the limited amount of road haulage undertaken from the port in 1951 (7 % domestic, 0,4 % international).

Table 3.4. Share of transit in in- and outward maritime throughput of the port of Antwerp (average percentages 1947-1994)

	Imports			Exports		
NSTr	47-50	50-70	71-94	47-50	50-70	71-94
0	32%	39%	59%	37%	66%	69%
1	49%	47%	52%	55%	54%	55%
2	30%	32%	13%	40%	26%	68%
3	33%	9%	20%	4%	5%	7%
4	13%	15%	15%	27%	53%	61%
5	27%	37%	73%	20%	45%	67%
6	8%	25%	50%	13%	13%	24%
7	10%	12%	37%	2%	17%	35%
8	43%	54%	66%	37%	55%	64%
9	58%	53%	70%	41%	34%	59%
XX	28%	22%	34%	24%	33%	47%

Sources: NIS, Jaarstatistieken over de internationale trafiek der havens (1947/52-1983). NIS, Statistiek over de internationale trafiek in de havens van de BLEU (1984-1989/94) and own calculations. Note: 0: Agricultural produce; 1: Foodstuffs and fodder; 2: Solid fuels; 3: Petroleum and products; 4: Ores and metal waste; 5: Iron and steel manufactures; 6: Building materials; 7: Fertilisers; 8: Chemical products; 9: Vehicles, other goods; XX: Total.

Table 3.1. additionally shows that the truck as a means of international transport only really broke through in the mid 1980s. Initially the truck was only successful when transporting foodstuff, chemicals and finished products (Table 3.5.). It is remarkable that international continental throughput was dominated by inland shipping. In domestic cargo flows, all three transport modi held approximately equal shares (Table 3.1.). Domestically, the truck soon (mid 1960s) accounted for ¼ of all continental port traffic. Already by 1969 the truck overtook the overall share of the railways in international cargo flows (Table 3.1.). The dominance of inland shipping was based on the transportation of rather bulky goods, especially petroleum, building materials and fertilisers (Table 3.5.). By acquiring virtually the entire oil flow (towards the domestic hinterland, Table 3.4.), inland shipping had succeeded in re-assuring one of the most lucrative cargo flows of the time. Table 3.5. also shows that inland shipping competed with the railroads in agricultural produce and coal. The railways on the other hand, never really dominated any cargo flow, although they did have a major share in ores and semi manufactures.

The port's modal split as well as its throughput would however change dramatically in the wake of the oil crises. Total throughput dwindled with 10 % in 1971 and with another 7 % in 1972 to 67 million tons. Due to the favourable economic climate, exports continued to rise until 1975 while imports were decaying (Fig. 3.1.). In 1975 a second downturn hit total throughput (- 20 %), because contrary to 1971, both in- and outgoing cargo-flows now plummeted. This meant an abrupt end to the upward spiral of the silver 1950s and the golden 1960s. The initial decline can be attributed to the introduction of the Rotterdam Antwerp Pipeline, which considerably reduced transhipment of crude petroleum. A second explanation concerns the oil crises, which boosted the short-term negative effect of the pipeline on the maritime cargo flows.

The Belgian economy, open and vulnerable, was severely affected by the world-wide crisis of 1975-1985. The higher energy prices and the reduction in world demand led to a bad trade balance. Originally the government reacted with an anti-cyclical policy Keynes would have been proud of. The welfare state was not dismantled after 1974, but continued to expand even though its economic base had shrunk dramatically. This policy maintained the illusion of prosperity, but caused an enormous deficit and left little if any financial means to stimulate new innovative industrial sectors. Tensions of a linguistic nature exacerbated the situation and slowed the government's structural regeneration policy. The situation worsened with the departure of many multinationals on account of the high wages and social burdens. The rise in oil prices of 1973 had pushed up consumer prices and caused, due to the system of automatic wage-indexing, a wage-price spiral. These high wages destroyed the international competitive position of several industries. The second oil price rise of the late 1970s prompted the government to battle unemployment with a tight monetary policy, export oriented growth policy, wage cuts, price freezing and a devaluation by 8,5 % (1982). The devaluation of the franc and the accompanying wage restraint restored competitiveness so that Belgian companies could participate in the revival of the world economy from the end of 1982. Exports soared and remained one of the engines of economic growth. The spectacular plunge in oil prices at the beginning of 1986, reinforced by a sharp depreciation of the dollar, brought about a serious strengthening of purchasing power. Between 1986 and 1990 however, the country took full advantage of strong growth in world trade (Buyst 1997).

This favourable development of the economy was reflected in the throughput of the port of Antwerp. From 1975 onwards a new increase announced itself. Already in 1982 throughput matched the peak of 1970, while the symbolic cape of 100 million tons was rounded in 1990. Anno 2000 maritime cargo-flows added up to 120 million tons. This implies an average growth of 3 %. The very low standard deviation (0,07) indicates that this growth was far form mercurial (Fig. 3.1.).

Table 3.5. Positioning of the continental cargo-flows of the port of Antwerp (average percentages: 1947-2000)

	1947-1972			1973-2000			1973-1988		
NSTr	IS	RR	RH	IS	RR	RH	IS	RR	RH
0	61%	9%	31%	24%	7%	69%	29%	8%	63%
1	32%	12%	56%	32%	14%	54%	37%	11%	52%
2	59%	40%	0%	43%	51%	7%	48%	46%	6%
3	80%	2%	18%	85%	5%	11%	88%	3%	9%
4	42%	58%	0%	23%	74%	4%	20%	77%	3%
5	45%	49%	6%	43%	28%	29%	48%	29%	23%
6	82%	13%	4%	71%	9%	20%	73%	10%	18%
7	82%	16%	2%	69%	11%	20%	75%	10%	15%
8	29%	19%	52%	27%	10%	63%	26%	8%	65%
9	37%	15%	48%	29%	10%	60%	20%	11%	69%
XX	56%	27%	17%	45%	21%	35%	46%	21%	33%

Sources: GHA, Statistieken over de zee- en binnenvaart en over het goederenverkeer (1947-1969); GHA, Jaarverslag van de werkzaamheden van de HKD (1970-1985); GHA, Statistisch jaarboek (2000); GHA, Statistisch overzicht (1958); NMBS, Spoorwegvervoer in de haven van Antwerpen (1950-2000); GHA, Statistisch overzicht van het havenverkeer (1970); NIS, Jaarstatistieken over de internationale trafiek der havens (1947/52-1983); NIS, Statistiek over de internationale trafiek in de havens van de BLEU (1984-1988/94) and own calculations. Note: 0: Agricultural produce; 1: Foodstuffs and fodder; 2: Solid fuels; 3: Petroleum and products; 4: Ores and metal waste; 5: Iron and steel manufactures; 6: Building materials; 7: Fertilisers; 8: Chemical products; 9: Vehicles, other goods; XX: Total. Time-series on road haulage for the period 1988-2000 were constructed according to the composition of road haulage in 1987. The small impact of the choice can be seen when comparing the middle and the last three columns. The table should be interpreted as follows: in the years between 1947 and 1972 on average 61 % of agricultural produce was transported to the hinterland via inland shipping (IS), 9 % via railroad (RR) and 31 % via road haulage (RH).

In the inward bound cargo-flow the share of petroleum was reduced to ¼ (Fig. 3.2.). Agricultural produce (American grain shipments to Soviet Union) and coal (from 1978 onwards due to closure Belgian mines) experienced a comeback with average shares of respectively 9 % and 10 %. Import of ores dropped slightly to 22%. Remarkable is the growth of rather unconventional imports like chemical products and finished goods. Throughput of finished goods even tripled to 3,9 million tons. These figures foster the thesis that ingoing traffic was a lot more diversified than in the first half of the century. Exports on the other hand, only now exceeded the 40 million ton-mark. Exports sustained some losses due to the crises in the steel manufacturing industry. The market share of steel shipments in the 1970s and 1980s dropped from (on average) 37 % to 24 % (Fig. 3.3.). From now on, Antwerp relied on new goods like petroleum derivatives (23 % share in 1973-1994), chemicals (12 %) and finished goods (11 %). Just like steel, chemicals (etc) would find their way to the port because of the unique cargo handling facilities and know-how; in other words thanks to the port's distribution function. This hypothesis is corroborated by the remarkable fact that 60 % of the loaded chemical and finished products had a foreign origin (Table 3.4.). Both turn out to be the new driving force behind throughput. This implies that the dependence of the port of Antwerp on the foreign part of its hinterland has increased dramatically.

Does the rise in transit (in the new and decisive commodities) put the port of Antwerp in a bad position? In comparison to the period 1945-1970, overall transit has grown: 1/3 of incoming and ½ of outgoing maritime cargo flows has a foreign origin/destination (Table 3.4.). Veraghtert situated the final breakthrough of transit in the aftermath of the French-German War of 1870 when large quantities of German industrial products joined Belgian steel exports. Until the industrial port era (1960s) Antwerp had however always been a "Belgian" port: it supplied Belgium. Contrary to Rotterdam, the port of Antwerp depended on its own national hinterland for economic survival. During the interwar period Rotterdam paid a high price for its dependence on German cargo-flows. From the 1960s onwards the "Belgian character" of Antwerp has continuously been diminishing as the percentage of transit increased. In other words, has Antwerp been acquiring a similar baleful secondary position like Rotterdam? To some degree it has undeniably done so. On the other hand this also implies that, on an international level, the competitive position of Antwerp has approved dramatically. If one compares 1950-1970 with 1971-1944, Table 3.4. shows a rise in transit in all commodities (except for coal import). Outward bound transit reached very high percentages (60-70 %) in agricultural produce, foodstuff, solid fuels, ores, steel manufactures, chemicals and finished goods. Inward bound transit reached equally high percentages in agricultural produce, steel manufactures, chemicals and finished goods. In all, transit accounted for half of the outgoing and a third of the total ingoing cargo flow. The percentages in Table 3.4. may be misleading because some categories are small, but they do indicate where Antwerp holds special trumps (e.g. importing steel is a tiny, but new and promising trade ...).

This rise in transit must also be explained by referring to one of the most important trends in post-war trade, namely the growth of intra-industry trade. Intra-industry trade can be defined as the simultaneous export and import of products belonging to the same industry and is opposed to inter-industry trade, which involves countries exchanging the products of different industries. In the latter case each country specializes in a particular industry in which it enjoys a comparative advantage. Such inter-industry specialization results in a relocation of economic activity. Although this kind of specialization does still take place, specialization between advanced industrial countries has since World War II been much narrower and within a particular industry[6]. This intra-industry specialization has dramatically increased international trade. Most intra-industry trade takes place in commodities that are differentiated, i.e. goods that are close but not perfect substitutes. A large number of studies have been carried out to measure the level of intra-industry trade in different countries. They show that Western-European countries have the highest level of intra-industry trade. The highest levels of intra-industry trade were especially to be found in chemicals and machinery (Grubel and Lloyd 1975, Aquino 1978, table 1). Both commodities not surprisingly feature among the forerunners of maritime throughput in Antwerp.

Intra-industry trade traditionally concentrates on Western-European countries. This is also apparent from Table 3.1. and 3.2.. The former confirms that by 1980 45 % of total continental traffic in the port of Antwerp had a destination/origin in the port's foreign hinterland. A decade later this had even increased to 48 %. The latter table support this as well. It shows virtually no changes in the origins and destinations of the maritime cargo flows, safe for the decrease of the Middle East's share in imports. The rise in intra-industry trade went hand in hand with the diffusion of the truck as a means of international transport. After a century long dominance the inland barge seems to lose the battle on the international scene. In the domestic cargo-flows, railways and canals continuously lost ground. Fortunately, the figures in Table 3.1. indicate that the advance of the truck has halted domestically. This may be explained by the fact that barges and wagons can now also participate in the transportation of high value general cargo (containers), which since World War II used to be the sole privilege of the truck. Table 3.5. supports this thesis only partly, though. Compared to the period 1947-1972, the truck continued to concentrate on foodstuffs, chemicals and finished goods. It has however managed to acquire a large share of the agricultural produce (69 %) at the expense of inland shipping. It has also made important progress in the field of steel manufactures, building materials and fertilisers, also at the expense of inland shipping. The latter clung on to petroleum and coal and largely lost ores to the railways.

The fact that the truck hasn't completely taken over transporting chemicals and finished goods, can probably be explained by the introduction of the container. This trend allowed general cargo to be transported in a bulky way, suitable for inland barges and trains. The ascent of the container in the late 1960s facilitated intra-industry as much as the truck. Containerization confronted the port with new infrastructural demands. The planned Eighth and Ninth Harbour dock were therefore converted into one dock, the Delwaidedock (1982), which allowed Antwerp to keep pace with the process of scaling-up in shipping. This evolution prompted the cargo-handlers to construct two container terminals in front of the two north-

[6] Some economists have posed questions as to the exact definition of this phenomenon. It has been argued that intra-industry trade is largely a statistical and exaggerated phenomenon because it is due to a large number of different products being treated as belonging to the same industry. After all, it isn't easy to measure the level of intra-industry trade. Research has indeed confirmed the existence of an "aggregation bias", but has simultaneously emphasized that the bias only accounts for a small proportion of the observed intra-industry trade (Grimwade 1989, 89-141).

ern sea locks. In the future several additional tidal container terminals will be opened on the Left Bank of the river Scheldt. Until now, the "distributional" expansion was largely accommodated on the newly developed Left Bank. As early as 1962 this area had already been conquered by some petrochemical plants, not in need of maritime access and connected by pipelines to the factories on the Right Bank. A further industrial expansion appeared only possible with the construction of a lock and a new system of docks. The Oil Crises dampened the demand for land on the Left Bank. Only thanks to the spectacular containerization of the last decade will the Left Bank be given a clear assignment (Himler 1986, Thues 1988).

Conclusion

At the outset of this paper we emphasized the importance of putting the growth of the port of Antwerp in a larger context. By using the functional approach and by building on existing economic as well as geographic port transition models, we have designed a paradigm explaining the evolution of the seaport of Antwerp and framing it in the wider development of its surrounding hinterland-foreland continuum. We discerned three functional shifts, which can be explained by a number of exogenous as well as endogenous determinants.

This paper also confronted the paradigm with the history of the port of Antwerp. We have relied on an extensive database regarding maritime as well as continental throughput in the port (1901-2000). In so doing we have, at least to some extent, supplemented Veraghtert's seminal quantitative work on the evolution of the port during the nineteenth century. The limited scope of this paper didn't allow a full-out discussion of the model in its every aspect. We have primarily concentrated on the development of international trade and the Belgian economy. We have e.g. hardly said a word about technological innovation in cargo-handling or, more importantly, in shipping itself.

In theory, the "Hanseatic model" that results from this study is applicable to any Western-European seaport as long as the local municipality manages it. We are aware how easily the edge can be taken off this paradigm. Like any other model it is vulnerable, because exceptions to the rule will be readily found. We hope, nonetheless, to have identified some patterns in port development and shed at least some light on the bigger picture.

References

Aquino A (1978) Intra-industry trade and inter-industry specialization as concurrent sources of international trade in manufactures. Weltwirtschaftliches Archiv, CXIV-2: 275-296

Baer W (1972) Import substitution industrialization in Latin America. Latin American research review, VII-1: 95-122

Baetens R (1991) A survey of maritime relations between Belgium and the United States of America. In: Koninckx C (ed) Proceedings of the international colloquium "Industrial revolutions and the sea". Collectanea Maritima, V. Brussel, pp 229-255

Baldwin RE, Martin P (1999) Two waves of globalization: superficial similarities, fundamental differences. Cambridge (NBER Working Paper 6904)

Baudez L (1960) Hinterlands et "forelands" portuaires. La vie économique et sociale, XXXI: 203

Baudhuin F (1946) Histoire économique de la Belgique, 1914-1919. Bruxelles, 2 vol

Bird J (1971) Seaports and seaport terminals. London

Blumenhagen D (1981) Containerization and hinterland traffic, Maritime management and policy, VIII-3: 197-206

Buyst E (1997) The decline and rise of a small open economy: the case of Belgium (1974-1990). In: Van der Wee H, Blomme J (eds) The economic development of Belgium since 1870. The economic development of modern Europe since 1870, VIII. Cheltenham Lyme, pp 67-76

Cardoso E, Helwege A (1992) Latin America's economy: diversity, trends and conflicts. Cambridge

Chang S. (1978) In defense of port economic impact studies, Transportation journal, XVII-3: 79-85

Charlier J (1981) Contribution méthodologique à l'étude des arrière-pays portuaires. Ph.D. thesis, University of Louvain-la-Neuve

Coeck et al. (1995) The unreliability of maritime trade statistics. International journal of transport economics, XXII-2: 217-224

De Baets G (et al.) (1995) Van wieg tot zeemansgraf. Hulp- en voorzorgskas voor zeevarenden. Antwerpen

De Kesel L (1964) Structurele ontwikkeling van de haven (1803-1914). In: Bouwstoffen voor de geschiedenis van Antwerpen in de XIXde eeuw. Antwerpen, pp 124-168

De Lombaerde P (1994) The unreliability of maritime trade statistics. International journal of transport economics, XXI-1: 93-97

De Rousiers P (1909) Les fonctions économiques des ports maritimes modernes, Revue économique internationale, IV: 822

De Rousiers P (1909) Les grands ports de France. Leur rôle économique. Paris

Degrève D (1982) Le commerce extérieur de la Belgique (1930-1913-1939). Bruxelles

Deprez J (1939) Le port d'Anvers: ses zones d'influence et son trafic. Louvain

Devos G (1991) German ocean shipping and the port of Antwerp (1875-1914). An introduction. In: Koninckx C (ed) Proceedings of the international colloquium "Industrial revolutions and the sea". Collectanea Maritima, V. Brussel, pp 217-229

Drèze J (1961) The standard goods hypothesis. In: Jacquemin A, Sapir A (eds) The European internal market: trade and competition. Oxford, pp 13-32

Dubois E., Theunissen M (1906) Anvers et la vie économique nationale. Les ports et leurs fonctions économique. Louvain

Dumoulin M (1993) Belgische investeringen in Latijns-Amerika. In: Stols E (et al.) Vlaanderen en Latijns-Amerika. 500 jaar confrontatie en métissage. Antwerpen, pp 283-294

Ehlers P, Bultman H (1915) Die Verkehrswirtschaft des Antwerpener Hafens. Hamburg Bremen

Federico G, Tena A (1989) On the accuracy of historical international foreign trade statistics. Morgenstern revisited. EIU Working papers, 89/373

Frankel EG (1987) Port planning and development. New York
Grubel HG, Lloyd PJ (1975) Intra-industry trade: the theory and measurement of international trade in differentiated Products. London
Hayuth Y (1982) Intermodal transportation and the hinterland concept, Tijdschrift voor economische en sociale geografie, LXXIII-1: 14
Henau B (1985) De Belgisch-Britse handelsbetrekkingen (1919-1939). Belgische tijdschrift voor nieuwste geschiedenis, XVI-3-4: 271-305
Himler A (1993) De Antwerpse haven vanaf de Franse periode. In: De Nave F (ed) Antwerpen, geschenk van de Schelde. De Antwerpse haven door de eeuwen heen. Brussel, pp 48-50
Hogg RL (1986) Structural rigidities and policy inertia in interwar Belgium. Brussel
Hoyle BS (1988) Development dynamics at the port-city interface. In: Hoyle BS, Pinder DA, Husain MS (eds) Revitalising the waterfront: international dimensions of dockland redevelopment. London, pp 3-17
Jackson G (1983) The ports. In: Aldcroft DH, Freeman MJ (eds) Transport in the Industrial Revolution. Manchester, pp 220-231
Jarvis A (1999) Port history: some thoughts on where it came from and where it might be going. In: Fischer LR, Jarvis A (eds) Harbours and havens: essays in port history in honour of Gordon Jackson. (Research in maritime history, XVI). St. John's, pp 13-34
Jolmes L (1966) Die Funktionen der Seehäfen für die Volkswirtschaft. In: Jolmes L (ed) Seewirtschaft. Beiträge zur ökonomischen Entwicklung in Seehäfen und Seeschiffahrt. Hamburg
Kenwood AG, Lougheed AL (1999) The growth of the international economy (1820-2000). An introductory text. London
Kinart F, Bollengier K (1931) Administration du port d'Anvers. In: Kinart F (ed) XVième congrès international de navigation. Bruxelles, pp 1-24
Kuiler HC, Verhoeff JM (1973) Inleiding tot de vervoers- en haveneconomie. Rotterdam
Layton IG (1981) The evolution of Upper Norrland's ports and loading places (1750-1976). Geographical Reports, 6. Umea
Loyen R (2001) De consumptiemaatschappij vanuit een havenperspectief. Een gevalstudie voor de Antwerpse graantrafieken (1860-1960), In: Segers Y, Loyen R, Dejongh G, Buyst E (eds) Op weg naar een consumptiemaatschappij. Amsterdam, pp 103-137
Mingret P (1976) La croissance industrielle du port d'Anvers. Bruxelles
Murphey R (1989) On the evolution of the port city. In: Broeze F (ed) Brides of the sea: port cities of Asia form the 16th-20th centuries. Honolulu
Notteboom T (2000) De invloed van ruimtelijke en logistieke ontwikkelingen in het voorland-achterlandcontinuüm op de positie en functie van zeehavens. (Ph.D. thesis, University of Antwerp)
Oboussier M (1917) De haven van Antwerpen en de economische conferentie van Parijs. Antwerpen
Peeters C et al. (1995) De haven als economische motor van de regio. Financieel-economische relaties van stad en de mainport Antwerpen met haar omgeving. Leuven Apeldoorn
Possemiers J (1993), De Belgische handel en scheepvaart op Latijns-Amerika (1830-1914). In: Stols E (et al.) Vlaanderen en Latijns-Amerika. 500 jaar confrontatie en métissage. Antwerpen, pp 263-282
Robinson R (1960) The hinterland-foreland continuum. Concept and methodology. The professional geographer, XXII-6: 307

Romus P (1944) L'économie portuaire et sa terminologie, Bulletin de la société belge d'études géographiques, XIV-2: 164-168

Sargent AJ (1938) Seaports and hinterlands. London

Seidenfus HS (1987) European ports in the context of the world economy and the European economy: changes in sea transport. International journal of transport economics, XIV-2: 133-138

Slack B (1985) Containerization, interport-competition and port selection. Maritime policy and management, XII-4: 293-303

Sohr F (1919) Le port d'Anvers: le causes de sa prospérité, le rôle réel du commerce et des navires. Bruxelles Paris

Stengers J (1968) Léopold I et le chemin de fer d'Anvers au Rhin. In: Henne H (ed) Mélanges offerts à G. Jacquemyns. Bruxelles, pp 573-599

Stols E (1978) Colonisation et intérêts belges en Argentine (1830-1914). In: Schneider J (eds) Wirtschaftskräfte und Wirtschaftswege. IV. Übersee und allgemeine Wirtschaftsgeschichte. Bamberg, pp 295-296

Suykens F (1985) Administration and management at the port of Antwerp, Maritime policy and management, XII: 181-194

Suykens F (1986a) "Ports should be efficient. Maritime policy and management, XIII-2: 105-126

Suykens F (1986b) Physical distribution and European ports. In: Charlier J (ed), Port et mers. Mélanges maritimistes offerts à André Vigarié. Caen, pp 97-108

Suykens F (et al.) (1986) Antwerp, port for all seasons. Antwerp

Taaffe EJ, Morril RL, Gould PR (1963) Transport expansion in underdeveloped countries: a comparative analysis. Geographical review, LIII: 503-529

Thues G (1988) Haven van Antwerpen: havenrenovatie rond het Albertdok. Het ingenieursblad, pp 23-28

Tongzon JL (1995) Determinants of port performance and efficiency. Transportation research, XXIX-A3: 245-252

UNCTAD (1992) Review of maritime transport. New York

Van der Wee H (1997) Investment strategy of Belgian industrial enterprise between 1830 and 1980 and its influence on the economic development of Europe. In: Van der Wee H, Blomme J (eds) The economic development of Belgium since 1870. The economic development of modern Europe since 1870, VIII. Cheltenham Lyme, pp 186-204

Van der Wee H, Veraghtert K (1978) De economie van 1814 tot 1944. In: Twintig eeuwen Vlaanderen. Hasselt, vol VIII, pp 129-211

Van Hooydonk E (1996) The legal aspects of the Hanseatic tradition. In: Bekemans L Beckwith S (eds) Ports for Europe: Europe's maritime future in a changing environment. Brussel, pp 347-378

Van Klink H.A. (1995) Towards the borderless mainport Rotterdam: an analysis of functional, spatial and administrative dynamics in port systems. Amsterdam

Van Rompuy V (1978) Vlaanderen 1944-heden. In: Twintig eeuwen Vlaanderen. Hasselt, vol VIII, pp 213-232

Veraghtert K (1976) Overzicht en kritiek van de kwantitatieve bronnen voor de Antwerpse havenbewegingen (negentiende eeuw). Mededelingen van de marine academie, XXIV: 78-85

Veraghtert K (1983) Buitenlandse handel. In: Algemene Geschiedenis der Nederlanden. Haarlem, Part XII, p 49

Veraghtert K (1986) The growth of the Antwerp port traffic (1850-1900). In: Fischer W et al. The emergence of a world economy (1500-1914). Wiesbaden, pp 573-591

Veraghtert K (1988a) Antwerp and the Baltic sea during the nineteenth century. In: Heeres WG (ed) From Dunkirk to Danzig. Shipping and trade in the North Sea and the Baltic. Hilversum, pp 447-455

Veraghtert K (1988b) The port of Antwerp and America (1790-1900). In: Reynolds CG (eds) Global crossroads and the American seas. Missoula, pp 53-66

Veraghtert K (1994) The Antwerp grain trade. In: Friedland K (ed) Maritime food transport. Köln, pp 81-91

Vigarié A (1979) Ports de commerce et vie littorale. Paris

Waters RC (1977) Port economic impact studies: practice and assessment. Transportation journal XVI-3: 14-18

Weigend G (1956) The problem of hinterland and foreland as illustrated by the port of Hamburg. Economic geography, XXXII-1: 2-3

Williams DM (1993) The progress of maritime history. Journal of transport history, XIV-2: 126-141

Winkelmans W (1972) De moderne havenindustrialisatie: een empirisch-kwantitatief onderzoek van de lokalisatiemotieven en de relaties produktie-zeetransport van de olie- en chemienijverheid in de havens van Antwerpen en Rotterdam. Gent

Winkelmans W (et al.) (1993) De economische impactstudie als instrument voor het zeehavenbeleid in Vlaanderen. In: Blauwens G (et al.) De dynamiek van een haven. Kapellen, pp 512-530

Port traffic in Rotterdam: the competitive edge of a Rhine-port (1880-1914)

Paul Th. van de Laar

Erasmus University Rotterdam, The Netherlands

Introduction

In the nineteenth century the north-western European port landscape changed considerably. The commercial staple market ports, with their focus on trade in relatively high value goods shipped in low volumes, became more and more involved in the transhipment of raw materials and the efficient handling of industrial commodity flows. Most ports in north-western Europe had to adapt their port infrastructure, built railway stations, construct docks and so on. In goes without saying, that the industrial era brought about a change in European port hierarchy. Some commercial ports lost their dominance, but others strengthened their positions and benefited from the new role the industrial era demanded. The ports of Rotterdam and Antwerp both played a significant role in this nineteenth century transformation process, but either port followed a different path of development.

In January 2001 the University of Leuven and the Erasmus University Rotterdam started the project: "Rotterdam and Antwerp, a century and a half of port competition in the Rhine-Scheldt-Meuse delta (1860-2000)". The inter-port comparison will be based on an exhaustive databank concerning the cargo-flows of the port of Antwerp and the port of Rotterdam and their respective fore- and hinterlands. By working with comparable data-sets and by using an uniform classification of the maritime and non-maritime time-series, the Antwerp-Rotterdam research group aims to evaluate the development of both ports. The result should give us a reliable picture of the strengths and weaknesses of both Antwerp and Rotterdam. The development of the port of Antwerp, is discussed in the preceding chapter by Reginald Loyen. At the time of the conference, the Rotterdam research has just started. Therefore, the Rotterdam data are still not available to make adequate comparisons between these ports. In order to do so in time a critical evaluation of throughput of the port of Rotterdam in the period 1880-1914 is necessary. That is the main focus of this paper. It will present a new estimation of the throughput in the port of Rotterdam in this period that will be used to review the development of the major cargo-flows. Time-series analyses, however, are important but they should be evaluated against an institutional urban port context. Although lack of space prevents me from going into great detail, the first section of this paper discusses the features of Rotterdam's Rhine-port development in this period.

1. Rotterdam's urban and port development 1880-1914

Rotterdam has been looked upon as a dynamic city where industrious people have lived, willing to take new changes whenever possible (van de Laar 2000) However, contrary to popular belief, in general, Rotterdam's business elite feared any kind of new developments in the first part of the nineteenth century. It was opposed against free trade, the abolition of Rhine tolls that would stimulate the port's transit function, and it did not like any modern railroad connections that could jeopardize the distributive function of the old merchant families. In sum, the old merchant class dreaded a loss of its central position in trade and Rotterdam's staple markets. The business elite that depended on the economic functions of the older staple market, used its political power to slow down the transformation process. The Rotterdam Council and Chamber of Commerce coalesced aiming to revive the Rotterdam staple market and made sure that improvements in the commercial infrastructure did not conflict with their staple market interests. In the 1830s and 1840s, the merchant elite closed ranks as a consequence of external pressure on Dutch staple-market institutions that hindered the economic development of Britain and Germany. These countries needed continental port facilities in combination with cheap inland water borne transport and adequate railroad connections.

The British and Prussian governments enhanced the pressure on King William to submit to new international standards of free trade. In the case of Germany the Prussians forced the Netherlands to put an end to Dutch seaport monopolies. A railroad connection between Antwerp and Cologne, and an aggressive Rhine policy pursued by Prussia, were more effective than a diplomatic offensive. Most Rotterdam members of the elite were convinced that railways, free trade and free Rhine transit would be the final blow to their staple-market interests. Of course, not all the members of the Rotterdam merchant elite resisted to the challenges a new era could offer. Some of them supported a further liberalization of the Dutch economy. Newcomers in Rotterdam port business hoped to open this tight older network of commercial interests for their own benefits. In circa 1870 Lodewijk Pincoffs, a successful merchant and wealthy member of the city council, appeared to be the central entrepreneur. He functioned as an intermediary between the old and new business network. The Rotterdam Chamber of Commerce, once a body that acted on behalf of the staple-market interests, turned toward a new policy that would end the hegemony of the old network (Callahan 1981). Once the resistance of the old commercial class slackened in the third part of the nineteenth century, Rotterdam was able to enjoy the advantages of both its favourable geographical location (connection to the North Sea, a highly efficient inland waterway via the river Rhine, and its central position in Europe).

The central government financed the major part of constructing the *Nieuwe Waterweg* (1864) –an open waterway to the sea to improve the access route to

Rotterdam– and also by building a railway connection between Rotterdam and the southern part of the Netherlands. From 1870 onwards the local government started its own investment programme, pushed forward by Pincoffs and his Rotterdam friends who backed his aim to promote Rotterdam's port development. Pincoffs founded the Rotterdam Merchant Association ("Rotterdamsche Handelschvereeniging") in 1873. Based on the London docks this new complex was installed on the south bank of the river *Maas*. Nowadays it forms part of a huge river-front redevelopment scheme. The Rotterdam Merchant Association was not a success, however, and went bankrupt in 1879. Its managing director Pincoffs turned out to be a trickster. However, the misfortune of this company was not only the result of embezzlements of its chairman of the board. The Rotterdam Merchant Company had not appealed to many companies, because it was not designed for transit-port purposes. Its rectangular and comparatively small docks, its quays, warehouses and dock facilities were not developed to meet the demands of an efficient cargo handling industry. Notwithstanding its modern appearance, the installations of the Rotterdam Merchant Association can be regarded as the last convulsions of the staple-market era. The Rotterdam Merchant Association got into financial difficulties, and the city took over its assets and paid one third of its total investments costs, the estimated market value at that time. The take-over of the company put an end to an era of public-private partnership in the port of Rotterdam. From the 1880s onwards the municipality had full responsibility for port development. It could do so, since there were no private companies that were able to take the lead.

In order to understand why the local government could play such a decisive role, a closer look is needed towards the business network. Rotterdam housed several major shipping lines, e.g. the Holland-America Line and the Rotterdam Lloyd, but around the 1880s shipping agents and ship-brokers dominated the port business landscape. Most of these firms worked in commission of German and English traders and, therefore, played a significant intermediary role between the Rotterdam and the German industrial network. Some of these companies like Van Ommeren, Pakhoed and Wm.H Müller & Co. tried to realize synergy from diversification and developed into maritime conglomerates, who own ships, Rhinebarges, warehouses, stevedore companies and other port related businesses. Most companies, however, belonged to small sized, mostly family owned firms. These shipbrokers and shipping agents had no direct involvement in transhipment and delegated the cargo handling to foremen. These stevedores, as they were called, operated on an individual basis and not as a firm and contracted dockers on a irregular basis. As a result, casual labour became the rule in the port of Rotterdam. Before the rise of international operating trading companies that integrated cargo handling and transport operations in one firm hand, and the foundation of professional managed stevedore firms that invested in modern cargo handling equipment, the development of the port infrastructure at large was left to the public sector.

This Rotterdam port context –the abundance of small agencies and the lack of large international trading and stevedore firms– paved the way for an increase in public involvement in the development of the port. Gerrit Johannes de Jongh, Surveyor of Municipal Works of Rotterdam (1879-1910), is credited with the transformation of Rotterdam. This genius engineer pioneered in the construction of docks with open access from the river that facilitated the transhipment of bulk goods. He realized that Rotterdam needed docks suitable for quick dispatches. Great basins where transhipment could take place on-stream were more important than conventional docks used by line-shipping companies with warehouse facilities. From the mid-1880s onwards he built three river docks, *Rijnhaven*, *Maashaven* and *Waalhaven* (Rhine, Meuse and Waal docks) that reshaped the river landscape south of Rotterdam. Between 1880 and 1914 the city of Rotterdam spent almost eighty million guilders in port facilities. In general, port income (port duties and tariffs) was insufficient to meet depreciation and interest costs. However, although it was recognized that on average a rate of return on port investments was low, a large majority of the Rotterdam Council backed the port development plans at large. Not until, the interwar period opposition grew against a port policy that depended too heavy on the transhipment trade with Germany (Van de Laar 1999).

2. Estimation of throughput in the period 1880-1914

2.1. The problems of interpreting statistics of import, export and transit

There are various ways in evaluating port performance and throughput is just one of them, but an essential one to assess the development of cargo-flows in both ports. Therefore, the researchers started to construct a comprehensive database with data on maritime and non-maritime cargo-flows. The constructed continuous time-series are classified according to an universally accepted table of classifications, the "Nomenclatuur voor Vervoers Statistieken" (NVS), that can be used for grouping the Antwerp and Rotterdam data. The NVS lists ten groups: (0) agricultural products and live stock, (1) foodstuffs and fodder, (2) solid mineral fuels, (3) crude oil and petroleum products, (4) iron ore and metal waste, (5) iron and steel manufactures, non-ferrous metals and semi-manufactured products, (6) raw and building materials, (7) fertilizers, (8) chemical products and (9) machinery, general cargo and miscellaneous goods. But before we were able to group the seaborne and inland time-series, a critical evaluation of the statistics is needed.

The SIUD-statistics (Statistics on Import, Transit and Export) are the most relevant statistics for measuring port throughput, since these national statistics listed the major trade and shipping statistics for the ports of Amsterdam and Rotterdam. Most port historians have, therefore, relied on these statistics in the past, although many have doubted the reliability of the underling series and questioned the usefulness of the data (Sanmann 1956). They had every reason to do so. Until the reorganization of the Dutch national trade statistics, which took place in 1917, these series should be handled with care. This was recognized by the Rotterdam Chamber of Commerce, which published summaries of the national statistics. But it was unwilling to publish abstracts of the outgoing cargo-flows before 1900, because they were thought useless at all. Several attempts were made to improve the

Dutch export statistics, but in 1888 the Rotterdam Chamber sent a public address to the Treasurer and complained about the reliability of the statistics, which had not been improved since the 1880s (Chamber of Commerce 1928, 625-634).

Thomas Lindblad and Jan Luiten van Zanden have reviewed the statistics extensively (Lindblad and van Zanden 1989, 231-269). As other historians have done before, they do confirm that the SIUD-statistics are troublesome, but they are able to show that they can be used when the series are re-arranged. In particular, with respect to the volume of transit goods in the statistics, an important issue whenever one is studying the port of Rotterdam at the end of the nineteenth century.

Lindblad and Van Zanden showed that the SIUD statistics do not make a clear distinction between real incoming and outgoing goods and the volume of transit goods. In fact, due to the liberalization of trade and shipping in 1872 most goods that the Netherlands imported and exported were exempted from import- and export duties. As a result, importers and exporters were indifferent whether raw products of (semi)-finished goods were either used for consumption or production in the Netherlands or shipped abroad after discharge in one of the Dutch ports. In a period where import and export duties no longer hindered the free transit of goods, it made less sense to keep records of the volume of transit goods. Instead, all goods were mostly considered as if they were consumed or processed in the Netherlands, and it did not matter whether imported goods were in fact transhipped abroad. The same goes for the export firm who did not care whether the shipping documents revealed whether the exported goods were produced in the Netherlands or elsewhere. In the latter case, goods were imported first and then exported via the Netherlands. To summarize: the import and export series underestimate the volume of transit for particular goods. Since this cannot be concluded from the underlying time-series these goods are called "disguised transit goods".

2.2. A review of the Rotterdam cargo-flows

In the foregoing section we set out the main problems with the national statistics on import, export and transit. This means that the Rotterdam series on incoming and outgoing cargo need to be assessed carefully. Especially, those cargo-flows relating to the goods the port of Rotterdam transferred to the German hinterland and other foreign countries. Without recalculations, the time-series make the reconstruction of the throughput before the First World War troublesome.

Fig. 4.1. gives an impression of the development of general incoming and outgoing cargo of the port of Rotterdam in the period 1880-1914. The series are based on the national Statistics in Import, Export and Transit. Although, generally these statistics make a distinction between the import by sea-going vessels, water borne transport and inland transport by rail or road, these specifications are only recorded on an national level and not published for Rotterdam and Amsterdam. That means, that the series do not specify the modal split for the port of Rotterdam. However, it is save to assume probably more than 80% of the general import in the port of Rotterdam relate to maritime cargo-flows. This can be concluded from two studies by the leading Rotterdam Banker and liberal member of the

Rotterdam council Marten Mees. He had access to certain custom documents that revealed that in 1896 and 1904 most goods were imported by sea vessels. In 1896 almost 83% of the imported goods were shipped by sea, especially bulk goods. Certain general cargo goods (mineral water, bottled wines, glass products, paper and finished metal goods) were almost exclusively imported by land or riverside. But in most cases, even general cargo was sea-borne. Mees repeated his calculations some years later and his sample of port statistics in 1904 brought him to a similar conclusion. In that year, about 82% of the imports was sea-borne, 15% came by river transport and 4% by road (Mees 1898, 1-45 and 1909, 68).

Fig. 4.1. Incoming and outgoing goods in the port of Rotterdam (1880-1914; ton)

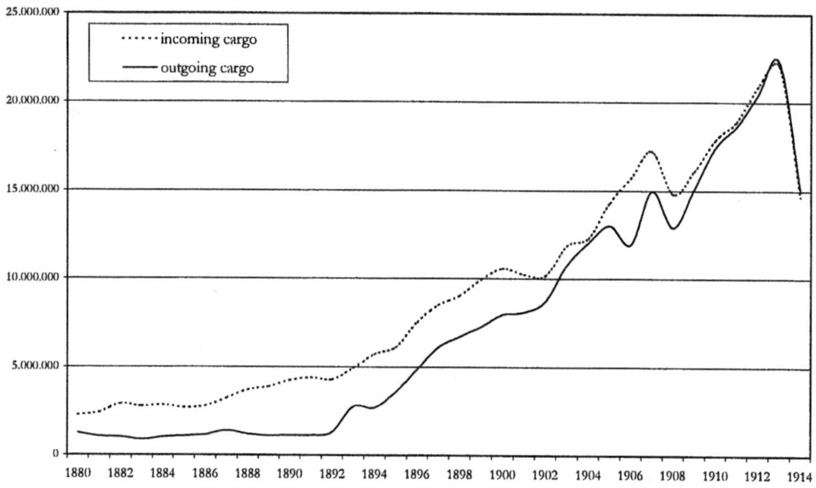

Source: SIUD-statistics (1880-1913)

In the period 1880-1914, the incoming cargo-flows in Rotterdam grew on average with more than 7% per annum, from 2 million tons in 1880 to more than 22 million tons in 1913. The outbreak of the First World War led to a serious downfall. In August 1914 370.000 net tons were cleared, just 26% of the total shipping tonnage the port had done a month earlier. The export in the period 1880-1914 grew on average with 11% per annum, from something more than 1,2 million tons in 1880 to more than 22 million tons in 1913. Again, the outbreak of World War I led to an considerable decrease of the export volume. Compared to the incoming goods the export growth rate, calculated on the basis of the period 1901-1914, exceeded the import growth rate. In absolute numbers, the export of the port of Rotterdam almost tripled from 1901 until 1913, whereas in the same period imports had doubled.

If we would rely on the same import and export series it would be tempted to conclude that the throughput of the port of Rotterdam grew from less than 3,5 million tons in 1880 to more than 40 million tons in 1913. However, the chart reveals that both import and export series are highly correlated. Moreover, the annual changes in both incoming and outgoing cargo-flows more or less have the same pattern and this suggests that both time-series are correlated. In essence, the correlation coefficient is 0,99. In particular, there is a strong relation from 1890s onwards. Apart from the fact that these series were subject to the same underlying business trends, this high correlation coefficient indicates that there is more to be explained[1]. Even if the series are transformed in stationary series by taking first differences, the correlation coefficient is circa 0,75. These correlation coefficients signal the effect of disguised transit goods, as some goods were probably, firstly, enlisted as incoming cargo's and, secondly, recorded as export goods as well. This means, that is very likely that a substantial part of the outgoing goods were in fact imported cargo's transhipped abroad after discharge in the port of Rotterdam. Therefore, the series overestimate the real import and export respectively and underestimate the volume of transit goods. As the correlation becomes stronger in the early nineties, it is clear that the problem of disguised transit increased over time (Lindblad and van Zanden 1989, 236-241). This becomes particular evident, when the incoming and outgoing cargo-flows are compared with the development of the Rhine traffic between Rotterdam and the German hinterland.

Fig. 4.2. Rhine traffic in the port of Rotterdam (1882-1914; tons)

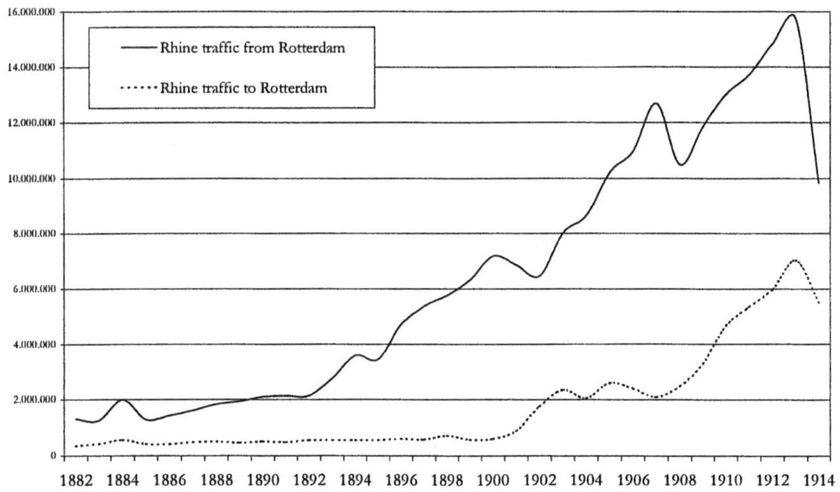

Source: Jahresberichte der Zentralkommission für die Rheinschiffahrt (1882-1914)

Fig. 4.2. shows the development of the Rhine traffic as had been recorded and published by the Central Commission of Rhine Traffic in their *Jahresberichte der Zentralkommission für die Rheinschiffahrt* (Annual Reports of the Central Commission of Rhine Traffic). The depicted time-series relate to the shipments from Lobith up the river Rhine to Germany and from Lobith down the river towards the port of Rotterdam. As no specific comparable statistics were published regarding

[1] For a discussion of the problems with non-stationary time-series and spurious regressions see the paper of S. Janssens *et. al.* in this volume.

the Rhine shipments from and to Rotterdam before 1882, the time-series concern the period 1882-1914. In this phase the export towards Germany up the rive Rhine grew on average with 9%, from about 1,3 million tons in 1882 to more than 16 million tons in 1913. The import from Germany down the river Rhine to Rotterdam mounted to 350 thousand tons in 1882 but in 1913 Rotterdam imported almost 10 million tons, an annual growth rate of 10%. As will be discussed below, due to a strategic alliance of the leading coal works in Germany and the Dutch "Steenkolenhandels Vereniging" (Coal Trade Union) the industrious town at the river Maas became the coaling station of Western Europe and handled the bulk of coal the Rhine-land exported via Rotterdam (Nusteling 1946, Sneller 1946).

A re-estimation of throughput, 1880-1914

The findings of Lindblad and Van Zanden were used as a starting point to calculate a new time-series on Rotterdam's port throughput. Table 4.1. summarizes the correlation coefficients for a number of products for which Lindblad and Van Zanden concluded that disguised transit was a problem. That is for goods with low or zero import duties that were produced abroad and transhipped to the hinterland, like cereals, iron ore, wood, hides, petroleum, as well as certain chemical and metal products, machinery and engine parts. To test whether these products were shipped to the hinterland up the river Rhine, the correlation coefficients between the imports and exports and Rhine-traffic are given as well.

Lindblad and Van Zanden used simple criteria to decide whether disguised transit was a problem or not. They argued that if a correlation coefficient is below 0,70 the problem of disguised transit is very unlikely. When, however, the correlation coefficients are above 0,95 re-adjustment is necessary. But when a coefficient lies between 0,70 and 0,95 it is not easy to draw a conclusion. Other information and sources need to be evaluated in order to assess whether re-adjustments are necessary or not.

Lindblad and Van Zanden concluded that disguised transit was the case with iron ore, wheat, barley, oats, hides, petroleum products, chemical and metal products and paper products. The results of table 4.1. confirm their conclusions for the Rotterdam case. Furthermore, the import/Rhine-traffic and export/Rhine-traffic correlation coefficients can be used as evidence that these goods were directly transferred to the hinterland after arrival in Rotterdam, i.e. the cereals and iron ore and oil products. Rice, rye, corn, chemical products, metal and paper manufacturers were, however, dubious cases. The same goes for coffee with a correlation coefficient below 0,70. There is not a strong relation between import and export of coffee export through Lobith. This suggests that most imported coffee was consumed in the Netherlands and distributed by a number of large coffee trade houses in Amsterdam, the major staple market for colonial products and colonial manufacturers. However, Rotterdam played a part in the transit of coffee that came from South-America. Coffee was shipped to Germany directly, or distributed from several warehouses located in the docks, managed by specialized storage companies, like Pakhuismeesteren (Van Driel 1997 and Mees 1909, 14). The interpretation of coal is not without problems either. Rotterdam imported coal from Great-Britain and Germany, being the major European suppliers. The British coals were mostly consumed in the Netherlands and the same goes for the import of German coal until the 1890s. From that period onwards most coal from Germany was used to fuel ships or exported to other countries and should therefore be classified as a transit good.

Table 4.1. Correlation coefficients import-export series (1880-1914); import and export-Rhine traffic upstream: Rotterdam-Germany, 1884-1914

	Import export	Import/Rhine-traffic	Export/Rhine-traffic
Wheat (NVS=0)	0.98	0.98	0.97
Rye (NVS=0)	0.86	0.87	0.74
Barley (NVS=0)	0.98	0.98	0.99
Oats (NVS=0)	0.98	1.00	0.98
Rice (NVS=0)	0.93	0.57	0.65
Corn (NVS=0)	0.83	0.97	1.00
Wood (NVS=0)	0.99	0.99	0.97
Hides (NVS=0)	0.96	0.86	0.90
Coffee (NVS=1)	0.67	0.78	0.75
Coal (NVS=2)	0.77	0.56	0.95
Petroleum (NVS=3)	0.94	0.78	0.77
Iron ore (NVS=4)	0.99	1.00	0.99
Iron/ steel products (NVS=5)	0.88	0.70	0.36
Raw materials (NVS=6)	0.88	0.87	0.89
Fertilizers (NVS=7)	0.93	0.94	0.84
Chemical products (NVS=8)	0.96	0.75	0.73
Metal products (NVS=9)	0.94	0.79	0.70
Paper products (NVS=9)	0.95	0.70	0.57

Source: SIUD-statistics, Jahresberichte der Zentralkommission für die Rheinschiffahrt (1880-1913) and own calculations.

In order to estimate a new time-series on port throughput the following adaptations were made for goods listed in table 4.1. when (1) the correlation coefficients between incoming and outgoing cargo was equal to and larger than 0.95; (2) when the import/Rhine-export and export/Rhine-export coefficients indicated that these disguised transit goods were discharged in Rotterdam and shipped to the German hinterland via Lobith by water borne transport. This was particular evident in cases of wheat, barley, oats, wood, hides and iron ore, but also for petroleum products, until the start of the twentieth century when the emergence of the crude oil production started in the port of Rotterdam and part of the export was produced by the refinery of Royal Dutch and other oil producers[2]. When the relation with the Rhine-statistics was not so evident, that is with chemical products, iron and steel products, paper manufacturers, the incoming cargo-flows were taken in case of an import-surplus; and the outgoing cargo-flows in case of an export surplus. In either cases, the volume of goods transhipped by the Rhine from Rotterdam to Germany *vice versa* were added. As referred to above, the calculations of the throughput of coffee and coal were based on the fact that coffee and coal were consumed in the Netherlands, but for the latter just until the turn of the century. Therefore, recalculations were necessary in case of the throughput of coal after the 1890s when Rotterdam became a major transit port for coal.

For those goods not listed in table 4.1., for which the problems of disguised transit could be neglected, no adaptations were made. This means, that the incoming and outgoing series of the cargo-flows listed in the SIUD-statistics were used and to these series were added the Rhine imports and exports. This was done because, as the banker Mees showed, the SIUD-statistics referred almost exclusively to sea-borne cargo-flows. Most Rhine shipments were, therefore, not included in the general time-series on incoming and outgoing goods. In general, these relate to duty free goods cleared at the Rhine borders that were shipped down or up the river Rhine to and from Rotterdam but not recorded as incoming or outgoing cargo. Of course, it is not sure whether these duty free goods were enlisted in the import and export series at all and the possibility that these are counted twice had to be considered. However, there is reason to believe that errors due to double counting are small. As Mees' calculations show for 1896 and 1904 perhaps less than 1% of the total volume listed in the series of the Central Commission of Rhine-traffic overlapped with those of the SIUD-statistics. Unfortunately, there are no data available to estimate the import by rail in Rotterdam as only unspecified national accounts are available. Therefore, the re-adjusted import series may still underestimate the import in the port of Rotterdam. This will be the case, especially with reference to the import of coal by train, as before the turn of the century Rhine-transport did not dominate the coal transit shipments with the Netherlands (Nusteling 1978, 274-289). At the same time, it has to be considered that the Dutch railroads transported (semi)-finished products to Germany, which were not recorded either. Thus, the export may still be underestimated.

The re-calculations, as referred to above, lead to the construction of a new series of throughput in the port of Rotterdam. The new series are compared with the general incoming series (until 1900) and from 1900 onwards with the throughput figures that were published by the "Stichting Havenbelangen Rotterdam" (Foundation for Port Interest Rotterdam) as Hugo van Driel and Ferry de Goey used in their recent book on cargo handling technology (van Driel and de Goey 2000, 13 and 126). It is unclear how these series of the "Stichting Havenbelangen" were put together. Probably, these statistics relate to maritime cargo-flows and do not include other modes of transport and may, therefore, underestimate the total throughput. On the other hand, the new estimates may overestimate the develop-

[2] The adjusted throughput of a good x was calculated by the formula throughput = (incoming cargo + outgoing cargo)– (Rhine-export) where x= iron ore, cereals, timber, hides, oil products.

ment of the throughput just before the First World War. But there is reason to believe that this time-series is more reliable than throughput estimates based on the total of imported and exported goods. In particular when the problems of disguised transit are faced. Perhaps at least 25% of the total throughput, based on the sum of incoming and outgoing cargo-flows, may have been liable to disguised transit from 1890 until 1914 (which increased from 1890s onwards).

Fig. 4.3. Estimation of throughput in the port of Rotterdam (1880-1914)

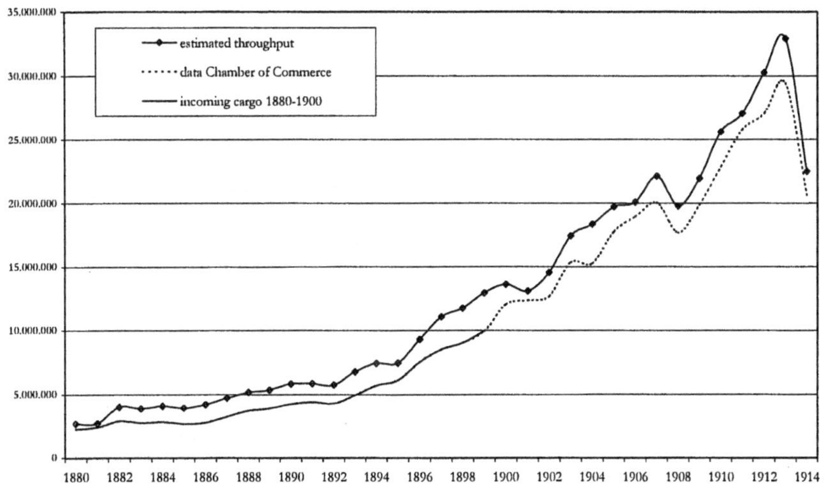

Source: SIUD-statistics, Jahresberichte der Zentralkommission für die Rheinschiffahrt (1880-1913) and own calculations.

Fig. 4.3. shows that the growth of throughput in the port of Rotterdam accelerated at the mid-1890s. Apart from a temporary set back at the turn of the century and a sharp decrease in 1908, a short period of crisis, the port of Rotterdam witnessed a remarkably annual growth rate of almost 8%. According to the new calculations the port of Rotterdam handled about 2,7 million tons in 1880 and in 1913 the total volume of cargo increased to around 32 million tons. The period of fastest growth coincided with the major expansion of the port infrastructure in which the port-relationships between Rotterdam and the German hinterland tightened, As the first section of this paper showed, Rotterdam developed into a major continental transit-port. Between 1895 and 1914 the annual investment rate in port infrastructure amounted to 8% and Rotterdam expanded its port area significantly from about 70 to more than 320 hectares at the outbreak of the First World War. Just before the war, the port of Rotterdam employed fourteen thousand dockworkers, although most of them worked on an irregular basis. In 1890 the numbers of dock workers amounted to about six thousand. In less than 25 years the labour productivity had risen remarkably and in 1913 every labourer handled three times as much goods as in 1890. As is discussed elsewhere in this volume, the rise in productivity was the result of the mechanization of the cargo handling which became particular successful in the discharge of cereals, iron ore and coal.

3. The development of throughput in the port of Rotterdam

In order to give a summary of the recalculations, table 4.2. lists five-year averages, except for the period 1910-1913, of the relative development of these cargo-flows series, grouped according to the NVS-table.

Table 4.2 shows that agricultural products and other food products dominated port traffic in the period 1880-1884 (45% of the total volume of cargo handling). The share of these products even rose in the following decades– to almost 50% in the five-year period 1895-1899, but thereafter its relative importance declined somewhat. However, in the four-year period 1910-1913 agricultural products and other food products compromized still 39% of the total cargo handling in the port of Rotterdam. Iron ore, already an important cargo in the 1880s, became more dominant than before. In the period 1910-1913 this bulk good accounted for 25% of the total throughput in Rotterdam. Together with agricultural and food products these three cargo-flows made up about 64% of the total cargo handling in the port of Rotterdam at the end of the period under study. The table witnesses that the handling of solid mineral fuels, like coal, briquettes and cokes became important as well. Rotterdam became an important import port for English coals and turned into the major export port for the German coal cartel at the turn of the century. This bulk good accounted for 13% of total cargo handling in 1913. In this period, the handling of oil was modest and fertilizers had a larger share in the total throughput in 1913. In the 1880s, a significant part of the port handling consisted of machinery, general cargo and iron and steel products but their relative weight declined significantly at the turn of the century, as had been the case with machinery and general cargo. Below the different categories will be discussed in more detail, but the table confirms that, although the total throughput in the port rose considerably form 1880 to 1914, the port of Rotterdam became more and more specialized in the handling of bulk goods. As a consequence, the relative share of general cargo products diminished.

3.1. Agricultural products

Cereals (wheat, rye, barley, buckwheat, rice, oats, corn, spelt and other cereals) were the prominent agricultural products. Most of these products were imported form overseas, as a small share of the agricultural products came from Germany, on average less than 2% of the total Rhine-import. This is not surprisingly, as this country, once a major exporter of grains to the Netherlands, changed into a grain-importing country. The industrialization of Germany reduced the share of German labourers in the agricultural sector who migrated to the cities. Consequently, less cereals were produced and imports were necessary to feed the urban populace.

Table 4.2. Specification throughput cargo-flows, port of Rotterdam, 1880-1913 (five years average)

	1880-1884	1885-1889	1890-1894	1895-1899	1900-1904	1905-1909	1910-1913
(0) agricultural products	24.9	26.4	27.2	32.5	27.2	25.9	25.1
(1) other food products	20.5	22.1	19.7	17.4	16.0	14.0	13.2
(2) solid mineral fuels	7.3	5.3	5.2	4.5	5.6	9.5	13.4
(3) crude oil and oil products	0.1	1.0	2.3	2.7	1.9	1.9	1.4
(4) iron ore and metal scrap	15.0	14.4	18.5	20.6	24.8	25.9	24.8
(5) iron and steel products	12.3	9.0	6.8	6.3	7.4	5.9	6.0
(6) raw and building materials	3.2	4.3	4.5	3.0	5.6	6.6	5.4
(7) fertilizers	0.4	0.9	1.9	1.8	1.5	2.0	2.7
(8) chemical products	5.6	5.4	4.3	3.2	2.7	2.0	2.8
(9) machinery, general cargo	10.6	11.2	9.6	8.1	7.3	6.3	5.2
	100.0	100.0	100.0	100.0	100.0	100.0	100.0

Source: SIUD-statistics, Jahresberichte der Zentralkommission für die Rheinschiffahrt and own calculations (1880-1913).

The socio-economic transformation of Germany, coincided with the Great Depression (1878-1895) during which large quantities of cereals were shipped at relatively low transport costs by steamers form the America's to the European continent. The prices of feed stuffs and fodder on the continent dropped significantly. Many farmers changed to other crops or were forced to quit their business. On the other hand, the population of the large cities in Europe benefited from the decrease in food prices and rise in net-income (Nusteling 1978, 305-317 and Vervelde 1997).

Before the 1870s the Rotterdam grain business was concentrated on supplying local and regional markets. After that, the position of Rotterdam changed at great length due to the transformation of the German economy. The importance can be illustrated by the share of cereals the port of Rotterdam transhipped to Germany. On average 26% of the incoming maritime cargo-flows were cereals. In 1880 Rotterdam imported about half a million ton and in 1913 the total volume rose to about five million tons. Although, the emerging port-city became not the international centre of the grain trade, it developed into the major grain transit point on the continent. As the German hinterland became more and more dependant on the shipments of grain from Rotterdam, a number of German grain traders settled in Rotterdam and expanded their agency networks in order to be able to guarantee the deliveries of cereals to the hinterland.

Compared to other cereals the other agrarian products were less important, albeit not insignificant, in particular timber that accounted on average for 5% of the total throughput. Especially, in the third part of the nineteenth century, did the transhipment of timber became more important. The import of timber in the period 1880-1914 grew with 12% and the export in the same period with more than 18%. As Hubert Nusteling explained in his study on Dutch Rhine traffic, before 1850 the shipments by Rhine barges from Germany to Rotterdam were negligible, as most of the time, wood was transported to Rotterdam by log rafts (Nusteling 1978, 317-323). After bringing them down, the trees were thrown in the water and floated to the Rhine, collected and tightly mixed and bound together to huge log rafts. The so-called "Dutch rafts", floating islands which measured sometimes 1000 by 130 feet, became less important after 1850. Economic considerations and technical requirements reduced the popularity of rafts. Due to expansion of Rhine-traffic the large wooden islands became too dangerous and turned to be obstacles for the regular Rhine-ships. In the twentieth century, this means of transport from Germany to Rotterdam lost its importance all together. Wood was seldom transported form Rotterdam to Germany by rafts, as shipment by Rhine barges was the dominant mode of transport. Most of the times it arrived in Rotterdam in bundles of timber already sawn by the sawmills in wood-producing countries (Mees 1909, 31-32).

3.2. Other foodstuffs

Rotterdam handled a lot of other foodstuffs and fodder, on average more than 8% of the total volume of incoming cargo and even 17% of the outgoing cargo-flows. These products relate to different kinds of food products, like grain-manufacturers (flour, bread, biscuits), agrarian natural and industrial products, such as vegetable oil products, cheese, butter, margarine, but also colonial products as spices, coffee, tea, sugar and so on. On average, 23% of the imported food products were so called traditional colonial staple goods. But compared to the 1880s and 1890s the portion of staple products fell down at the end of the period, because of the reduced imports of coffee and sugar. In 1880 coffee compromized 15% of the staple products and in 1913 the share dropped to circa 5%. The import of sugar, first, started to rise in the 1880s but its relative weight diminished due to the sugar crisis of 1884. This crisis led to a sharp decline in prices of sugar cane and countries started to protect their home markets for sugar refined in the Netherlands. The Dutch refused to levy import duties on sugar refined elsewhere and its own market became abounded with cheap sugar (Chamber of Commerce 1885, 90 and 108-109, Bakker 1989). As a result, the share of export of sugar fell down as well - from on average 15% in the early 1880s to around 2% in the early 1890s, but then started to rise again. The export of sugar stood out in 1897 (almost 20%) and reached an average of 10% in the period 1900-1914. From the 1890s Rotterdam exported a considerable volume of sugar to Germany, which was still an important export product.

The Dutch industries manufactured a range of agrarian products. Margarine was one of the modern products where Dutch manufacturers became important international players. Margarine was a French invention, which became a cheap alternative for butter. As The Netherlands were a large exporter of butter the country developed a great interest in the making and selling of margarine. Rotterdam became an important centre for the import of soot, oil, talc, neutral lard and all other greasy or oily substances that were shipped from Boston and Chicago and used for fabricating margarine. Because Rotterdam developed as a centre for the shipping lines with the America's and imported a high volume of these raw materials, several producers of margarine decided to build a factory in this port-city. Margarine became, thus, one of these new traffic industries and had a large impact on the industrial development of the port, like the sugar refineries, beer and gin distilleries had done in the seventeenth and eighteenth centuries. Van den Bergh, a former butter merchant, who owned a margarine plant in the southern part of The Netherlands, decided to move his premises to Rotterdam and built a new modern plant in the southern part of the city near the new transit docks in 1891 (Wilson 1945). The development of the margarine, however, stocked in the early nineties, since it became more difficult to obtain cheap neutral lard from Chicago. Due to a substantial rise in purchase power the living-conditions in the Americans improved and more people could afford meat. The import of fats and neutral lard became more expensive for margarine producers and the competition between the Dutch firms increased. Apart from business reorganizations, which stimulated small firms to merge with their rivals, producers started to look for other ingredients to make margarine. Although, neutral lard was still used for the production of margarine, more and more firms started to use vegetable oils. The import statistics show that Rotterdam imported less neutral lard and more oils. In fact, the port became the major European port for the transhipment and storage of vegetable oils the margarine industries and other fat and edible oil consuming industries used.

3.3. Solid mineral fuels

Until the 1880s the position of Rotterdam as a transhipment port of coal was modest, as most of the times the imported coal was used for consumption in the Netherlands (Sneller 1946 and Nusteling 1978, 274-289). Apart from the sea-borne coal imports from Great-Britain, the city handled coal from Germany shipped by the Rhine-railroad company. Until the 1890s this company had a strong position in the transport of coals as the services offered were competitive towards water borne transport. However, due to a change in German marketing tactics, the railroad companies position deteriorated in favour of the Rhine-shipping firms. The Germans mines planned to boost their export to the Netherlands and increased their shipments. To that purpose the German coal producers joined their forces and founded in 1893 the Rheinisch-Westfälische Kohlen-Syndikat (Rhine-Westphalia Coal Syndicate) that sought co-operation with the Dutch Coal Trade Union, which started business in 1896. This Dutch organization represented the German cartel and got the sole selling and distribution rights of coal from Westphalia. D.G. van Beuningen, the leading figure of the Coal Trade Union, decided to set up a business in Rotterdam in 1901 to augment its competitive position towards the importers of English solid fuel. Due to the activities of the Rotterdam-based firm, the shipments from Germany boosted. Soon it turned out that it was cheaper to transport and unload coal from Rhine barges than from rail wagons. As is discussed by Hugo van Driel elsewhere, this strategic response in the coal business was an important impetus to mechanize the cargo handling of coal as well. The decision to move the coal trade to Rotterdam, stimulated the position of this port in becoming the leading coal transhipment port of the Netherlands. In particular, Rotterdam developed into the major continental bunker port and ships sailed to Rotterdam to fuel their ships by coal delivered by Van Beuningen. In the period 1882-1913 the import of coals from Germany grew on average with 12% annually, from 115.000 tons to around 5 million tons. From 1900 until 1913 the Rhine-statistics show an annual growth rate of 28%. In 1913 the coal transhipment from Germany to Rotterdam compromized 70% of the total volume of Rhine transport.

3.4. Crude oil and oil products

Table 4.2. illustrates that the transhipment of oil had not been an important business in Rotterdam yet. But this situation changed just before the First World War when several oil multinationals had chosen Rotterdam as production, transhipment and storage centre. This situation was quite different from what had been the case before the 1860s, as the petroleum trade was a local business. Until then Rotterdam did not develop remarkable initiatives in this particular field. The storage company Pakhuismeesteren was the first firm to start selling oil and began to dominate the local market, i.e. supplying local customers with oil to fuel oil lamps. Germany and Belgium were more interested in other refined oil-products, like gasoline, and began to develop oil-transhipments in the 1880s. Petroleum was initially carried in wooden barrels by sailing ships which after discharge were transported by rail. As

Rotterdam had no part in the oil-transhipment business, Antwerp and Bremen were far more important than Rotterdam.

This situation changed following the arrival of the first tanker in Rotterdam and sail quickly made way for steam after 1888. Pakhuismeesteren lost its local monopoly in the last decade of the nineteenth century when the American Standard Oil Company located its subsidiaries American Petrol Company and Deutsch-Amerikanische Petroleum Gesellschaft, next to Pakhuismeesteren in Rotterdam to serve the Dutch, Belgian and German markets. Other competitors were to follow. The concentration of multinational companies in the port of Rotterdam led to the change in transhipment and storage politics. It became more efficient to use tank lighters to transport petroleum than by railroad. As early as 1886, Deutsch Russische Naphtha Import Gesellschaft requested permission from the municipal executive to carry petroleum on the Rhine (Gerretson 1971, 267). In fact, the change in selling strategies of major international firms, as had been the case in the coal trade, reinforced the position of Rhine-shipping firms.

At the turn of the century the arrival of Royal Dutch to Rotterdam stimulated the development of the oil business. In November 1901 Royal Dutch's notorious chairman Henri Deterding started the construction of two storage tanks and a petrol refinery. Deterding challenged his rival American Standard Oil and attacked its monopoly in German. Royal Dutch established Benzinwerke Rhenania G.m.b.H. and financed the construction of the facilities in Düsseldorf. In 1902 Royal Dutch granted Van Ommeren a monopoly for the transport to and in Germany. Until then, petrol had never been carried by tankers on the Rhine, only petroleum had been carried in that way. Van Ommeren was one of the leading shipping agents in the port of Rotterdam and became an influential firm. It had diversified into a shipping company, ship management firm and started tank storage operations in the twentieth century, and entered into rivalry with Pakhuismeesteren (Boele and van de Laar 2001). The combination of the presence of major oil companies and cheap transhipment and storage facilities in the port, strengthened Rotterdam's position. However, compared to other bulk cargo-flows, the shipment of oil products to the German hinterland lagged behind. From the turn of the century until the outbreak of the First World War, the annual growth rate was around 3%.

3.5. Iron ore

Table 4.2. tells us that iron ore was the most important bulk good in the period under study. The development of Rotterdam into a major iron ore port cannot be explained without stressing the role of the German steel industries. As they needed ore with a higher content of iron than the German mine-companies were able to deliver, the bulk of iron had to be imported abroad. The major German industrialist, like Krupp, exploited their own mines in Spain. But Sweden and Russia also exported large volumes via Rotterdam to the German hinterland. Especially, the Russian high quality ore was widely asked (Nusteling 1978, 295-305). From the beginning, the transport of iron ore by rail road was not insignificant, as the Swedish mines exported their ship load in summer and autumn before the start of the winter season when it was impossible to ship ore. In summer and autumn the river Rhine often had to cope with low water levels, which reduced the competitiveness of the shipment by Rhine-barges. During periods of low water levels, less tons per unit could be transported than under normal conditions and consequently the relative transport costs rose. The railroads benefited from the temporary relative price differences, especially German companies which were partially subsidized by tariffs arrangements.

However, at the turn of the century the Swedish mines were connected to the ice-free Norwegian ports of Narvik and Kirkenas. Then it became possible to ship ore the whole year round. In a short period of time, the Rhine became the dominant mode of transport and within a few years the railroad lost its position in ore shipments to Germany: in 1903 circa 95% of the transport went by river. Rotterdam, thus, became the major transhipment port. In 1899 the German city Dordtmund became connected to the Rhine through the Eems-canal, but it was still much cheaper for German industries to import their large quantities from Rotterdam than order deliveries by the German town.

From 1880 until 1913 the total tonnage of iron ore imported in Rotterdam grew with an average rate of more than 10%. In less than twenty-five years the imports increased from 400.000 tons to almost 9 million tons in 1913. The bulk of these huge volumes of ore the port handled went to the German hinterland. About 40% of the exports from Rotterdam up the river Rhine compromized iron ore.

3.6. Iron and steel products

The development of the handling of metal products underwent a remarkable shift in the period under study. Until 1902 the import of iron and steel products exceeded the export of these goods, but from that period onwards the port of Rotterdam witnessed an export surplus. In the period 1880-1914 the import of these goods showed an annual growth rate of 4%, whereas the average annual export growth rate was 8%. As table 4.1. shows, the correlation coefficient signalled that there was a strong relationship between the import and export, but the relation between import and Rhine-export was less clear. In fact, the Rhine-series show that the volume of goods that were shipped from Germany down the Rhine to Rotterdam exceeded that of the shipments of iron and metal goods up the river Rhine.

This opposite directions in Rhine-shipments can partly be explained by the expansion of the German industry. Before the turn of the century, the metal industries were busy conquering their home markets and competed with foreign, foremost British firms. However, beyond 1900 the German home market became saturated and the steel manufacturers could not expand without increasing the export possibilities. In fact, a parallel can be drawn with the coal trade where an aggressive sales policy pushed the export of coals abroad. The same strategy was taken by the metal producers to stimulate the export of their products from Germany. Again, as had been the case with other bulk goods, as the volume of transports rose, it became more economical to ship manufacturers by river than by rail. Until then most metal products from German were used by Dutch firms, but as Nusteling stressed (Nusteling 1978, 290-295), from 1900 onwards Rotterdam became an transit-port for those metal products that the German exported to other countries. The share of pig iron of the total import from Germany to Rotterdam declined after 1900, whereas the Rhine-import of steel and iron manufacturers augmented to more than 70% of the total shipments from Germany.

The metal products that were exported from Rotterdam, therefore, represent part of the transit-trade from Germany to other foreign countries. The correlation coefficient of 0.92 between export of metal products and the Rhine-import series for this particular good underlines this fact. However, not all metal products the Dutch exported via Rotterdam were imported from Germany. At the turn of the century, the production of metal products in the Netherlands increased significantly and a considerable share of these goods were exported as well. In 1873 the national export of industrial products was less than 26% of the total volume but rose to 40% in 1913 (van Zanden and van Riel 2000, 357-358). For the port of Rotterdam, the handling of iron and steel products was important, as was confirmed by table 4.2. On average, almost 8% of the throughput related to these cargo-flows, although the relative importance of this good declined in time.

3.7. Raw materials and building materials, fertilizers and chemical products

The throughput of raw and building materials was not substantial in the period under study, on average less than 5% of the total volume, as summarized in table 4.2. Rotterdam imported these materials that were mostly used for the Dutch home market. Round 1900 the export of these goods exceeded the total import. In the same period, the import of raw materials from Germany by Rhine-barges increased. On average, in the period 1900-1914 about 17% of the total volume of Rhine-shipments from Germany to the Netherlands compromized raw materials. As far as the Rhine-import of raw materials and construction materials exceeded the export flows, the surplus was taken up by the Dutch home market. This is in accordance with the fact that in the first decade of the twentieth century the building activities in the Netherlands increased significantly.

Compared to the raw materials and building materials the share of fertilizers in the total volume of cargo handling was limited. The import from Germany of fertilizers increased from the 1890s, as slag, waste matter remaining from metal extracted form ore in the so-called Thomas steel process, became converted into fertilizers. This by-product of the ore-industry had a large concentration of phosphor and competed with other fertilizers. The import of slag from Germany reduced the competitiveness of the infant Dutch super-phosphate industry, which started in the third part of the nineteenth century. Compared to slag the concentration of phosphor in sulphuric acid the super-phosphate firm used, was relatively low and their product, therefore, less wanted. In order to remain competitive, firms merged and started looking for alternatives to sulphuric acid, and within time they turned to phosphoric acid as a raw material (de Wit 1990, 12-20).

Table 4.3. Share of import and export of general cargo in Rotterdam, 1880-1913 (five year averages)

	1880-1884	1885-1889	1890-1894	1895-1899	1900-1904	1905-1909	1910-1914
Import							
Metal products	46,7	37,5	32,8	31,7	33,3	27,7	29,4
Machinery	7,0	6,0	7,2	7,9	8,4	8,5	8,0
Textiles	17,3	17,1	15,7	14,7	9,8	10,6	9,1
Paper manufactures	4,1	5,1	7,7	8,5	9,6	9,6	9,7
Miscellaneous cargo	24,9	34,4	36,6	37,2	38,9	43,6	43,8
	100,0	100,0	100,0	100,0	100,0	100,0	100,0
Export							
Metal products	64,5	60,0	47,9	49,3	50,4	43,2	47,7
Machinery	4,0	3,8	5,2	5,6	6,6	7,4	6,5
Paper manufactures	13,8	14,8	15,1	15,5	10,2	9,9	9,3
Textiles	5,8	6,3	9,2	8,8	12,9	15,9	16,0
Miscellaneous cargo	11,9	15,1	22,6	20,8	19,9	23,6	20,4
	100,0	100,0	100,0	100,0	100,0	100,0	100,0

Source: SIUD-statistics, Jahresberichte der Zentralkommission für die Rheinschiffahrt (1880-1913) and own calculations.

The throughput of chemical manufacturers was directly connected to the production of fertilizers, but also the production of talc acid, used for the fabrication of candles and other by-products that the margarine and soap manufacturers applied (Berkers and Homburg 1993a and 1993b). The bulk of the chemical products consisted of chemicals, dyes and other products, on average, 66% of the imports and 67% of the exported cargo. As could be concluded from table 4.1. the import and export series were highly correlated, but there was no indication that there was a strong relation between import and Rhine-export. In fact, the Rhine-statistics are difficult to evaluate as there is a sharp distinction between the data before and after 1909 when chemicals and dyes were specified for the first time. However, as far as conclusions may be drawn from table 4.2., it will be clear that on average chemical products were not a major cargo-flows in the port of Rotterdam.

3.8. Machinery and general cargo

This category of goods lists a bunch of goods, ranging from machine part, steam-engines, finished products, textiles, yarns, packing materials, glass works, potteries, paper manufacturers, tools and implements and other general cargo. In table 4.3. the import and export series are split into four main categories, i.e. metal products, machinery, textiles, paper manufacturers and miscellaneous general cargo. The table shows that the fluctuations in the share of import and export of general cargo more or less have the same pattern.

Firstly, the share of miscellaneous cargo became more important as an import and export product. The share of import increased in the first five-year period from 25% to almost 44% in the period 1910-1914, whereas the export share of these goods rose from 12% to more than 20%. In 1880 Rotterdam imported 83.000 tons of metal products and in 1913 this number had tripled. In absolute numbers, the export-figures are comparable, but as table 4.3. shows the relative importance of the export of metal products fell down. The average share of textile manufacturers declined as an import and export good. On the other hand, the import and export of machinery remained more or less stable. Although the relative share of the export of paper manufacturers declined, the average annual growth rate of the export of this product with 8% exceeded the import growth rate. In 1913 Rotterdam exported 120.000 tons of paper manufacturers.

As has been discussed before (see table 4.1.) there has been a close relationship between the import and export of metal finished goods and the same goes for the correlation between import and export of paper manufacturers. Table 4.3. confirms this for the import and export of machinery and general cargo, as the series show a parallel direction. However, there has not been a strong relationship between the import series and the Rhine-export series. Although it must be recognized, that the Rhine statistics of general cargo in the period 1880-1909 are not very reliable, one has to consider the possibilities that a substantial part of the export of general cargo were products made by Dutch firms, which became more competitive than before, as the relative costs of the input of labour and capital declined (Van Zanden and Van Riel 2000, 285).

Conclusion

This paper has discussed the development of the port of Rotterdam in the period 1880-1914, an era in which port functions changed significantly. This process was not unique for Rotterdam, as will become clear to readers of the Antwerp case. In order to study the competitiveness of both ports we need to discuss the strength and weaknesses of both Antwerp and Rotterdam by means of analysing the data. The first step, therefore, is to get the facts and figures right, how many goods and – equally important – what kind of goods these competitors handled. After a short introduction on the institutional development of the port of Rotterdam, attention was paid to the port statistics and how these should be interpreted. On the basis of these statistics, a estimation was made of the volume and growth of throughput in this period and classified accordingly to criteria that will make comparisons with the port of Antwerp possible in due course. This exercise confirmed the general accepted idea that the port of Rotterdam became more and more dependant on the close relationship with Germany. The function of Rotterdam as a transit-port has, therefore, to be stressed. Indeed, the new throughput estimates show that, when the relative part of the cargo handling of cereals, timber, hides, coal, iron ore and petroleum products are taken together, almost 60% of the total volume consisted of transit-goods. This percentage is probably too low, since, as the review of the diverse goods has revealed, a lot of other products were more or less shipped to Germany after arrival in the port of Rotterdam. However, as a close review of the Rhine-statistics made clear, several industrial products that were exported to the hinterland had stamps on it "made in the Netherlands". But it is important to stress, that this industrial expansion was made possible thanks to the efficient services the port of Rotterdam offered. Especially, the Dutch industry benefited from the increase in scale the port of Rotterdam made possible.

Rotterdam's transit-port system was a strategic response to the demands of an industrial era. Rotterdam developed, in the first place, its intermediary function as a transit-port connecting the industrial power of Britain with that of rival Germany. As the review of the major bulk goods has revealed, this development was stimulated by a concentration of multinational capital and the business interests of large firms in Germany. However, Rotterdam did not industrialize at a large scale. The primacy of shipping, Rhine traffic and cargo-handling reduced the possibilities of a more diversified industrial development. Most industries that developed in Rotterdam were more or less dependant on the same shipping cycle, like shipbuilding, or the processing of raw materials imported from abroad. It must be recognized that many ports did not develop into major industrial diversified locations (Lee 1998, 160). However, perhaps few ports, like Rotterdam, depended on transit-trade. The next step in the discussion will be to compare the data for the port of Antwerp and Rotterdam and find out whether the strong position of the Belgian port in transhipment of general cargo resulted in a more balanced growth rate.

References

Berkers E and Homburg E (1993a) Van "unvollkommene Waare" tot kwaliteitsprodukt. De ontwikkeling van de kaarindustrie in Nederland, 1800-1880. Jaarboek voor de Geschiedenis van Bedrijf en Techniek 10: 100-133

Berkers E and Homburg E (1993b) Stearinekaarsen. In Lintsen HW (ed) Geschiedenis van de techniek in Nederland. De wording van een moderne samenleving, 1800-1890. Delfstoffen, machine- en scheepsbouw, stoom, chemie, telegrafie en telefonie, part IV. Zutphen, pp 241-259

Boele C and van de Laar P (2001) The history of Koninklijke Van Ommeren. Rotterdam

Callahan M (1981) The harbor barons; political and commercial elite's and the development of the port of Rotterdam (Ph.D. -dissertation Princeton University)

De Wit D (1990) Windmill, wieken naar de wind gekeerd. Van boerencoöperatie naar internationale organisatie. Vlaardingen

Gerretson C (1971) Geschiedenis der "Koninklijke". Baarn

Lee R (1998) The socio-economic and demographic characteristics of port cities: a typology for comparative analysis, Urban History, 25: 160

Lindblad JT van Zanden JL (1989) De buitenlandse handel van Nederland, 1872-1913. Economisch- en Sociaal-Historisch Jaarboek 52: 231-269

Mees (1909) Tegenwoordige staat van handel en scheepvaart. Rotterdam in den loop der eeuwen. Rotterdam

Mees M (1898) Eenige cijfers betreffende het scheepvaart- en handelsverkeer te Rotterdam, reprint De Economist: 1-45

Nusteling HPH (1974) De Rijnvaart in het tijdperk van stoom en steenkool 1831-1914. Amsterdam

Sanmann H (1956) Die Verkehrsstruktur der nordwesteuropäischen Seehäfen Antwerpen, Rotterdam, Bremen und Hamburg und ihre Wandlungen vond der Jahrhundertwende bis zur Gegenwart. Hamburg

Sneller ZW (1946) Geschiedenis van de steenkolenhandel van Rotterdam. Groningen

Van de Laar P (1999) Het rendement van de Rotterdamse haven ca. 1870-1940. In: Bindinga AJ, van Hoepen MA, Maat J (eds.), Bericht gegeven. Opstellenbundel aangeboden aan prof. drs. F. Krens bij zijn afscheid als hoogleraar in de bedrijfshuishoudkunde, in het bijzonder de Kosten- en Winstbepalingsvraagstukken aan de Faculteit der Economische Wetenschappen van de Erasmus Universiteit Rotterdam. Deventer, pp 259-271

Van de Laar P (2000) Stad van formaat. Geschiedenis van Rotterdam in de negentiende en twintigste eeuw. Zwolle

Van Driel H (1997) Uitschakeling van de Nederlandse koffiehandel in de negentiende en twintigste eeuw. NEHA-Jaarboek voor economische, bedrijfs- en techniekgeschiedenis 60: 159-203

Van Driel H and de Goey F (2000) Rotterdam cargo handling technology 1870-2000. Zutphen

Van Zanden JL and van Riel A (2000) Nederland 1780-1914, staat, instituties en economische ontwikkeling. Amsterdam

Vervelde K (1997) De Rotterdamse graanhandel bemonsterd en bewogen, 125 jaar Koninklijke Vereniging Het Comité van Graanhandelaren 1872-1997. Rotterdam

Commentary on the papers of Loyen and Van de Laar

David J. Starkey

University of Hull, United Kingdom

In his pioneering work on British ports, Gordon Jackson commented that *transport systems, though they might appear to have a certain permanence, have nevertheless been in a state of almost continuous evolution for the best part of two centuries* (Jackson 1983, 10). One of the most striking examples of this continuous evolution has been the changing configuration of the port provisions of north-west Europe. While the period down to 1914 witnessed the rise to pre-eminence of major UK ports such as London, Liverpool and Hull, these "gateways to Europe and the wider world", as contemporaries liked to call them, have declined fitfully since 1918. However, even as these gateways were approaching their relative peaks in the late nineteenth and early twentieth centuries, the European ports that were soon to eclipse the British trading centres were beginning to develop rapidly. Antwerp and Rotterdam were at the fore of this "continental" development. Located on deep, navigable rivers, with easy access by river, rail and road to an industrial hinterland that was far more extensive and populous than even the "workshop of the world" could offer, Antwerp and Rotterdam possessed many advantages in the changing economic environment of the twentieth century. In this setting, throughput, or transit traffic, to and from the interior emerged as a dynamic sector of the business of both ports.

The papers of Reginald Loyen and Paul van de Laar are essentially concerned with measuring and explaining the extent and significance of the throughput of Antwerp and Rotterdam respectively. The two papers differ in a number of respects. They deal with different time periods, Van de Laar focusing on Rotterdam's throughput in the 1880-1914 period, while Loyen covers the twentieth century. They cover different topics. In contrast to Loyen, who discusses methodologies and concepts as well as the pattern of transit trade growth, Van de Laar provides a good deal of historical background to his account of the rapid rise of Rotterdam's throughput in the late nineteenth and early twentieth centuries. The two authors adopt different approaches in seeking to explain the development of traffic in their respective ports, Loyen preferring a chronological framework and Van de Laar opting for a commodity by commodity line of enquiry. Moreover, the depth of coverage in the two papers differs, largely because Loyen's paper is the fruit of a project that has been underway for some years, while Van de Laar's investigation into Rotterdam's transit trade is in its early stages.

Due to these differences in parameters, approach and depth of coverage, the two papers do not readily lend themselves to comparative analysis. Rather, they complement each other, and it is therefore more appropriate to discuss them together. Five aspects of the papers warrant particular comment. First, both authors have produced time series pertaining to the throughputs of their respective ports. To achieve this, they have drawn on national sea-borne trade statistics and local inland trade statistics, as well as data concerned with road, canal and rail traffic. Various contemporary accounts and secondary studies have also been used to yield comprehensive annual figures on the volume and composition of the throughput of Antwerp and Rotterdam. Though the datasets are somewhat understated in the two papers, the production of these time series is a great achievement in itself. More importantly, it would seem that the data has been assembled in a systematic, scientific manner. Accordingly, there are signs in both papers that the authors, in considering their primary evidence, have asked the right questions of their material; thus,

- Why was the information produced initially?
- How was it generated?
- Is it comprehensive, accurate and compatible with data from other ports and other modes of transport?
- Can the data be corroborated?
- If there are gaps and problems, can they be alleviated or overcome by estimation, extrapolation, or a resort to alternative sources?

In other words, both Loyen and Van de Laar have been very professional in the provenance of their primary source material, and in the assembly and presentation of the evidence derived from these sources. While this is an extremely important and admirable facet of their work, I have one slight misgiving about the technical procedures that they have followed. My concern is that neither author has devoted much space in his paper to the data evaluation process that has been employed. This is not because I am an advocate of long, detailed and potentially distracting primary source descriptions and methodological treatises, but because I believe that historians need to be especially careful in their treatment of quantitative data. Our sources need to be assessed thoroughly and our methods need to be rigorous and transparent. We need to learn from our colleagues in the science disciplines that the validation of data is a vital aspect of historical enquiry, and we should not be reticent in writing about it.

A second notable – and notably strong – element of the two papers is the discussion of conceptual approaches and models that have been applied to port development. This features prominently in Loyen's paper, mainly because the Antwerp project is at a more advanced stage than that pertaining to Rotterdam, but it is also implicit in Van de Laar's study. Loyen's discussion of this matter rests on an impressive survey of a broad range of literature which embraces the works of geographers, economists and historians. Having considered and discarded a range of paradigms and models, Loyen devises an integrated functional approach to port development. This combines the functional approach advanced by De Rousier and others with the foreland and hinterland concept championed by Vigarie and Robinson. The product is a framework in which the flow of goods from place of production to place of consumption is in the form of a continuum. This analytical apparatus entails three functional shifts in the ports that form part of the continuum: from primary to commercial; from commercial to industrial; and from industrial to distibutional, wherein ports act as "hubs". Such an approach, it is argued, provides a model - the Hanseatic paradigm - that can be applied to the major ports in the spatial range from Hamburg to Le Havre. A significant element of Loyen's paper, it will be instructive to see whether or not his hypothesis stands up to the rigorous testing that will be facilitated by the empirical data generated by the Antwerp-Rotterdam comparative project. Whether it does or not, the authors should be applauded for engaging in type of theoretical debate that historians shy away from all too often.

The third point arising from the papers relates to their structure, an area in which neither is particularly strong. While Loyen promotes his thesis of the "integrated functional approach", his paper is hardly an integrated piece of work. It is really a paper in three parts, or perhaps parts of three papers joined together. Accordingly, there is a discussion of concepts and models, a brief discussion of sources, and then a long section, occupying two-thirds of the paper, on cargo flows during the 1860-2000 period. This is not only unbalanced, but also ordered in an odd way with the concept and the model placed before the empirical data. I would prefer it if this order of discussion is reversed so that the theory derives more closely from the evidence. Van de Laar's paper is likewise unbalanced and slightly stilted, with an historical introduction, and a review of the sources, somewhat eclipsed by a long explanation of the trends evident in the datasets.

This leads to a fourth point - the clarity of the analyses advanced by the authors. In discussing Antwerp's twentieth-century throughput traffic, Loyen essentially adopts a chronological approach. Within this framework, various exogenous factors - notably world trade - are melded with a range of endogenous factors - dock building, local politics, land policies - to explain the fluctuations in the level and composition of the port's throughput. This is logical, but given the extent of Antwerp's foreland and hinterland, it does entail consideration of an extremely broad array of causal factors. In essence, the integrated functional approach gets somewhat lost in a long discussion that amounts to a short economic history of the industrial world in the twentieth century. Van de Laar's paper also suffers in this respect, though in a slightly different way. Choosing to examine the throughput of Rotterdam on a cargo by cargo basis not only leads to repetition of points that apply to all the commodities traded, but also tends to obscure, rather than illuminate, the central trends in the growth of the port's transit traffic. In both papers, a simpler, more thematic structure might render the argument more accessible. For instance, the explanatory factors - exogenous or endogenous - might be discussed in order of significance, with examples drawn from the statistical data and wider literature selected to serve as evidence to support the point being made.

A fifth and final comment concerns the causal factors identified by the two authors. While their explanations are generally sound, a little more emphasis might be afforded to the role of geography in determining port development. Though a somewhat obvious point, the location of Antwerp and Rotterdam in relation to the extensive and dynamically growing German hinterland was of great significance from the late nineteenth century onwards. A further explanatory factor that is given short shrift in both papers is the role of shipowners in the development of port traffic. Historically, shipowners, at least in Britain, have generally been in a strong negotiating position in their dealings with port operators, largely because they can re-route their vessels to another port if the right facilities are not provided at the right price. The same applies today, as the great alliances and combinations in the contemporary container shipping industry are not entirely passive agents in determining the scale and composition of traffic flows in even the greatest of ports.

These are minor criticisms. Reginald Loyen and Paul van de Laar have written strong papers based on an impressive range of largely statistical evidence. They should both be congratulated and thanked for their efforts to make sense of throughput, a vital - but, as Jackson suggests, not necessarily permanent - feature of the business of the ports of Antwerp and Rotterdam.

References

Jackson G (1983) The History and Archaeology of Ports. Tadworth

Port throughput and international trade: have port authorities any degrees of freedom left?

Sabine Janssens, Hilde Meersman, Eddy Van de Voorde

University of Antwerp, Belgium

Introduction

Ports have always been at the heart of economic activity. They were and still are the places of transhipment between maritime and hinterland transport, they supplied storage facilities, they were locations for all kind of service providers and they attracted industrial and trade companies.

The functions of a port are closely related to the different types of freight handled within the perimeter of that same port, and vice versa. Especially the transhipment from sea to land and vice versa depends to a large extent on the international trade of the hinterland. Changes in trade directions might have considerable impacts on the flows of goods arriving at and departing from the port. Recent examples are a number of Polish ports being confronted with the fact that Poland switched from being a coal exporter to a coal importing country, and also the consequences of the South-east Asian crisis some European ports where confronted with. From a policy point of view it is necessary to have reliable estimates of the relation between economic and port activity.

This paper focuses on the relation between throughput in the port of Antwerp and international trade. The first part gives a brief overview of the evolution of the quantities handled at the port in the post World War II period. In the second part the relation between throughput and international trade is quantified by using modern econometric techniques such as unit roots, cointegration and error correction models. It investigates whether there is a long run, stable relation between international trade and port traffic in Antwerp and how this relation might vary for different commodity groups. Attention also goes to the short-term relation and to other factors, which may have an impact on the evolution of the throughput, such as capacity and indicators for the competitive position of the port. Although the evolution of international trade has an impact on port traffic, it cannot fully explain the fluctuations in port throughput.

Even if there is a historical relationship between port traffic and international trade, a port such as the port of Antwerp still has to face other challenges, which will affect its competitive position. Ports and port authorities are facing new, strategic objectives. The relation between the port authorities and the users of their infrastructure gets a number of new dimensions. Ports are forced to go in search for a good position in important networks and for all kinds of co-operation. As a consequence, the success or failure of a port is no longer determined by the costs of transhipment, handling and related activities. A successful port will be able to become a part of important logistics chains. This implies that the strategy of port authorities should not be restricted to their own, specific activities. They have to become an important player in the field of national and international logistics.

1. The evolution of throughput, international trade, capacity and costs in the port of Antwerp in the post war period

After the Second World War radical changes occurred in maritime traffic (Stopford 1997, 54-67). During the first twenty-five years after the war (the period 1950-1973), world sea trade rose sharply at an average annual rate of 22.5 percent. This growth was driven by an increase in international trade and by technical changes in the shipping industry (cf. also the two "revolutions" in the maritime business, i.e. bulk transport and unit loads). There was a clear trend to specialized ships and to an increase of ship size. The first chemical parcel tanker was put into service in 1954, the first car carrier in 1956 and the first LNG tanker in 1964. The average size of tankers increased exponentially over the period 1956 (closing of the Suez Canal) - 1980. The introduction of the container and of container vessels did not only affect the organization of sea trade and ports, it changed the entire transportation sector.

The growth of maritime trade was not uniformly distributed over the entire post-war period. A number of cycles can be identified, driven by economic and/or political events. Recessions alternated with periods of expansions in the sector. The Suez crisis in 1956 resulted in an increased tanker demand, stimulating the construction of new and bigger tankers. The recession of the world economy in 1958 and the reopening of the Suez canal resulted in a reduction of seaborne trade. Overcapacity led to reductions of profitability in the sector. The recession was turned by the closure of the Suez Canal in 1967 following the Six-Day War and by the growth of international trade leading to the boom of 1973. The slowdown and recession generated by the first oil crisis of 1973 resulted in a contraction of seaborne trade. The consequences of the second oil crisis of 1979 were even more severe and lasted until 1985 when the globalization of the world economy started of a new recovery.

Throughput in the port of Antwerp over the period 1947-1990 has a pattern, which is partly in line with the cycles in world maritime trade as is clear from Fig. 6.1.. But at the same time some fluctuations in Antwerp cannot be explained simply by looking at world seaborne trade.

Fig. 6.1. Throughput in the port of Antwerp (1947-1990)

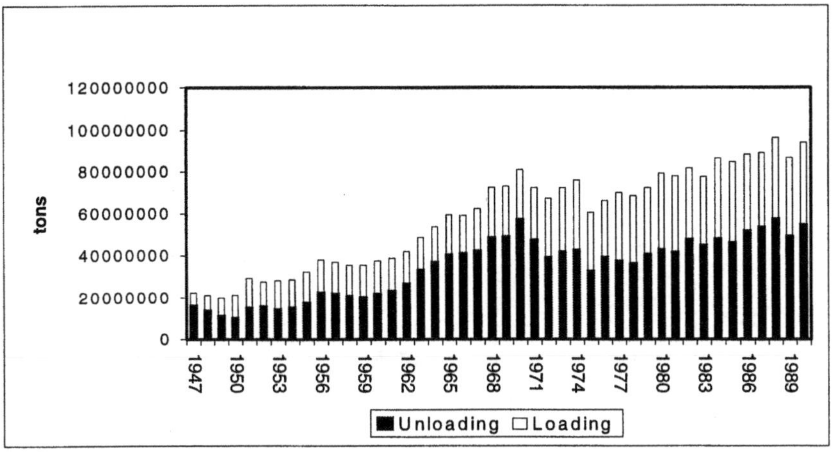

Splitting up total throughput in the volume loaded and the volume unloaded clarifies already part of the picture, but more information is given if a number of commodity types are considered. Fig. 6.2. gives the evolution of goods handled (both loading and unloading) for the following 10 NVS categories.

Table 6.1. Shares of different good categories loaded and unloaded in Antwerp (based on tons)

cat.0	Agricultural products and living animals
cat.1	Food and cattle feeding products
cat.2	Solid mineral fuels
cat.3	Petroleum and derivatives
cat.4	Ore, metal waste, roasted pyrite
cat.5	Iron, steel and non-ferrous metal
cat.6	Raw minerals and products; building material
cat.7	Fertilizers
cat.8	Chemicals
cat.9	Vehicles, machinery and remaining

Fig. 6.2. Tons loaded and unloaded in Antwerp: shares of different good categories

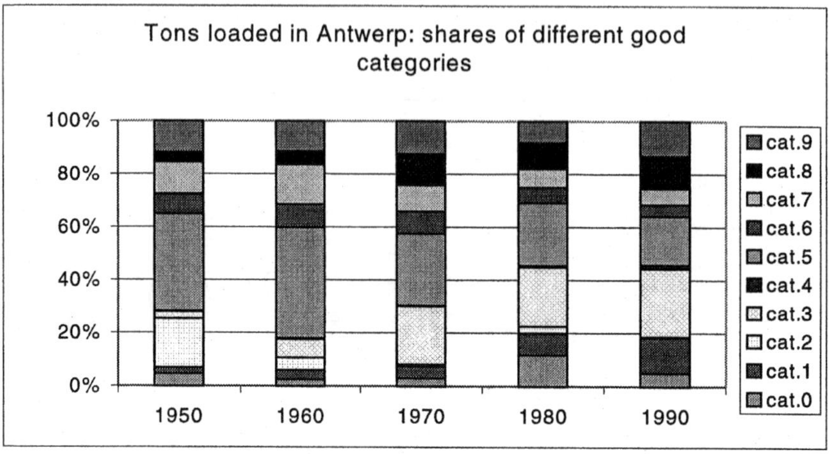

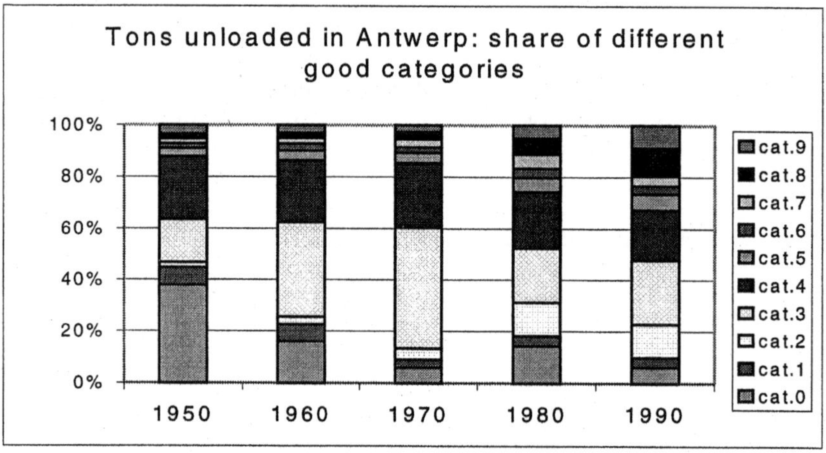

It is clear that there have been large differences in the evolution of port traffic over the 10 categories. Fig. 6.2. gives the share of each of the categories in the global tonnage loaded and unloaded in Antwerp. Up until the seventies the major share of the number of tons unloaded consisted of agricultural products (cat.0), petroleum and derivatives (cat.3) and ore, metal waste, roasted pyrite (cat.4) with a reduction of the share of agricultural products in the sixties and seventies and of petroleum starting in the seventies. Within the tonnage loaded in the port of Antwerp, iron, steel and non-ferrous metals (cat.5) represented an important share, together with, starting from the second half of the sixties, petroleum products (cat.3).

Fig. 6.3. Tons loaded and unloaded for different commodity types

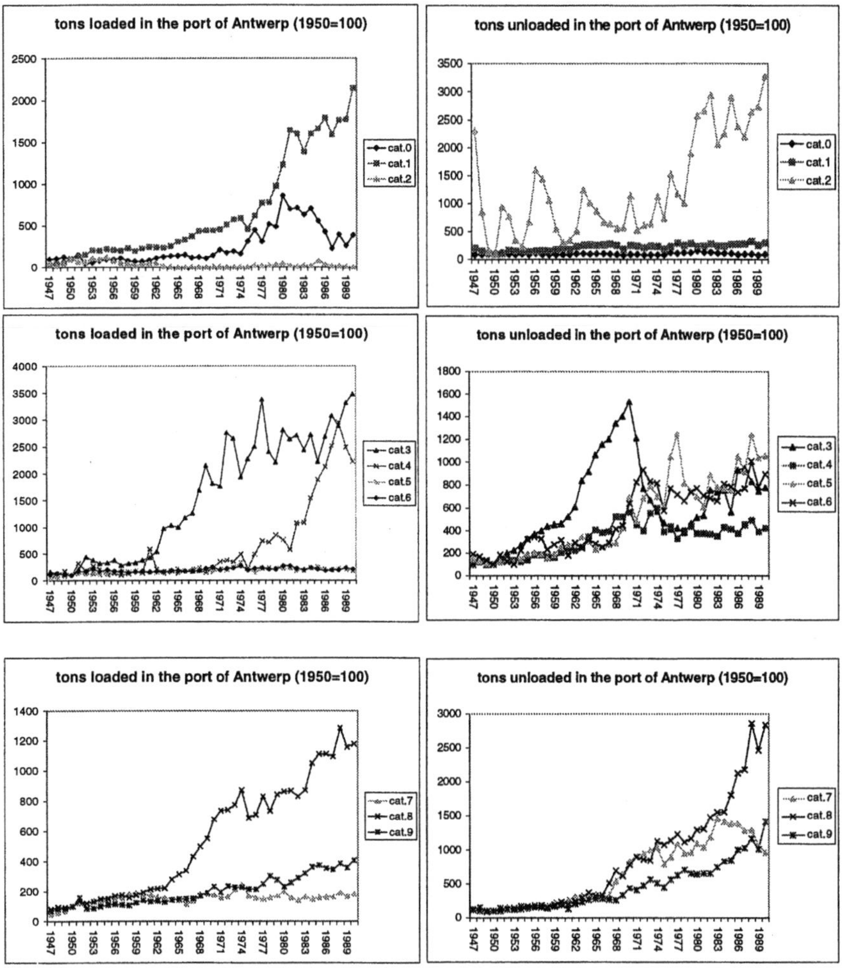

Fig. 6.3. shows the evolution of port traffic for each of the commodity groups. Most striking is the increase of the unloading of petroleum until 1970, followed by a spectacular reduction due to the start-up of the Rotterdam-Antwerp Pipeline (1974) in combination with the oil crises (with a start in 1973 and 1979). The major reason for the construction of this pipeline was the increase in tanker size and the fact that, due to the limited draught of the Scheldt, VLCC's (Very Large Crude Carriers) could not call at the port of Antwerp. As a consequence the share of petroleum in the total volume unloaded was reduced to half its value.

Fig. 6.4. The import and export of the Belgian Luxembourg Economic Union (BLEU) (1951-1990)

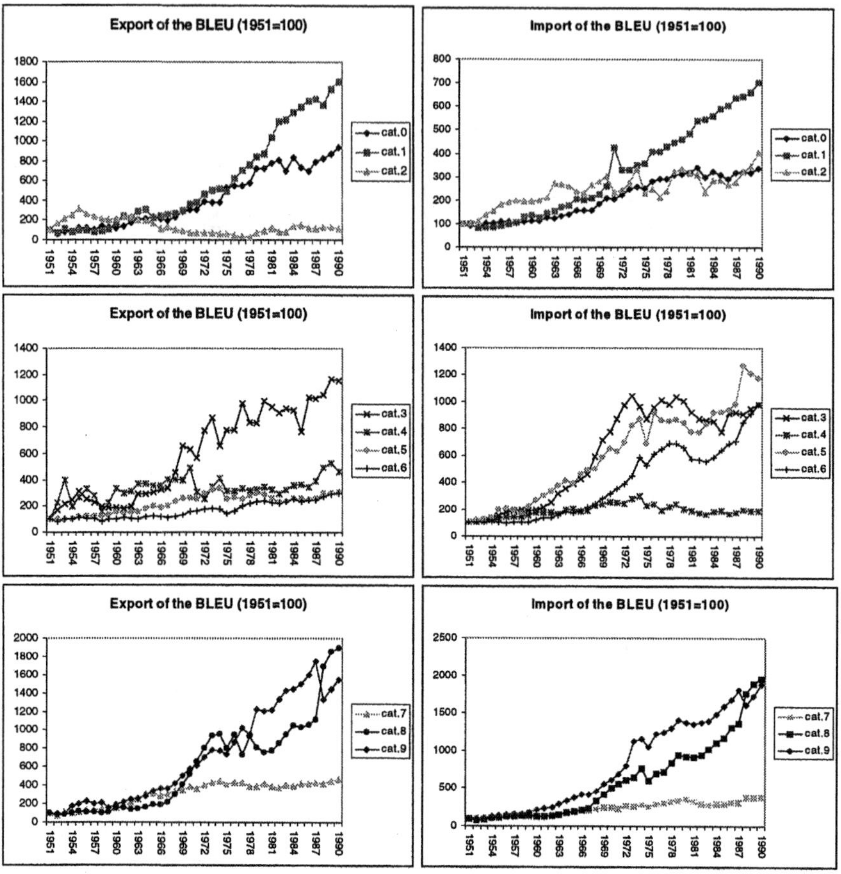

Some categories are characterized by very high growth rates in the volumes handled at the port of Antwerp. The strong growth of the tons of chemicals loaded and unloaded, starting in the sixties, can be attributed to the increased number of companies of the chemical and petrochemical sector and the growing importance of this sector in the industrial production of the hinterland of the port. The advent of petroleum refineries explains the strong growth of the volume of outgoing petroleum products, which becomes, in tons, one of the important categories leaving the port of Antwerp. In the eighties the number of tons of ore, metal waste, roasted pyrite, rose at a spectacular rate.

Port traffic is closely related to economic activity and also, especially for Antwerp, to the international trade of the hinterland. As it is difficult to identify exactly the hinterland because it may change considerably over time, Fig. 6.4. gives, as an approximation, the import and export of the Belgian Luxembourg Economic

Union (BLEU). There are clearly some similarities in the growth patterns of trade and the growth patterns of port throughput. But it is also obvious that the relation between trade and port throughput is not a perfect one.

The international trade can be considered as an indicator for the potential throughput of the port. How much of this potential the port can actually realize depends on a number of factors among which the capacity of the port and the competitive position are the most important ones.

The notion of "port capacity" is not always interpreted in the same way. But whatever definition is used, two elements always seem to be present (Meersman, Steenssens and Van de Voorde 1997, 6). First, it is pointed out that a distinction must be made between the overall capacity of the port and its constituting parts (i.e. maritime access, locks, docks, services supplied, terminals, hinterland connections). In addition, emphasis is put on the variable nature of port capacity.

It becomes even much more complicated if one makes a distinction between physical capacity, effective capacity and economic capacity (Vlaamse Havencommissie 1992, 94). The physical capacity refers to the maximum capacity at which the port infrastructure could be used on a permanent basis if no external limitations were imposed. This capacity is in other words fixed and determined solely by the size and other physical characteristics of the port. The effective capacity can be described as the greatest possible capacity at which the port can operate in the real world, taking into account external limitations (working hours, maintenance, repairs, legal constraints,...). The economic capacity represents that part of the effective capacity, which can be utilized with maximum economic and commercial return.

Fig. 6.5. Useful berth length in the port of Antwerp

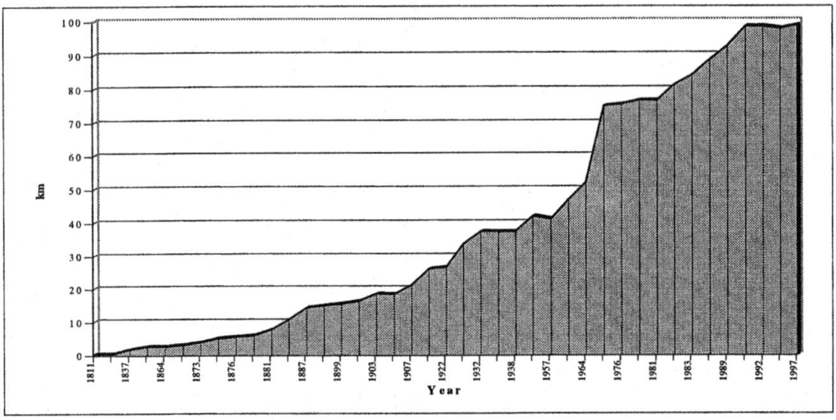

In the short run, the available capacity undeniably puts an upper limit on the total traffic a port can handle. In the long run it is one of the most important decision variables of a port. In a similar way as for a private company, investing in the appropriate capacity is crucial for profit generation and the survival of the port. Only if sufficient capacity is available it will be possible to benefit from growth in the maritime transport market (Meersman, Steenssens and Van de Voorde, 1997, 6).

Determining the capacity of a port and/or a terminal is a complex matter. As an approximation we use the length of the quay which can be used for mooring as presented in Fig. 6.5. In the sixties the quay length increased considerably with the construction of the "Vijfde haven" dock, the "Industrie" dock, the "Zesde Haven" dock, the "Graan" dock, the Churchill dock, and the "Kanaal"-docks B1, B2 and B3. In the eighties there was another big expansion with the Delwaide-dock and the development of the left bank.

The competitive position of a port is determined by a large number of factors among which productivity and costs take an important position[1]. Productivity and costs are closely related as is illustrated for container handling in table 6.2. However, this table only considers the handling costs for containers. In order to have an idea of the impact of costs on the competitive position of a port one should consider the total generalized costs, not only for the handling but also all the costs involved when a ship is calling at a port. The latter consist of the out-of-pocket costs (port dues, towing costs, pilotage dues, payments to the Shipping & Signalling Services N.V., police dues, agency fees), cost of spending time in the port (operational costs of the ship, value of the cargo) and costs due to unreliability of port operations.

It is till now practically impossible to find good information on the evolution of the total generalized costs over time. Even for the majority of the cost components consistent time series are hard to find. Therefor one is obliged to use an approximating indicator such as the labour costs in the port. For Antwerp and Rotterdam the rate of change of the standard wage per task is represented in Fig. 6.6. The increase in throughput in Antwerp in the early sixties may be explained partly by the slower increase of wage costs in Antwerp compared to Rotterdam.

Fig. 6.7. gives the evolution of real wages in the port of Antwerp. There was a strong increase up until 1975 followed by a rather stable period with a reduction of real wages in the early eighties.

[1] A detailed analysis can be found in (Haezendonck, Huybrechts and Meersman et al. 2000).

Table 6.2. Productivity and costs for container handling (1993)

Port	Terminal Productivity					Container handling costs (USD)			
							Import/Export		Transshipment
	Moves per call	Moves per hour	Average Crane Intensity	Moves per hour and crane	Net crane productivity	Operational cost	Total Cost	Operational cost	Total cost
Antwerp	>1000	132	4	33	35	104	108	143	152
Rotterdam	>500	105	3.5	30	35	139	151	164	183
Hamburg	>1000	69	3	23	27	156	191	128	163
Marseille-Fos	>1000	68	2.5	27	29	145	168	176	191
Venise	100-500	30	1.4	21	23	140	162		
Genoa	>750	33	1.85	18	20	128	151	178	207
Trieste	>750	36	2	18	20	123	136	119	135
Naples	500-750	40	2	20	23	139	139	220	220
Piraeus	500-750	28	1.2	23	24	124	136	124	136

Source: MARCONSULT (1994, data 1993)

Fig. 6.6. Evolution of wages Rotterdam-Antwerp

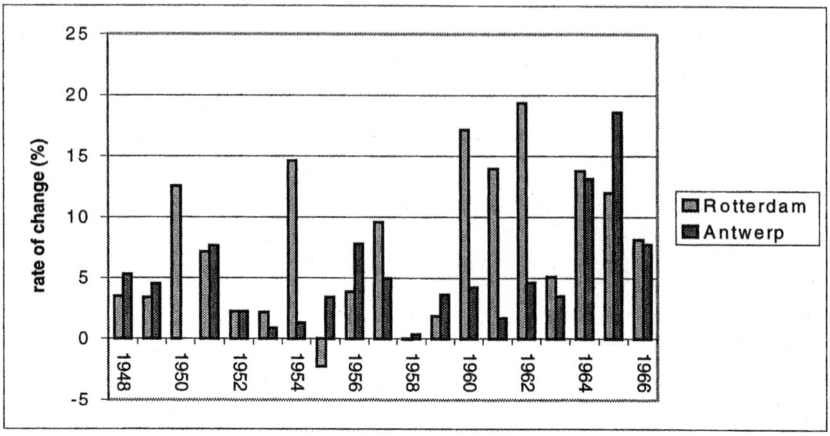

Fig. 6.7. Real wages in the port of Antwerp

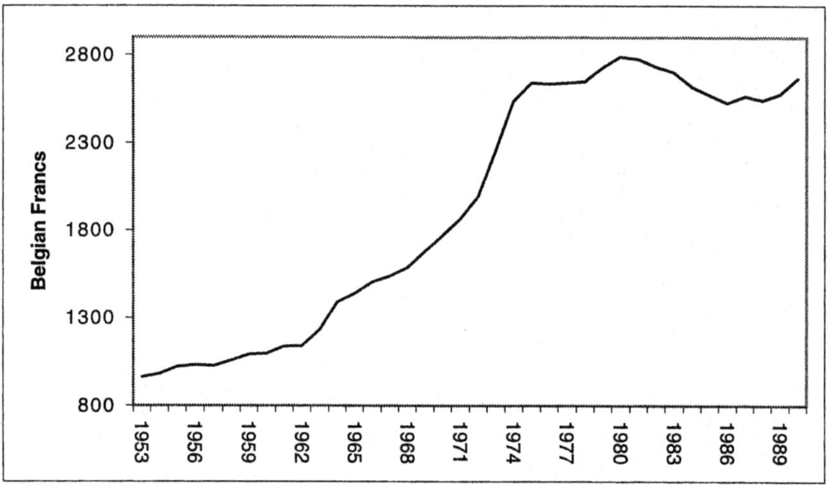

2. Modelling port throughput : have port authorities still any degrees of freedom?

In order to have an idea of the magnitude of the impact of trade, capacity and wages on throughput, it is necessary to quantify the relations between those variables for each commodity group. For each good category the relations that needed quantification can be represented by the following general specifications:

$$\text{unload} = f(\text{import, quay, rw}) \quad [1]$$
$$\text{load} = f(\text{export, quay, rw}) \quad [2]$$

with

unload	the number of tons unloaded in the port of Antwerp;
load	the number of tons loaded in the port of Antwerp;
import	import of the BLEU;
export	export of the BLEU;
quay	quay length in the port of Antwerp;
rw	real wage in the port of Antwerp.

The data used for modelling the relations and covering the period 1951-1990 is described in Appendix 1.

Traditionally, up until twenty-five years ago, relations between time series were modelled and estimated using regression analysis in a very simple, straightforward way. One started from a linear or a logarithmic specification such as

$$Y_t = a_0 + a_1X_{1t} + a_2X_{2t} + \dots a_kX_{kt} + u_t \quad [3]$$

or

$$\ln(Y_t) = b_0 + b_1\ln(X_{1t}) + b_2\ln(X_{2t}) + \dots b_k\ln(X_{kt}) + u_t \quad [4]$$

with

Y_t	the endogenous variable at time t
$X_{1t}, X_{2t}, \dots, X_{kt}$	the exogenous or explanatory variables at time t
u_t	the stochastic "error" term at time t
ln(.)	logarithm

and estimated the coefficients $a_0, a_1, \dots, a_k$ or $b_0, b_1, \dots, b_k$ with ordinary least squares (OLS). One also calculated the coefficient of determination R^2, which gives the percentage of the variation in the endogenous variable, explained by the estimated relation.

However, this method will only give reliable results under specific conditions. One of the conditions is the absence of autocorrelation in the error terms, meaning that the error term in one year is not allowed to be correlated with the error term in another year. Another condition is that the variables included in [3] or [4] must be stationary time series[2]. Using non-stationary time series has the severe consequence that neither the estimated coefficients, nor the coefficient of determination

[2] Definitions of stationary time series are given in Appendix 2

are reliable. One may even come to biased and absurd conclusions. This is illustrated with an example in Appendix 2[3].

Within the field of econometric time series analysis, a lot of research has been done to develop statistically sound methods to cope with non-stationary time series. The main fields of the research are focused on the design of statistical tests for stationarity of time series (a.o. unit root tests), the construction of stationary combinations of non-stationary time series (cointegration) and the correct dynamic relations between non-stationary time series (error correction models)[4].

In order to find the correct specification for [1] and [2] it is necessary to test whether all the variables included are stationary, whether there are cointegrated variables, and then estimate the suitable dynamic specification. Applying the appropriate unit root tests led to the conclusion that all the variables are non-stationary and integrated of order one.

This implies that the relations [1] and [2] have to be specified in first differences.

In a second stage, for each relation, the existence of a long run equilibrium relation between the variables of that relation was tested. The Johanssen cointegration test revealed for each relation exactly one cointegrating vector. As a consequence, using Granger's equivalence theorem, the relations have to be represented by an error correction model (ECM). The estimates for the 10 commodity groups are given in appendix 3.

Table 6.3. Trade elasticities of port throughput for different goods categories

Commodity Type	import elasticity of tons unloaded		export elasticity of tons loaded	
	short run	long run	short run	Long run
Cat.0	0.33	0.14	0.59	0.93
Cat.1	0.38	0.29	0.31	0.86
Cat.2	1.75	0.74	0.99	0.89
Cat.3	1.04	0.88	0.95	0.59
Cat.4	1.22	0.97	0.45	0.90
Cat.5	1.18	0.97	0.50	0.53
Cat.6	1.00	0.51	0.58	0.27
cat.7	0.80	0.94	0.77	0.22
cat.8	0.55	0.68	0.17	0.39
cat.9	0.86	1.25	0.15	0.34
Total	1.26	1.15	0.56	0.72

[3] Appendix 2 gives a brief description of the problems arising when using non-stationary time series.

[4] Appendix 2 gives a rather intuitive description of unit root tests, cointegration and error correction models. For a more detailed approach we refer to (Verbeek 2000), Chapter 8 and 9

International trade had clearly an impact on the throughput for each of the goods categories in the port of Antwerp. There were however considerable differences in the sensitivity of the number of tons handled to changes in import and export of the BLEU. Table 6.3. contains the short and long run elasticities of the number of tons loaded and unloaded with respect to exports, respectively imports.

What about the two other explaining variables incorporated in the model, i.e. the quay length as a capacity indicator and the real wage? For some categories the capacity indicator and/or the real wage had a significant impact on the number of tons handled, where for other categories no significant impact could be identified. Sensitivity estimates to changes in capacity and real wages are summarized in table 6.4.

One of the major conclusions from this analysis is that international trade, capacity and wages can only explain to a certain extent the variation in port throughput. On average approximately 40 to 50 percent of the variation is explained by the model. This implies that there are still other factors playing an important role in the determination of the throughput of the port of Antwerp.

Table 6.4. Impact of a 1% change in capacity and real wages on port throughput for different goods categories

	1% change in quay length				1% change in real wages			
	unloaded		loaded		unloaded		loaded	
	short run	long run	short run	long run	short run	long run	short run	long run
cat.0	-	-	-	-	-	-	-	-
cat.1	0.58	-	-	0.57	-	-	-	-
cat.2	-	0.81	-	-	-1.13	-	-8.93	-
cat.3	0.38	0.61	0.59	1.60	-0.91	-	-	-
cat.4	0.37	0.74	-	2.13	-	-	-	-2.89
cat.5	-	-	-	-	-0.89	-	-	-
cat.6	-	0.88	-	-	-	-	-	-
cat.7	-	0.61	-	-	-	-	-	-
cat.8	1.26	1.09	0.59	1.28	-	-	-	-
cat.9	-	-	-	0.43	-1.24	-1.23	-	-
total	-	-	-	-	-0.50	-	-	-

The question now is whether those factors give the port authorities some degrees of freedom to play an active role in the design of short and long term policies for the port, or whether their function is just simply reduced to a kind of coordination of the necessary facilities for handling the incoming and outgoing traffic. This will depend largely on the behaviour of all the parties involved in the maritime and transport sector.

3. The function of port authorities in a changing transport environment

The pressure of competition in the maritime and port industry, especially in the container trade, inherently encourages the setting up of joint ventures, mergers, strategic alliances and cartels. It is noticeable that shipping companies in particular have been taking the initiative in this move towards closer integration. These developments had and still have their effect on seaports and their competitive position. To what extent will, for example, liner shipping companies remain real negotiating partners (either directly or indirectly through subsidiaries such as stevedores, railway companies etc.) of the port authorities? And are port authorities responding similarly or differently to the new challenge[5]?

Table 6.5. offers a brief overview (with examples) of the kind of co-operation agreements that have been established in recent years between the predominant maritime market players (shipping companies, stevedores, hinterland transport modes, port authorities).

By looking into detail into the underlying causes for all the different forms of co-operation in the container shipping business, we come to a number of conclusions which are emphasising the changing role and functions of the port authorities (Heaver, Meersman, Moglia and Van de Voorde 2000, 372-373). The increasing power of shipping companies threatens to force ports in a subordinate position.

Port authorities have responded to this development, by, among others, a greater willingness to dedicate terminals to shipping companies and, to a lesser degree, by becoming active partners in the capital of stevedoring companies. The dedication of terminals is not exclusive of any danger. In the short term, dedicated terminals indeed offer a possibility for increasing market share and protecting employment. But in the long term, one needs to take into account the striving towards a greater return on port investments.

---

[5] Those topics have been treated in detail in (Heaver, Meersman, Moglia and Van de Voorde 2000) and (Heaver, Meersman and Van de Voorde 2001).

Table 6.5. Co-operation agreements between various market players

MARKET PLAYERS	SHIPPING COMPANIES	STEVEDORES	HINTERLAND TRANSPORT	PORT AUTHORITIES
SHIPPING COMPANIES	⇒ Vessel sharing agreements ⇒ Joint Ventures ⇒ Conferences ⇒ Consortia ⇒ Strategic (global) alliances (e.g. Grand Alliance, New World Alliance) ⇒ Cartel agreements ⇒ (e.g. TAA) ⇒ Mergers			
STEVEDORES	⇒ Financial stake of shipping company in stevedore (e.g. CMB in Hessenatie, Nedlloyd in ECT) ⇒ Joint ventures (e.g. MSC and Hessenatie in Antwerp) ⇒ (Dedicated terminals) (e.g. ECT Maersk in Rotterdam)	⇒ Participation in capital (e.g. Hutchison Whampoa in ECT, PSA in Voltri Genova)		
HINTERLAND-TRANSPORT MODES	⇒ Block trains and capacity sharing (e.g. from Rotterdam to Italy) ⇒ Alliances (e.g. CSX with DB and NS)	⇒ Joint ventures (e.g. in Antwerp between NMBS and Noordnatie for operating of a terminal)	⇒ Takeover strategy of railway companies (e.g. DB and NS cargo, NMBS and THL)	
PORT AUTHORITIES	⇒ (dedicated terminals) (cf. land-use and concession policy)	⇒ Financial stakes port authorities (e.g. 30% ECT by Rotterdam, ECT in Trieste, Seaго in Zeebruges)	⇒ Antwerp in Rijn shipping terminal of Germersheim	⇒ Alliances (e.g. Rotterdam and Vlissingen, Antwerp and Zeebruges)

Source: (Heaver, Meersman, Moglia en Van de Voorde 2000, 365).

Conclusion

Nobody will and can deny the role international trade has played and still plays for the throughput of the port of Antwerp. By applying the wrong tools to quantify this role, one could come to the misleading conclusion that the evolution in international trade explains almost fully the volumes loaded and unloaded in the port, leaving the port authorities with as good as no degrees of freedom. If so, their sole function would be to create the environment needed to handle the increasing volumes of throughput.

However, by using the correct methodology to analyse historical data, we come to a more realistic and reliable conclusion. Imports and exports over the period 1951-1990 explained, depending upon the goods category, on average about 40 to 50 per cent of the variation in throughput, even when other factors such as capacity and wage cost are incorporated in the model. This implies that there are additional forces which drive the throughput activity in the port.

One of these forces undeniably is the search for scale increases and cost-saving in the shipping sector, resulting in vertical and horizontal forms of co-operation dominated by the shipping companies. This has resulted in a rationalization and compression of the market. Shipping companies, consortia and alliances have thus acquired a more powerful negotiating position vis-à-vis port authorities, stevedores and hinterland transportation modes. The final outcome of this process is not clear because the other parties have responded.

It is in any case clear that the market balance is shifting all the time. What will the ultimate result be? Will one arrive at a fully vertically integrated logistics chain? In order to answer this question, one first needs to gain insight into the cost structure of the individual market players as well as the logistics chain as a whole (i.e. including cargo handling and storage costs, feeder costs, ...).

But the crucial question remains what role port authorities will be able to play in the future if the concept of the logistics chain is indeed translated into a more pronounced vertical integration of shipping companies, stevedores, hinterland transport modes and (possibly) shipping agents. Will port authorities become fully-fledged partners in the logistics chain, will their involvement be restricted to a supporting role (safety, land-use and concession policy, ...), or might they disappear from the scene entirely?

In order to find answers to these questions, further research, more in particular disaggregated empirical research, is urgently required. From a scientific and transport policy perspective, this will allow us to gain a quantified insight into the complexity of and interaction between the various links in the logistics chain.

References

De Gooijer JG, Klein A (1989) Forecasting the Antwerp maritime steel traffic flow: a case study. Journal of forecasting: 381-398

Heaver T, Meersman H and Van de Voorde E (2001), Co-operation and competition in international container transport: strategies for ports. Antwerp. (Research Paper 2001-02

Heaver T, Meersman H, Moglia F and Van de Voorde E (2000) Do mergers and alliances influence European shipping and port competition? Maritime policy and management: 363-373

Klein A, Verbeke A (1987) The design of an optimal short term forecasting system for seaport management: an application to the port of Antwerp. International journal of transport economics: 57-70

McLellan RG (1997) Bigger vessels: how big is too big. Maritime policy and management: 193-211

Meersman H and Van de Voorde E (1998) Coping with port competition in Europe: a state of the art. In: Sciutto C and Brebbia CIRCA (eds) Maritime Engineering and Ports. Southampton, pp 281-290

Meersman H, Steenssens C and Van de Voorde E (1997) Container throughput, port capacity and investment". London (IAME International Conference)

SERV - Vlaamse Havencommissie (1992) Rapport over de uitwerking van een lange termijn strategie voor de Vlaamse havens. Brussel

Stopford M (1997) Maritime economics. London/New York

Suykens F and Van de Voorde E (1998) A quarter of a century of port management in Europe. Objectives and tools. Maritime policy and management: 251-261

Verbeek M (2000) A guide to modern econometrics. Chichester

Appendix 1: Description of time series used in modelling port throughput

unload: the volume of goods unloaded (i.e. import and ingoing transit of the Belgian Luxembourg Economic Union) in the port of Antwerp, classified by NVS[6]-category (tons); 1951 - 1990

load: the volume of goods loaded (i.e. export and outgoing transit of the Belgian Luxemburg Economic Union) in the port of Antwerp, classified by NVS-category (tons); 1951 - 1990
Source: National Institute of Statistics: "Statistiek over de internationale trafiek in de havens (BLEU)"Data for the greater part collected and where necessary converted to NVS-classification by Reginald Loyen.

import: import of the Belgian Luxembourg Economic Union, classified by NVS-category (tons); 1951-1990

export: export of the Belgian Luxembourg Economic Union, classified by NVS-category (tons); 1951-1990

[6] NVS: Nomenclature for Transport Statistics

Source: National Institute of Statistics: "Statistisch Jaarboek van België" Converted from Standard International Trade Classification (SITC) - to NVS-classification

quay: useful berth length in the port of Antwerp, jetties and talus included (kilometre); 1951-1990
Source: Antwerp Municipal Port Authority; based on A. Himler, "De Antwerpse haven vanaf de Franse periode" in *Het Tijdschrift van het Gemeentekrediet*, 47TH year of publication, no. 185. Antwerp Municipal Port Authority, *Havenatlas van het havencomplex op de Rechter- en Linker-scheldeoever.*

rw: wage, walking compensation included, of corporations and stevedores (day-shift) deflated using consumer price index (National Bank of Belgium) (Belgian Francs)
Source: "Nationaal Komitee van de haven van Antwerpen" CEPA-jaarverslagen" Data up to 1972 collected by Stephan Vanfraechem

Appendix 2: Stationarity, unit roots, cointegration and error correction models

Regression analysis using time series, will only give reliable estimates if the dynamics of the underlying data generating process are modelled in the correct way and if the variables included in the model are stationary. If this is not the case one may end up with results that seem rather good, but which are in reality unreliable. An example can clarify this reasoning.

The number of tons loaded at the port of Antwerp is related to the exports of the hinterland. This gives the following model:

$$\ln(load_t) = a_0 + a_1 \ln(export_t) + u_t \qquad [A1]$$

Using annual data for the period 1951 until 1990 for the port of Antwerp, OLS estimation of [A1] gives (numbers between brackets are standard errors of the estimated coefficients):

$$\underset{(0.025)}{\ln(load_t) = 4.14} + \underset{(0.45)}{0.72} \ln(export_t) \qquad [A2]$$

with $R^2 = 0.96$. This implies that 96% of the variations in the number of tons loaded in Antwerp is explained by the variations in the export of the BLEU and only 4% is due to other factors, amongst which port policies. If this were correct, the port and the port authorities would only have a very small impact on the realized throughput and the success of the port would mainly depend upon international trade, exchange rate and trade policies.

Figure A1 :Upward trend in number of tons loaded in Antwerp and in the export of the BLEU

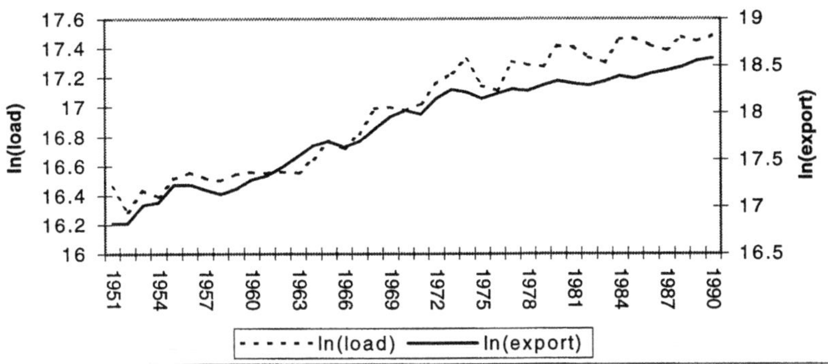

Figure A2 : Rate of change of number of tons loaded in Antwerp and of exports of the BLEU

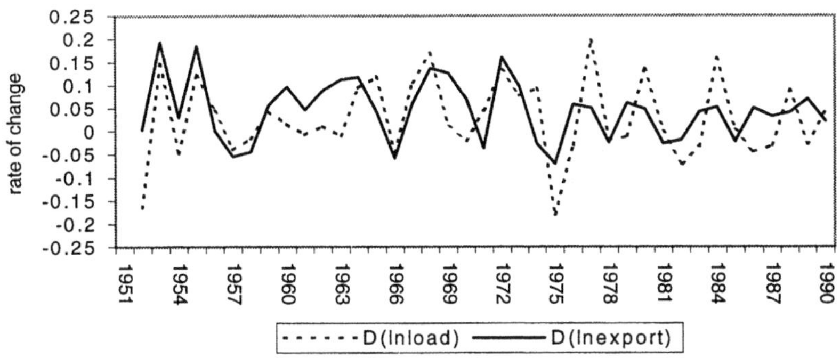

One of the reasons for the unreliability of the results is the presence of autocorrelation. This is mainly the consequence of a poor dynamic specification and can be cured by introducing lags of the exports (distributive lags) and/or lags of the numbers of ton loaded (autoregressive terms) in [A1]. To find the most appropriate dynamic specification, one has to rely on a battery of statistical tests, a lot of experience, a good knowledge of the sector and a healthy dose of common sense.

Including non-stationary time series in the model will also give unreliable results. Non-stationarity of time series can have several causes. One of the major causes can be the presence of an upward or downward stochastic trend. From figure A1 it is clear that both series have an upward trend. The presence and dominance of this trend may mask the true relation between the two variables. This phenomenon is known as spurious regression and is caused by the non-stationarity of both series. The major consequence is that the estimates in [A2] are not reliable and the R^2 is overestimated.

Most non-stationary trending time series can be transformed to stationary series by taking first differences. If the resulting new time series is stationary, the original series is integrated of order 1. Figure A2 illustrates clearly that there is no longer a trend present in the first differences of the number of tons loaded and of the export.

To avoid spurious regression, the relation between the non-stationary time series should be replaced by a relation in first differences

$$\Delta \ln(load_t) = b\Delta \ln(export_t) + v_t \qquad [A3]$$

where Δ indicates first differences, b is the coefficient to be estimated and v_t is a stochastic error term. Estimation with OLS gives (standard error between brackets)

$$\Delta \ln(load_t) = \underset{(0.15)}{0.66}\Delta \ln(export_t) \qquad [A4]$$

with $R^2 = 0.28$. This implies that exports are not the sole determining factor for the variation in the number of tons unloaded. Other elements, deterministic or stochastic, will also have an impact on throughput.

From this example, it is clear that, before estimating a model with time series, one should be sure that only stationary variables are included. There exist a large number of statistical tests, designed to test for the stationarity of a time series under several conditions and which fall mainly under the heading of unit root tests.

One of the disadvantages of [A4] is that the estimated coefficient b=0.66 only measures the immediate, short run impact of a percentage change of exports on the number of tons loaded. It does not measure the full, long run impact. This problem can be overcome under the specific condition that the variables "ln(load)" and "ln(export)" are cointegrated. This means that there has to exist a stationary linear combination of the two non-stationary series. If this is the case, according to the Granger Equivalence Theorem , the only correct way to model the dynamics is by means of an error correction model (ECM), or

$$\Delta \ln(load_t) = b_1\Delta \ln(export_t) + b_2[\ln(load_{t-1}) - a_0 - a_1\ln(export_{t-1})] + v_t \qquad [A5]$$

The expression within squared brackets is the cointegrating, long run or equilibrium relation. The negative coefficient b_2 indicates in what way an error from the previous period is used to correct the change in the number of tons loaded as a consequence of a change in the quantity exported. The long run impact of export on tons loaded is given by a_1, the short run impact by b_1.

So it is not only crucial to test whether the variables in a model are stationary, one should also test whether non-stationary series are cointegrated. The most well-known test procedure is the one from Johansen.

In the example the variables "ln(load)" and "ln(export)" are cointegrated which results in the following estimated ECM

$$\Delta \ln(load_t) = 0.56\Delta \ln(export_t) - 0.50[\ln(load_{t-1}) - 4.14 - 0.72\ \ln(export_{t-1})] \qquad [A6]$$

An increase of exports by 1% will lead to an immediate increase in the number of tons loaded by 0.56% and a total, long run effect of 0.72%.

Appendix 3: Impact of international trade, quay length and labour costs on the number of tons loaded and unloaded in the port of Antwerp (numbers between brackets are asymptotic standard errors)

TOTAL

$$\Delta \ln(unload_t) = \underset{(0.21)}{1.26}\Delta \ln(import_t) - \underset{(0.32)}{0.50}\Delta \ln(rw_t) - \underset{(0.078)}{0.18}\Delta D71_t - \underset{(0.11)}{0.38}\,[\ln(unload_{t-1}) + \underset{(1.21)}{3.69} + \underset{(0.067)}{0.46}D71_{t-1} - \underset{(0.067)}{1.15}\ln(import_{t-1})]$$

$R^2=0.59$ sample 53-90

$$\Delta \ln(load_t) = \underset{(0.13)}{0.56}\Delta \ln(export_t) - \underset{(0.12)}{0.50}\,[\ln(load_{t-1}) + \underset{(0.45)}{4.14} - \underset{(0.025)}{0.72}\ln(export_{t-1})]$$

$R^2=0.51$ sample 51-90

Cat.0: Agricultural products and living animals

$$\Delta \ln(unload_t) = \underset{(0.28)}{0.33}\Delta \ln(import_t) - \underset{(0.14)}{0.53}\,[\ln(unload_{t-1} - \underset{(1.54)}{17.33} - \underset{(0.095)}{0.25}D75_{t-1} + \underset{(0.099)}{0.14}\ln(import_{t-1})]$$

$R^2=0.35$ sample 51-90

$$\Delta \ln(load_t) = \underset{(0.28)}{0.59}\Delta \ln(export_t) - \underset{(0.14)}{0.59}\,[\ln(load_{t-1}) - \underset{(0.0036)}{0.93}\ln(export_{t-1})]$$

$R^2=0.41$ sample 51-90

Cat.1: Food and cattle feeding products

$$\Delta \ln(unload_t) = \underset{(0.17)}{0.38}\Delta \ln(import_t) + \underset{(0.30)}{0.58}\Delta \ln(quay_t) - \underset{(0.13)}{0.62}\,[\ln(unload_{t-1}) - \underset{(0.55)}{9.85} - \underset{(0.036)}{0.29}\ln(import_{t-1})]$$

$R^2=0.43$ sample 51-90

$$\Delta \ln(load_t) = \underset{(0.020)}{0.048} + \underset{(0.12)}{0.31}\Delta \ln(export_t) - \underset{(0.12)}{0.37}[\ln(load_{t-1}) + \underset{(0.55)}{0.30} + \underset{(0.10)}{0.60}D60_{t-1} - \underset{(0.073)}{0.86}\ln(export_{t-1}) - \underset{(0.24)}{0.57}\ln(quay_{t-1})]$$

$R^2=0.26$ sample 51-90

Cat.2: Solid mineral fuels

$$\Delta \ln(unload_t) = \underset{(0.40)}{1.75}\Delta \ln(import_t) - \underset{(1.39)}{1.13}\Delta \ln(rw_t) - \underset{(0.12)}{0.25}\,[\ln(unload_{t-1}) - \underset{(5.83)}{0.61} - \underset{(0.45)}{0.74}\ln(import_{t-1}) - \underset{(0.48)}{0.81}\ln(quay_{t-1})]$$

$R^2=0.44$ sample 53-90

$$\Delta \ln(load_t) = \underset{(0.42)}{0.99}\Delta \ln(export_t) - \underset{(2.79)}{8.93}\Delta \ln(rw_t) - \underset{(0.11)}{0.37}[\ln(load_{t-1}) - \underset{(0.011)}{0.89}\ln(export_{t-1})]$$

$R^2=0.34$ sample 53-90

Cat.3: petroleum and derivatives

$$\Delta\ln(unload_t) = 1.04\Delta\ln(import_t) - 0.91\Delta\ln(rw_t) + 0.38\Delta\ln(quay_t) - 0.38\Delta D71_t - 0.28[\ln(unload_{t-1}) + 0.78 + 1.31D71_{t-1} - 0.88\ln(import_{t-1}) - 0.61\ln(quay_{t-1})]$$

$R^2=0.45$

(0.25) (0.69) (0.36) (0.15) (0.099) (1.68) (0.15) (0.17) (0.44) sample 53-90

$$\Delta\ln(load_t) = 0.95\Delta\ln(export_t) + 0.59\Delta\ln(quay_t) - 0.29[\ln(load_{t-1}) - 0.59\ln(export_{t-1}) - 1.60\ln(quay_t)]$$

(0.13) (0.39) (0.12) (0.15) (0.34) $R^2=0.58$ sample 51-90

Cat.4: Ore, metal waste, roasted pyrite

$$\Delta\ln(unload_t) = 1.22\Delta\ln(import_t) + 0.37\Delta\ln(quay_t) - 0.36[\ln(unload_{t-1}) + 3.87 - 0.97\ln(import_{t-1}) - 0.74\ln(quay_{t-1})]$$

(0.16) (0.26) (0.14) (1.52) (0.10) (0.091) $R^2=0.66$ sample 51-90

$$\Delta\ln(load_t) = 0.45\Delta\ln(export_t) + 0.68\Delta D71_t - 0.66[\ln(load_{t-1}) - 10.49 - 1.55D71_{t-1} - 1.37D75_{t-1} - 0.90\ln(export_{t-1}) - 2.13\ln(quay_{t-1}) + 2.89\ln(rw_{t-1})]$$

(0.27) (0.36) (0.14) (6.18) (0.43) (0.29) (0.44) (0.87) (0.91) $R^2=0.41$ sample 53-90

Cat.5: Iron, steel and non-ferro

$$\Delta\ln(unload_t) = 1.18\Delta\ln(import_t) - 0.89\Delta\ln(rw_t) - 0.42[\ln(unload_{t-1}) + 0.17 - 0.97\ln(import_{t-1})]$$

(0.22) (0.63) (0.13) (0.67) (0.046) $R^2=0.52$ sample 53-90

$$\Delta\ln(load_t) = 0.50\Delta\ln(export_t) - 0.80[\ln(load_{t-1}) - 7.27 - 0.53\ln(export_{t-1})]$$

(0.23) (0.17) (0.89) (0.055) $R^2=0.48$ sample 51-90

Cat.6: Raw minerals and products, building material

$$\Delta\ln(unload_t) = 1.00\Delta\ln(import_t) + 0.73\Delta D5560_t - 0.69[\ln(unload_{t-1}) - 2.84 - 0.56D5560_{t-1} - 0.51\ln(import_{t-1}) - 0.88\ln(quay_{t-1})]$$

(0.29) (0.14) (0.15) (0.77) (0.12) (0.14) (0.40) $R^2=0.54$ sample 51-90

$$\Delta\ln(load_t) = 0.58\Delta\ln(export_t) - 0.51[\ln(load_{t-1}) - 10.12 - 0.27\ln(export_{t-1})]$$

(0.14) (0.15) (0.68) (0.044) $R^2=0.49$ sample 51-90

Cat.7: Fertilizers

$$\Delta\ln(unload_t) = 0.80\Delta\ln(import_t) - 0.58[\ln(unload_{t-1}) + 1.48 - 0.94\ln(import_{t-1}) - 0.61\ln(quay_{t-1})]$$

(0.075) (0.12) (0.36) (0.067) (0.16) $R^2=0.73$ sample 51-90

$$\Delta\ln(load_t) = 0.77\Delta\ln(export_t) - 0.21\Delta D75_t - 0.35[\ln(load_{t-1}) - 10.99 + 0.098D75_{t-1} - 0.22\ln(export_{t-1})]$$

(0.16) (0.12) (0.12) (0.93) (0.063) (0.057) $R^2=0.56$ sample 51-90

Cat.8: Chemicals

$$\Delta\ln(unload_t) = 0.55\Delta\ln(import_t) + 1.26\Delta\ln(quay_t) - 0.66[\ln(unload_{t-1}) + 0.41 - 0.68\ln(import_{t-1}) - 1.091\ln(quay_{t-1})]$$

(0.12) (0.25) (0.14) (0.29) (0.067) (0.23) $R^2=0.48$ sample 51-90

$$\Delta\ln(load_t) = 0.17\Delta\ln(export_t) + 0.59\Delta\ln(quay_t) - 0.22\Delta D75_t - 0.31[\ln(load_{t-1}) - 0.39\ln(export_{t-1}) - 1.28\ln(quay_t)]$$

(0.088) (0.22) (0.087) (0.15) (0.060) (0.21) $R^2=0.43$ sample 51-90

Cat. 9: Vehicles, machinery and remaining

$$\Delta\ln(unload_t) = \underset{(0.023)}{0.031} + \underset{(0.24)}{0.86}\Delta\ln(import_t) - \underset{(0.56)}{1.24}\Delta\ln(rw_t) - \underset{(0.070)}{0.41}\Delta D61_t - \underset{(0.17)}{0.42}[\ln(unload_{t-1}) - \underset{(0.51)}{4.27} + \underset{(0.13)}{0.49}D61_{t-1} - \underset{(0.14)}{1.25}\ln(import_{t-1}) + \underset{(0.32)}{1.23}\ln(rw_{t-1})] \qquad R^2=0.61 \quad \text{sample 53-90}$$

$$\Delta\ln(load_t) = \underset{(0.10)}{0.15}\Delta\ln(export_t) - \underset{(0.12)}{0.75}[\ln(load_{t-1}) - \underset{(0.40)}{7.68} - \underset{(0.073)}{0.34}\ln(export_{t-1}) - \underset{(0.22)}{0.43}\ln(quay_t)] \qquad R^2=0.52 \quad \text{sample 51-90}$$

LOAD	number of tons loaded at the port of Antwerp
UNLOAD	number of tons unloaded at the port of Antwerp
EXPORT	number of tons exported by the BLEU
IMPORT	number of tons imported by the BLEU
QUAY	quay length
RW	real wage indicator

Commentary on the paper of Janssens, Meersman and Van de Voorde

Honoré C. Paelinck

Port and transport consulting, Antwerp, Belgium

The paper incorporates a limited and incomplete number of elements that can or should be followed closely by Port Authorities in order to maintain or expand their existing role. These comments should therefore be considered as a stimulant to further research, as already suggested at the end of the concluding remarks.

Ingredients of competition between ports are changing but can be influenced by politics, changing regulations on the national or international level or by local or regional subsidies.

Strategy for Port Authorities should analyse the importance of the role of the major players, customers of the ports, i.e. shipping lines and shippers, on the one side and the providers of services in the ports on the other. On some occasions the providers of services can be one (the Port Authority as operator of some or all of the services), in most ports they are a combination of public and private entities whereby co-action and co-thinking are vital requirements in order to obtain coherent results.

In comparing the growth of tonnage in Antwerp with the rest of the Hamburg-Le Havre range it is remarkable that figures have expanded exponentially for all ports during the last 20 years. Little variations appear in evaluating the comparative competition between ports. It is therefore important to also take into account the economic evolution of a wider area than just one port.

Errors of appreciation may occur through inaccurate indication of statistical figures when in the indicated categories "agricultural products" and "cattle feed" are considered separate whereas corn (maize) can be both feed stock of for human consumption (maize-flour, corn flakes,...). Also "chemicals " and "petroleum and derivatives" may get mixed up. This may be at the bottom of the 40 to 50 % unexplained differences.

Port capacity is another element of confusion. Changing techniques have influenced capacity per meter-length (ml) of quay walls. Break bulk cargo generated 1000 tons per ml per year; container quays now produce 10.000 tons and more per ml. per year. In bagged cargo, handled with cranes, slings and manhandled in the holds a productivity of 700 to 800 tons per gang shift (with 14 people) was considered a record performance whereas toboggan installations produce 1.500 to 2.000 tons per gang shift with two people.

At the same time break bulk quays are left un(der)used but the total sum of quay length for a port built over decades, is used in the model. A corrector for berth occupation should be applied.

In a colloquium in Washington DC, five years ago, labour cost came as number seven in a list of preferential items for choosing investments after political stability, transport capacity, communications, tax advantages, space availability, energy supply. Labour cost in ports is translated in handling tariffs and is not considered as a direct input element as such. It is used in general as input to justify higher tariffs. Too high labour costs result in more automation, less labour.

Not mentioned but very important is the capacity of commerce and industry in and around the port to produce a high percentage of cargo, independent of a hinterland that may be shared by a number of ports in the same region. (For Antwerp the figure is said to be around 60 % of all loaded cargo).

Although some port authorities do deserve to disappear because of their inefficiency, in general their role will not be sub-ordinate in the future if they play their cards right. The risk, that is not mentioned, is that via the extrapolation of old politics, they may continue doing investments whereby, as a result of a changed attitude of ship owners, they may be left holding the bag of uneconomic investments in infrastructure.

What is definitely required for port authorities is intensive co-operation between ports in the same region and overseas in order to respond to sometimes exorbitant demands of ship owners.

It should not be forgotten that shippers might not, without a tough fight, surrender their independent thinking of choosing their port of handling, whatever the pressure of other parties may be.

Thirty-five years of containerization in Antwerp and Rotterdam: structural changes in the container handling market

Theo Notteboom

Institute of Transport and Maritime Management Antwerp, Belgium

1. Introduction: the history of containerization

Prior to containerization, all products other than bulk commodities were moved piece by piece in break bulk. Not only was the freight handling slow, other modes of transport, such as railroads, basically added to the inefficiency. Moreover, the cargo was exposed to potential damage and pilferage. In 1956 the McLean Trucking Company started experiments with standardized boxes in an attempt to streamline a distribution system from shipper to consignee. The Ideal X, the first cargo ship carrying containers, sailed from Newark, New Jersey. This marked the first scheduled containership service in the world. Matson, another US pioneering company, started to experiment with containers in 1958 (Gilman 1977 and UNCTAD 1985).

Container shipping was seen by many as a rather risky business. It involved a big investment in new vessels and new equipment, which differed radically from the existing ones. Containerization was a form of automation. Consequently, numerous jobs were bound to be eliminated. Container ships also needed extensive docking and special shipbuilding and repair facilities.

In the early days of containerization the concept of intermodality was just an idea. Crucial for true intermodality was the issue of standardization of container sizes and fittings. The first container vessels were able to carry 226 boxes in "trailerships", which conformed to the maximum length for trailers allowed on the US highways at the time: 35 ft long x 8 ft wide and 8 ft high. Later, the standard size agreed upon became the 20 ft and 40 ft units, although high-cube and 45 ft units are still used today. The standardization of sizes meant that any box could lock on to any other box, trailer chassis or ship.

In the early 1960s containerization was yet to be tested on an international scale. The first trans-Atlantic container service was Sea-Land's SS Fairland. The cargo arrived in Europe four weeks faster than its equivalent had before. Previously, it took a crew of twenty longshoremen to load twenty tons per hour into a ship's hold. With containers and gantry cranes, a crew of just ten can load twice as much in a matter of minutes.

The concept of containerization proved to be safer, faster and cheaper than the existing methods of transporting commodities. It minimized damage and pilferage, and precluded other types of perils. It cut labour and insurance costs dramatically. And it was the catalyst for new and improved types of cargo ships. Containerization changed more than the way we transport goods around the world. It is responsible for the economic success of port cities and their surrounding regions. By enabling easier access to the exchange of goods, it has opened up new markets for export and import. The requirements imposed by containerization contributed to the decline of some established ports and to the growth of new ones and partially reshaped port hierarchy. The concept of containerization extended ports' hinterlands in a way it redefined port competition.

2. The evolution of container throughput in Antwerp and Rotterdam

The ports of Antwerp and Rotterdam were among the first European ports to engage in large-scale containerization. The container era in the port of Rotterdam started on 4 May 1966 when SS Fairland of Sea-Land loaded and discharged a number of 35' containers in light of the first transatlantic container liner service. In the same year the port handled about 60.000 TEU. The port of Antwerp recorded a total throughput of 43.820 TEU in 1966, the first year of container operations. Containerization in Rotterdam boomed to about one million TEU in 1971. Antwerp reached one million units seven years later. In 1980 container throughput in Rotterdam approached two million TEU, a traffic level Antwerp would only reach in 1993. Container growth in Antwerp accelerated from 1993 onwards: it took the port merely four years to increase throughput from two million to three million TEU and only three years to add another million. Rotterdam also added two million TEU to its cargo volume in the period 1993-1999, but in 2000 the Dutch load centre witnessed a (temporary) setback (Fig. 8.1.).

In the 1970s the port of Rotterdam recorded an average market share in the total container throughput of the Hamburg-Le Havre range of 40%. This share gradually decreased to some 35% in 1999. The strong growth of Bremerhaven, Hamburg and Antwerp, combined with a traffic decline in Rotterdam, dropped the market share of the Dutch load centre to 31 % in 2000. The share of the port of Antwerp surpassed 20% in 2000, compared to 10 to 15% in the early days of containerization (Fig. 8.1.).

Fig. 8.1. Container throughput of Antwerp and Rotterdam in the period 1966-2000 (in 1000 TEU) and market shares in the Hamburg - Le Havre range

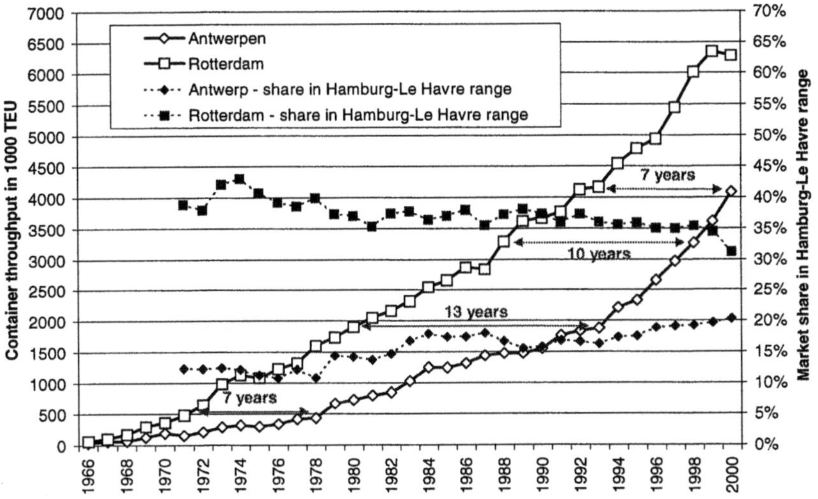

Source: based on data port authorities

Rotterdam has always been and still is the biggest container port in Europe. Antwerp was number two in Europe till 1975 and in the period 1983-1986. In the other years of observation Hamburg kept the position of the second biggest European container port (table 8.1.).

Table 8.1. Container throughput of the load centres of the Hamburg – Le Havre range (in TEU)

	1970	1975	1980	1985	1990	1995	1998	1999	2000
Rotterdam	363492	1078661	1900707	2654906	3665955	4786576	6010502	6343020	6274555
Antwerp	189097	297268	724247	1243009	1549113	2329135	3265750	3614246	4082334
Hamburg	81400	326217	783323	1158776	1968986	2890181	3546940	3738307	4248000
Bremen	195821	404967	702764	986265	1163347	1518206	1811014	2201220	2712420
Le Havre	107995	231675	507289	565914	857765	970425	1319278	1378379	1464901
Zeebrugge	92400	184383	181010	218258	334382	528476	776357	850164	965345
Other (*)	47379	123052	326012	330583	268658	293716	228180	267286	359983
TOTAL	1077584	2646223	5125352	7157711	9808206	13316715	16958021	18392622	20107538

(*) Gent, Amsterdam, Flushing, Dunkirk, Rouen

Containerization in Antwerp and Rotterdam was triggered by trans-Atlantic liner services. In 1967 about 64% of the container throughput in Antwerp consisted of American container volumes. This share slowly dropped to reach 36% in 1999. The relative importance of the Atlantic volume in Rotterdam decreased from 42% in 1968 to 18% in 1999.

Fig. 8.2. Container distribution in the large load centres of the Hamburg – Le Havre range according to foreland regions, figures in TEU (loaded and discharged) for 1999

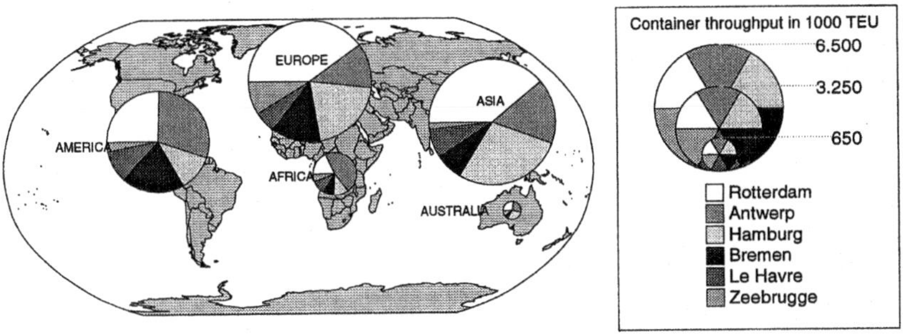

Source: T. Notteboom on the basis of data respective port authorities

Rotterdam has gradually acquired an important position in Europe for what feeder and short sea flows are concerned. Intra-European container flows in Rotterdam represented 2,4 million TEU in 1999 or 40% of the total intra-European container throughput in the Hamburg – Le Havre range. Shortsea and feeder flows have always been relatively small in the upstream port of Antwerp. However, efforts to stimulate coastal shipping and the decision of the shipping line MSC to use Antwerp as a north European hub have resulted in an increase of intra-European container traffic from 259.000 TEU in 1994 (12% of Antwerp's container throughput) to 712.000 TEU in 2000 (19,7%). Antwerp is the market leader on the Atlantic (1,3 million TEU in 1999 or 30% in the observed range) and the north-south position routes to Africa (456.000 TEU or 46%). Rotterdam dominates the Asian trade. The Dutch load centre recorded 2,4 million TEU in relation to Asia in 1999, which equals a share of 38,8% in the observed range. Fig. 8.2. illustrates the above findings.

Fig. 8.3. The degree of containerization in Antwerp and Rotterdam (1980-2000)

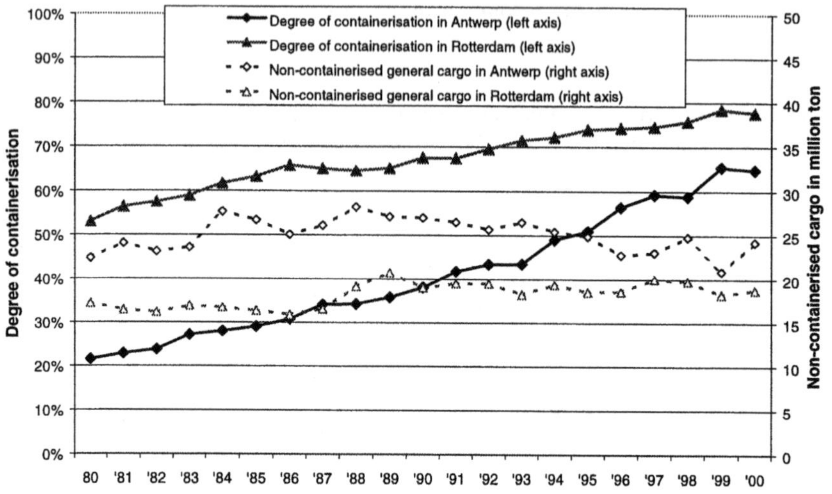

Source: T. Notteboom on the basis of data respective port authorities

The sharp increase of containerized cargo in Rotterdam coincided with a moderate growth of non-containerized general cargo. Consequently, the degree of containerization in the Dutch load centre evolved from 53% in 1980 to 78% in 2000. Antwerp still is the largest European port for non-containerized general cargo, but the port was not able to realize growth in this traffic category. The combination of a stagnation or even a decline in conventional cargo flows on the one hand and an exceptional growth in container volumes on the other, tripled the degree of containerization in twenty years time (see Fig. 8.3.). Compared to other load centres in the Hamburg-Le Havre range the degree of containerization in Antwerp still remains rather low (cfr. Hamburg reached a degree of 93% in 2000, Bremen more than 81%).

3. Spatial development of container facilities in Antwerp and Rotterdam

The spatial structure of ports changes all the time. Several studies have mirrored the development of ports through time. A well-known geographical model on port development is the Anyport model of Bird (1971). The Anyport model of Bird describes the evolution of the physical lay-out and installations in a port in six successive stages. It is a generalization of the tendency of port development to move downstream towards deeper water. The sixth and final stage in the model consists of specialized quayage developments far away from the port city. Although Bird conceived his model in the 1970s, it is still valid in the context of container terminal developments in Antwerp and Rotterdam.

3.1. The early years of containerization

3.1.1. Rotterdam

The first containers in Rotterdam were handled by Quick Dispatch on the Müller-Progress terminal, situated in the Prinses Beatrixhaven (part of Eemhaven). In the first year of operations the containers were placed directly from ship to trailer, as terminal operators had no equipment for moving full containers on the terminal. With the introduction of reach stackers and low straddle carriers in 1967-1968 indirect transhipment from a vessel to truck or rail became possible. From that moment on containers could be stacked on the terminal floor.

The founding of ECT (Europe Combined Terminals) in 1966 proved to be crucial for the development of a specialized container stevedoring business in Rotterdam. ECT was founded by the Dutch Railways (NS) and five stevedoring companies specialized in the handling of general cargo (i.e. Quick Dispatch, Thomson, Müller-Progress, Cornelis Swarttouw and Pakhuismeesteren). In 1967, ECT opened the first full container terminal in the Eemhaven port area. Three years later a dedicated terminal for Sea-Land was inaugurated in the Prins Willem Alexander port area (Rotterdam Port Authority 1996, Van Driel 1990).

3.1.2. Antwerp

In the late 1960s Stevedoring Company Gylsen, Hessenatie, Noord Natie, Müller-Thomson Antwerp and Antwerps Havenbedrijf Pays developed container operations along the Leopold Dock and the Churchill Dock (built in the framework of the ten-year expansion programme 1956-1967). At the end of 1967 Hessenatie-Neptunus was the first operator to start container operations at the Churchill dock. In 1968 already five companies handled containers along the Churchill dock (Hessenatie-Neptunus, Westerlund Corporation, Noord Natie, Gylsen Stevedoring Company and Antwerps Havenbedrijf Pays). Seven container gantry cranes were installed along the berths. Some argued that the container capacity created at the end of the 1960s was far too big: "If the currently available container quantities are compared with the potential capacities of the terminals, it is clear that the existing equipment can not be used at full economic capacity. The over-investment is at present so large that even in the years to come the container volume cannot offer prospects for achieving a balance" (Coppieters 1968, 53). History proved that demand would soon outgrow the capacity of the Churchill dock.

3.2. The 1980s

3.2.1. Rotterdam: the Maasvlakte or the move to the sea

The sustained growth of container throughput in Rotterdam soon led to the idea of constructing massive container facilities on the Maasvlakte. The Maasvlakte, the most westerly port complex, differed from previous projects in that it was not a case of converting land into water, but water into land. At this location, just off the coast, lay a sandbank which was raised to the desired height. The construction of the Maasvlakte extended the total area of the port of Rotterdam by 3000 hectares to 10,000 hectares. The first container terminal on the Maasvlakte, now the Delta Multi-User terminal (DMU), welcomed a first container vessel in September 1984 (Rotterdam Port Authority, 1985 and 1995). The Maasvlakte terminals handled less than 0,6 million TEU in 1988 or approximately 18% of the total container throughput in Rotterdam.

3.2.2. Antwerp: scale increases and a first wave of market concentration

The completion of the Delwaide Dock in 1982 gave a real impetus to strong growth in the Antwerp container business (see chart 8.1.). Seven years after the opening the three container terminals situated along this dock handled some 75% of the total container throughput in Antwerp. Terminal depth along the dock reached 600m compared to merely 300m for the older facilities.

Mergers and acquisitions characterized the stevedoring business at the end of the 1980s:

- Antwerp Combined Terminals (ACT) was founded in January 1987 as a result of the merger between Müller-Thomson Antwerp and Stevedoring and Transport (Pays). Van Ommeren (owner of Pays) and Internatio-Müller (owner of Müller-Thomson) sold ACT in 1990;
- In 1988 Compagnie Maritime Belge (CMB) bought Hessenatie and integrated Stevedoring Company Gylsen in Hessenatie. At that time Stevedoring Company Gylsen operated terminals along the Leopold Dock and the Churchill Dock. Hessenatie offered container handling services at the Delwaide Dock and the Churchill Dock;
- In 1989 Furness sold Seaport Terminals to Katoen Natie.

3.3. The 1990s

3.3.1. Rotterdam: Delta 2000-8 or the introduction of automated facilities

In the 1990s ECT developed a strong technological focus. This ultimately led to the construction of fully automated terminals equipped with AGV (Automated Guided Vehicles) and ASC (Automated Stacking Cranes). The fully automated and dedicated Delta-)Sea-Land terminal (DSL), recently renamed to DDN (Delta Dedicated North), opened its doors in 1993.

Fig. 8.4. Spatial distribution of the container throughput in the Rotterdam port area (DD = diversion distance)

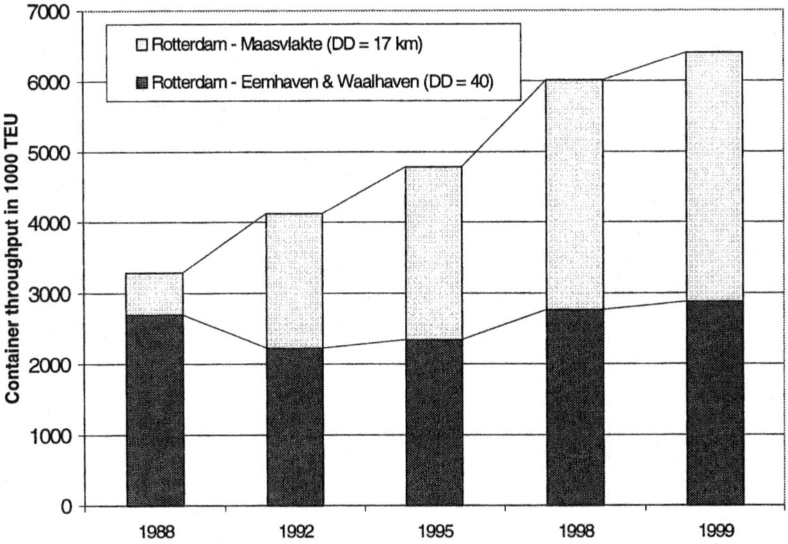

The further development of container facilities on the Maasvlakte was concretized in the plan Delta 2000-8. The Delta Dedicated East terminal (DDE) was the first module of some 60 ha to become operational in the framework of this development plan (Nierop 1996). The Delta Dedicated West terminal (DDW) opened in 2000. The Maasvlakte terminals handled 3,5 million TEU in 1999 or approximately 55 % of Rotterdam's container throughput. In 1988 this share was only 18% (Fig. 8.4.). The Maasvlakte clearly is an example of a deconcentration tendency within a port area. The Home Container Division of ECT at Eemhaven port are accounted for some 22 % of total container traffic in 1999. Hanno and Uniport handled a large share of the remaining container flows in the Waalhaven.

3.3.2. Antwerp: the development of on-stream facilities

Even today the Delwaide Dock remains a very important container centre in the port of Antwerp. The three container terminals situated along this dock handled nearly half of the total container throughput in 1999 compared to 75 % in 1989. The relative decline in importance is explained by the strategic decision of the Antwerp port community and the Flemish government to build container capacity along the river Scheldt in front of the sea locks, thereby allowing considerable savings in the port turnaround time of conatiner vessels. Both the Churchill Dock and the Delwaide Dock are part of an extensice dock system located behind locks (Fig. 8.5.).

Fig. 8.5. Spatial distribution of container throughput in the Antwerp port area

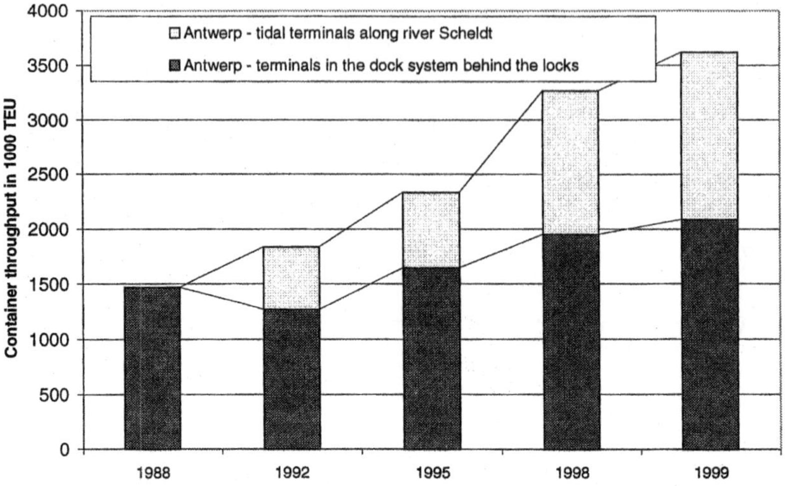

The first Scheldt terminal, the Europaterminal operated by Hessenatie, started operations in 1990 and has reached its maximum effective capacity utilization (container throughput of some 1,1 million TEU in 1999). The second Scheldt terminal, the Noordzeeterminal operated by a combination of the stevedoring company Noord Natie (67 %) and Belgian Rail (33 %), handled 477.00 TEU in 1999, just three years after it welcomed the first vessel.

3.4. The new millennium

3.4.1. Rotterdam: dedicated terminals and ECT shake-up

At the end of the 1990s the shareholder structure of ECT changed substantially. Pakhoed, Nedlloyd, Internatio-Müller and the Dutch railways decided to sell their shares. After long negotiations and the intervention of the Merger Task Force of the European Commission, the new shareholder structure became 35% for Hutchison Port Holding, 35% for the Rotterdam Municipal Port Management, 28% for ABN-Amro and 2% for the employees. The new shareholder structure brought the start of a restructuring phase at ECT, which came into full effect in the new millennium. In 2002, the shareholders were HPH (79 %), RMPM (19 %) and the empoyees (2 %).

Maersk reached an agreement with ECT in the beginning of 1999 to dedicate a part of the DMU terminal to Maersk vessels. The dedicated Maersk Delta terminal opened its doors in 2000. In the medium term the whole DMU terminal will be transferred to Maersk Delta b.v., initially a 66/33 joint venture between Maersk Sealand and ECT, but at present a 100 % subsidiary of the Maersk group. Maersk Sealand shifted about 300.000 TEU to Bremerhaven in 2000, because of start-up difficulties at the Maersk Delta terminal and ECT's lack of efficiency and productivity before and during the transition phase.

In 2000, ECT and P&O Nedlloyd agreed to build the so-called Euromax terminal at the Maasvlakte. The Euromax terminal will open its doors in 2004 (first phase) and will be operated by a 50/50 joint venture between ECT and P&O Nedlloyd. Terminal capacity should reach at least 2,4 million TEU. The Euromax facility will primarily accommodate vessels of P&O Nedlloyd and the partners of the Grand Alliance.

The port of Rotterdam has developed ambitious infrastructure plans to meet further container growth, i.e. a second Maasvlakte of which a part would be dedicated to the container business. At present a broad so-called "utility and necessity discussion" is taking place in the Netherlands to determine the structure and functions of a sustainable second Maasvlakte.

3.4.2. Antwerp: concentration among players and massive terminal developments

To meet growing container volumes in the future, the Antwerp Port Authority plans a tidal container dock on the left bank of the River Scheldt to be completed in three successive phases by 2006. The new dock will then consist of more than five kilometres of quay wall and will cover an area of some 230 hectares. The first phase and the second phase (west) encompass the building of a dedicated terminal allocated to the joint venture Hessenatie/MSC with an annual capacity of at least two million TEU. The terminal is under construction and should be ready by early 2004. The second phase (east) was granted to Hessenatie and will most likely accommodate container flows generated by the CP Ships group (CAST, Canmar, Contship and Lykes Lines). In 2000, the concession for the third phase (west) was granted to the combination Hessenatie / Noord Natie, while the Board of the Antwerp Port Authority awarded the concession for the third phase (east) to the combination P&0 Ports/Duisport. When completed the tidal dock should reach an annual capacity of 5.5 to 6 million TEU.

The years 2000 and 2001 have really transformed the container handling business in Antwerp:

- Early in 2000, P&O Ports acquired the business of Seaport Terminals which operates two stevedoring facilities in Antwerp. This investment forms part of the broader strategy to link an inland container terminal in Duisburg (Germany) with a major marine facility. A few months later P&O Ports took over ACT/MT (Antwerp combined Terminals/Maritime Terminals), a stevedore who handles 3 million tons of general cargo and 100,000 containers a year;
- In 2000 Hessenatie, a wholly-owned subsidiary of CMB, and Noord Natie announced to join forces. Hesse Noord Natie became operational in 2001;

- On 8 March 2001, PSA Corporation (PSA) as the purchaser and CMB and Noord Natie as the vendors have signed a Heads of Agreement (HOA) in which PSA is set to acquire a majority stake in Hesse Noord Natie (HNN). The HOA is subject to the completion of a Sale and Purchase Agreement and satisfactory fulfillment of regulatory and commercial conditions, including local competition clearance and completion of the merger between Hessenatie and Noord Natie[1]. The take-over was completed in 2002, with PSA taking a 80 % stake in Hesse Noord Natie.

4. Containerization in Antwerp and Rotterdam: (dis)similarities

4.1. Background: the liner industry in transition

One of the most striking impacts of container and intermodal transport developments is the realignment of traffic flows. New patterns of freight movements have emerged as a consequence of the changes in port hierarchy and the extension of ports' hinterlands. These spatial developments are going hand in hand with dramatic changes in the organization of logistic chains and liner networks.

Container carriers have achieved considerable cost savings at sea through a gradual scale enlargement in vessel size. In 1970 the biggest container vessel afloat was the Sea-Land Navigator with a capacity of 2.361 TEU and a draft of 11,1 metres. The Nedlloyd Houtman broke the 3.000 TEU-barrier in 1977. The Nedlloyd Holland (4.534 TEU and a draft of 12,68 m) was the first vessel to surpass 4.000 TEU. Till 1994 no container vessel had a breadth of more than 32,3 metres, this to allow transit of the Panama Canal. With a beam of 40m the OOCL California (4.960 TEU) was the first post-panamax vessel. In 1996 Maersk dramatically increased ship size with the introduction of the Regina Maersk with an official capacity of 6.418 TEU and a draft of 14 metres (Gilman 2000). At present all leading shipping lines have introduced 5.000+ units or will do so in the short term.

Liner service networks have evolved from end-to-end services to world encircling hub-and-spoke networks. The emphasis of such services lies on a few selected hub ports of call, linked to all the other destinations by feeder services and or inland shuttle services. Such networks offer great advantages in terms of the consolidation of cargo flows and in terms of potential market coverage (Slack 1999). In the eighties some container shipping lines (e.g. Evergreen and United States Lines) started to abandon traditional routing systems in favour of round the world services (Lim 1996). But the breakthrough of RTW-services has always been hindered by the capacity constraints of the Panama Canal. In the early 1990s some carriers introduced pendulum services. The system relies on hub ports that act as turntables between liner services of two different trades. This kind of liner

[1] Press release of PSA and HNN, 8 March 2001.

service design allows the use of post-panamax units and is well suited for high-volume international trade routes such as the trade Europe-Far East-US West Coast.

Shipping lines have always co-operated, but the intensity and scope of carrier co-operation is changing. The impact of liner conferences (i.e. a form of trade agreements) is decreasing. Vessel sharing agreements and consortia (i.e. widespread forms of horizontal integration in the 1970s and 1980s) have made room for strategic alliances (e.g. Grand Alliance, United Alliance and New World Alliance). Furthermore, the shipping business has never witnessed so many large-scale mergers (e.g. P&O Nedlloyd in 1997) and acquisitions (e.g. the take over of Sea-Land by Maersk in 1999). Improvements in terminal effectiveness and landside operations must ensure that the savings at sea are not lost on land. Many shipping lines are therefore expanding their scope to include terminal operations and hinterland transportation.

The power of these large intermodal carriers, reinforced by strategic alliances between them, is used to play off one port or group of ports against another. Consequently, if a seaport does not succeed to attract or retain some of the megacarriers, it will be exposed to high risks for substantial losses of container traffic. These developments force ports to make every effort to be competitive in terms of cost and quality of services and to develop the port area to a multimodal transport and distribution service centre.

Antwerp and Rotterdam have responded in their own way to the above structural changes in the shipping business. This section explores similarities and dissimilarities between the two container load centres and identifies common challenges in three interrelated areas: (a) the container handling market, (b) port competition and (c) infrastructure and accessibility.

4.2. Structural changes in the container handling market

4.2.1. Concentration at the port demand side and new entrants in the stevedoring business

Ports are confronted with a concentration of power at the port demand side. The terminal operators and seaport authorities of Antwerp and Rotterdam have to deal with larger port clients with a strong bargaining power vis-à-vis terminal operations and inland transport operations. It is quite striking in this respect that even the large stevedoring company ECT in Rotterdam eventually had to yield to the demands of Maersk and P&O Nedlloyd.

Another relatively new element is that large transport and industrial companies are entering the stevedoring market. New entrants in the market include railway companies and shipping lines. Belgian Rail has a stake of 33% in the joint venture that operates the Noordzeeterminal in Antwerp. Sea Land was the first shipping line to acquire a dedicated facility in Rotterdam, i.e. the Delta SeaLand terminal (DSL) at the Maasvlakte (in 2000 renamed to DDN). Maersk Delta is a relatively new dedicated terminal. The plan for the construction of the dedicated terminal Euromax (P&O Nedlloyd/ECT) further proves that large carriers are engaging in stevedoring activities. The Deurganck dock will offer dedicated or semi-dedicated facilities for MSC and CP Ships, both in joint venture with Hesse Noord Natie.

4.2.2. Concentration and integration at the port supply side

As mentioned earlier, the port of Antwerp went through two phases of horizontal integration in the container stevedoring market: one at the end of the 1980s and one that started in the new millennium. The port authority of Antwerp has always tried to ensure a high level of inner-port competition, even while the number of major container handling companies gradually decreased from six in the 1970s to only two in 2001.

Müller-Thomson, Pays, Stevedoring Company Gylsen, Noord Natie, Seaport Terminals and Hessenatie-Neptunus were the main container handling companies till half of the 1980s. The 1990s were marked by fierce inner-port competition, primarily between Hessenatie, Noord Natie, Katoen Natie and ACT. The granting of the first Scheldt terminal to Hessenatie and the second Scheldt terminal to Noord Natie gave these stevedoring companies a competitive advantage over the other operators. Well aware of the strategic importance of the Scheldt facilities, Katoen Natie filed an official complaint against each of the granting procedures. Katoen Natie completely shifted its attention to industrial subcontracting and distribution when the company realized that its container growth potential in Antwerp was restricted. At present, only two companies offer large-scale container facilities in Antwerp: Hesse Noord Natie with a share of 85% of Antwerp's container throughput in 2000 and P&O Ports. Fig. 8.6. illustrates the growing dominance of Hessenatie in the container business in Antwerp.

In Rotterdam, two events have had an important impact on the level of concentration in the container handling market. In order to cope with the high capital requirements and risks linked to container operations, five conventional stevedoring companies and the Dutch Railways founded ECT in 1966. ECT was set up at the instigation of the Municipal Port Management. The plan 2000-8 led to a second major event with respect to market concentration in the stevedoring business: Unitcentre merged with ECT in 1992. Pakhoed, the owner of Unitcentre, was told by the Rotterdam Municipal Port Management that the merger with ECT was needed to create a powerful player in view of operating the Maasvlakte facilities. Half of the equipment of Unitcentre was sold to Uniport. Today Hanno and Uniport are the main competitors of ECT (shipping lines not included), but the draft conditions at the Waalhaven are less favourable compared to the Maasvlakte.

The Rotterdam Municipal Port Management has always given ECT a preferential treatment in order to meet its objective of having a strong container operator in Rotterdam. RMPM even gave ECT some financial back-up for the development of the Maasvlakte facilities (Wildenberg 1998). The strong links that have always existed between RMPM and ECT were formalized in 1999 when RMPM acquired a share of 35% in ECT (afterwards lowered to 19%). The market share of ECT in Rotterdam's container throughput increased from 61.5% in 1992 to 73% in 1999, mainly as a result of capacity increases at the Maasvlakte.

Fig. 8.6. Container throughput in Antwerp by terminal operator

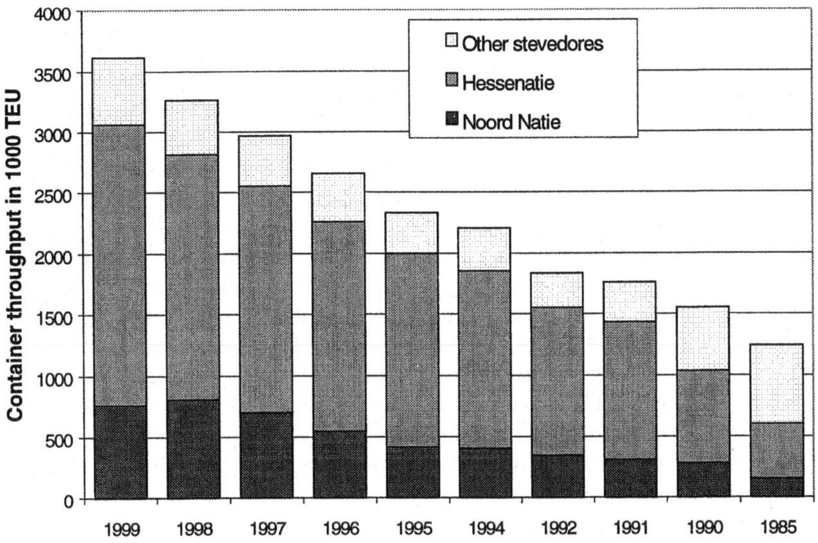

Source: Hessenatie, Noord Natie and Antwerp Port Authority

Hesse Noord Natie and ECT clearly are the dominant players in Antwerp and Rotterdam. These dominant players are compelled to perform efficiently as shipping lines demand cheaper and better service and as port competition remains fierce (see section 4.3). The agreements of these operators with shipping lines to jointly develop dedicated container facilities (P&O Nedlloyd/ECT, Maersk Delta and MSC/Hessenatie) shows how the balance of power is still shifting to the carrier.

4.2.3. Foreign players move in

The events in the last couple of years have proven that the European container handling industry is ripe for consolidation. The European container scene has become a magnet for top global investors. The European arrival of Hutchison Port Holding, PSA Corporation (Singapore) and P&O Ports and the expansion schemes of leading European stevedoring groups such as Eurogate have changed the dynamics of the business. Competition is gradually shifting from port authorities to private terminal companies who are trying to build a regional terminal network.

Also Rotterdam and Antwerp witness an influx of foreign players. In 1999 Hong Kong's Hutchison Port Holding (HPH) acquired a strategic stake in ECT. Hutchison Port Holding controls around 10% of world container port moves. In the United Kingdom, HPH operates container terminals in Felixstowe, Thamesport and Harwich. The total European container throughput of HPH amounted to 8,17 million TEU in 1999. P&O Ports entered mainland Europe through the acquisition of the container activities of Seaport Terminals and ACT/MT in Antwerp. P&O Ports is co-owner of the container facilities in Southampton and Tilbury and is expected to build a new one million TEU-a-year terminal on a former Shell site along the river Thames. P&O Ports operates about twenty-one terminals around the world with a total throughput of 8,3 million TEU in 1999. As indicated earlier PSA Corp has taken a majority participation in Hesse Noord Natie. PSA handled approximately 17 million TEU in 2000, of which only one million TEU in Europe (740.000 TEU at the Voltri terminal in Genoa and 220.000 TEU in Venice).

The influx of overseas capital in Antwerp and Rotterdam and the consolidation in the cargo handling business have created circumstances in which international stevedoring companies have acquired a very strategic position in the ports' future. The key position of such terminal operators can attract a higher direct involvement of central governments and "landlord" port authorities, as the latter want to make sure that not all economic rents of these terminal operations are transferred abroad. In Rotterdam, this objective ended up in an actual financial participation of a semi-public port authority in the shareholding of a stevedoring company (i.e. the share of RMPM in ECT). With an eye to the future of the port, RMPM has opted for a participation in ECT once the company went up for sale. Such developments might not be very legitimate to the ports industry, as other terminal operators fear preferential treatment and limited market entry to new players. It is clear that ECT at all times should compete on a fair basis with private sector firms and not enjoy any net competitive advantage by virtue of their public sector involvement.

The Antwerp Port Authority still swears by the model of internal port competition. This port business model contributed to the port's strong competitive position, but at the same time inevitably introduced mergers and acquisitions. In the near future the stevedoring business in Antwerp is expected to be controlled by two large international players, i.e. PSA of Singapore (via a majority stake in Hesse Noord Natie) and P&O Ports. At present, the Antwerp port authority does not intend to participate in container stevedoring companies. However, in the terms of the concessions for the third phase of the Deurganck Dock a clause has been included which entitles the port authority the right to take a minority participation in the working companies of the strategic Scheldt terminals at such times as the port authority is legally permitted to do so[2] (decisions taken by the Board on 20 June 2000). Pending this, alternative control and supervisory modes will be elaborated for the benefit of the Antwerp Port Authority.

4.3. Port competition

The presence of fewer players in the container handling industry so far has not implied less competition. On the contrary, the expansion of global shipping companies and port operators is supposed to have actually increased competition.

---

[2] At this moment, the Antwerp Port Authority is only permitted to take majority participations.

The container ports of Rotterdam and Antwerp have always competed with each other and with other large and medium-sized load centres in the Hamburg - Le Havre range, i.e. Hamburg, Bremen, Le Havre and Zeebrugge. History taught that a lot of container shipping lines regularly shift cargo from Antwerp to Rotterdam or vice versa[3].

However, competition is no longer limited to the six load centres in the Hamburg – Le Havre range. Port competition has become broader in several ways:

- Notteboom demonstrated that distant seaports are starting to compete directly as a result of changes in the carriers' liner service networks (Notteboom 1997). Container shifts between the northern ports in the Hamburg-Le Havre range and ports situated in the Mediterranean have risen considerably since the beginning of the 1990s. Major shipping lines started to include more Mediterranean ports in their intercontinental service networks. The growing number of deepsea vessels calling directly at Mediterranean load centres boosted the development of new transhipment hubs in the area (e.g. Gioia Tauro, Taranto and Cagliari in Italy and Marsaxlokk on Malta). The quality improvements and major investments in Med hubs have already contributed to a partial shift of traditional north-south land and water feeder flows. Rotterdam is more vulnerable for the Mediterranean revival than Antwerp, because the Dutch load centre has a much stronger orientation on container services that pass the Med area to reach the Far East;
- The UK ports of Felixstowe, Thamesport and Southampton can to some extent threaten the competitive position of Antwerp and Rotterdam for what transhipment flows to the United Kingdom, Ireland, the Baltic and Southern Europe are concerned. The competitive pressure of the UK load centres on Antwerp and Rotterdam evolved from weak in the 1980s to substantial in the 1990s, together with a growing sea-sea transhipment business in northern Europe;
- Antwerp and Rotterdam are facing competition from new load centres in the immediate vicinity. The coastal port of Zeebrugge is determined to attract more intercontinental container traffic, by manifesting itself as an alternative for the big load centres Antwerp and Rotterdam. The Dutch seaports Amsterdam and Flushing will start large-scale container operations in the short or medium term. The city of Amsterdam and the stevedoring company Ceres opened a container terminal with an initial capacity of some 950.000 TEU. ESM (Exploitatiemaatschappij Schelde Maas), a joint venture between the port authority of Flushing/Terneuzen and the Rotterdam Municipal Port Management, will invest in the infrastructure for the Westerschelde Container Terminal in Flushing, with a maximum capacity of 1,75 to 2,5 million TEU and a quay length of 2,6 kilometres. The first phase should be ready by early 2004. The Antwerp stevedoring company HNN will operate the facility and will make the necessary investments in terminal equipment. Amsterdam and Flushing are examples of the so-called "peripheral port challenge" phenomenon that was first introduced by Hayuth (Hayuth 1981). It is expected that these new terminals will depend heavily on the cluster effects in and the existing hinterland networks of the

[3] A few examples: Maersk moved from Noord Natie (Antwerp) to Zeebrugge in 1995 and afterwards to Rotterdam and ACL concentrated all calls in Antwerp from 1996 onwards.

large load centres. The additional terminal capacity gives the big shipping lines and alliances more opportunities to use their bargaining power to play off one port against another.

4.4. Infrastructure and accessibility

The requirements imposed by shipping lines on deepsea container terminals has changed considerably, not only in terms of productivity, handling costs and service, but also in terms of location-bound elements such as the maritime access profile and the access to the cargo-generating hinterlands.

4.4.1. Terminal infrastructure development

Terminal infrastructure is a necessary ingredient for attracting cargo, but it is not a sufficient one. In the early days of containerization Antwerp and Rotterdam were in the middle of massive port extension works (e.g. ten year plan 1956-1967 in Antwerp and Europoort in Rotterdam) primarily aimed at accommodating large petrochemical complexes (Winkelmans 1973 and de Goey 1990). Ports are increasingly confronted with serious constraints to further port extensions, caused by a growing environmental consciousness[4], an increasing scarcity of space and the NIMBY syndrome (not in my backyard). Recent examples are the discussion in the Netherlands on the second Maasvlakte and the juridical fights related to the Deurganck Dock in Antwerp.

The increased scarcity of space forces ports to intensify the occupancy of terminal surfaces. For instance, the annual TEU-capacity per square meter on the new MSC/Hessenatie terminal will be much higher compared to the existing Scheldt terminals. Spatial constraints also make the renovation of older port areas more feasible. However, the terminal surfaces and draft conditions in older port areas are generally too small for the development of large container facilities.

Since the 1980s Antwerp and Rotterdam have intensified the downstream development of massive container terminals with a high draft, multiple berthing facilities, large back-up land and specialized container cranes with a sufficient outreach. *Spatial concentration* and *automation* are important in this respect:

- The Delwaide dock and the plan 2000-8 on the Maasvlakte are both examples of a spatial concentration of container terminals, created mainly for reasons of operational efficiency. At present the container terminals in Rotterdam are all situated in the Eemhaven (Home Terminal of ECT and Rotterdam Shortsea Terminal), Waalhaven (Hanno, Morcon, Uniport) and on the Maasvlakte (DDN, DDE and DDW of ECT and Maersk Delta). The initial spatial concentration of container cargo at the Churchill dock in Antwerp somewhat shifted to the Delwaide dock in the 1980s. The terminal facilities on the river Scheldt

[4] More than ever port projects have to comply with a whole set of environmental and safety regulations. Moreover, port projects are subject to extensive evaluation procedures (cost-benefit analysis, economic effect analysis, environmental impact assessment, mobility impact study, etc.).

have created a second large container centre. The Deurganck dock will add a third container concentration zone to the Antwerp port area;

- ECT has developed a strong focus on technologically advanced terminal solutions (cfr. AGV and ASC at DDN, DDE and DDW). Not all shipping lines are in favour of such automated terminals. For instance, Maersk opted for a more conventional handling equipment at the Maersk Delta terminal, as the carrier feared the productivity and flexibility at automated terminals is too low. Terminal operators in Antwerp have always opted for traditional container terminals equipped with gantry cranes and straddle carriers. The MSC/Hessenatie terminal will become the first facility to use another handling technique, based on a combination of stacking cranes and "runners" (i.e. low straddle carriers used for the transfer of containers between quay wall and stacking area).

4.4.2. Maritime accessibility

Rotterdam is a downstream port at the estuary of the Rhine and can accommodate the largest container vessels at any time at the Maasvlakte facilities. Antwerp is a river port situated upstream of the river Scheldt. Container vessels can sail closer to the economic markets in the hinterland. However, the nautical accessibility is time costly and draft conditions are less optimal than in Rotterdam. At the time when container vessels were still limited in size, the port of Antwerp wanted to increase the maritime accessibility in view of receiving large dry bulk carrier and tankers. Since the 1990s the main focus has shifted to guaranteeing access for container vessels. A dredging program in the late 1990s resulted in a tide-independent draft of 38'. Ships with a draft of 43' can sail down the river in one tide. The largest container vessels need to take into account some tidal window restrictions. A second deepening program should further improve the accessibility for post-panamax vessels. At present a broad discussion on a long-term vision for the Scheldt estuary (Lange Termijn Visie Schelde-Estuarium) is going on to determine to what extent a further deepening of the river is desirable and necessary.

4.4.3. Hinterland transportation

4.4.3.1. Changes in the modal split

The growing container volumes in Antwerp and Rotterdam have made efficiency improvements and rationalizations in the hinterland transportation not only possible but also necessary. In both ports a modal shift from road haulage to intermodal initiatives in the area of sea-rail, sea-inland navigation and sea-sea (feeder) can be observed in order to cope with the increasing distribution requirements (Fig. 8.7.). The intermodal solutions can be exploited profitable on a number of traffic corridors (e.g. the Rhine axis and the crossing of the Alps) or in some specific niche markets, but they are not suitable to become a European-wide alternative for road haulage.

4.4.3.2. Structural changes in the rail sector in Antwerp and Rotterdam

For a long time most container terminals in Antwerp and Rotterdam provided on-dock rail facilities. As such, rail operations were scattered all over the port

Fig. 8.7. Modal split for hinterland transportation in Antwerp and Rotterdam, containers only (basis = TEU)

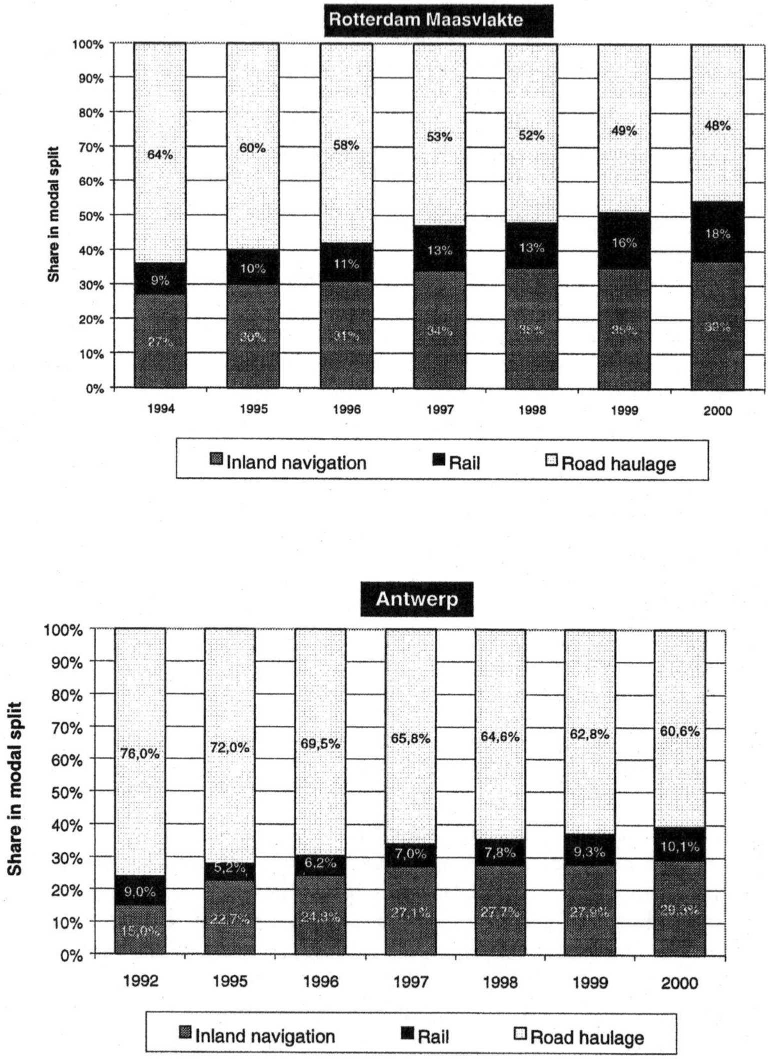

Source: RMPM and AGHA-SEA

area. In 1994 the port of Rotterdam introduced the RSC-concept (Rail Service Centre). This concept gradually led to a strong geographical concentration of rail operations in two locations: RSC Rotterdam in the Eemhaven and RSC Maasvlakte. At present, nearly all shuttle trains leave at the RSC-facilities. The Zomerweg terminal, the first specialized rail terminal in the port of Antwerp, opened in 1972. Ten years later about two thirds of all container traffic by rail still used on-dock rail facilities. The opening of the Cirkeldyck rail terminal in 1996 and of the rail hub of IFB in 2000 drastically reduced the share of on-dock rail operations.

In the early days of containerization containers were loaded onto mixed cargo trains. With the increasing volumes dedicated container shuttles became possible. The container growth in Antwerp and Rotterdam gradually generated enough critical mass to install a number of direct shuttle trains to a limited number of destinations in the hinterland. For other destinations the volumes remained too low to allow direct shuttle trains on a frequent basis. Since the 1990s intermodal railway networks centred around inland hubs emerged (e.g. North European Network with the inland hub Dry Port Muizen and Qualitynet of Intercontainer-Interfrigo with an inland hub in Metz-Sablon).

Until half of the 1990s, only national rail companies and Intercontainer provided regular rail services to the hinterland. The gradual liberalization of the EU rail sector allowed some new entrants, who buy capacity from the national railway companies and sell it to their customers. New rail operators in Antwerp and Rotterdam include sea carrier combinations (e.g. European Rail Shuttle - a joint venture between Maersk SeaLand and P&O Nedlloyd), some new licensed rail operators (e.g. Short Lines and ACTS), operators of inland rail terminals (e.g. ECT Venlo and Rail Terminal Born) and former members of ICF who decided to start their own operations independently from ICF.

4.4.3.3. Structural changes in inland navigation in Antwerp and Rotterdam

Rotterdam is blessed with a central location at the mouth of the river Rhine. The port of Antwerp realized an excellent direct connection to the Rhine through the opening of the Scheldt-Rhine Canal in the early 1980s. Antwerp and Rotterdam are almost equidistant from the Rhine. The Rhine basin with its tributary rivers is by far the most important inland waterway in Europe. Nevertheless, inland waterway transport played a very modest role in the initial stages of containerization. Pioneers in barge container transport such as Koeningsfeld and NRM (Nieuwe Rijnvaart Maatschappij) carried small containerized volumes at irregular intervals by conventional barges to conventional transhipment points on the Rhine. In the mid-1970s, liner container services by inland waterway developed gradually, based on the principle of line concentration within a particular navigation area (i.e. upper, middle and lower Rhine). Specialized container barge carriers arose in the mid-1970s to provide scheduled barge services from Antwerp and Rotterdam to a whole new range of inland terminals along the Rhine. No less than twenty new Rhine terminals were opened in the period 1980-1987. The growing realization of the potential offered by barge container shipping has led to a wave of investment in new terminals over the past few years, in northern France, the Netherlands and Belgium. The Benelux and northern France now have more than 30 container terminals (about as many as in the Rhine basin) compared to only six terminals in the early 1990s.

Antwerp and Rotterdam account for around 95% of total barge container transport to and from the European port system. In 2000, Antwerp handled a barge freight volume of 1,5 million TEU compared to only 128.700 TEU in 1985. The river-linked container business in Rotterdam reached an estimated 1,7 million TEU in 1999 versus 225.000 TEU in 1985.

A large proportion of the hinterland flows is generated by the Antwerp-Rotterdam route. In 1999, the volume of containers carried by barge between the two ports was around 680.000 TEU, representing a share of 77% in the modal split on this transport axis. Shuttle trains between Antwerp and Rotterdam carried 130.000 TEU in 1999 (Notteboom 2000).

5. Concluding remarks: containerization, port clustering and distribution

This paper has demonstrated how the containerization process materialised in Antwerp and Rotterdam. The focus was mainly on the container handling market or the loading and discharging of containers. However, it is crucial to realise that during the containerization process the functional focus of the Antwerp and Rotterdam port communities shifted somewhat from the pure loading and unloading operations to value added logistics within the port boundaries. Containerization has allowed Antwerp and Rotterdam to become important logistics centres. In the past, Antwerp developed its distribution function much more than Rotterdam, whose distriparks fill only part of the huge gap between the two ports in the field of physical distribution. Three Distriparks were built in Rotterdam from 1992 onwards. Distripark Maasvlakte, next to the ECT container terminal on the Maasvlakte, opened in 1996. The port of Antwerp has a rich history in distribution, supported by an impressive supply of covered warehouse facilities. The growing container volumes in the port have increased the supply of distribution facilities for containerized cargo (e.g. consumer products, sportswear, ..). There are several advantages in attracting port-related distribution activities: an additional flow of goods, additional value added and extra employment.

The container activities in Antwerp and Rotterdam have also triggered huge logistics developments in the hinterland and vice versa. Logistical spill-over zones of Rotterdam are located in Moerdijk/Dordrecht and Flushing. This process has been encouraged by the co-operation agreements between the Rotterdam Municipal Port Management and these logistics zones/ports. Locations on the axis Eindhoven-Tilburg-Venlo and the region Arnhem-Nijmegem have proved that they are in a good position to accommodate some European distribution centres and other logistics activities. The suburbs of Antwerp, the axes to Brussels and Ghent and the logistics zones along the Albert Canal to Liège have become other successful locations for European distribution facilities. These logistics sites and zones intensively use Antwerp and Rotterdam. More significantly, it is quite unlikely that they would have been located in the Benelux were it not for the seaports.

The functional interactions between Antwerp, Rotterdam and logistics zones in the hinterland have created a large logistics pole. Antwerp and Rotterdam are the central nodes driving the dynamics in this logistics pole. But at the same time Antwerp and Rotterdam rely heavily on the hinterland nodes to preserve their attractiveness (Notteboom 2000). As such, Antwerp and Rotterdam are becoming increasingly interrelated with each other and with other multimodal nodes. The future of Rotterdam and Antwerp is partly in their own hands, and partly beyond their control. Antwerp, Rotterdam and other nodes have become part of the same functional port cluster, notwithstanding the fact that each port has its separate port management staff and that competition remains fierce in many fields. The growing private company interrelations support the cluster idea. The resulting cluster effects allow companies to offer a more differentiated product to the customer and to optimise hinterland flows. The private sector has rightly assessed the increasing symbiosis among the nodes in the Rhine-Scheldt delta area.

This symbiosis also exists at the port management level. On the maritime side even simple forms of co-ordination can help to counterbalance carrier power. The port authorities of Rotterdam and Antwerp up to now have always limited their interactions to co-ordination on matters of mutual interest, for instance with respect to port policy outlines advocated by the European Commission. Although local interests are still important, Antwerp and Rotterdam are slowly disconnecting the private objectives from the public objectives by becoming more autonomous vis-à-vis the respective city councils and by creating separate commercial entities. It is likely that the increased networking capabilities of the port management will result in more co-ordination and co-operation in the port cluster. This serves not only the containerization process in the individual ports, but increases the logistical attractiveness of the whole region. Hence, it is needless to say that logistics and containerization are closely linked in the global economy.

References

Bird J (1971) Seaports and seaport terminals. London

Coppieters J (1968) Konventionelle Schiffsliegeplätze und Container Terminals. Beschreibung und Leistungsvergleich. Hinterland LVI: 53.

de Goey F (1990) Ruimte voor industrie: Rotterdam en de vestiging van industrie in de haven (1945-1975). Rotterdam

Gilman S (1977) The economics of port location in through transport systems. International Journal of Transport Economics, 4: 257-269.

Gilman S (2000) An evolutionary approach to large container ships. The World of Cargo Handling - ICHCA Annual Review: 41-44.

Hayuth Y (1981) Containerization and the load centre concept. Economic Geography, LVII: 160-176

Lim SM (1996) Round-the-World service: the rise of Evergreen and the fall of US lines. Maritime Policy and Management XXIII: 119-144

Nierop T (1996) Delta 2000-8: limitless container centre. Port of Rotterdam Magazine XXXV-3: 8-13.

Notteboom T (1997) "Concentration and load centre development in the European container port system", Journal of Transport Geography, V, 99-115.
Notteboom T (2000) De invloed van ruimtelijke en logistieke ontwikkelingen in het voorland-achterland continuüm op de positie en functie van zeehavens (met toepassing op het containervervoer in de Rijn-Scheldedeltahavens). PhD Thesis: University of Antwerp
Rotterdam Port Authority (1985 en 1995) Annual Report. Rotterdam
Rotterdam Port Authority (1996) Container Yearbook. Rotterdam
Slack B (1999) Satellite terminals: a local solution to hub congestion? Journal of Transport Geography VII: 241-246
UNCTAD (1985) Seminar on container terminal management. Antwerp
Van Driel H (1990) Samenwerking in haven en vervoer in het containertijdperk. Rotterdam
Wildenberg (1998) Het kaartenhuis van Rotterdam (unpublished)
Winkelmans W (1973) De moderne havenindustrialisatie. Antwerpen

Fig. 8.8. Container facilities in the port of Antwerp

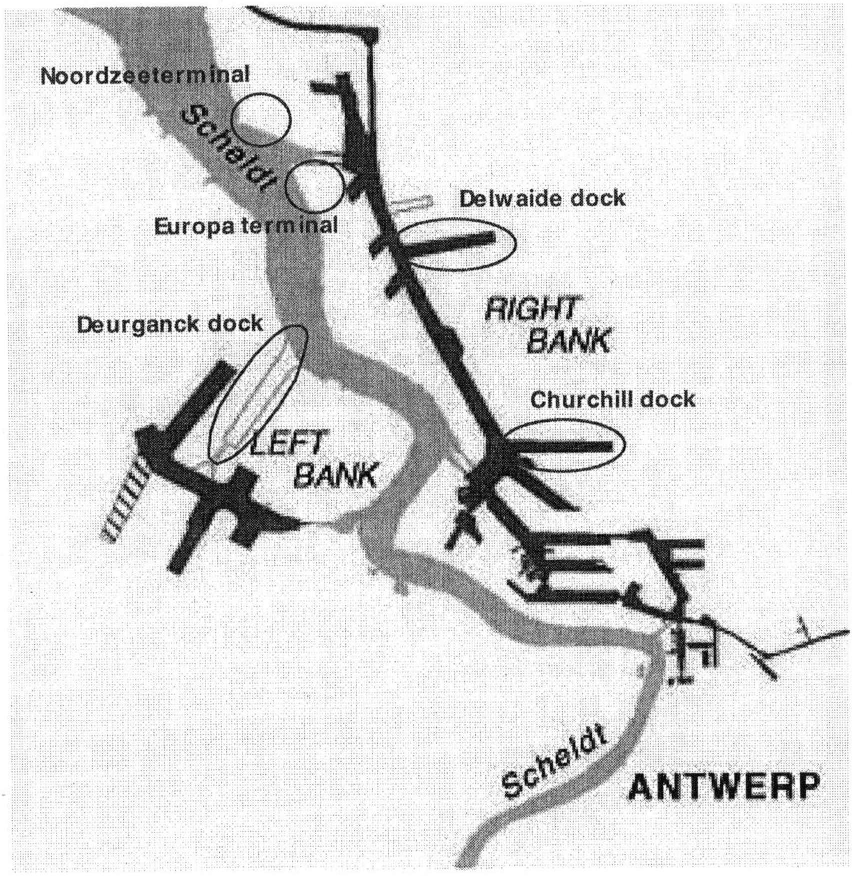

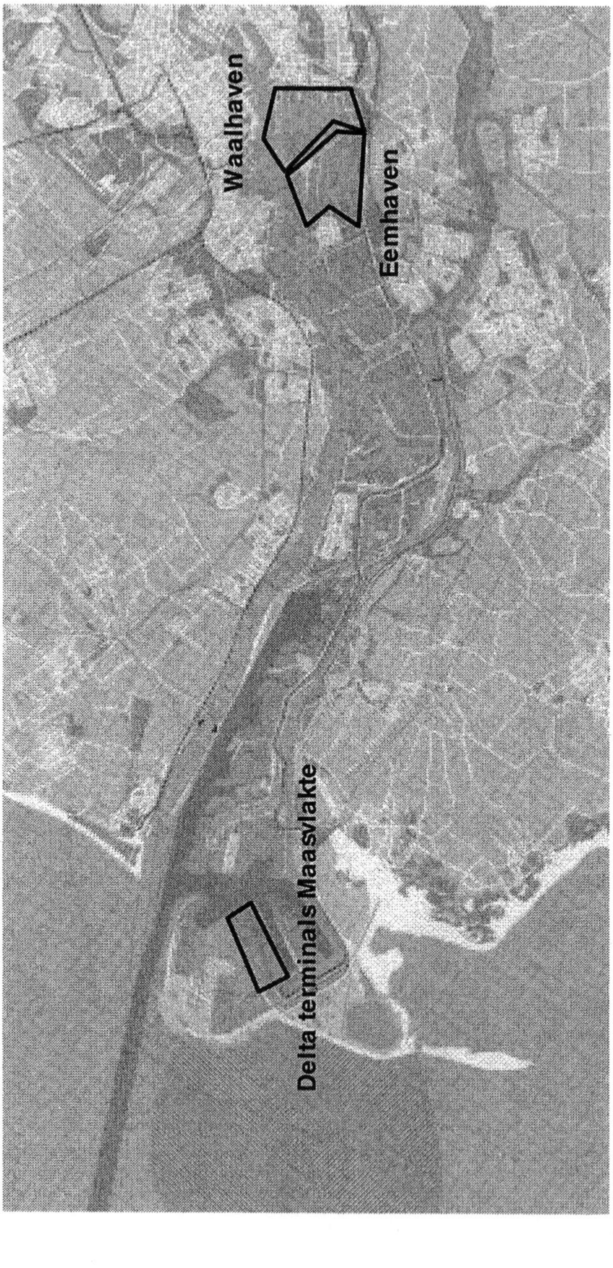

Fig. 8.9. Container facilities in the port of Rotterdam

The Kempen Nexus. The spatial-economic development of Rotterdam and Antwerp

Arjen van Klink

Rabobank Corporate Clients, Utrecht, The Netherlands

Introduction

From the dawn of modern industrialization, concentration and deconcentration of production have both had their effects on the spatial-economic landscape (Scott 1988). This applies to both urban systems (Van den Berg 1985) and port systems. While in the past, storage and distribution of maritime goods flows took place on or near the quays of a seaport, today these activities are often located at a considerable distance from the waterfront. Secondary centres arise around major seaports, resulting in port networks (Van Klink 1995). The process of deconcentration stems from diseconomies of scale in the ports combined with the changing location requirements of port-related activities and better accessibility of inland locations.

This contribution analyses the history of port development in Rotterdam and Antwerp from the perspective of the widening spatial scope of seaports. This perspective has been chosen because not only do both ports show spatial-economic spill-overs, but the process of spatial deconcentration of the two ports also results in the spatial integration of the port systems: some companies have established operations in both ports and several port-related activities located in the hinterland are orientated towards both Antwerp and Rotterdam. The interrelationship especially becomes clear in the location pattern of port-related activity in the crossborder region of Belgium and the Netherlands. We call this area, which consists of the Belgian provinces of Antwerpen and Limburg and the Dutch provinces of North Brabant and Limburg, the *Kempen,* the historic name of a part of the region.

1. Port development and location behaviour

Through history, port operations have changed and consequently the port's spatial structure has been transformed. In the literature on port development, various spatial patterns have been deducted and several models explaining the transition of ports have been developed (Bird 1987, Hoyle 1988, Hayuth 1981). Most of the models have a purely descriptive nature, based on changes in the physical structure of specific ports. A closer look at the descriptions of land use in seaports reveals that the location behaviour of port-related companies is a key determinant. Location behaviour is driven by structural breaks in economy, technology and society. These changes have an impact on a company's strategy and operations, which is reflected in increased mobility and new location requirements. Mobility is the propensity to migrate (Klaassen 1988); a high degree of mobility implies that the cost constraints for locating further from the quay are low and that the spatial tie to the port is weak. Together with the level of transport costs, an activity's mobility determines its spatial reach from the port. Whether fundamental developments indeed result in a new location behaviour is, in addition to location requirements and mobility, also determined by the availability of land. The supply of additional land is the outcome of a political process, which is also influenced by the structural breaks.

On the basis of fundamental changes and their impact on location requirements, mobility, and supply and demand of business sites, we have structured the development of the functional and spatial structure of seaports in four successive stages (see Table 9.1.) (Van Klink 1995). This generic framework makes it possible to understand the pattern of development of individual ports and to signal the transition towards another phase of development. As we believe that history serves as a guide for the future, understanding the spatial and functional development of a port in the past helps to identify relevant factors for the location behaviour of relevant actors in the port in the future. We extend the analysis into the future, as the fourth stage of port development is based on the rise of information and communication technology. The impact of this new development as yet allows only the most tentative conclusions.

The port city. The rise of overseas commerce is at the basis of the development of modern ports. The foundation of colonies can be considered a fundamental tendency that stimulates port development. At this stage, the seaport is a local cluster of trade, storage and craftsmen's manufacturing. Because the mobility of activities is rather low, all business is located in the port city, which has a market for most of the cargoes. The volume of throughput is only limited and is treated as general cargo. The role of the port authority, if it exists at all in this phase of development, is limited to providing nautical services and some basic infrastructure.

The port area. In this phase of development, the port has the characteristics of an industrial complex. Manufacturing activities with massive overseas goods flows are located at maritime industrial development areas outside the original port city. Port industrialization is driven by the strong demand for oil and petrochemical products, as a consequence of the growth in car traffic and general welfare. The throughput of bulk cargoes increases considerably and the facilities become more capital intensive. The port authority provides industrial sites and infrastructure.

Table. 9.1. Stages in the development of seaports

	Stage 1	Stage 2	Stage 3	Stage 4
Fundamental development	Rise of trade	Industrialization	Globalization	Informatization
Main functions of the port	Cargo handling Storage Trade	Cargo handling Storage Trade Industrial manufactur-ing	Cargo handling Storage Trade Industrial manufacturing Container distribution	Cargo handling Storage Trade Industrial manufacturing Container distribution Logistics control
Dominant cargo flow	General cargo	Bulk cargo	Containers	Containers + data
Spatial scale	Port city	Port area	Port region	Port network
Role of port authority	Nautical services	Nautical services Land and infrastructure	Nautical services Land and infrastructure Port marketing	Nautical services Land and infrastructure Port marketing Network management

Source: Van Klink 1995

The port region. The port has changed into a centre of container stevedoring, driven by the globalization of the economy as a fundamental development. The distribution of container cargoes is a new focus function. As containers are relatively mobile and container handling requires considerable land, container freight stations are concentrated at sites in the environs of the port. The regionalization of the port is also driven by the high labour costs in the port territory itself. In addition to its traditional tasks, marketing is given a prominent and structured place within the activities of the port authority as a response to the stronger port competition.

The port network. The port is the heart of a network that locates port-related activities in a number of logistics poles: distribution, trade and manufacturing. Secondary locations arise, because the port itself is confronted with congestion and land scarcity, while inland locations offer attractive locational conditions. In addition to containers, "data" becomes a new strategic focus. Given its centrality, the seaport can accommodate "virtual" services related to logistics and transport management in the network. Cargo flows are handled in the port network in multimodal operations, which further reduces the sense of distance. Coordination of location and infrastructure policies in the port network is a new task for the port authority.

The successive stages of port development show that the set of port functions is expanding and the spatial scale of the port is widening through time (Fig. 9.1.). Indeed, the increasing number of port functions, together with the growth of throughput, is a determinant of the process of spatial deconcentration, because it causes diseconomies of scale and thus stimulates port users to seek alternative locations. Moreover, the growing number of activities implies that guiding the process of port development becomes an increasingly complex task. That is reflected by the increase in the port authority's range of tasks.

The model described above is based on the development of Rotterdam. The following sections analyse the ports of Rotterdam and Antwerp together and look at their combined future. With the help of the above model, several topics are addressed and questions answered. For instance, what was the location pattern of port-related activity in the past? What stimuli were relevant? What are the differences and similarities in the spatial development of both ports? Is there any evidence of the rise of a port network in Rotterdam and Antwerp and do spatial patterns indeed converge?

Fig. 9.1. Spatial pattern of port development

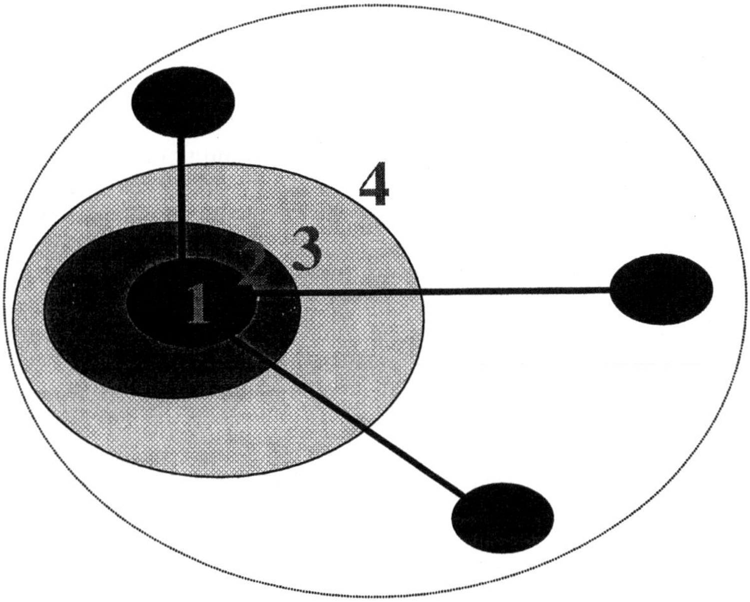

Source: Van Klink (1995).

2. Rotterdam and Antwerp in stage 1

The history of Antwerp and Rotterdam began along the river Scheldt and Rotte respectively. In the eleventh century, Antwerp developed as a town with maritime activity. Rotterdam originated at a fishery port one century later. The port was long overshadowed by Dordrecht and Amsterdam (De vries and van der Woude 1995). It only got a chance to grow into a commercial port when the city of Dordrecht lost its right to raise tax on cargo flows (staple place) in 1597. Moreover, after the closure of the Scheldt, traders from Antwerp fled to Holland, giving the trade in Rotterdam an extra impulse.

The foundation for their development into modern ports was laid when in the second half of the nineteenth century fundamental developments placed Rotterdam and Antwerp at the crossroads of growing international trade. The industrialization of the Ruhr area, and of the Wallon region for Antwerp, was crucial; the establishment of the iron, steel and coal industry stimulated imports and exports. Another fundamental development was the advent of steamships and the introduction of techniques for handling bulk cargoes. For Antwerp, the end of the "Scheldt toll", imposed by the Dutch, in 1863 was a political breakthrough (Delwaide 1963). The Franco-German war in 1870 was a stimulus to the traffic in the port of

Antwerp and the development of the railways in its hinterland. For Rotterdam, the Act of Mannheim (1886) that liberalized the traffic on the river Rhine was important. Thanks to the opening of the New Waterway in 1872, Rotterdam was able to further strengthen its position.

In the first period of port development, activities concentrated at the level of the port city. The mobility of activities was rather low. Alternative locations were difficult to reach because the inland transport system was very limited, making transport from the port expensive. Moreover, the mobility of labour was limited; dockworkers depended on walking or cycling to work because public transport was almost non-existent. This stimulated the development of living quarters in the direct vicinity of the docks (van der Hout 1992). The growth of business in the late nineteenth century led to the need for new land, both for constructing new docks and for building dwellings for new dockworkers from the countryside. In Rotterdam and Antwerp, new land was created by annexing surrounding villages. Delfshaven (1886), Kralingen (1895) and Pernis (1917) are illustrations in Rotterdam. In the case of Antwerp, Oorderen, Wilmarsdonk and Austruweel (annexed in 1929) are examples.

Additional capacity in the ports was not only necessary due to increased throughput, but also because the character of cargo flows had changed. From the mid-nineteenth century, the cargo base of the ports shifted from (former) colonial goods such as cotton, sugar, wood, and coffee to less expensive bulk goods such as coal, cereals, ores and oil. The latter were transported in bulk rather than general cargo and this demanded different handling in terms of quays and sites. In Rotterdam, port extension took place at the southern bank of the river with the Koningshaven (1874), the Rijnhaven (1894), the Maashaven (1905) and the Waalhaven (1930). With the construction of the Merwehaven (1932) and the first Petroleumhaven (1933), the port reached the municipal borders of the city of Rotterdam. Antwerp constructed the Kattendijk dock (1860), the Hout docks (1869) and the Merksem docks (1875) (Himler 1987). Major port works in Antwerp took place at the so-called "Noordergronden", north of the city itself, in the 1920s and 1930s (1st - 5th Harbour docks). Owing to its distant location from the city, the America dock was popularly called "Siberia dock" (van Cauwenbergh 1961). Given the strong growth of bulk cargoes in Rotterdam at the turn of the twentieth century, the change in the port layout manifested itself more clearly in Rotterdam than in Antwerp. With the newly constructed docks at the southern bank of the river, Rotterdam created a "transit port landscape" (Meyer 1997).

In the era before the Second World War, the intervention of the government in economic life in general and in port development in particular was rather limited. Local government took care of nautical safety and basic infrastructure, but a general strategy to stimulate port development was non-existent. A policy aimed at enhancing the economic contribution from the seaports only arose after the economic crisis of the 1930s. One reason was the sensitivity to the economic climate in Germany, given the transit function of both ports for that country. The involvement of the municipal government in port management was streamlined by the establishment of a separate port authority in 1923 in Antwerp and in 1932 in Rotterdam (one reason for establishing the Rotterdam port authority was the good experiences with a separate port management in Antwerp reported by Backx (Backx 1929).

Table 9.2. summarizes the changes in Rotterdam and Antwerp during the first phase of their development into modern ports in terms of land use and throughput. Both the beginning and end of this stage are arbitrary; the dates should be viewed as a longer period of transition.

Table 9.2. Key indicators of port development stage 1

	1870		1940	
	R'dam	A'werp	R'dam	A'werp
Gross area (in hectares)	700	340	2,100	1,400
Throughput (in million tons)	1.2	1.5	42.3	20.5

Source: Port Authorities

3. Rotterdam and Antwerp in stage 2

Port industrialization was driven in Rotterdam and Antwerp by the oil and petrochemical industry. Shipbuilding and food processing were traditional industrial branches in the ports. The development of processing industries in the ports ensued from the cargo flows that passed through the ports. Processing arose based on the availability of storage facilities. Fundamental developments influencing the spatial behaviour of port users were the invention of the internal combustion engine and the strong economic growth after the Second World War. This boosted the demand for petrol and petrochemical products and thus for refinery and petrochemical installations in the oil consuming countries, whereas before the war most oil was refined in the oil producing countries. An essential factor for locating oil refineries in Europe was maritime accessibility, as the growing volume of crude oil called for larger tankers (their maximum draught changed from 16.000 dwt in 1945 to 100.000 in 1960 and 300.000 in 1970).

Crude oil has been stored in the ports of Rotterdam and Antwerp since the nineteenth century. The America Dock was the location of oil storage in Antwerp, while in Rotterdam oil was stored and processed at the Sluisjesdijk. Because storage was increasingly combined with refinery, the oil industry required more land. Moreover, for safety reasons, oil storage and processing had to be located at a distance from other port operations and living quarters. Therefore, new plots of land were made available and a port area was created, which exceeded the territory of the original port city. In the case of Rotterdam, Shell opened its refinery near the village of Pernis in 1936. In the case of Antwerp, oil activities were initially relocated to the southern part of the city and, at a later stage, to newly constructed docks in the north, on the right bank as well as on the left bank of the Scheldt river. In Rotterdam, major port extensions were realized in the 1950s (Botlek) and 1960s (Europoort). The ten-year plan of Antwerp (1956-1965) was at the basis of the construction of new docks, such as the sixth Harbour dock, the Canal docks and the Churchill dock, as well as the construction of the Zandvliet lock. Between 1965 and 1970, industrial land in the ports of Rotterdam and Antwerp grew from 1,450 ha and 480 ha respectively to 2,075 ha and 1,925 ha. The port areas of Rotterdam and Antwerp were administratively integrated in the port city, and the newly constructed sites were managed by the port authorities. In the case of Antwerp, the annexation of Lillo, Berendrecht and Zandvliet (in 1958) provided the land for port expansion.

The development of the petrochemical industry in Rotterdam and Antwerp can be divided into three stages (see Fig. 9.2.) (Winkelmans 1973): the phase of petroleum (before 1960), the petrochemical phase (1960-1965) and the phase of chemical industry (from 1965 onwards). In Rotterdam, the rise of the petrochemical industry started earlier than in Antwerp and created a larger cluster of producers of basic petrochemicals than in Antwerp. The presence of Royal Dutch Shell, the rapid increase in the number of business sites for industrial development since 1950, and the excellent nautical conditions gave Rotterdam a competitive edge over Antwerp. Not for long, however. Antwerp also hastened to supply land, which it could issue to the chemical industry that ensued after the development of the refinery and petrochemical industry. Moreover, contrary to Rotterdam, producers could buy land in Antwerp. That appeared to be a crucial selling point for attracting huge investments from, among others, BASF and Bayer in the mid-1970s. The location of activities in refinery and chemical industry turned the ports into petrochemical complexes. Several activities were located in the ports not because of maritime accessibility, but rather because of (technical) linkages with other petrochemical producers. Thanks to the development of extensive pipeline networks, the maximum distance from the quay was extended and industrial activities could be located at sites without direct access to the water.

Fig. 9.2. The development pattern of the oil-related industry in Rotterdam and Antwerp

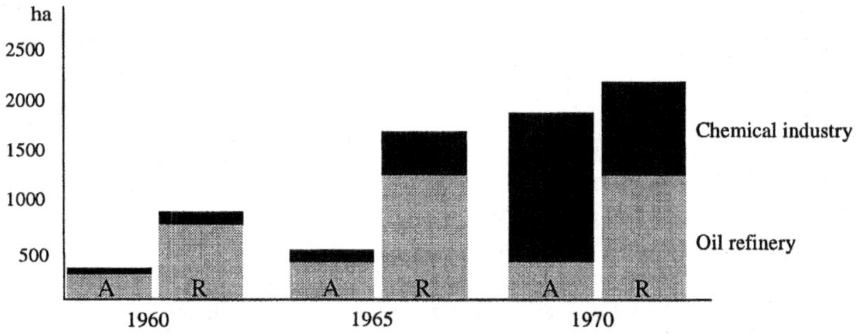

Source: Winkelmans (1973)

The different pattern of industrialization in the ports implies that Rotterdam and Antwerp have petrochemical complexes with a relatively high degree of complementarity. Several producers have facilities in both ports, managed jointly to optimise their total production. Since 1974, the Rotterdam-Antwerp pipeline provides Antwerp with crude oil from Rotterdam. In addition to oil, various raw materials and semi-finished products are transported between both ports. The development of petrochemical production at Moerdijk in the 1960s, halfway between Rotterdam and Antwerp, led to a further integration of both petrochemical complexes. The development of (petro-)chemical industries in Flushing and Terneuzen in the 1970s added to the interwoveness.

The earliest industrial activities met with opposition in the port community, as it was feared that those activities would cause congestion and would raise land prices. However, the crisis of the 1930s gave advocates of port industrialization a strong argument: industrial activities could help to bind cargo flows to the port and to reduce the port's sensitivity to economic cycles in the hinterland. In Belgium and the Netherlands, port industrialization appeared to be an important line of economic policy after the Second World War. Port industrialization changed the role of the port authority. It entered a new market of capital intensive activities and multinationals. The provision of industrial land was costly and risky, especially because the port authorities had to anticipate new industrial developments (de Goey 1990). Land leases became an important source of income.

Table 9.3. summarizes the changes in Rotterdam and Antwerp during the second stage of port development in terms of land use and throughput.

Table 9.3. Key indicators of port development stage 2

	1946		1970	
	R'dam	A'werp	R'dam	A'werp
Gross area (in hectares)	1,800	1,400	6,200	10,600
Throughput (in million tons)	5.8	n.a.	218.9	78.1

Source: port authorities

4. Rotterdam and Antwerp in stage 3

In 1972, the Maasvlakte added another 2.500 ha to the port of Rotterdam. While the Maasvlakte was built to provide additional space for the industrial complex in Rotterdam, the industrial climate changed dramatically as a consequence of the oil crisis in the mid 1970s and the changing community attitude towards further industrial development (Club of Rome) (Pinder 1980). The Maasvlakte came too late to play a role in the industrialization stage of the port, but it became the focal point for a new activity: container handling.

The first container box arrived in Rotterdam and Antwerp in 1966. The arrival of the container set a dramatic process of change in motion in many perspectives. Firstly, general cargo stevedores recognized the container as a substitute for their traditional markets and identified it as a growth area. Secondly, it appeared that the layout of port sites was no longer adequate. A container terminal takes more square metres of land and less metres of quay than a traditional terminal for general cargo. The port authorities and stevedoring companies consequently had to invest in new docks and container facilities. Thirdly, port competition intensified, as container cargo appeared to be more footloose than non-containerized cargo. Operations can be rerouted rapidly. This applies to both handling of container vessels and to loading and stripping of containers.

With respect to the attitude of stevedores, Rotterdam cargo handlers, more than their Antwerp competitors, seemed to have decided to put all their eggs in one basket. They rapidly concentrated on container handling and gradually neglected their operations in other segments of the general cargo market. Consequently, Rotterdam lost much traditional general cargo. One reason of the Rotterdam attitude was the tension between the stevedores and their dockworkers; mechanization helped to reduce the power of the labour unions. In line with the strategic choice for containers was the decision of several stevedores to establish a common container operator - Europe Container Terminus (ECT) - in 1966. The decision was made at the instigation of the Rotterdam port authority, as it had only one plot of land (the Eemhaven) available and it considered container operations to be too risky for a single stevedore (van Driel 1990). The monopolistic situation was reinforced by the merger between ECT and Unitcentre in 1984. In Antwerp, the operators and the port authority reacted differently to the introduction of the container: they invested in container facilities, but they also maintained their interests in general cargo. Moreover, in Antwerp, several container operators being active, container handling had an oligopolistic structure. Antwerp could remain competitive longer in non- containerized cargo thanks to its labour climate and the system of "Naties". However, containerization also changed the business structure here, as the traditional Naties gradually were replaced by the stevedoring concept and traditional general cargo by the container.

The difference in orientation on container traffic between Rotterdam and Antwerp resulted in a different growth pattern of the container throughput. Antwerp handled one million teu (twenty feet equivalent container unit) in 1984, while Rotterdam had already surpassed this figure in 1974. The difference is also illustrated by the different share of containers in the total volume of general cargo. In 1990, the general cargo throughput in Rotterdam amounted to 58 million tons, 51% of which was containerized; Antwerp loaded and unloaded 44 million tons of general cargo, 31% of which was containerized (van de Voorde en Dewulf 1993).

With respect to the land use, both ports heavily invested in container facilities. In Rotterdam, the Eemhaven was the earliest centre of container handling. In 1984, ECT opened its first terminal at the Maasvlakte, as the number of containers grew rapidly and carriers deployed larger vessels. In Antwerp, the Delwaide dock was the first location that was largely dedicated to container handling (1982). In 1990 and 1997 respectively, Antwerp opened the Europa terminal and Noordzee terminal at the Scheldt river. Today the container terminals in Rotterdam have a surface of 344 hectares and those in Antwerp 228 hectares. The overall productivity in terms of containers handled per hectare in Rotterdam is somewhat higher than in Antwerp, but the highly automated terminals at the Maasvlakte do not perform better than the newest facilities of Antwerp with their semi-automated layout (Notteboom 2000).

Containerization has had dramatic consequences for the port's labour force. Fig. 9.3. shows that parallel to the rise of the container, direct port employment in Rotterdam and Antwerp decreased. The container can be considered to be the most important cause of the job losses, although there are other reasons for the reduction of port employment as well, such as the loss of competitiveness of shipbuilding in Antwerp and Rotterdam and the mechanization in bulk handling and the petrochemical industry. The container drastically stimulated labour productivity in the ports and caused less work in general cargo. Labour conflicts were the result (Heygele 1982).

Fig. 9.3. Container throughput and direct employment in Rotterdam and Antwerp

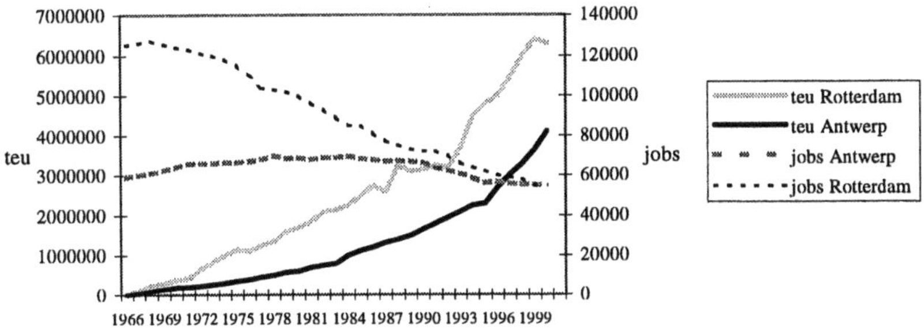

Source: Port Authorities (teu = twenty feet equivalent container unit)

The loss of employment induced the local governments of Rotterdam and Antwerp in the 1980s to develop a policy to generate more added value in the port. The focal point of these policies was the distribution sector. It was planned to raise the number of containers opened in the ports by distribution and assembly operations (Port of Antwerp 1995, Port of Rotterdam 1991). In the port areas several sites for container freight stations and distribution centres came available, such as the Logistics Parcs Zandvliet and Waasland in Antwerp and the Distriparks Eemhaven and Maasvlakte in Rotterdam. In 1995, the proportion of containers opened in the port of Rotterdam and Antwerp was 7% and 15% respectively (Notteboom 2000).

Despite the distribution parcs in the port area, the majority of business in loading, stripping and distributing container cargoes developed outside the territory of the ports. The choice for the suburbs was made for several reasons. Firstly, operations in container freight stations are relatively labour intensive, while dockworkers are costly and have a relatively inflexible deployment. Municipalities in the environs of the ports are not included in the regulations of the port labour agreement, so cheaper labour could be hired. Secondly, outside the port land costs were lower and, in the case of Rotterdam, land could be bought instead of leased. Finally, these excentric locations along the highways to the hinterland could offer better accessibility to the hinterland than the ports themselves. In the case of Antwerp, the business sites in Boom, Wommelgem and Waasland illustrate the rise of a port region. In Rotterdam, Spijkenisse, Ridderkerk and Albrandswaard are examples of excentric locations with a functional link to the port. The development of a port region, covering the jurisdiction of the port authority as well as several surrounding municipalities, can compensate for the sharp decline of direct port employment, as illustrated in Fig. 9.3.: a part of direct port employment was not actually lost, but transferred from the port to the port region.

With the development of a port region, the functional territory of the port (the spatial pattern of port-related activity) exceeded the administrative territory of the port (the area managed by the port authority), creating problems of coordination between the port and the surrounding municipalities. The case of Albrandswaard demonstrates that the development of the port region beyond the administrative boundaries of the port was not unproblematical. In the early 1980s, the port of Rotterdam decided to develop a Distripark south of the Eemhaven on territory of the municipality of Albrandswaard. Only after a struggle of years was it agreed that the port authority could develop the business park, but it remained in the jurisdiction of Albrandswaard and the port authority had to invest in a green buffer around the business park (Van Klink 1995).

Table 9.4. gives a summary of the development of Antwerp and Rotterdam in the third stage of port development.

Table 9.4. Key indicators of port development stage 3

	1970		1995	
	R'dam	A'werp	R'dam	A'werp
Gross area (in hectares)	6,200	10,600	8,700	14,055
Throughput (in million tons)	218.9	78.7	282.3	106.5

Source: port authorities

5. Rotterdam and Antwerp towards stage 4

Between 1990 and 2000, the average annual growth rate of container throughput in Rotterdam and Antwerp was 7% and 12% respectively. The massive increase of container volumes has been primarily caused by the strong growth of international trade, based on liberalization and globalization of the world economy. Another determinant is the efficiency of container transport, in which global container carriers increasingly have a dominant voice. These shipping lines not only control the maritime leg of the transport chain, they also control port operations through their own terminals and inland transport through their involvement in shuttle services. Bypassing merchant haulage, they meet with global logistics service providers that are also striving for chain leadership.

Information and communication technology enables the integration of the transport chain, which is stimulated by new logistics demands and concepts. Examples are the centralization of distribution operations from national to European levels and the introduction of just-in-time delivery. Information and communication technology - such as SEAGHA in Antwerp - simplifies document flows and facilitates tracing and tracking of individual shipments. Moreover, it contributes to the rise of multimodal transport by combinations of barge, rail and truck transport. With its historically strong focus on the railways, Antwerp has become a hub in a network of rail services. Rotterdam has a stronger position in container barge operations on the Rhine than Antwerp, although the modal share of rail transport has risen in the last few years and Antwerp also has a considerable traffic in inland shipping of containers.

The "informatization of transport and logistics" changes the role of seaports such as Antwerp and Rotterdam. From locations where the transport route is interrupted for technical and commercial reasons, they have become efficient links in integrated logistics operations where disruption is minimized by sophisticated technology and extensive infrastructure. Together with the rise of multimodal transport, the informatization of transport and logistics dramatically enhances the mobility of port-related activities and thus reduces the physical relationship with the quay. For some categories of port-related activity, especially those with a high inland traffic intensity and high labour intensity, being located in the port is no longer necessary or even desirable (Kuipers 2000). Consequently, a process of deconcentration from the port to the hinterland ("subharborization") (Buck Consultants 1996) is set in motion. Push factors - locational bottlenecks stimulating relocation from the port - are traffic congestion, high land costs and inflexible labour conditions in the port region. Pull factors - locational advantages in surrounding regions attracting business from the port - are the reversal of the location disadvantages of the ports together with a better centrality in Europe and a better quality of living.

The process of spatial deconcentration especially becomes clear in the location pattern of European distribution centres (EDCs). The majority of these centres is located in the Benelux and concentrated in regions in the surroundings of the ports of Antwerp and Rotterdam (and the Brussels and Amsterdam airports). Focal point is the area that we call the "Kempen" in the borderland of the Netherlands and Belgium. Examples of EDCs in this area are Nike (Meerhout), Chrysler (Puurs), Duracell (Heist op den Berg), Chrysler (Diest), Adidas (Moerdijk), Nashuatex (Roosendaal), Daewoo (Breda), Samsung (Tilburg) and Lexmark (Venlo). Companies located in the Kempen region profit from the vicinity of both ports. Many consider Rotterdam and Antwerp as part of one port complex; they pursue a multiport focus and determine the routing of their cargoes on purely rational grounds: sometimes containers arrive in Rotterdam, sometimes in Antwerp. The equivalence between Rotterdam and Antwerp is enhanced by tariffs for inland transport that come close to each other (moving a container from Rotterdam or Antwerp to a place in the Kempen costs some 150 EURO and 130 EURO respectively).

With the dynamics in the transport industry, Fig. 9.4. illustrates the rise of a port network in the case of Rotterdam; it appears that while inland regions have shown considerable growth of jobs in the transport and distribution industry, the port region itself has lost employment. In Antwerp, the relocation process seems to be less forceful than in Rotterdam, but even in the case of Antwerp surrounding regions have located logistics companies (Notteboom 2000). One reason for the limited off port location in Antwerp is its role in the storage of goods traded at futures markets, such as coffee and cacao. Futures markets require the goods to be stored within the administrative borders of designated ports in order to safeguard product quality.

Fig. 9.4. Regional dynamics in the employment of transport and distribution (1987=100)

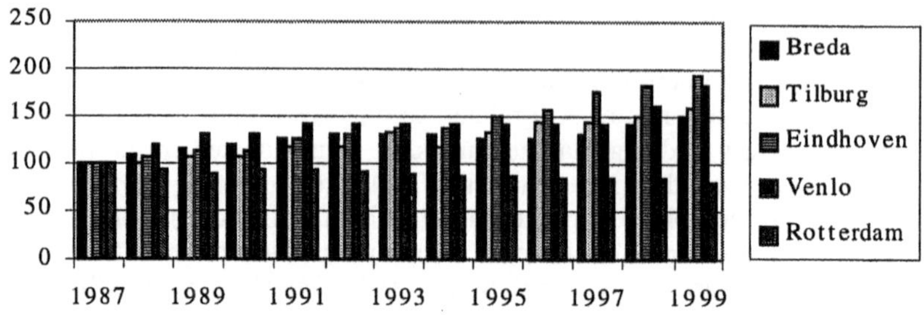

Source: CBS

In addition to the location behaviour of EDCs, the spatial integration of the ports of Rotterdam and Antwerp can be illustrated by the inter-port traffic; for instance, boxes arriving in Rotterdam continue their journey to the hinterland on a rail shuttle from Antwerp. The inter-port traffic is stimulated by so-called port equalisation schemes of container carriers, with which they balance their transport flows between the ports. Total container traffic between Rotterdam and Antwerp amounted to 881.000 teu in 1999 (Notteboom 2000). The intensity of traffic between both ports has increased strongly in the last decade. This is particularly true for inland shipping. The volume of containers shipped by barges grew from some 19.000 teu in 1981 to 680.000 teu in 1999 (van den Arend et al. 2000).

The development of multimodal transport is an important determinant for the rise of a port network. In the case of Rotterdam, the establishment of a rail terminal in Venlo, operated exclusively by ECT, has enabled Venlo to make a great leap forward in the development of its logistics pole (van Klink 1995). The terminal was opened in 1982 and significantly improved the access to Venlo from Rotterdam. As a result of this "time-space convergence", numerous value-added logistics services have been located in the city. Between 1985 and 1994, an area of one million square meters has been issued to the logistics industry. The newly established companies included Rotterdam-based forwarders that chose to extend their operations in Venlo rather than in the port region itself. The lobby of Venlo for rerouting the Iron Rhine - the historical railway from Antwerp to Germany that is being reopened - to pass by the city illustrates that logistics companies in Venlo concentrate on the port of Antwerp as well.

While inland locations become attractive for port-related companies, some business sites in the port become obsolete, because their spatial and maritime configuration has become outdated. This brings new challenges to the port cities. In line with waterfront redevelopment elsewhere, Antwerp and Rotterdam are putting a lot of effort into renovating docks for new purposes. Examples are the Bonaparte dock in Antwerp and the Leuvenhaven in Rotterdam and, with a more strategic focus and a much larger volume of new buildings, the Kop van Zuid in Rotterdam. In addition to new dwellings, the focus of waterfront redevelopment is especially on offices in order to benefit from the rise of the information economy and to find a new balance in the economic structure of the port city (Meyer 1999). The creation of an attractive location climate for office activities is, among other things, intended to anticipate the development of new high-grade services based on the informatization of transport and logistics. Fourth-party logistics service providers - organising and managing complete logistics chains - are examples, as are software bureaus and providers of training services. However, in practice it appears that the port cities have to compete with Amsterdam and Brussels on the one hand and logistics poles in the hinterland, such as Venlo, on the other. The capital cities offer a more attractive international living climate, while the logistics poles have much state-of-the-art logistics knowledge available (de Haan 1998).

The changing spatial-economic setting with which the ports are confronted induce the port authorities to reconsider their position. Firstly, the provision of conditions for a viable port economy is shifting from nautical services and physical infrastructure to a broader package that includes information services, logistics engineering, multimodal transport services, and business development support. Secondly, these conditions should be offered to clients within the port and, at the level of the port network, outside the traditional territory of the port management as well. To cope with those challenges, the Antwerp and Rotterdam port authorities seek to position themselves at one remove from local government in order to create more freedom of action. In Antwerp, the port management was corporatized in 1998, while in Rotterdam the discussion on the future constellation of the port authority began in 2001.

The fact that traditional boundaries no longer apply is illustrated by the development of partnerships among port authorities and the investments of stevedores outside their home ports. An example of the latter is the decision of Hessenatie to exploit a deepsea containerterminal in Flushing ("The Maasvlakte of Antwerp") and the investments of ECT in inland terminals in Willebroek and Duisburg. The Rotterdam port authority has developed several cooperative ventures with, for example, the ports of Flushing and Terneuzen, to benefit from the integration of the port economy in the Rhine Scheldt Delta region.

Conclusions

The analysis of Rotterdam and Antwerp from a spatial-economic perspective shows that the ports have much in common. *Grosso modo*, both ports can be placed in the same model of port development. Structural breaks in economy, technology and society have left their traces in both port communities. Despite often-cited cultural and socio-economic differences between both countries, the location behaviour of port-related activities changed in the same way and the port management of Rotterdam and Antwerp developed comparable strategies to adapt to new circumstances. This applies to both the port industrialization in the 1960s and the orientation on value added activities in the 1980s and 1990s. Moreover, in line with the theoretical model, both ports exhibit a widening spatial scale of activity. The similar (hanseatic) orientation on competitiveness - to attract new business and cargo flows by providing infrastructure, business sites and competitive services - can be considered to be at the heart of the common development pattern.

However, below the surface of commonality, various differences in the spatial and functional development and its stimuli can be identified as well. In Rotterdam, the development of the petrochemical industry started earlier thanks to the rapid availability of industrial land. However, Antwerp was able to develop much more industrial land, as it could use rural land while Rotterdam had to undertake more costly construction works. Although the ports service a similar hinterland, they have different relationships: Rotterdam still depends on the river Rhine, while in Antwerp the railways are crucial for its relationship with the German hinterland, although here inland shipping is also important. In Antwerp, containerization followed a more gradual path than in Rotterdam, because the Antwerp Naties had a more viable position in general cargo, in part thanks to the more flexible labour force and their traditional orientation towards cargo flows rather than vessels (van Driel 1994). This situation is also a determinant of the slower deconcentration in Antwerp compared to Rotterdam up to now. Besides, the policy of the Dutch government to stimulate inland locations and to create a structure of transport nodes has also contributed to the relatively strong development of a port network in the case of Rotterdam.

Despite the weaker process of spatial deconcentration in Antwerp, both Antwerp and Rotterdam increasingly have a common region in their hinterland where port-related activities, such as European Distribution Centres, are located. Both ports consequently meet in the "Kempen". Kuiler (1967) already stated that national boundaries are a bottleneck in the development of a common port complex in the Rhine Scheldt Delta. The present dynamics in transport, logistics and industrial activities call once again for the demolition of those boundaries in order to develop a common vision on the future of both ports on the basis of the strong parallels of their past.

References

Backx J (1929) De haven van Rotterdam: onderzoek naar de oorzaken van haar economische betekenis in vergelijking met Hamburg en Antwerpen. Rotterdam

Bird J (1987) Seaport and seaport terminals. London

Buck Consultants International (1996) Seaports and their hinterland. Nijmegen

de Goey F (1990) Ruimte voor industrie. Rotterdam

de Haan P, van Klink HA, van Winden W (1998) Logistieke ketenregie: van pretentie naar praktijk. Rotterdam

de Vries J, van der Woude A (1995) Nederland 1500-1815 – de eerste ronde van moderne economische groei. Amsterdam

Delwaide L (1963) De vrijkoping van de Scheldetol. In: Antwerpen, IX-2: 41-50.

Hayuth Y (1981) Containerization and the load centre concept. In: Economic Geography, LVII-2: 160-176

Heygele Y (1982) Meer loon voor minder werk – arbeidersstrijd in de Rotterdamse haven 1960-1980. Rotterdam

Himler A (1987) De Antwerpse haven vanaf de Franse periode. In: de Nave F (ed.), Antwerpen, een geschenk van de Schelde, Tijdschrift van het Gemeentekrediet, CLXXXV-3: 33-56.

Hoyle BS (1988) Development dynamics at the port-city interface. In: Hoyle BS, Pinder DA, Husain HS (eds.) Revitalising the waterfront, international dimensions of dockland redevelopment. London

Klaassen LH (1988) Exercises in spatial thinking. Aldershot

Kuiler H (1967) Deltahavens: polen in een krachtenveld. In: Tijdschrift Vervoerswetenschap III-4: 312-325.

Kuipers B (2000) Havenplan 2010: weg van de Maasvlakte? In: Tijdschrift Vervoerswetenschap, XXVIII-1: 74-92

Meyer H (1999) City and port – urban planning as a cultural venture in London, Barcelona, New York and Rotterdam. Utrecht

Notteboom T (2000), De invloed van ruimtelijke en logistieke ontwikkelingen in het voorland-achterland continuüm op de positie en functie van zeehavens. Antwerpen

Pinder DA (1980) Community attitude as a limiting factor in port growth – the case of Rotterdam. In: Hoyle BS, Pinder DA (eds.) Cityport industrialization and regional development. Oxford

Port of Antwerp (1995) Masterplan. Antwerp

Port of Rotterdam (1991) Port Plan 2010. Rotterdam

Scott AJ (1988) Metropolis – from the division of labour to urban form. Berkeley

van Cauwenbergh G (1961) Antwerpen – de haven. Antwerpen

van de Voorde E, Dewulf B (1993) Maritieme ontwikkelingen en het effect op de havencompetitiviteit: een toepassing voor de haven van Antwerpen. In: Blauwens G, de Brabander G, van de Voorde E (eds.), De dynamiek van een haven. Kapellen

van den Arend M (et al.) (2000) Waterlogistiek – vaart in de ruimtelijke ontwikkeling van logistieke dienstverlening. Utrecht

van den Berg L (1985) Urban systems in a dynamic society. Aldershot

van der Hout A (1992) De sociale quaestie. In: de Klerk L, Moscoviter H, En dat al voor de werkende klasse – 75 jaar volkshuisvesting in Rotterdam. Rotterdam

van Driel H (1990) Samenwerking in haven en vervoer in het containertijdperk. Delft

van Driel H (1994) Verschillen tussen Rotterdam en Antwerpen zijn historisch bepaald. In: Nieuwblad Transport, 26 april 1994

van Klink HA (1995) Towards the borderless mainport Rotterdam – an analysis of functional, spatial and administrative dynamics in port systems. Amsterdam

Winkelmans W (1973) Moderne havenindustrialisatie. Rijswijk

The Antwerp port: elements of spatial planning

Jan Blomme

Antwerp Port Authority, Belgium

1. Historical and geographical situation

Antwerp is an outspoken inland port, located along the river Scheldt at about ninety kilometres from the North Sea. In the sixteenth century, the city was the unrivalled centre of international trade. Due to religious wars, the Scheldt and thereby the city's access to the sea, was blocked in 1585. It would take until the nineteenth century before the river was reopened to shipping again. From that moment on the expansion of the port and its activities rapidly gained momentum.

In the earliest days, ships moored alongside the quays situated near the town centre. However, both the considerable tidal movement (actually amounting to five metres near Antwerp) and the lack of handling capacity alongside the city quays, led to the construction of a series of docks in the beginning of the nineteenth century. During the twentieth century the docks were expanded at the Right Bank of the river Scheldt to the north of the city. When at the end of the 1960s the area was almost used completely, the construction was started of a new harbour area at the Left Bank of the river. The reasons for the expansion of the port to the north were obvious. The low-lying polder lands were particularly suitable for docks, while at the same time the area was relatively scarcely populated. Moreover, the downstream expansion of the port alongside the river corresponded to the increase in size of sea-going vessels.

The rapid expansion of the port in the afterwar period was based on a concept of planning that made a clear distinction between industrial and transhipment areas. This implied that transhipment companies were concentrated in the outer parts of the harbour. Similarly, port-related industries were located in the centre of the port area, as far as possible from urban areas for reasons of environmental effects and safety. For the latter industries, the area between the docks and the river Scheldt turned out to be the most suitable location.

2. The evolution towards a multifunctional port

During the past fifty years, in terms of value added and employment, the port of Antwerp changed from a classical transhipment port towards a multifunctional one. In the latter, the classical function of transhipment is complemented by a large range of logistical services (storage, distribution, VAL and semi-industrial activities) as well as by port-related industries.

The afterwar expansion of the port of Antwerp on the Right Bank of the river Scheldt gained momentum with the Ten-Year Plan (1956-1965). Transhipment traffic almost tripled between 1950 and 1975 (from 21 million tons to 60,4 million, i.e. an annual growth rate of 4,3 %). The remarkably fast growth before 1975 relates to the extraordinary economic growth in that period, known as "Silver fifties" and "Golden sixties". It can be attributed most of all to the sharp increase in imports of raw materials and fuel (ore, coal and most of all crude oil) for the expanding manufacturing industries.

After 1975, the growth in maritime traffic was marked by a moderate slowdown (from 60,4 million tons of transhipment in 1975 to 130,5 million in 2000, i.e. an annual increase of roughly 3,1 %). The nature of the post-1975 growth, however, differed considerably from the previous period. The driving force behind growth in the past few years consisted of general cargo, that is mainly consumer goods and semi-finished products. Containerized general cargo in particular, recorded spectacular growth rates, more than doubling its volume in the seven-years period between 1993 and 2000. The evolution of these categories generally exhibits a steady upward trend. The volume of solid bulk cargo, on the other hand, hardly grew or even stagnated.

Fig. 10.1. Transshipment Antwerp 1975-2000 (tonnes)

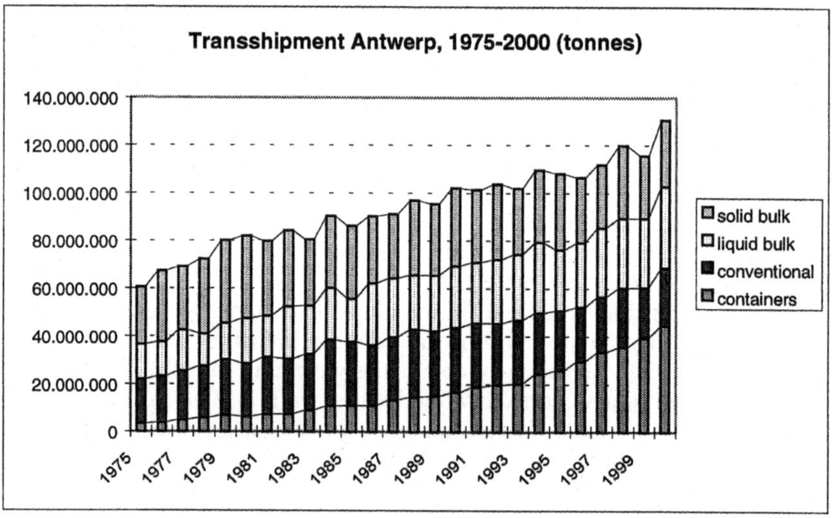

Source: Antwerp Port Authority

The afterwar period at the same time meant a break-through as far as the presence of manufacturing industries was concerned: a considerable part of the newly opened areas were occupied by petrochemical industries. Thus the industrial area in the port increased from roughly 300 ha shortly after the Second World War, to about 3.000 ha in the mid 1990s.

3. Consequences for the lay-out and policy of the port

After 1975 the general cargo sector continued its development, requiring more and more space area for transhipment. The marked increase in scale of maritime traffic also led to a rising demand for larger areas for transhipment, storage and distribution, in order to meet the steady increase in the size of cargo handled. More particularly, stevedoring companies in the general cargo sector saw a rapid expansion of their activities as consumer goods increased their share in international trade. As a consequence, the last remaining areas on the Right Bank were developed into an important transhipment and distribution centre (*Delwaidedok*, opened up in 1982). Thereafter this evolution was continued on the Left Bank (*Vrasenedok* developed in 1990).

A remarkable feature in this development is the trend towards larger terminals in terms of surface. Until the Second World War quays generally didn't exceed a depth of 100 metres. During the period of the Ten-Year Plan these depths increased to 270 meters. From 1980 on, inland depths varying between 500 and 700 metres were very common. This increase of the surface of terminals offered the possibility for an integrated handling of cargo, in which logistical services and semi-industrial activities were added to the classical transhipment operations.

A second, and related, feature is the gradual disappearance of the classical "*multi-purpose* conventional cargo" terminal in favour of modern and highly specialized ones (most of all container terminals, but also those equipped with special superstructures for steel products, forest products, kaolin, fruit, coffee, sugar, petrochemical products, scrap, fertilizers, etc.). Since the specialization of terminals required specific superstructures, expenditures on investment and thus the commercial risks involved, increased considerably. Specialized terminals also required additional technical expertise, especially in the field of value added logistics. Mainly as a result of this development, the Antwerp Port Authority abandoned its active role in transhipment of goods gradually. As a result, the management of new terminals was exclusively granted to private companies and more and more municipal terminals were transferred into private stevedores. Consequently, transhipment on municipal terminals decreased from up to two thirds of all general cargo traffic in the mid 1960s, to almost negligible proportions today. Further, a number of areas were created situated around the terminals that were specifically designed for distribution purposes.

The increase in size of maritime shipping and the congestion of the existing locks necessitated the construction of a fourth sea lock, called *Berendrechtsluis* (1989), which today still is the largest lock in the world. The steady increase of the importance of rotation time for ships of the large international container shipping companies, led to the development of terminals situated along the riverbanks (*Europaterminal*, 1990, and *Noordzeeterminal*, January 1997), in order to cope with the tremendous growth of the container traffic. Actually, a specialized tidal container dock (thus without having to pass the locks) is under contruction (first terminals planned to open in 2003).

Last, but not least, the impressive growth of port-related industries completely changed the characteristics of the port. Right from the beginning, port-based industries started to occupy large areas, which at first were used only partially. This enabled the companies to expand their activities in later phases without requiring them to adjust their entire previous layout. As a result, the area of 2.900 ha occupied by port-related industries exceeded the area for maritime services in 1994 by almost 50 %.

4. The expansion of port infrastructure : more traffic with less infrastructure

As explained in the previous section, during the past one and a half century the Port of Antwerp went through a number of cycles of intense construction and expansion activity. The first small docks in the early nineteenth century, the construction of the docks in the area which is now called "Eilandje" (1860-1873), the straightening of the Scheldt quays along with the construction of the Amerika and the Lefebvre docks (1884-87), the lengthening of the Scheldt quays and the construction of the Albert dock and side docks between 1903 and 1914, the construction of the Kruisschans lock and the connected dock system (1928), the Ten-Year Plan (1956-66), the Delwaide dock, the river container terminals and the expansion of the Left Bank (1971-). A fascinating and fundamental policy question is whether that infrastructure has well been employed. Have the new docks and quay walls been utilized as intensively as has been the older infrastructure? Have possible productivity gains been made so that relatively more traffic could be handled with less means? Another related question is whether the extension of the Antwerp port in the past was inspired either by supply or by demand driven forces. In other words, was new infrastructure built in order to attract additional cargo or was it built with some delay in order to be able to handle an ever-growing cargo supply?

A development could be described as "negative" when the extension of the infrastructure goes faster than the growth of the cargo transhipment because this way there is a permanent situation of (partial) insufficient use of capacity.

A "good" development is a situation where the extension of facilities is circulating around the traffic growth curve. This means that at a continuing traffic growth, after some time the authorities take corrective measures and build sufficient handling capacity in order to meet future demand for transhipment facilities. The trick is (one can hardly call it exact science) to construct a "good average", not developing too much (spare)capacity which would be used insufficiently for too long ("not too much and not too little, not too early and not too late").

Finally the "ideal" or most favourable approach is a slower capacity extension related to a faster traffic growth. This means that important productivity profits are being made and that ever growing volumes are being handled with relatively less infrastructure. In other words, considerable savings are being realized on space utilization as well as on the means deployed. Here too some nuancing is needed: the "ideal" approach does not mean that no further extension of the infrastructural facilities is needed. Even in a process of constant technological innovation the physical possibilities per meter of quay length or per ha of storage space, will always be limited. And even if the "sky were the limit", in a given situation there will always be limits where the economic cost effectiveness is exceeded at a certain moment in time. These three variants are presented in the chart 10.2.

Fig. 10.2. Relation traffic evolution and supply of infrastructure

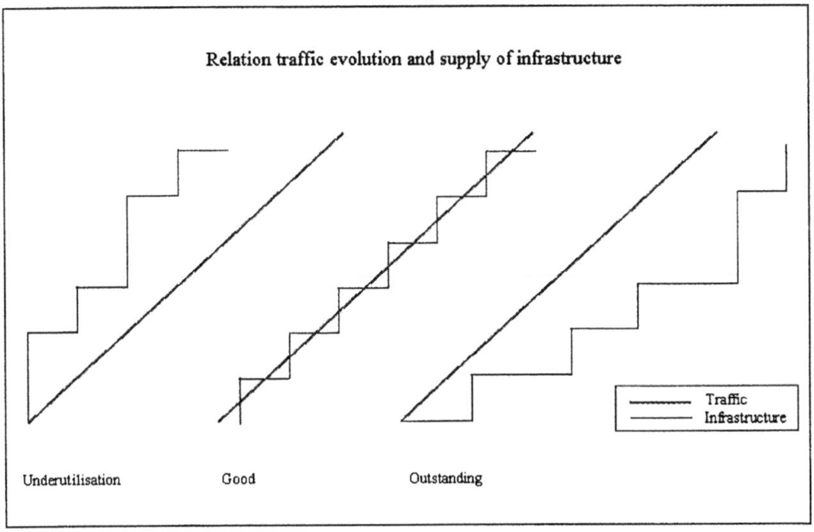

Source: own calculation

For the Port of Antwerp an exercise is made by comparing the increase of the maritime cargo turnover with the construction of new infrastructure, in this case the so called profitable mooring length (quay walls, slopes and landing stages or "jetties"). The results of this exercise are presented in Fig. 10.3.

The diagram shows that more than once in the past divergence between the evolution of realized traffic and the infrastructural facilities occurred.

The straightening of the quays in the years 1880 meant a tremendous expansion of the handling capacity that however coincided with the economic crisis of that time. The chart gives a distorted picture, because the straightening of the river quays was in fact a catching-up manoeuvre to meet the tremendous trade growth of the preceding years 1860.

As a result of the next economic recovery, the turnover increased again during the 1890s (with e.g. massive imports of cereals), and the construction of new infrastructure became necessary as from the turn of the century. These were the years when the Albert dock with inlet basins was dug. The pace at which the new mooring facilities became available now forms a stepped curve round the turnover increase.

Fig. 10.3. Comparison traffic evolution and quay length, 1875-1998 (1928 = 100)

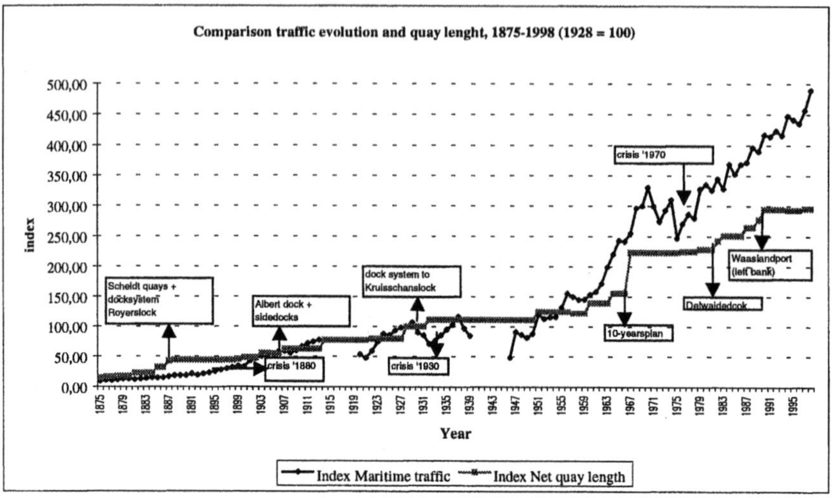

Source: Antwerp Port Authority

When after the First World War and the subsequent recovery traffic volumes increased strongly, a new large-scale project was started in the euphoria of the late 1920s (already prepared before the war). It comprized the construction of a dock system, starting from the Royers lock downstream in the direction of a new lock, the Kruisschans lock (now called Van Cauwelaert lock). In fact this was a "dock version" of the "Big Short-Cut", a (fortunately) never executed project to reposition the bed of the river Scheldt. Short after the start of this very large scale project, the big depression of the years 1930 reduced the international maritime traffic to a level never seen before. The result was an insufficient use of the brand new infrastructure. It was only used after the Second World War, during the rebuilding of post war Europe, for importing food and investment goods from overseas. Mid 1950s, an accelerated expansion of the capacity was carried out by means of the Ten-Year Plan, which could more or less keep pace with the explosive growth of the turnover (especially oil and coal). At the same time, a large area of land was opened up for the development of the petrochemical industry. After the regression of maritime turnover in the 1970s (Rotterdam Antwerp Pipe Line or RAPL and oil crisis) the growth of the turnover volumes in the eighties and the nineties increased much faster than the extension of the infrastructure (Delwaidedock, Waasland port and river container terminals).

Until a quarter of a century ago the strategy persued was mainly demand oriented and despite the unstable economic climate it was attempted to develop sufficient basic infrastructure to keep up with the traffic development.

The last twenty five years however were characterized by a much more efficient use of the newly built infrastructure than before. This remarkable increase of the infrastructure productivity is even more remarkable if we exclude liquid bulk turnover. In this case the "jetties" (mooring places for tankers) are excluded from infrastructure, but the full length of the slope docks (also Doeldock), which also have a transit function and are sometimes used for inland navigation vessels, remains considered in the infrastructure supply.

The results of this exercise are presented in Fig. 10.4.

Fig. 10.4. Comparison traffic growth (excl. liquid bulk) and infrastructure (excl. jetties) 1950-1998 (1950 = 100)

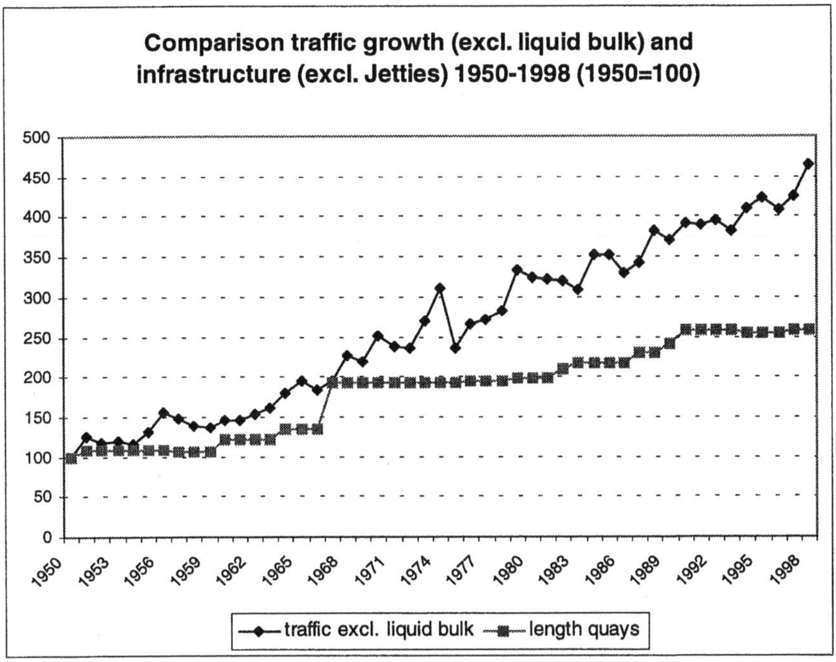

Source: Antwerp Port Authority

The chart shows that the length of the maritime infrastructure increased by only 25 % after 1970 whereas the turnover of general cargo and dry bulk increased by a factor 2.25 which resulted in a productivity growth of 80 % of the available capacity. When the surface area of the docks is taken as a criterion for infrastructure extension, the growth of the productivity slows down but still remains impressive. Through the construction of larger docks (in order to meet the increase in scale of the shipping trade), the dock area increased by approximately 50 % after 1970.

The main explanation for this remarkably improved utilisation is the containerization. Container vessels are loaded and unloaded faster so that their stay in the port is shorter which results in a better utilisation of the quay walls. On shore the container boxes can be stored more efficiently. At full container terminals per m of quay, performances of 9,000 tonnes/m are reached. At classical general cargo terminals this is only 900 to 1,100 tonnes/m, which demonstrates the enormous efficiency of the loading and unloading operations of container vessels. Also, in the field of land use container transhipment is relatively environment-friendly with performances of approximately 16.5 tonnes of general cargo/year/m2 at full container terminals arranged in accordance with the straddle carrier concept to approximately 30 tonnes general cargo/year/m² at full container terminals equipped with transtainers (i.e. automated storage space). This is two to three times higher than the average for the port of 6 to 7 tonnes of general cargo/m2 at classical general cargo terminals. This leads us to the somewhat surprising conclusion that probably the port, without containerization, would literally have reached its spatial expansion limits already.

A second related consideration is that, taking into account the limited expansion possibilities of the port, it might be an excellent choice to make container handling a spearhead of the future port development and port strategy.

Port authority cluster

Port and politics in Antwerp: a prudent approach

Frank Seberechts

Archive and Documentation Centre on Flemish Nationalism, Antwerp, Belgium

During the twentieth century, the port of Antwerp was one of the most important ports on the European continent, together with Rotterdam and Hamburg. There was considerable influence of national and international politics on the development of this port. Trade and port are the point where foreign and domestic politics meet. Consequently the development of trade policy and of the ports is fraught with controversy between nations, between the affected interests and policy makers etc.

It is important to reconstruct the ties and relations between the several players in the field. This is the key to understand why Antwerp went the way we know it did, leaving behind it the other ways of (non-)development. By tracing the life and the functions of the political and economic leaders, we managed to determine the important role of port firm managers in the catholic and liberal parties. These parties used to play an important role in Antwerp politics and in the development of the port - e.g.: the alderman in charge of the port always belonged to one of these two parties. Between the political and economic leaders there used to be a very intense circuit of informal contacts in cultural and social organizations.

There are also a second and even a third level of interference between politics and economy, i.e. the national and international level. Antwerp politicians and representatives of port, business and trade took part in the government's decisions concerning the development of the port. They also had their influence on the international level, sometimes even as participants in the talks between different countries. The Belgian government always had to bear in mind the interests of the port whenever it negotiated the economic and trade relations with other countries.

1. A network analysis of the Antwerp port: a theoretical approach

It is useful to make a network analysis in order to study the possible influence of the port and the trade circles on politics and government. By this you try to learn the actors' membership of different organizations or groups of interest. Thus you can get an indication of the possible and even the probable contacts between people. The analysis we made is not limited to the economic or port related organizations. We made some researches into judicial and cultural organizations and institutions as well.

The persons, who were the subject of our researches, played an important role in the political and economic - mainly maritime and port related - life in Antwerp. Most of them were member of the committee of the organization concerned. This was not entirely the case as for the cultural organizations: sometimes we included the honorary freedoms.

We admit that we cannot give you a complete survey. Some organizations were not taken into account; the sources are rather poor, indistinct and ambiguous. There has been little or no research on the Antwerp case. We can only give an impulse to it.

1.1. The interest groups

In a network analysis you make researches on the membership of people of different groups of interest. An interest group is an organization of persons having a common interest and trying to influence the political decision making to the advantage of these sectional interests (De Clercq and Naert 1985, 39). The interest group does not aim to obtain any political responsibility, but it tries to exert an influence on the political world. This process is called "lobbying".

Lobbying always occurs in two directions: to lobby and to be lobbied. This way an intellectual process is created, focusing on two needs. The interest group needs to reach a certain aim; the politician, on the other hand, wants to stay in power. There are different ways of lobbying (De Clercq and Naert 1992, 74-77):

An interest group may bring in votes needed by the politician in times of elections. In exchange for this support, the group expects the politician to defend more or less their interests. Thus the trade unions generally support the politicians having the same political colour. These politicians usually defend the trade unions' points of view in the political decision making process. An example of the twenties and thirties: Piet Somers was at the same time leader of the Belgische Transportarbeidersbond (Belgian Transport Workers' Union) and member of the city counsel, an alderman and a senator for the Belgische Werklieden Partij (Belgian Labourers' Party).

Because of their knowledge of a particular problem, the interest groups may procure some useful information to the politician. Organizations like the Fédération Maritime d'Anvers (Antwerp maritime federation) dispose of businessmen who were at work every day on the maritime problems. These men were able to take in at a glance the needs and interests of the port and the transport industry.

The interest group may contribute financially to the election campaigns of the politician. Often the campaign is paid, entirely or partly, by organizations belonging to the same ideological family.

The interest group may organise a strike in order to exert pressure on politicians to make some concessions or to defend its points of view. Examples: the general strike of 1936 and the Royal Question strikes of 1950.

Finally the interest group may participate in the party politics or even directly in the decision making process. Representatives of this group are invited to attend, as participants or as experts, to the international or social conferences. Several interest groups were involved in the social deliberations in the port of Antwerp.

1.2. The network

Network relations in fact are exchange transactions: you help a partner because you know you can count on him when necessary. The partner in such a network enlarges the possibilities to improve the position of himself, his business or his organization. He may avoid obstacles and learn some interesting pieces of news before his rivals may.

The interpretation of the network needs some qualification. On the one hand: every network is imperfect. It deals with a certain time span during which one has been a member of or a collaborator to one or another organization or institution. This may have happened in the beginning of a decade, but not at the end of the same. The indication of the participation leaves the intensity of the collaboration an open question: in every organization you have active and less active members, members of the committee, honorary members etc. It may even be possible that two people, belonging to the same society, cannot stand the fellow-member and try to avoid or even work against each other. Lots of contacts take place in an informal or even anonymous atmosphere, by means of telephonic contacts, scrawls or back-room conversations, the contents of which - if ever they happen - most of the time are unknown to the historian. The character of some organizations may change, as well as their relations to other organizations. Besides there is that threat of intrigue theories: the fact that two people belong to the same organization at the same time does not mean that they are at the origin of (the absence of) some events.

The presence, on the other hand, of persons, organizations and networks can be an indication of what may have happened. They create a background to an event or contribute to the explanation of what happens. The networks can help us to estimate a situation, to sense an atmosphere, to judge a society.

1.3. The participants

It is clear that the common memberships are important for this research. They show the possibility of contacts between business and politics. We chose to limit our research to the three "traditional" parties - liberal, catholic/Christian-democrat, socialist - because the levers of the political power were concentrated with these tree parties until many years after the Second World War. The other parties in fact were rather insignificant in Antwerp political life. The period we studied lies between 1920 and 1950: the rise of the port after the First World War and the twenty years of crisis till the beginning of a new golden era in the fifties.

We looked for members of the city council, aldermen, burgomasters, members of the province council, members of the chamber of representatives, senators and cabinet ministers, regardless the duration of the mandate. We also selected party militants: people who show their adherence to one of the political parties by participating in the elections. Sometimes we suppose that a relation exists, e.g. because of the collaboration with a newspaper or with an organization with strong ties to the party.

There were different organizations and institutions the politicians and the businessmen were involved with. We found memberships of the "Algemeen Belgisch Vakverbond" (ABVV), a socialist trade union. The ABVV arose after the Second World War, as a fusion of the pre-war socialist "Belgisch Vakverbond" with communist and independent leftist trade unions, to become an overall socialist organization (Huyse and Hoflack 1995, 178). The branch ("centrale") in charge of the port labour was the "Belgische Transportarbeidersbond" (BTB), founded in 1913 at the initiative of the "Antwerpse Zeemansbond" (Van Isacker 1966, 150). There were the "Association Maritime Anversoise", a local maritime organization, and the "Bond van Belanghebbenden van Dokken en Kaaien", an interest group that plead the cause of the users of the docks and quays. In the late twenties there was a "Commission d'Etudes concernant l'Administration de l'Escaut", a study commission on the Scheldt administration, in which businessmen and politicians met. The "Comité des Intérêts Maritimes d'Anvers" tried to defend the local maritime interests. The "Fédération Maritime d'Anvers" was established in 1901 to become the most important union of the port industries (Antwerpen 1960, 479). In 1930 the "Groupement des Agents Maritimes d'Usines", another business union, was founded (Antwerpen 1960, 481). There was the "Intercommunale Maatschappij voor de Linker Scheldeoever" (IMALSO), an interlocal organization for the economic and social development of the Scheldt left bank, established in 1929 (Denys 1980, 113). The first traces of the Antwerp Chamber of Commerce date from 1802: a chamber was established by Napoleon (Devos 1996, 1). It became one of the most important overall business organizations in Antwerp. Some businessmen were member of the "Ligue Maritime Belge" or the "Nationaal Verbond der Verzenders van België", maritime and shipment organizations. The "Union pour la Protection du Travail au Port" was a rather paternalistic social and economic society in the Antwerp port. The "Vereeniging van Belgische Reeders" was a shipowner organization. It was established in Antwerp in 1909 (Antwerpen 1960, 480). In 1945 the "Vereeniging der Expediteurs van Antwerpen" succeeded to the pre-war "Cercle des Expéditeurs et Exportateurs réunis" which was founded in 1905 (Antwerpen 1960, 479). There was also the "Vereeniging van Verzenders, Uit- en Invoerders", another shipment organization. The "Vlaamsch Economisch Verbond" (VEV) arose in 1926 to replace the "Vlaamsch Handelsverbond" as the Flemish employers' union (Luyten 1998).

Several businessmen acted as judges in the trade courts. In the Netherlands, the first trade courts were established in 1795, one of them in Antwerp (Van den Eeckhout and Vanthemsche 1999, 483).

Businessmen and politicians participated in the cultural and social life as well. The "Aéro Club, the Automobile Club" and the "Antwerp Aviation Club" were established in the beginning of the twentieth century to join in the modern trends of the upper classes driving a car and supporting aviation. "Beerschot" arose shortly before the turn of the century as a split from the "Antwerp Football Club", considered to be too vulgar. The new society disposed of a football team as well as tennis, polo, golf and athletics facilities, players and teams. "Mars et Mercure" was a circle defending the cultural, social and economic interests of former army officers who went into business. The "Cercle La Métropole" and the "Cercle Philotaxe" were clubs where nobility, higher classes and businessmen met. The "Rotary" service club got a first branch in Antwerp in the twenties. The "Zoologie or Antwerpse Maatschappij voor Dierkunde" dated from the nineteenth century and kept on managing the Antwerp zoo. Several organizations like the "Amitiés françaises" and the "Cercle français" together with the newspapers "Le Matin" and "La Métropole" testified to the flourishing French social and cultural life in Antwerp.

1.4. Politics in Antwerp (1918-1950)

Before the First World War, the city council of Antwerp consisted almost entirely of liberal politicians, due to the election system: 31 members of the liberal-socialist cartel, 4 liberals, 2 socialists ("Belgische Werklieden Partij" - BWP) and 2 catholics. After the war, the election system changed. This caused a complete change in the presence of the different parties in the city council.

There were three important parties: Catholics, socialists and liberals (Antwerpen 1960, 38-39). In 1921 and 1926 there was a split in the catholic party between the conservatives and the Christian-democrats. Twice the second faction made an agreement with the socialist party to rule the city. The Christian-democrat leader Frans Van Cauwelaert became the new burgomaster and at the same time the alderman in charge of the port. In 1933 socialists and liberals agreed to govern the city, with the socialist Camille Huysmans as burgomaster and the liberal alderman Paul Baelde in charge of the port. The three big parties decided to go together after the 1938 elections, maintaining C. Huysmans as the burgomaster and appointing the catholic Leo Delwaide sr. as the new alderman of the port.

After the Second World War, Antwerp was governed exclusively by the Belgische Socialistische Partij (socialists) and the Christelijke Volkspartij (Christian-democrats) during almost half a century.

2. Network analysis for the port of Antwerp

2.1. Network analysis for the port of Antwerp (1920-1930)

A network analysis for this period leads to several conclusions. Most of the representatives of the Antwerp trade and shipping obviously sympathized with the Liberal Party, though the Catholic Party managed to appeal to some of them as well. Not surprisingly the socialist BWP did not appear at all in Antwerp business life. The Chamber of Commerce and the "Fédération Maritime" were the two most important interest groups dealing with the port. Some representatives of the port bound economic life played an active role in the trade courts.

The Antwerp business life was a liberal and, to a lesser extent, a catholic matter. There certainly existed some contacts with the socialists, but probably within the framework of other organizations and institutions, such as the city council or the early consultation structures on social themes.

In social and cultural matters, the Antwerp port circles preferred to join the "Automobile Club", "Beerschot", the "Cercle artistique", the "Philotaxe" and the "Zoologie". People with catholic sympathies as well as with liberal ones liked to spend their leisure by supporting these organizations. Some businessmen and politicians seemed eager for collecting an impressive amount of memberships. People like the liberal shipowner and politician Léon Dens, his fellow party-members Louis Joris and Louis Strauss, and the catholic shipowner and politician Gustave Van den Broeck, all of them member of the parliament in this period, were able to show a large number of member's tickets. But less important businessmen and politicians were very active in cultural and social societies as well.

2.2. Network analysis for the port of Antwerp (1930-1940)

In the course of the thirties, the interest of the Antwerp port circles for the Catholic Party increased slowly. This may be caused by the action of F. Van Cauwelaert as the burgomaster and the alderman in charge of the port. While being into power he managed to prove that the catholic politicians ware able, too, to defend the interests of the port, the trade and the shipment industry. Yet the Liberal Party continued to obtain most of the sympathy of the Antwerp business circles. The socialists still were not able to penetrate in this part of the society. The political representatives of the BWP came from circles that were totally different from the Antwerp business circles.

The Chamber of Commerce of Antwerp and the "Fédération Maritime" continued to act as the representative organizations of the Antwerp port and trade circles. The "Vereeniging van Verzenders, Uit- en Invoerders" became important as well.

The scene of the social and the cultural life of the Antwerp politicians and businessmen in this period was laid in practically the same circles and societies as it was in the period before. Besides, the "Aéro Club", "La Concorde" and the newly established "Rotary Club" managed to attract the interest of these persons. Again we have to notice that there was little or no difference between the appearance of the liberal and the catholic clientele, and that there was no sign of the presence of any socialist representatives.

2.3. Network analysis for the port of Antwerp (1940-1950)

During the forties, some new organizations tried to conquer their place in the port of Antwerp. This was the case with the "Groupement des Agents Maritimes d'Usines" and the "Vereeniging der Expediteurs van Antwerpen". Meanwhile the Chamber of Commerce and the "Fédération Maritime" kept on playing their role as the main representatives of the Antwerp business life and port circles.

In politics the Antwerp port and trade circles still preferred the Liberal Party, although its importance in city politics diminished dramatically after the Second World War. It only came back into power in 1994. There was also some sympathy for the Christian-democrat CVP. There still was no interest at all for the socialist party in leading port circles.

Some changes occurred in post-war cultural and social life in Antwerp as well. The French speaking cultural life gradually fell into decay: the French clubs and *circles* lost their adherence. Instead the Rotary clubs welcomed more and more members. It strikes that socialist politicians such as burgomaster Lode Craeybeckx and province governor Richard Declerck joined in this society as well as liberal or catholic colleagues. It seems that for the first time the socialist manage to break out of their own groups and organizations and are accepted in the "higher" social circles.

Conclusion

The network analysis makes it clear that business circles, through the intermediate of several and different organizations and institutions, had contacts with the political world. This means that they may have had considerable influence through these organizations etc.

The interest of the Antwerp business and port circles for the Liberal Party turned out to be constant, probably even during the decline of the party after the Second World War. The Catholic Party - later on the CVP - gradually made up its arrears The socialist party - BWP, later on BSP - had to keep out of the economic strongholds. It was difficult to them to penetrate into the social and cultural elites as well. It was not before the end of the Second World War that the first impulses to this appeared.

We may conclude that contacts between businessmen and politicians with liberal and catholic sympathies were possible within the economic, social and cultural life that was flourishing in Antwerp. As yet the socialists were kept out of the game despite their important presence in the city council. If there were contacts with the labour representatives, then they took place in other places and institutions, such as the city council and the social negotiations, which became more important since the interwar period.

References

Antwerpen (1960) Antwerpen 1860-1960. Antwerpen

De Clercq M, Naert F (1985) De politieke markt. Deurne

Denys L (et al.) (1980) Tentoonstelling «Antwerpen 1830-1980». Antwerpen

Devos G (1996) De Kamer van Koophandel en Nijverheid van Antwerpen op de drempel van twee eeuwen. Antwerpen

Huyse L, Hoflack K (eds.) (1995) De democratie heruitgevonden. Oud en nieuw in politiek België (1944-1950). Leuven

Luyten D (1998) Vlaams Economisch Verbond. In: Nieuwe Encyclopedie van de Vlaamse Beweging. Tielt, p 3316
Naert F (1992) De uitgeperste democratie. Lobby's in actie. Leuven
Van den Eeckhout P, Vanthemsche G (ed.) (1999) Bronnen voor de studie van het hedendaagse België 19^{e}–20^{e} eeuw. Brussel
Van Isacker K (1966) De Antwerpse dokwerker. Antwerpen

The end of the sea

Henk Molenaar

Erasmus University Rotterdam, The Netherlands

1. The port-policy arena: the two main-actors

The historic position of most nation-states is that they wanted (and want!) to consider the seaports within their territories as "basic good". As a facility that is - under certain conditions - open for all potential (port)users on a non-discriminatory basis, at least for their own citizens. With the social goal to optimise the possibilities offered by unrestricted connections with the "outside world", not jeopardized by the self interest of individuals. Safeguarding this "open" character of their seaports was not only seen as a political desire but also considered as an executive obligation of the relevant governmental institutions. It made them important players in the port-scene. On the basis of this prime "public" interest in port-matters, gradually other public interests were linked up. Originally mainly related to generating public income by taxing the port-visitors. But also in a more indirect way by stimulating public feelings on collective pride and chauvinism about "our" port, or by creating public threat over other cities or regions located within the captive hinterland of "our" port. It is only after World War II that the public function of (sea)ports actively is enlarged to socio-economic matters. To use the port as instrument for economic policy. First of all to stimulate industrialization in the post-agricultural society, later on to stimulate employment and the generation of added value in the mature industrialized society and nowadays in the stimulation of value adding services in the post-industrial society.

The second main-actor in the port is the collective of private port-operators. Several models do exist about the division of port-related activities over governmental institutions and private enterprises. Sometimes based on the political system as such, but more often because of imperfections deemed to be present for the "other" actor. According to this line of thinking the required "open" character of the port makes it impossible in the eyes of the public actor to have the management of the - by definition restricted - capacity of the port-infrastructure in the hands of private business. Whereas in the eyes of private business it is undesirable to have the actual handling of cargo executed by bureaucratic governmental agencies. These more or less fixed negative feelings about each other are not merely an expression of general discontent. The two main-actors are in fact different. As can be seen from the totally different way they are reacting on changing circumstances.

In the public domain adaptation to changing circumstances is in principle re-active. At least 51% of the people must recognize the necessity of the change, and the process to reach that change is prudent and therefore long-lasting. The driving force is social change and the whole complex of all social changes is to be reached within budgetary limitations. In the private domain the simple objective is to earn money. It is not so relevant in this respect whether the beneficiary of the earned money is the director/owner (like for most stevedoring companies in Rotterdam shortly after World War II) or the workers (like for the "naties" in Antwerp until recently) or the shareholders (like for the big petrochemical and logistic industries in both Antwerp and Rotterdam nowadays). This gradual historic shift in the nature of the beneficiaries from individual person, to "internal" group and finally to "external" group, only implies that more attention is to be paid to the social limitations within which the earning of the money takes place. To remain competitive and thus to remain in the situation to earn money, the private company is to be pro-active. Either by improving its processes, for instance by making use of ICT or economy of scale, or by improving its products, by putting emphasis on revolving innovative activities. The allowable incubation-time for improvement is far more restricted than in the public domain, it being that the "scene" also is more restricted.

As far as ports are concerned the social goals of the governmental institutions are - at least - related to three fields of interest: safety and order, planning, and capacity-management of available infrastructure. The direct social contents evidently diminishes in the same sequence. No doubts do exist that safety and order, setting standards, enforcing rules and regulations, is a governmental obligation. For centuries already the Harbourmaster personifies this obligation as far as shipping is concerned. Just before World War II the planning-task evolved. Primarily spatial (and thus evidently belonging to the public domain), but later on also economic (and thus moving into the direction of the activities of the private enterprises). And the third mentioned task, the capacity-management of available infrastructure, comes even closer to the private domain, in particular when not concessions and permits but taxes, tariffs and rents are used as steering-instruments. Widening the field in which the governmental institutions were expected to be active entailed at the same time that the discipline of the market gradually entered the public domain.

Notwithstanding the paradoxical goals and limitations of governmental institutions as compared with private enterprises, in ports the two domains got mixed up to an ever growing extent. A number of examples in the field of logistics may elucidate the existing paradoxes and the "mixed up" counter-paradoxes:

- the mode of transport paradox; the public actors want a modal shift towards train, barge and coaster, whereas the private actors require a free modal choice, even so knowing that this free choice will mean more trucking;
- the parcel-size paradox; the private actors know that their customers ask for individualized services, whereas the public actors are in favour of massive and therefore not-individualized transport;
- the proliferation paradox; the public actors stimulate settlements in places where space is still available, or a "grand design" for the distribution of cargo

over the various ports, whereas the private actors only can live with a free choice;

- the employment paradox; to remain competitive the private actors are forced to make use of replacing activities to low wage countries or to "delabourize" their activities in the wealthy countries, whereas the public actors are willing to pay a lot of money to prevent loss of employment.

Following the same examples the "counter-paradoxes" are:

- for private actors, too, the reduction of trucking might become an option, either on the basis of costs (economy of scale) or on the basis of reliability (congestion);
- also public actors realize the force of individualization; the compromize might be a far more developed system for distribution and collection, making use of ICT;
- public actors are also discovering the advantages of concentration in clusters (less transport, concentrated hindrance);
- private actors accept as well that keeping alive of outdated industries is counter-productive and that stimulation should be directed to new knowledge-services.

This fragile equilibrium between the paradoxical and counter-paradoxical attitude of the two main-actors in seaports leads to a complicated and ever shifting interaction. Between the re-active approach and the pro-active approach. Between the long-term social goals and the short-term financial results. Between strict ruling and free enterprise. Between de-personalized equality for all and personalized equivalence of customers. Between long-lasting hierarchic structures and "fluid" networks.

In most ports there is a "gatekeeper" to regulate, or at least watch, the interaction between the two domains. Sometimes in the form of an official body, entrusted specific powers to influence both domains, sometimes in the form of a rather complicated institution, where the two domains meet, but mostly in the form of a governmental agency, that has learned to understand the private domain and that acts as a "window" for the public domain. Quite often these bodies, institutions or agencies call themselves port-authority. But most of them have hardly any formal authority over either of the two domains. Their authority is at best restricted - apart from the formal authority of the Harbourmaster - to the authority of their plans and their individual representatives.

Antwerp and Rotterdam are examples of ports where for a long period of time a municipal agency was (and in Rotterdam still is) acting as "gatekeeper".

Over the past decades the unmistakable trend for "port authorities" is towards privatization, or at least corporatization and commercialization. The pressure of the market, both regarding earning-capacity and avoidance of bureaucracy stimulates the movement of port-authorities from the public domain into the private one. Apart from these evident pro's there are, of course, also cons. The problem not being so much that executive tasks related to well described governmental obligations are outsourced to an actor in the private domain, but the safeguarding of public interests in general. For instance when dealing with developments in the field of perceived safety and order and how to interpret the monopoly-status that each port has for its catchment-area. To overcome this problem partly, normal practice for port-authorities aiming at privatization is to replace their existing direct governmental steering - via the port-authority being a governmental agency - by an indirect governmental steering - via the port-authority being (indeed) privatized, but with all (or the great majority of) shares in the hands of governments. Even so, the privatization-approach creates a new entity in the private domain and, as a consequence, brings the discussion between the privatized port-authority and the relevant governments on the level of an "external" negotiation between two autonomous bodies with their own interests. Only recently more "modern" solutions are appearing in the form of bringing within the corporatized but not privatized port-authority a separated corporation with limited commercial and participative tasks. By doing so the "external" discussions between two autonomous bodies, as is the case for a truly privatized port-authority, is "internalized". It takes the shape of a network-configuration, with emphasis on mutual influencing rather than on negotiating with "strangers"

2. Historic notion of port-policy in the Rotterdam case

For most interested observers in port-matters the factual development of the port of Rotterdam only starts after the end of World War II. The historic notion of the prior centuries of port-development is reduced by them to the fact that before the Second World War Rotterdam was extremely dependant on the situation in the German industry. A well-known saying in that time was: "if the Ruhr only sneezes, Rotterdam already has a cold".

Just before the end of the war in 1945 the Germans destroyed a major part of the port-infrastructure and its equipment. With the effect that the Rotterdammers had both an economic and an emotional reasoning to make themselves less dependant of the Germans when shaping their renewed port. The - also politically supported - answer was: industrialization. Our "own" industry was expected to tie the cargo-flows to our own Rotterdam -port far better than the transit-flows for the German industry, knowing from hard experience that the Germans could easily divert their cargo-flows to another port for just a few pfennig cheaper freights. Moreover our "own" industry could - was the rationalized explanation - offer the necessary new employment for the thousands of workers that were expected to loose their jobs in agriculture.

Looking backward over more than half a century we are to admit that, with the glorious exception of the oil-industry (refineries and the related production of bulk chemicals), this industrialization-policy has failed. The historic notion of what happened in the port of Rotterdam is, however, for decades not jeopardized by the one-sidedness of the industrial port-complex. The "hollow curves" of ever growing cargo-flows determined the picture. Each year more tonnes, more seagoing vessels, more basins and more chemical industries was considered the ultimate proof of a good port-policy. The turning-point appeared a quarter of a century ago.

Since then the general feeling about the port-policy seems to be far more dispersed, an intriguing mixture of chauvinistic remembrances and gloomy thoughts about the future.

3. The historic development of port-policy: various perspectives

The complex arena of port-policy can be viewed from many angles. Each perspective is not merely a choice between do and don't. In practice these two positions are only the far ends of the spectrum between which development takes place. Any major historic change involves a complicated journey in a space filled with numerous perspectives, some desired, others not, some easy to steer, others not, some quick movers, others slow and steady, some with a strong coherence, others rather solitary. Moreover each perspective is "filled" with a combination of cognitive contents and social context. With a combination of "vertical" learning and "horizontal" learning. "Vertical" learning, in this interpretation, is to do with science, with knowledge that is generally applicable and that is reproducible. The object of the "vertical" learning might be extremely specialized, but will never be specific. "Horizontal" learning is dealing with understanding, with personal experience, it is by definition specific and specialized knowledge might even hamper the applicability. Each perspective is determined by the interacting effects of both impersonal "vertical" learning and personalized "horizontal" learning. It explains how difficult it is to convince others about the righteousness of a personal positioning within the spectrum of a specific perspective. And port-policy can be judged by an almost infinite number of perspectives. Because of this complicated character of a double helix the study of port-policy is often narrowed down to the "beta-elements" The idea, however, that understanding a port-policy can be restricted to a scientific approach of beta-elements, neglecting not only the elements related to social sciences and behavioural sciences, but even more importantly leaving out all feelings and emotions of individuals, is a fatal mistake.

Three observations emerge. First of all that our surrounding world is not only affected by our activities, but that our acting is at the same time affected by influences from the world around us. Secondly that the natural tendency to reduce the ever growing complexity of our arena's to just one single perspective and to reduce the interpretation within that one single perspective to impersonalized facts and figures, is not only confining reality in an impermissible way, but also ignores the effects of the mutual affecting mechanisms. And thirdly that affecting always means positioning in a spectrum, knowing that each spectrum is part of a polyperspective complex.

The four perspectives mentioned below to illustrate the historic development of port-policy in Rotterdam are to be considered as an elaboration of these three observations.

3.1. The perspective social context: establishment-professional politicians-groupings-individuals

The rebuilding of the port after the war was an enormous effort. The old establishment, the "port-barons", the ship-owners, the traders and the stevedores, they all did a marvellous job. Only in retrospect we realize that they rebuilt their "own" pre-war-port. Their common interest was loading and discharging of seagoing vessels and the storage of commodities for trading. Hence, the new port became a modernized old port. Doing things better and not so much doing better things. It made, on the other hand, reconstruction easier, quicker and more successful. All the available experience, all old authority and all new money was directly applicable. The resulting strength washed away all bureaucratic resistance and political planning. The gossip is that when a new plan for rebuilding a quay-wall was presented to the city-council, the politicians first started to applaud and only then prudently inquired what it was all about and what budget they were expected to admit. This may be exaggerated, but the fact remains that until the end of the sixties the standing committee for the city-council regarding port-matters not only consisted - as the only exception - of both elected politicians and nominated experts from the circles of port and industry, but also was chaired - again as the only exception - by the mayor of Rotterdam himself, so by a man nominated by our queen and supposed to stand above the political parties. The unwritten rule in those days was that the port was that important that discussing port-matters in the standing committee or in the city-council was not to be degraded to the level of party-policy. The private domain was deeply penetrated into the public domain. And everybody felt happy and proud about the results. On the waves of post-war successes the necessity of building and constructing from directly after the war was gradually transformed in the believe in constructing. The port of Rotterdam as one of the striking examples of the really "constructable" future.

Retrospectively the report of the Club of Rome and the oil-crises in the seventies can hardly be considered a surprise. At a great pace the world became more prudent. Economic, resource-wise, environmentally, financially. But also mentally. No longer "oversized" plans and "gigantic" expansions. The public domain switched its attention almost completely to the introduction of new and more strict limiting boundaries for the activities of the private actors: space, environment, public money. The effects of this new attitude were twofold. On the one hand the interests and thus the representatives of the private domain were more or less radically pushed out of the public domain and on the other hand the political part of the public domain was professionalized, under the creed "primacy for politics". The public domain became extremely inward oriented and the private domain was so little accustomed to that attitude that it experienced the relation with the public actors as hostile. Both the self-selected separation of the public domain and the experienced segregation of the private domain gave rise to the formation of "internal" groupings. Or, probably better to say, made already existing "internal" groupings more outspoken and more active. The environmentalists, the "NIMBY-ists", the port employers society, the foundation for the interests of the industries in the Rotterdam port-area, and so on and so forth, in an almost endless row. Perhaps a typical phenomena for our Dutch culture. As it is a part of our culture that in the "cooling down" period - that naturally succeeds the period of "warming up" - the same groupings started to deliberate on improvement of the mutual relations.

During the years of downward economic development the for the greater part rather "classical" industries in the port of Rotterdam choose also a rather "classical" remedy to overcome the less favourable economic development: concentration, making use of the economies of scale. The inertia of the big, established and formerly so successful industries in Rotterdam proved to be a cumbersome limitation on the way to more "mean and lean" production,, more specialization and more outsourcing of not-core activities. With fewer "immured" activities, less resource-based strategies, reduced reliance on competitive offers of "strange" suppliers. For big, bulky and massive ports like Rotterdam the global alteration towards a growing resource dependant strategy, with stronger relations with a selected group of co-makers, is difficult to follow. It will take a lot of effort to convert the existing pattern, to change the relations with the outside world gradually from impersonal, short term and determined by incidental outcome into long-lasting highly personalized relations based on mutual trust in a constant process of collective change. One thing is clear, however: in the new era of the world-wide network-economy, the social context will be ascertained by global individualism, rather than by regional corporatism.

3.2. The perspective aimed output: horizontal growth-selective growth-dematerialization

The rebuilding of the destroyed port directly after World War II was conducted by the same notabilities which led port and city before the war. The shared feeling that the recuperation of the port, being considered the most important means of new prosperity, was the highest priority, gave a remarkable push to the process. Both regarding the physical output itself (quay-walls, basins, sites) and regarding the psychological output (no-nonsense image, covering up all "minor" differences). But also with all accompanying disadvantages: no room for other plans or thoughts than expeditious "horizontal growth" based on well-known pre-war structures. More of the same. Finally ending in plans to accommodate a tremendous plant for the German steelworks on Maasvlakte and to reshape thousands of acres of rural land on the islands south of Rotterdam into new port-area. The city-élite nor the port-élite were aware of the growing disharmony with the surrounding population that their plans brought about. The mayor of Rotterdam, when proposing the plans for the new steel-works in the city-council, seemed to be surprized of the aggressive reaction of present citizens (and not of the present politicians!). The leaders of the unions seemed to be surprized when their members demonstrated for higher wages after a long period of regulated thriftiness for the sake of the positioning of the port. There evidently was - and most probably still is - a pronounced "phase-difference" between the "ruling class" and the "ruled" people, and this was (and probably is) valid for both the public and the private domain.

Following the rather abrupt ending of the period of "horizontal growth" the two domains, both public and private, shifted their aimed output into "selective growth". For the public domain that meant in practice a philosophy or "zero-growth" with as little direct physical output (like the mentioned quay-walls, basins and sites) as possible and all efforts directed on the indirect output, e.g. safety and the environment. Examples are in the field of safety a new shore-bases RADAR-system and for the environment a project to clean up the Rhine and as a result also to improve the quality of the sludge to be dredged from the bottom of the harbour-basins. Combined with the construction of a huge "pond" to dispose of the polluted sludge during the cleaning period. It is illustrative that all the three mentioned projects were planned and executed in collaboration with the relevant institutions of the central government. The public actor in the port moved in the direction of the central public domain and away from the private actors in the port. These private actors translated the selective growth in improvement of efficiency and postponement of new activities. Resulting in "horizontal clustering" like for the conventional break-bulk stevedores and for the discharging of crude oil via a mutual facility of a number of oil-companies.

After the in essence mental recovery from the effects of the oil-crises in 1973 and 1979 the general feeling was that - like our then prime minister said - "it never will be in the future as it was before the crises". Both the public actors and the private actors became more interested in the restoration of their relations. As a proof of that, postponed plans for deepening the channel for deep-drafted vessels into the Northsea were reactivated. The expected output for the port-authority not only being a better competitive position - and thus relation - for its most "bulky" customers like the oil-industry and the German steelworks, but at the same time also safeguarding - via "the golden tail of the bulk cargo" - a prerequisite for "internal subsidies" in order to accommodate new promising activities. The public actors moved slowly into the direction of inspiring new plans. Recognising that globalized production and opportunities offered by new technologies like "telematics" were to cause fundamental changes in the aimed output of the port. "Transport" transformed in "logistics", cargo moving from port to port became cargo moving from door to door, or - on the basis of new philosophies like "just in time delivery" - even into cargo moving from floor to floor or from shelf to shelf. Stand alone industrial activities transformed in clusters of industrial production, semi-finished products or even "waste" of the one participant being used as resource for others, "reversed" logistics becoming as important as "supply chain management". The consequences of all these alterations being the necessity to get better acquainted with those directly adjacent in the emerging chains, but also with the "far ends" of it (the producer and the consumer). Moreover to better make use of the possibilities for VAL (value adding logistics), to pay more attention to the connections to the hinterland (e.g. the "Betuwelijn") and to take the initiative for improving the processes in the port by ICT (as we call it nowadays).

All in all the output in that period of renewed transition was rather diversified. Partly for the reactivation of post-crises activities, partly for the introduction of completely new activities. The "phase-difference", we mentioned before as one of the characteristics of the post-crises period, appeared again, but not any longer between the "rulers" and the "ruled", but between the solid block of conventional port-users and the modernists with their believe in "de-materialized" production. This "splits" in aimed output still exists. The fair supposition is that it will remain to be so for at least a few decades more. The complete transformation from "mainport" to "brainport" is impossible and dangerous. In the best years of the "mainport" the well-functioning was supported by activities we now consider as products of the "brainport" and only a strong "mainport" will be able to foster a healthy "brainport".

3.3. The perspective mutual behaviour of actors: consensus-conflict-consideration-selfregulation

During the period of reconstruction directly after the war the then establishment from both the governmental institutions and the private firms active in the port were not endeavouring to reach consensus, they were simply the exponents of it. Decisions were taken, quickly and efficiently, within a rather small group of powerful people. All kinds of influences from less powerful circles could be -and in fact were- disregarded. It made them less sensible -to put it mildly- to growing resistance. Resistance partly on the social level, with as the most striking examples the ignored relation with the unions and the poor democratic procedures, partly on the physical level, with the well-known examples of unlimited consumption of restricted resources and pollution beyond the limits of perceived acceptance. It is remarkable that the "phase-difference" for the physical constraints was far shorter than for the social shortcomings. The exploding prices for energy and the forced cleaning up of all kinds of hidden refuse dumps may explain the reaction within a restricted time-horizon. The adequate reaction on the ignorance on the social level took, in general, much longer: the frequent strikes of the port-workers reached their top in the mid-eighties and the democratic procedures involved in major infrastructural works are still a subject of rather bitter discussions.

The attitude of conflict was deepened by the circumstance that the main-actors in the various camps were not acquainted with each other. Meaning that every proposal for improvement or even simple change was always received by the other actors with suspicion. Resulting in formalized reactions, putting emphasis on negative elements. The former dividing lines between the public domain and the private domain were combined with as grave dividing lines within the private domain as such. The port-authority felt obliged in a number of cases to present itself as mediator, but the effect often proved to be quite opposite: the opponents were offered an escape to avoid a direct confrontation and discussion with each other. Yet the public domain gained new esteem by doing so. It created the possibility for the port-authority to bring forward its ideas about the "post-crises-future" of the port. The platform and the contents of the discussion were replaced from yesterday's differences between various actors in the same (private) domain into deliberations about tomorrow's opportunities between representatives of the public domain and the struggling parties from the private domain. It goes without saying that those discussions created a climate not only for "vertical" learning, but at the same time for "horizontal" learning. Resulting in new configurations of common friends and common enemies, and, as a consequence, with new acceptance of consideration about each other's views. At some occasions this ongoing, more or less hidden, process of growing consideration was marked by "official" statements, like the "agreement of Wassenaar" about the reduction of wage-increases in order to stimulate employment, and the "kiss of Delft", regulating the loss of employment in the port-sector of the conventional break bulk cargo without one single worker being forced "to pass the gate". The effects of this consideration-approach proved to be extremely successful, not only on the national level but also on other levels, as in the port of Rotterdam. So successful, that we made it a national claim: the Dutch poldermodel.

Since the beginning of the nineties the ever stronger interconnected relations between the various actors have given rise to the formation of networks. The old authority, the old hierarchy, as well as the old rigid division between the public and the private domains and the old impersonal obedience belonging to those pyramidal command-structures, are fading away and replaced by personalized relations between the actors, through which each actor wants to affect the others but at the same time is willing to be influenced by those other actors, without any formalized order-sequence. The old organizational structures are becoming obsolete and are replaced by "fluid" networks, aimed to reach a by definition broad and temporary outcome. The old regulative systems are more and more taken over by systems of selfregulation in networks. The evident success of the "poldermodel", in which via long-lasting deliberations an outcome is reached that is acceptable for all, may act both as a stimulating steppingstone for the network-approach as well as a frustrating hindrance.

3.4. The perspective performance indicators: tonnes of cargo handled-social limitations-generated added value-growth potential

During the period of the "horizontal growth" the number of seagoing vessels that called at the port and the volume of the cargo that was loaded into or discharged from these vessels was the directly understandable indicator for success. The port was looking towards the sea and the indicator was restricted to that view. The potential customers were queuing at the front-door and the positive feelings were concentrated on the performance of the port as such. No necessity to worry about the "soft" characteristics of the port-product, even not about the infrastructure at the hinterland-side or the requirements of the shippers and the consignee's of the transports. The performance indicator was completely based on the activities of the private actors and from that group of private actors predominantly the Rotterdam based actors.

When the "horizontal growth" was overtaken by "selective growth" the dominance for selecting a performance indicator was shifted to the public domain, with the euphemistic indication of "quality port". In fact the "quality" was one-sided restricted to keeping the port-activities within ever severer social limitations, like pollution, noise, danger or hindrance. How successful the public actors may have considered themselves as measured in the performance indicator adhered by them, it covered up the poor performance of the private actors. With some exaggeration the "no"-indicator of the public actors overruled for some time completely the "yes"-indicator of the private enterprises. The new plans initiated by the port-authority to end this depressed period introduced the necessity of a new, more positive performance indicator. As such the economic added value generated by the port-activities was chosen. It still was a social economic indicator, but more directly coupled to the business of the private actors in the port. Stimulating new activities in a positive way and no longer restricting old activities to remain within dictated limitations in a negative way. After the period of the "volume-port" and the interregnum of the "quality-port" the era of the "value-port" was entered. It was clear right from the introduction of the new performance indicator that it had some practical disadvantages. The indicator can only be ascertained afterwards, with a time-lag sometimes mounting up to more than a year, and the indicator falls in case of improved efficiency (as earned wages form an important part of the added value). In that sense the indicator added value is an excellent instrument for planning and control, but less suitable for judging the day to day activities in an ever quicker changing environment.

The global economy, the reversed economy, the new economy, how vague they all may be, they are all indicating a stronger position of interconnected systems, of networks. Meaning that the performance indicator of the port is to be redefined as the capability to be or to become a nodal point in a number of strong networks, offering growth-potential for the future.

It is amazing how big the phase-difference again and again is between the real performance of the port according to the insights on that particular moment and the indicators applied by the general public. During the traditional speech of the alderman of the port on the last day of the year the highlight - still catching most attention from the media - remains the presentation of the figures about the seaborne cargo for the then almost passed year. Notwithstanding the fact that this indication of the performance of the port is outdated for at least a quarter of a century. It is even more astonishing that the same gap between real performance and applied indicator can be found in scientific publications. The ease and the readiness of the information about tonnes handled is not enough an excuse. The scientist should know that large volumes of handled tonnes means in general the loading and discharging of high-volume low-value bulky cargo, causing a fair amount of hindrance (the second performance indicator), generating a low added value (the third performance indicator) and the port only acting as "humble servant" and not as co-actor in networks meant for increasing growth-potential (the fourth performance indicator).

4. The steering-mechanisms in port-policy

We described so far a number of perspectives via which the historic development of port-policy can be reviewed. We saw sometimes rather loop-shaped developments, but also more or less linear evolution. The question than arises what steering-mechanisms apparently underlie these observed changes over time.

In the first mechanism the steering is initiated and executed by the singular actor. He is acting on the basis of self-interest and is making use of a resource-based strategy. His aim is to bring as many resources as possible under his own control, and, as a consequence, often will be forced in the direction of specialization. He is extremely powerful in his own domain, but often less sensible for developments and influences from outside his domain. This weak social receptivity makes him vulnerable for "strange" impulses. The craftsman and the artist as prototypes, but also the old-fashioned conglomerate and the modern global player, who is to share the world-market with only a few remaining competitors. Especially in the latter form the steering of these actors is extremely important and in some cases even decisive for big ports like Antwerp and Rotterdam.

The second steering-mechanism is related to a group of actors, rather than to the singular one. The group-interest is dominant over the self-interest of the members. The reason behind it is often the collective opponent(s) in the other domain(s). In case the gap between the feelings in the group and of those opponents is severe, a mediator may turn up, as we described in the Rotterdam case in the seventies and eighties. The groups mostly exist for quite some time, and the tolerated mandate normally is weak. The steering-power is long lasting but confined. All ports have to do with this type of representative, and because of that, impersonalized groups, acting as steering-mechanisms.

The essence in the third type of steering-mechanism, the network, is the personalized interrelation. It requires from each individual actor to be recognized and to be acknowledged as a strong identity, with enough mandate to effectively act as a negotiator. Instead of ultimate pictures of a desired future - as is the case for the first and second steering-mechanisms - the third steering mechanism is only meant to agree on the direction of the next step to be made. With a limited group of involved individuals, endeavouring to translate the data available at that very moment into a commonly negotiated outcome. Control and hierarchy are replaced by trust and contents. Especially for actors from the public domain the use of networks as steering-mechanisms is difficult. They are accustomed to work with impersonalized and "given" power and authority, with equality for all, and are now confronted with "earned" authority (and no power whatsoever) and the skill to negotiate with others on the basis of personal equivalence. In line with the historic development of the steering-mechanisms it may be worthwhile for corporatized port-authorities to start with negotiations in networks to establish new steps in port-policy, rather than to put all efforts in privatization of the group and falling back to the second steering-mechanism.

5. The end of the sea

Seaports are situated along the borders of the sea, and are, therefore, in the literal sense the end of the sea. In many ports the facilities to load and discharge vessels are named "terminals". Everybody knows that the cargo is not to terminate its transport at the terminal, but is to proceed over the sea or deeper inland. The most complicated part of the transport is to and from the hinterland. The period that the port could restrict itself to looking at the sea - or for that matter: the ship-owners - has passed and also in that sense we reached the end of the sea. People still counting the number of tonnes of cargo that has been loaded and discharged in and out seagoing vessels are apparently not aware of that end of the sea. Freight for sea-transport is extremely low, enabling producers and consumers to exercise a global economy. It seems no longer of any validity whether between production and consumption there is a sea or not. Once again: the end of the sea. The sea is large with the same waves all over. Symbolic for large groups of similar people. Modern ports realize that they have to deal with individual customers, that they are to offer tailor-made solutions in one to one relations. That also in this figurative way we reached the end of the sea.

The end of the sea? But the sea remains to be the raison d'être for ports like Antwerp and Rotterdam. Once again an explanation why port-policy is not merely a science but also an art.

6. Additional remarks

From the article a number of potential historic traps can be concluded. They will be presented as statements, followed by an illustration on the basis of the Rotterdam-case and a quest for historians regarding eventual new research.

A. To ignore the fundamental difference between the reactions of the public actors and the private actors in a port when confronted with essential paradigm-shifts; to consider ports as "black boxes", with a rather homogeneous and steady state and only externally effected by impulses for change.

The Rotterdam case illustrates that the relative strength of either of the two "internal" main-actors fluctuates with a wavelength of some 20 years: roughly from 1950 to the beginning of the seventies and from the seventies to the midst of the eighties.

Quest for historians: is a next period with more dominance in port-matters for the public actors due to appear, or will the interrelation between the two main-actors become more "fluid" and dissolved in "single issue discussions" about paradoxes and counter-paradoxes.

B. To restrict the study about port-policy to a scientific approach of beta-elements, neglecting not only the elements related to social sciences and behavioural sciences, but even more importantly leaving out all feelings and emotions of individuals.

The Rotterdam case illustrates that this mono-disciplinary approach of scientists has unduly widened the gap between scientific institutions and the port-community.

Quest for historians: May initiatives be expected from the circles of historians to close this gap, to accept that the counterpart of historic scientific studies being paid for by the public must be those studies also being of public interest.

C. To assume that wars are not only causing physical destruction and hence the necessity to rebuild in the materialistic sense, but are also causing the abandonment of pre-war ideas and thoughts and hence the appearance of totally renewed mental maps.

The Rotterdam case illustrates that the more severe the physical destruction is, the less space there is for radical mental redesign. Resulting in making directly after the war merely a modernized (bigger, deeper and larger) pre-war-port.

Quest for historians: is this "tolerated maximum degree of mental and physical disturbance" also recognisable for less "destructive" changes like containerization and if so, what does this mean for new emerging changes like ICT, dedicated terminals for shipowners, clustering of integrated process-industries, or, more in general, network-approaches and the related resource dependant perspectives.

D. To suppose that the coming about of hybris after a period of successful development may be avoided; that the inward looking attitude belonging to hybris and expressed by the tendency to tackle problems by endeavouring to get more grip on the situation, may be changed overnight by flexible adaptation to new circumstances.

The Rotterdam case illustrates that the higher the experienced summit of success is, the longer the period lasts to develop receptivity of the port-system for new impulses from the outside world.

Quest for historians: is there also a kind of "killing hybris", meaning that decline after a period of extreme forms of success are not followed by recovery, but by permanent degrading.

E. To overlook that the "phase-difference" (defined as the period between the first signs of a newly arising problem and the moment a commonly agreed reaction is available) for physical constraints is far shorter than for social shortcomings.

The Rotterdam case illustrates that port-related networks are as yet not functioning in such a way that in a broad sense social interaction and shared ideas about physical alterations are effectively combined.

Quest for historians: is this "two phases structure" hampering port development nowadays, adding predominantly a social aspect to "Schumpeterian creative destruction" that over the past decades was already active in the physical sense.

F. To misprize that existing patterns of hierarchy, given authority, impersonal obedience and the related rigid division between the public and the private domains are being replaced by acting in networks with limited objectives and on a temporarily basis.

The Rotterdam case illustrates that in particular the governmental institutions influencing the port "at arm's length" find it difficult to accept "networking" as steering-mechanism. For the port-authority it enables, however, "corporatization" as positioning instead of the difficult way to "privatization".

Quest for historians: is "privatization" belonging to the "pre-network" period and is that why governments do accept - or even promote - "privatization" (with its "given" authority) more easily than steering via personalized selfregulating networks.

G. To express the performance of a port by means of indicators that are at that moment already outdated for decades; and as a consequence mislead the outside world about what really its position is when judged against more modern aims and standards.

The Rotterdam case illustrates that it is difficult to find more modern indicators that are as easy to produce and to understand as the yearly throughput of sea-borne cargo. But the Rotterdam case also illustrates that remaining to use this "tons-indicator" hampers the understanding of what may be expected from a modern port and because of that the acceptance of plans by "higher" authorities.

Quest for historians: is the continued use of throughput as the (only!) performance indicator merely a matter of "intellectual idleness" or are also other motives at stake.

H. To position historians dealing with port-matters in the category of the steering-mechanism by singular actors; that is to say in the category of strong specialists in their own professional domain, but with a rather weak receptivity for the new impulses from both society as a whole and the port-community in particular.

The Rotterdam case illustrates how difficult it is to escape from this trap. That is why I am standing here today. To invite you to become part of the port-network. But you are to be aware of the price you have to pay for that inclusion: the willingness to be fundamentally affected by the port-world. That is, too, the reason why I am standing here today.

Commentary on the papers of Seberechts and Molenaar

Adrian Jarvis

Merseyside Maritime Museum, Liverpool, United Kingdom

I must make it clear at the outset that I was asked, in commenting on these two papers, to incorporate some comparative comments relating to British ports, particularly my home port of Liverpool as well, in the hope that this might help fuel a gainful discussion.

Molenaar's is a highly analytical paper with a complex logical structure which I need not summarize here as it is perfectly adequately set out in the paper. His oral presentation on the day was linked with the written version, but only loosely so. In the former he chose to identify a number of errors made by historians in dealing with ports. The historians whose tails he was tweaking were mainly too polite to refer to the errors that port engineers made - and make - in dealing with ports. (The first attempts at turning Bremerhaven into a container port were little short of scandalous)

His written version begins with a distinction between ports as a public good and ports as a source of private profit, which implies that port authorities should be above competitive money-grubbing, presumably in the hands of national governments. In Britain, of course, the furthest we got with the idea of public good in trading ports was the non-profit trust, pioneered at Leith but exemplified in the Mersey Docks & Harbour Board and imitated in the Port of London Authority. We did have, it is true, some nationalized ports of which Hull and Southampton were the most important, but they had got nationalized almost by accident along with the railway or canal companies which previously owned them. Here as elsewhere, Britain did not have a ports policy[1].

Both Rotterdam and Antwerp profited from the uncertainties of proposals for port nationalization in Britain during the 1970s. Liverpool was put in the impossible position of having been given powers to build its container terminal (without which its long-term future was virtually certain closure) only to have loan sanction cut off when construction had begun, leaving it with large costs but no corresponding income from a half built dock. Allowing it to be completed would increase the cost of nationalizing it. This is not just a local gripe: it is a disagreement with the underlying assumption that a national government necessarily has the national good at heart: it may - at least in Britain - be just as short-termist and

[1] It might be thought that Government funding for nineteenth century ports of refuge was a manifestation of a "ports policy", but in fact trading activity in, say, Dover or Holyhead, was entirely a secondary consideration. Similarly, Government funding for fishing ports was provided for social rather than economic reasons.

money-grubbing as any private company. A Labour government was willing effectively to bankrupt a major port in order to be able to buy it at a bargain price. These uncertainties were, naturally, greeted with a wave of labour problems in all the major British ports which our rivals, including Antwerp and Rotterdam, would have had difficulty in conjuring. The Australians were probably the only ones who got port operation more wrong in this period.

Seberechts' paper on Antwerp 1918-1950 exhibits a much more pragmatic and less philosophical approach. He looks behind the ostensible constitution of the port to try and grasp what really made it work. While he identifies many interest groups and networks, I was struck by the comparative lack of names of individuals. I have to say that I did not feel that the promised analysis of the networks really materialized, though the paper was still rather of the nature of a progress report. The fascinating thing in British port politics is the way in which we find the same men popping up in different places and wearing different hats but still grinding the same axe[2]. There are some who are always looking for minimal port charges while others are far more concerned with quality of service, with a relative disregard of price. Both papers have conflict among users and between users and the port authority as an underlying theme, so clearly the users of the Port of Antwerp must have exhibited divisions on this and other issues in the same way that Rotterdam and the major British ports did.

That dichotomy remained valid at least into the 1970s, probably longer, and of course the rust-bucket operators came into the former category, the reputable owners into the latter, because the capital costs of having a decent ship tied up were higher than those for a rust-bucket, especially if the latter's crew were Ukrainians who had not been paid for a decade or two[3]. In Britain as in Rotterdam or Antwerp the reputable owners sought to influence port policy mainly through the constitutional channels of the port authority, while the latter resorted (as they had for a century or more) to endless whingeing in the columns of the shipping press.

Or so it might seem. In fact, both papers suggest that there was far more to it than that in both Antwerp and Rotterdam. Both suggest that personal relationships in networks, the respectable version of England's "old school tie", became more rather than less important as time went on and informal contacts and relationships became institutionalized. Both see the port authority as a "gate keeper", a metaphor I might prefer to replace with that of a boxing referee, with the blood of both contestants splattered over his dress shirt. But because the port authority also had representatives of different factions within it, there was scope for internal quarrelling between different trades and interests, making the metaphorical referee schizophrenic. There was also the possibility that both fighters might decide to punch the referee instead of each other.

It was not one bout, however, but a tournament in which the owners of different sizes of ships might team up together to fight against merchants, but then split off

[2] Though they might occasionally change sides for short-term advantage vis-a-vis either their competitors or port authorities.

[3] In Liverpool we still get one or two vessels per year placed under arrest with their penniless crews literally cast on the mercy of local charities.

to fight each other - and it was just the same on the merchant side. The permutations for disagreement may not have been infinite, but they were certainly varied and extensive. This ever-changing scene prompted Professor Palmer to query in the discussion whether the concept of interest groups was actually any use, though it seems to me they were sufficiently coherent to remain helpful as an interpretative device provided that their fluidity is taken fully into account.

To summarize, I felt that both papers had something very useful to offer, but both needed a little further work. Molenaar really needed more hard reference to identifiable events[4] - his paper as presented was more philosophical than historical. Seberechts was clearly going along interesting lines and making good progress, but seemed to me to need some more prosopographical content.

That said, both these papers form part of an ambitious and extremely worthwhile project in comparative port history, and I fully endorse the complimentary remarks made by David Williams in his historiographical introduction. I found many other papers in the volume produced resonances with the British situation, and I only wish that we could get such a project going in UK: the success of this venture may make it easier for us to do so.

---

[4] Should I make a remark here about engineering being a "soft discipline" in which one can get by without the use of "hard data"? Perhaps not: some of my best friends are engineers.

Land-use policy in the port of Antwerp (1870-1994)

Greta Devos

University of Antwerp, Belgium

Introduction

Today, ports are more than merely places where ships are loaded and unloaded. Increasingly, customers expect a full package of services. Industry and integrated logistics with supply chain management offer added value. Moreover every possible kind of cargo must be shipped to and from virtually any port in the world as competently and as quickly as possible. Antwerp has always been an important link in international trade. As an inland port, it has the highest centrality index within the Hamburg Le Havre range, i.e. the best possible location vis-à-vis the shared hinterland and the largest European production and consumption centres. Today, a dense network of motorways, railways, waterways and pipelines connects the port to its hinterland. Initially, rail transport constituted the most important mode of inland transportation, as rail links, particularly with the east, were constructed from the 1840s onwards. Later, attention focused on the development of inland navigation and, in between the two World Wars, on road transport too. This is one of the many shifts that characterize the evolution of the port in the twentieth century.

Operating conditions in the port of Antwerp have changed constantly since the 1870s. One of the port authority's principal instruments for influencing traffic, and subsequently added value, was land-use policy, a policy that has clearly evolved over time. This paper tries to detect the shifts that have taken place in this respect, bearing in mind of course the port's characteristics and the technological innovation that has taken place.

2. Some characteristics of the port of Antwerp

Antwerp is a *tidal port.* The difference between high and low tide can amount to 4,5 metres. For this reason, an extensive dock system has been developed that is accessible only through a number of locks. With the exception of vessels unloading oil at a special jetty at the beginning of the twentieth century, all ships were moored at quays along the river or in the docks. From 1856, both State and City contributed to the continuous expansion of the port and its dock system in order to cope with growing traffic. The surface area of the dock system grew from 15,4 hectare in 1860 to 1.921 hectare in 1994. No fewer than eight locks, built in the period 1811-1983, provided access to these docks. The port was being expanded northwards on the Right Bank of the river Scheldt. The reasons were quite obvious: the low-lying polder lands were particularly suitable for digging docks, while they were also relatively scarcely populated. Several villages were integrated into the territory of the City and effectively disappeared. By the end of the 1960s, the construction had started of a new harbour area on the Left Bank of the river.

The Franco-German War of 1870 gave an important stimulus to port traffic. A shortage of mooring space in the overcrowded port required a better management and organization. Around the same time, steamships began to outnumber sailing ships in the port, so that liner shipping became increasingly important. The local Chamber of Commerce insisted on the allocation of fixed berths. Antwerp was at the time becoming an important *liner port*, as the number of regular shipping lines calling grew constantly:

Table 14.1. Recognized regular shipping lines

Year	Number of liner departures	Total arrivals at port	Proportion
1938	158	7.935	67 %
1950	159	6.295	65 %
1960	213	12.118	73 %
1970	244	14.537	76 %
1976	266	13.511	76 %

Source: Suykens 1979, 435.

Indeed, Antwerp was a not a particularly tramp-friendly port due to the constant need for mooring space and its internal organization of labour. Even in the 1930s, tramp ships carrying timber, grain and also iron and steel stopped calling at Antwerp because better facilities were available at the port of Ghent and at the Dutch port of Rotterdam.

Until the 1950s, tradition played an important role in transhipment. Originally, the crews of the sailing ships, assisted by so-called "naties" -organized groups of workers whose origins lay in the late fifteenth century- loaded and unloaded their own vessels. By the 1860s, the majority of vessels calling at the port were steamships, which occasioned the rise of a new group of goods-handlers, known as stevedores. Stevedores lifted cargo from the hold of vessels, after which the freight was passed on to the "natie" responsible for "reception" of the goods. The "reception natie" received the goods under the tackle of the ship, prepared consignments for the various addressees, distributed cargo all over town (and, from the 1930s, all over the country) or stored it in their warehouses. On arrival, stevedores controlled cargoes onboard. The goods were recounted, remeasured, reweighed and sorted on the quays, after which they were collected by different "naties". Conversely, goods for loading were placed at the perimeter of the ship by the "naties", after which the stevedores would take over and stow the cargo into the vessel's hold or on deck. This dual organization in dock work was maintained strictly up until the 1950s, though foreign (especially Dutch) stevedores had tried in between the First and the Second World Wars to centralize all goods-handling activities (Devos 1993, 190-194). Stevedores and "naties" did not operate at fixed quays. They performed their duties wherever they were required, though they did of course also have regular customers and/or shipping lines with fixed berths. The "naties" in particular had to spread their workforce over the entire surface area of the port. They transported the goods to and from vessels by means of very recognizable flat carts that were pulled along by horses. At first sight this did not seem a particularly efficient transport method. Yet it was thanks to their experience, and the level of co-operation and co-ordination attained, that Antwerp had already acquired a world-wide reputation in the nineteenth century as a *quick delivery port,* especially for general cargo.

This had consequences in terms of the required equipment, which up until the Second World War had been financed almost entirely by the City. Traditionally the quays were equipped for the purpose of handling conventional general cargo. Consequently hydraulically and, from 1905, electrically powered all-round cranes were installed along the new quays. This equipment was, however, a handicap when it came to the handling of bulk goods, especially with the emergence of more sophisticated lifting devices. Certainly in the inter-war period, the port had the intention of competing with Rotterdam for bulk goods. A fleet of floating grain elevators had already been taken into service in 1910, followed in the 1920s and 1930s by a number of loading bridges and heavy weight cranes.

3. Management of the port

Antwerp was a *municipal port.* The funding of infrastructure works depended on whether this infrastructure was located inside or outside the docks. The costs were borne respectively by the local or by the central authority. The State did, however, burden the City with the administration and the superstructure of the quays along the river. In 1923 separate balance sheets were drawn up. It would not be until 1 January 1988 that the port authority became independent of the City's other services. Henceforth it would be known as the "Antwerp Municipal Port Authority" (AMPA). The new structure led to a thorough evaluation of the port services, and it implied greater independence with respect to finance and administration. It also brought with it managerial flexibility, better financial insight and a clearer articulation of port policy. On 1 January 1997 AMPA was transformed from a traditional public service into a limited company.

Data on the gross surface area of the port prior to 1940 are not available, which is probably due to the fact that the port and the town originally constituted an entity. On the other hand, we do possess a complete series of data on the available berth length between 1811, when the first two docks were completed, and the present. Other data concern the surface area of the docks. Both can be compared with the volume of cargo handled. The gross surface area of the port, including the surface area on the river Scheldt and within the dock system, roads, railways, pipelines, locks and buildings, rose tenfold in fifty years.

Being public property, quays or plots inside the port could not simply be rented or sold. Instead, three different formulas have been applied in the course of time: short-term permits (one month to nine years), long-term concessions (over ten years) and the sale of land to certain industries. The principle of long-term concessions is somewhere between renting and buying land. The system gives more facilities than ordinary leasing. On the other hand it enabled the City to control better the situation. Various conditions were imposed upon applicants. The local authorities could unilaterally revoke all leasing contracts.

Table 14.2. Gross surface area of the Port of Antwerp (all included)

Year	Port area (hectare)	Industrial premises (hectare)	Proportion
1940	1.400	80	0,6 %
1950	1.400	127	9,1 %
1953	1.400	299	21,3 %
1957	5.340	350	6,5 %
1958	5.340	372	6,9 %
1960	5.340	600	11,3 %
1963	10.633	728	6,8 %
1966	10.633	1,969	18,5 %
1969	10.633	2.488	23,4 %
1994	14.055	2.955	21 %

Source: Antwerp Port Authority

The short-term rental of quays to shipping companies or their agents remained the rule up until the Second World War. These contracts were continuously renewed. Long-term concessions became more common in the Interwar period and, even more so, after 1945, particularly since the 1960s.

Table 14.3. Long-term concessions (number, total surface area, and average surface area)

Time-span	Number	Total surface area (hectare)	Average surface area (hectare)
1892-1914	33	30	0.90
1919-1940	71	91	1.28
1945-1994	990	2.679	2.71

Source: Calculations based on data collected by B. Lemayeur

The rental of fixed berths, quays, sheds, cranes and land was an important source of income to the City. Unlike in some other ports where quays were leased, prices did not depend on the amount of cargo handled; they were calculated per square meter. To the City, this source of revenue was less sensitive to economic fluctuations than the more important revenue generated by port dues. Indeed, the combined income from the granting of concessions and the renting of land, buildings, sheds; warehouses and quays to private enterprises never surpassed revenues from port dues. Until 1923, the port budget had not been separated from the City budget. They had in fact been fully integrated and an accurate specification had not been available. But the boom of the second half of the 1920s would eventually backfire: predictions of future financial results would prove too optimistic, leading to financial disaster during the economic crisis of the thirties.

During this crisis, the debt of the port began to grow. In the period 1932-1936, the deficit amounted to 127,7 million Belgian Francs (Van Tichelen 1942, 44). There was little the City could do. On the one hand it wanted to raise income by increasing dues and leasing prices. On the other, competition with such ports as Rotterdam and Hamburg was so fierce in the 1930s that the Antwerp Shipping Association -the professional association of shipping brokers and agents- and the Chamber of Commerce pressured the port authority into keeping prices low. But certain industries and services in the port were clearly suffering during the economic slump and asked for a reduction in taxes and leasing prices. Consequently the City found itself in a precarious situation. Ambitious new projects had to be cancelled. In a confidential report dated 1942, the Chamber of Commerce asserted that the Antwerp port had, in the late 1930s, fallen behind its competitors in terms of technology (Toekomstproblemen 1942, 2). Problems with the loading and unloading of vessels using older cranes resulted in longer berthing times. In 1939, with a view to cutting the port's debt, the so-called "Convention of the Northern Lands" was revised, and the Belgian State agreed to increase its financial contribution. But this decision on the eve of the Second World War failed to resolve the port's financial predicament.

4. Overview of the land-use policy during various periods

4.1. Land and quay policy before the First World War

In 1865, following the example set in English and French ports as well as in Hamburg and Bremen, a new company was established in Antwerp called "Compagnie des Docks-entrepôts et Magasins généraux d'Anvers", which by Antwerp standards was massive. The founders were thinking big. The company possessed a number of important and very modern warehouses. It equipped them with the newest devices and was prepared to install hydraulic cranes and closed sheds along the quays. In return, it asked for concessions for operating the existing quays as well as most cargo-handling operations. In addition the company demanded the sale of the land adjoining the docks. It would broaden the old Willem Dock, erect closed warehouses and mobile hydraulic cranes along all quays, build railways and fix fire-fighting equipment every 100 metres. Part of the net profit would be transferred to the City. However, the City blew the whistle on the project on grounds that it would result in an unacceptable quasi-monopoly (Devos 1994). A system whereby private companies would operate docks, as was already the case in several other Western European ports, was rejected outright. The fear for monopolies was simply too great.

Meanwhile, the development of the port continued. By 1914 the total surface area of the docks had been increased from 38,4 hectare in 1873 to 164.1 hectare. The useful mooring length increased from 3,7 to 25,9 kilometres. However, further conflicts arose before the start of the First World War, as the viewpoints of the various port users diverged. Traders and shipping agents were, of course, in favour of modernization, while other groups such as the cargo-handling firms were keen to protect their own interests and traditions. They called for investments by the City in land and in superstructure, and expressed fears that they would possibly be excluded from private concessions. On this basis they continued to oppose any form of privatization of harbour installations (Devos and Van Driel 2000, 151-152).

However, long-term concessions had been granted since 1892. The first was acquired by the "SA des Magasins à grains d'Anvers" (SAMGA). The company was granted a 45-year concession for a plot measuring 5.800 square metres on which a granary with silos was built and fitted with state-of-the-art equipment. As a committee established by the grain division of the Chamber of Commerce had taken the initiative, the City decided that there was no danger of monopolization. Moreover, everybody was aware that there was a shortage of grain storage facilities in the port. Another compelling matter was the transfer of oil storage from America Dock to a new site at the south end of the port, with larger and safer storage facilities. No fewer than 33 long-term concessions were granted before the outbreak of the First World War.[1] But not all parties interested in acquiring a plot near the waterside were successful in their bids. An attempt by a group of businessmen in 1914 to equip a quay plot was severely criticized and it failed.

Probably from the 1880s on, the harbour master and the municipal council assigned fixed berths for periods of between three months and one year to shipping companies and shipping agencies. The fact that Belgium's merchant fleet was rather modest in size explains why Antwerp was typically an *agency port* and *an important port of call.* Considering that demand for fixed berths on the Right Bank of the Scheldt - i.e. on the river itself - was much greater than supply (only 3,5 kilometres by 1885 and 5,5 kilometres by 1900), these facilities were only granted to postal and passenger lines. The allocation criteria applied included the frequency of the service - postal and passenger lines were given precedence - and the draught of the vessel, sometimes combined with intercession on the part of the Central Government. In short, all shipping companies preferred to moor their vessels along the river quay if at all possible, as this saved time and money. In time, fixed berths inside the dock area became more widely available, though there would continue to be a shortage of space. The harbour master, who was constantly swamped with applications, had the authority to allow tramp ships to moor at fixed berths, much to the dismay of the shipping companies or their agents.

4.2. The situation in the Interwar Period

In between world wars, the port expanded at an unprecedented rate. The surface area of the docks increased by 377 hectares (from 173,3 hectares to 550,7 hectares), while available mooring space was extended by 10,65 kilometres. An agreement between the City and the State in particular resulted in a huge expansion of over 3.700 hectares.

---

[1] Data gathered by former collaborator B. Lemayeur on the basis of information published in Gemeenteblad van de stad Antwerpen (Municipal Journal) 1892-1994.

Storage and distribution

The pre-war land-use policy was, by and large, continued in the 1920s and 1930s. The surface area taken up by short-term permits diminished, while an increasingly large area was reserved for long-term concessions.

Table 14.4. Evolution of short- and long-term permits in square metres

Year	Short-term permits (square metres)	Long-term concessions (square metres)
1921	456.225	256.225
1930	293.787	593.787
1939	146.632	704.011

Source: Lemayeur 1999, 9.

The long-term concessions were mostly granted for the handling of bulk cargo such as coal, ore, potash and grain, which was often transported by inland craft or Rhine barges. The City was keen to compete with Rotterdam in this particular market, and therefore set out to modernize its equipment, investing considerable sums in specific lifting devices, loading bridges and special warehouses. This equipment was subsequently rented in combination with land to interested parties. These were mainly newly established limited liability companies specialising in specific commodities. The traditional, undercapitalized co-operative companies or small stevedoring firms could not afford to rent these plots and equip quays or build warehouses inside the port area.

Port industry

Industrialization of the port came rather late. Initially, industry was located in the south of the city, near the river Scheldt. In the neighbouring suburbs of Hoboken and Hemiksem important processing facilities were established, including a non-ferrous metal plant founded by the Degussa Corporation and Metallgesellschaft in 1888, and a wool-combing plant opened by the Leipziger Wollkämmerei two years later. Both plants were typical port industries, where primary goods underwent initial processing before being dispatched to the hinterland. Also established around this time was the Cockerill Shipyard, and other companies would soon follow suit. Another industrialized area was the suburb of Merksem, near the Kempisch Canal, an inland navigation link with the hinterland. Here food-processing factories and traffic-friendly industries were established, some with the help of foreign capital. The storage of oil was initially concentrated near America Dock, but these facilities were transferred in the early twentieth century to the southern periphery of the city for safety reasons.

In 1927, after the State and City agreed on a Convention on the "Northern areas" (Noordergronden), a major expansion of the port offered new possibilities (Suykens 1991, 87-95). It provided the impetus for a new industrial function of the port. While trade and industry were long considered as antagonists in Antwerp (which in 1903 had led to the setting up of a Chamber of Industry besides the Chamber of Commerce) the City now attempted to promote industrial development in the port area. This would bind certain cargo flows to the port, which in turn would create employment and consolidate the economic development of the region. At the same time, the port authority hoped to make traffic less sensitive to the cyclical nature of the economy.

Fig. 14.1. Total surface in hectare of industrial and non-industrial companies in the port of Antwerp (1918-1945)

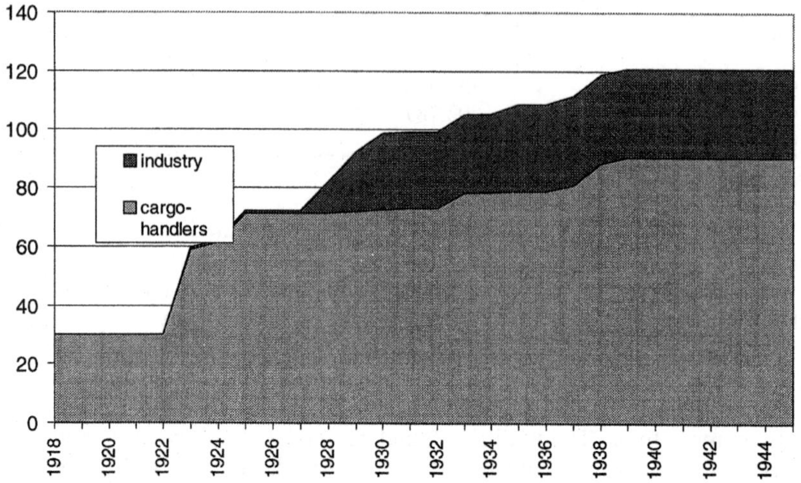

Source: City of Antwerp, *Municipal Journal.* Antwerp Port Authority.

In the late 1920s, car manufacturers such as General Motors Continental and the Ford Motor Company were among the first to transfer their operations from the city to the port. Shipbuilding and ship repairs, both closely related to ocean shipping, also constituted an important industrial branch. Although the City built three medium-sized dry docks in 1930, a private company called the Mercantile Marine Engineering and Graving Docks Cy built its own dry docks with adjacent yards, for which a permit had been obtained in 1929. As for mineral oils, these had up to then only been stored at Antwerp. However, in the early 1930s plans were drawn up for the construction of a first refinery. The project proposal for the construction of a refinery at Fourth Harbour Dock prompted fierce debate in the Municipal Council on, among other things, safety aspects. Even the Chamber of Commerce was opposed to the plan: the proposed site was located behind an expensive quay, and this would almost inevitably lead to an increase of insurance premiums for all port users. Nevertheless, towards the end of 1933, a 20-year concession was awarded for a refinery near Fourth Harbour Dock. Another industry to acquire concession plots were the sawmills for tropical wood, which was shipped in logs.

The attitude towards long-term concessions changed in the years between World Wars I and II. During this period, no fewer than 71 long-term concessions were granted. Some 25 % of the surface area involved was earmarked for industrial activity. Industrial initiative peaked in the period 1927-1932 (Fig. 14.1). The majority of concessions related to the construction of warehouses behind the quays, including special warehouses for frozen food, fruits and potash. Antwerp business circles pressurized the City into investing in more sophisticated installations, which it subsequently leased, together with the plots and sometimes deep-water quays, to private companies. A number of stevedores, specialized in the handling of specific bulk goods, benefited from the new policy. All-round cranes for the loading and unloading of general cargo, which were less efficient for the handling of bulk, were complemented with some electrical loading bridges. Competing with Rotterdam and catching up with technology were the primary objectives.

4.3. Land-use policy and port concessions 1945-1970

The pitiful financial situation of the municipality after World War II explains the shift that occurred in quay and land-use policy. The expansion of the port under a Ten Year Plan (1957-1967) was illustrative of a municipal investment drive in the superstructure of the quays and an altered concession policy with regard to deep-water quays and the adjoining land. The capacity of the port increased twofold. The water surface area more than doubled (from 592 hectare to 1.321 hectare) and the total surface area grew from 5.340 hectare to 8.600 hectare (Suykens 1993, 289). The useful mooring length increased by 33,6 kilometres. Throughput almost tripled between 1950 and 1975, from 21 million tonnes to 60.4 million tonnes, which corresponds to an annual growth rate of 4,3 %. In the mid-1960s, the first industries settled on the Left Bank of the river, as the land on the Right Bank was now fully occupied.

Cargo handling and distribution

Bare quays were now gradually leased to stevedoring firms and even "naties" who ventured onto the waterfront to take up stevedoring activities, as the strict division of labour between stevedores and "naties" was more relaxed after the war. These new "terminal operators", who obtained long-term concessions, were wholly responsible for paving the land, installing sewers, building sheds and warehouses, erecting cranes and/or loading bridges. As originally small firms were transformed into limited liability companies, they could now afford larger investments and, by reinvesting cash flow, they were able to expand or even specialize in certain types of traffic. Since the late 1960s the investment risks were eased by granting longer concession-terms and by giving more facilities by prolongation of a concession-deal. Shipping agencies and their customers, i.e. the shipping companies, were no longer interested in leasing berths because of the higher investments required and the inherent risks. Although their professional organization, the Antwerp Shipping Association, welcomed co-operation between the public and the private sectors, as well as private investment in more modern and sophisticated port equipment, it would not accept that these new terminal operators intended to attract shipping companies. The only Belgian shipping company to invest in 1948 in its own terminal by building two-storey warehouses was the *Compagnie Maritime Belge*, which provided the Congo service. Shipping agents tried to merge among themselves, or to collaborate and merge with other port actors. Horizontal and vertical integration resulted in stronger enterprizes and more interesting service packages for shipping companies.

In the mid-sixties the exclusive "reception natie", which was responsible for receiving cargoes from ships, disappeared. The new terminal operators attempted to take control of outgoing cargoes as well. This was quite a bold move, as forwarders and factory agents were in a strong position. From the sixties on, mergers between stevedoring companies and/or "naties" became quite common. Of course, this evolution went hand in hand with a technological revolution occasioned by the introduction of unit-loads, and with mechanization and specialization (containers, palletization, ro/ro ships). These developments also had consequences in terms of the surface areas of the conceded plots of land: while the small, narrow quays that were built around 1900 had a depth of up to 60 metres, those built in between the two World Wars were at least 100 metres deep. And by the time the Ten Year Plan was implemented, quays with a depth between 150 (Suykens 1978, 444) and 270 metres were no exception. Among cargo handlers, Hessenatie was the pioneer, followed by the Noord Natie and other "naties" or stevedoring companies. The former specialized among other things in iron and steel, the Noord Natie in the handling and storage of oil, sugar, fruit and coffee. Further specialized terminals were built for artificial fertilizers, forest products, automobiles and silver sand.

Table 14.5. Total surface area of warehouses and sheds (square metres)

Year	Municipal (square metres)	Index (1960=100)	Private	Index (1960=100)
1960	939.120	100	512.296	100
1961	937.677	99	565.914	110
1965	958.301	102	784.176	253
1970	984.783	105	1.157.391	226
1975	916.082	98	1.545.421	302
1980	895.269	95	1.965.023	384
1981	894.605	95	2.014.531	393
1982	964.017	102	1.990.824	389

Source: Antwerp Port Authority

The constant growth of private investments is quite apparent from the following data on warehouses, lifting devices and general cargo berths equipped by private terminal operators: Antwerp offers over 4,8 million square metres of covered storage space.

Table 14.6. Covered warehouses in the port area (1956-2000) (hectares)

Year	Surface (hectares)
1956	128.9
1960	145.1
1965	174.2
1970	214.2
1974	230.7
1980	286.0
1985	303.3
1990	379.0
1994	420.0

Source: Antwerp Port Authority

The newer loading bridges for containers were financed entirely by the private sector.[2]

Table 14.7. Length of berths equipped by private terminal operators

Year	Length (metres)
1960	4.244
1965	10.406
1970	10.863
1975	16.980
1980	17.059
1982	20.449

Source: Suykens 1982

These figures regarding the number of cranes and their capacity, as well as the surface area of quay sheds and warehouses and the growth of the available land illustrate how Antwerp gradually became a *landlord port*, a development that had previously unfolded in the Netherlands (Fig. 14.2). The gradual shift took place in order to allow private firms to generate enough cash flow for new investments. Indeed, loading and unloading activities in the port of Antwerp had traditionally been carried out by a large number of small companies.

[2] Antwerp Municipal Port Authority: the first loading-bridge was erected in 1967. In 1982 private enterprises had invested in no fewer than thirteen bridges.

Fig. 14.2. Total surface (hectare) of long-term concessions allocated to different types of companies in the port of Antwerp (1945-1994)

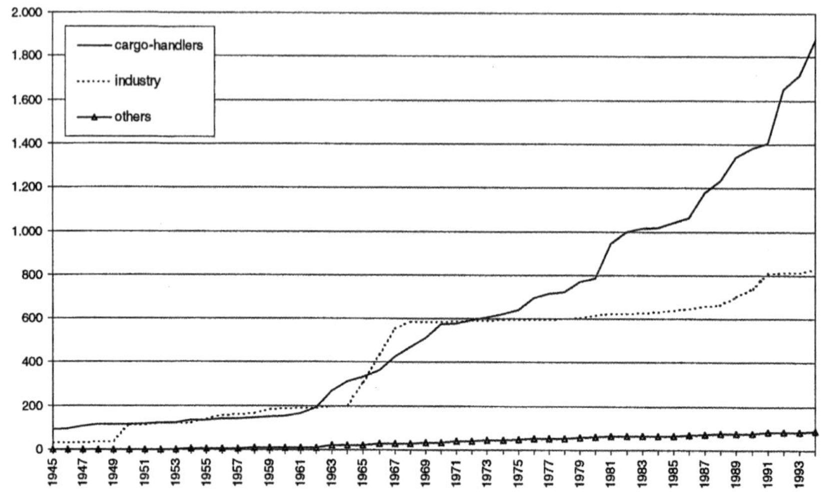

Source: City of Antwerp, *Municipal Journal.* (Note: sale of port territory not included)

Port industry

The rapid expansion of the port after 1956 was based on a planned approach that distinguished quite clearly between industrial and transhipment areas. Port-related industrialization of the European ports became important. The relocation of industrial activities to the port area was driven primarily by the introduction of new power sources and by the breakthrough of the petrochemical industry. The creation of so-called Maritime Industrial Development Areas (MIDAs) was made even more attractive by European economic integration, which necessitated larger production units and attracted American visitors to Europe.

Of course, port industrialization exerted a direct influence on the current quay and land-use policy. As a rule, the port authority applied, and indeed still applies, the principles of renting, leasing or conceding of industrial sites. Rarely was land sold. Still, some foreign investors insisted, and they were eventually able to buy land. This was a new formula, which allowed BAYER, BASF and General Motors Continental to acquire large plots at fairly reasonable prices. These plots of land were invariably located behind the quays. Only a few concerns were able to establish plants adjacent to deep-water quays.

As regards the term of leases or grants, it is obvious that several elements were taken into account. Among the most decisive factors were the planned investments, the nature of the industrial or other activity, the output or the resulting port traffic, and the labour intensity. The plots were leased for periods up to eighty years.

However, certain problems presented themselves. The first concerned the possibility of extending the rent period. The general principle was that tenants, hirers or leaseholders had right of priority when it came to contract renewal. The second problem had to do with the possibility to expand, which should be an option for any industrial plant located in the harbour area. Here the principle of option was applied, whereby preference was given to options involving payment of a reduced rent during a relatively short period of five years. It was indeed important to the port authority that sites should not remain unused too long. But some industries extended very gradually. BASF, for example, initially used just 90 hectares of the 440 hectares which it acquired, while Monsanto used a mere 10 hectares out of 102 hectares leased.

Table 14.8. Industrial sites on the Right Bank (1966)

Type	Proportion of total port surface
Chemical and petrochemical plants	54,8 %
Oil refineries	26,5 %
Automobile industry	13,4 %
Dry docks and ship repairing	3,9 %
Timber sawmills	0,4 %
Others	0,4 %

Source: Stad Antwerpen 1966.

Of course, the whole development was driven by Belgian legislation passed towards the end of the 1950s. The so-called "Expansion Acts" of 17 and 18 July 1959 opened the way for multinationals to settle in the port of Antwerp and absorb unemployment. By the mid-1960s, in no time at all, most of the land on the Right Bank (1.774 hectares) had been leased or, in some cases, sold to industry. The three remaining plots in 1966 were in huge demand.

From 1963 on, the imbalance between supply and demand prompted some industries to settle on the Left Bank. Polysar (30 hectares), Atlantic Polymers (65 hectares) and Cobenam (200 hectares) were the first to acquire land in the area known as Melselepolder. Some of these enterprises were connected with installations on the Right Bank by pipelines. From the beginning, the industrial development of the Left Bank maintained functional links with industry on the Right Bank. In some cases, there were also close financial links. By 1966, some 1.950 hectares of land on the Left Bank had already been sold.

Of course, the location of industrial plants within the port prompted protests from the traditional port users. Especially in forwarding and other maritime circles, the City was accused of applying a not very businesslike land policy. In response to this criticism, the port authority looked for a balance between investments in the expansion of the port and the preparation of sites for industry. This strategy implied careful environmental planning near the docks for general cargo, with a possibility of expanding warehouses and other installations, as well as the selection of new, mainly traffic-generating industries. It has since become obvious that the port has benefited greatly from this industrialization drive, both from a regional and from a national point of view.

4.4. New developments (1974-1994)

The number of concessions continued to increase as the expansion of the port went on. On the Right Bank, specialized container terminals were now being operated at Churchill Dock (opened in 1967) and at Delwaide Dock (opened in 1979). The general operators were Allied Stevedores, Antwerp Combined Terminals (ACT), (a merger of the stevedoring firms Pays and Müller Thomsen and a "natie" called Nieuwe Werk Natie), Hessenatie, Noordnatie and Seaport Terminals / Katoen Natie and Gylsen Stevedoring.

In 1971, a start was made with the construction of the new Kallo Lock, which heralded an expansion of the port on the Left Bank. The work was completed by the early eighties. The new Waaslandhaven, together with two mooring docks, was allocable to the private sector. The new dock area opened the road for investments in dedicated and multifunctional terminals.

The space granted to cargo handlers became increasingly substantial. The inland depth of terminals now varied between 500 and 700 metres, which created possibilities for integrated cargo handling with logistic and semi-industrial activities. Nevertheless, the port industry continued to occupy even more space, despite a slowdown since the 1973 crisis. So on the one hand there was a need for larger quays for container traffic; greater vessel perimeters and the introduction of integrated logistic handling of cargo required larger long-term concessions. On the other hand the consequences of the oil crises, a stricter application of environmental legislation and the restructuring of existing industry also played a role. Moreover, the very large plots of land conceded and sold to industry in the 1960s provided ample space for further expansion of plants in the seventies.

Table 14.9. Concessions granted to the three biggest cargo handlers

Company	1945-1970 (hectares)	1971-1994 (hectares)	Total (hectares)
Hessenatie	49,21	211,89	261,10
Noord Natie	31,99	132,47	164,46
Katoen Natie/Seaport Terminals	3,21	186,61	189,82

Source: Calculations based on data compiled by B. Lemayeur

Mergers between cargo handling firms created larger and more substantial groups. By 1994, the three biggest cargo handlers occupied at least 34 % of the land for which long-term concessions had been granted to cargo handlers and distributors (Fig. 14.3).

Local industry attracted interesting basic freight and stimulated exports. Many smaller cargo handlers, such as timber naties, specialized in chemical products for example. The possibilities for storage and throughput grew constantly. As "physical distribution" had become a new magic word and industry preferred to focus on core activities, the old naties, having lost their traditional cargo, concentrated on the logistic chain and on the handling of "new" products.

Fig. 14.3. Total surface (hectares) of long-term concessions allocated to the cargo-handlers Hessenatie, Noord Natie and Katoen Natie-Seaport Terminals in the port of Antwerp (1945-1994)

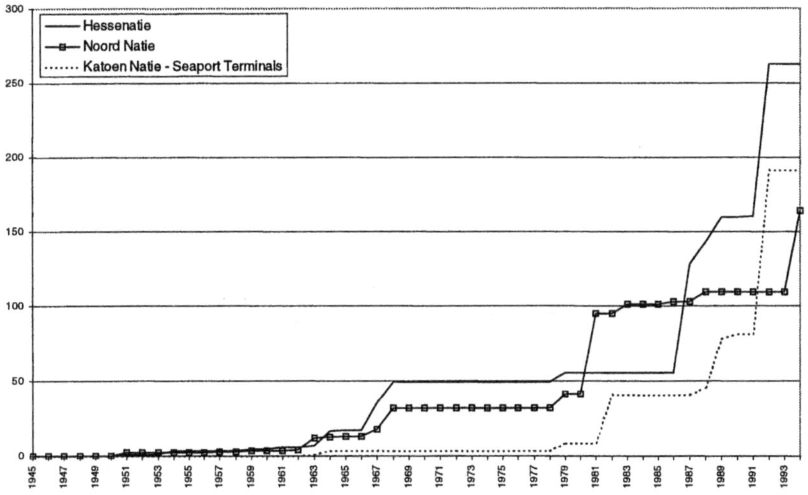

Source: City of Antwerp, *Municipal Journal.* (Note: sales of port territory not included.)

The second half of the 1980s was the beginning of a new chapter. In 1987 the Antwerp Municipal Council awarded the concession for the first Scheldt container terminal, located south of the new Zandvliet and Berendrecht locks, to NV Hessenatie-Neptunus. Again, objections were raised on the basis that this entailed a threat of monopolization. The attractive location of the terminal near the river, which would allow containerships with a deep draught to save time and money by avoiding locks, waiting times, possible claims and dock dues, was a provocation to all terminal operators in the docks. It was clear that the future in container handling belonged to cargo handlers possessing terminals outside the docks. Meanwhile other concessions were being granted for terminals on the riverside.

A new trend was unfolding: shipping companies, and especially large container shipping companies, were joining forces with terminal operators in an effort to acquire concessions together. Furthermore, scale increases and the enormous investments that were now required were conducive to mergers between even larger firms, as very recently between the Hessenatie and the Noord Natie.

Table 14.10. Net-surface area conceded and sold to port industry and port services (1994)

Sector	Right Bank (hectares)	Left Bank (hectares)	Total (hectares)	Proportion
Port industry	2.023	869	2.892	60 %
Port services	1.495	408	1.903	39 %
Total	3.518	1.277	4.795	100 %

Source: Antwerp Port Authority

Be that as it may, industry is the fastest grower when it comes to land occupation (leased and bought). During the 1960s, almost 80 hectares of land was made available to industry every year. Later, this amount dropped to 50 hectares a year.

Table 14.11. Industrial land policy (1994) (Right and Left Bank)

Type	Proportion of total port surface
Chemical and petrochemical industries	64 %
Oil refinery and oil processing	16 %
Car industry	5 %
Electricity plants	9 %
Storage companies (industrial)	5 %
Others	1 %

Source: Antwerp Port Authority

In the early 1990s, the chemical and petrochemical industries were able to strengthen their positions. Shipbuilding and repair disappeared altogether. Car manufacturing dropped to a third its previous level.

Conclusion

Over the past 125 years, land-use policy in the port of Antwerp has undergone some profound changes: it has shifted from a policy focusing on the maritime sector, with quays being rented to shipping companies and shipping agents, to a policy geared to industry and cargo handlers. Technological changes since 1945 have necessitated cargo-handling firms to adapt to the new unit-loads. Some of these firms were able to acquire different bases in the port area: storage, container handling, ro/ro quays, multifunctional and dedicated terminals and even pre-assembly of cars (JIT, JIST, SILS...) and management of goods flows before and after processing, including certain activities at industrial plants.

Over the past 50 years, the port of Antwerp has evolved from a traditional transhipment port to a multifunctional port. The classical transhipment function has been complemented with a broad range of logistic services (storage, distribution, value-added logistics, semi-industrial activities...) as well as port-related industries.

No fewer than 1.100 long-term concessions were studied using data published by the Antwerp Municipal Journal. These concessions were unevenly spread over various periods (Fig. 14.4 and 14.5). This study shows that quay and land-use policy in the port has been a permanent and invariably delicate issue. In spite of the expansion of the port, demand has always exceeded supply. Step by step, a systematic policy has been developed, especially in the second half of the twentieth century. But, as in the past, this policy is not always transparent. It was not until 1984 that standard conditions were introduced for the acquisition of long-term concessions.

Fig. 14.4. Average surface (hectare) of the long-term concessions allocated to cargo-handlers and industrial companies in the port of Antwerp (1945-1994)

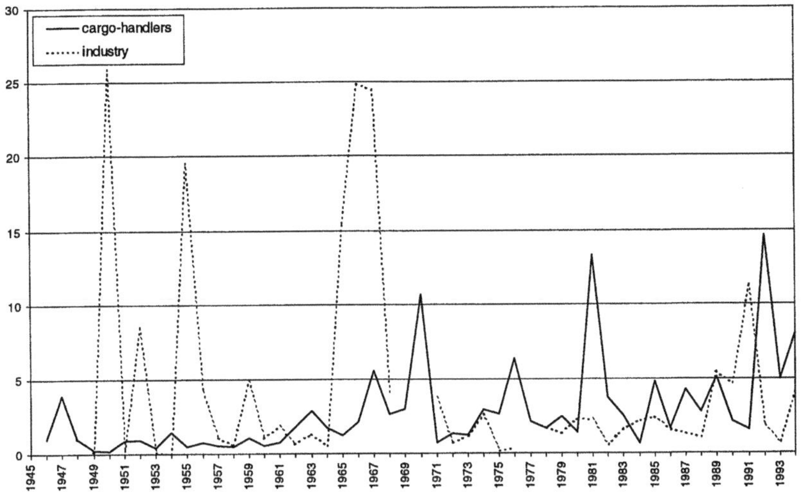

Source: City of Antwerp, *Municipal Journal.* (Note: sales of port territory not included)

Fig. 14.5. Yearly allocated new long-term concessions and changes in existing concessions in hectares in the port of Antwerp (1945-1994)

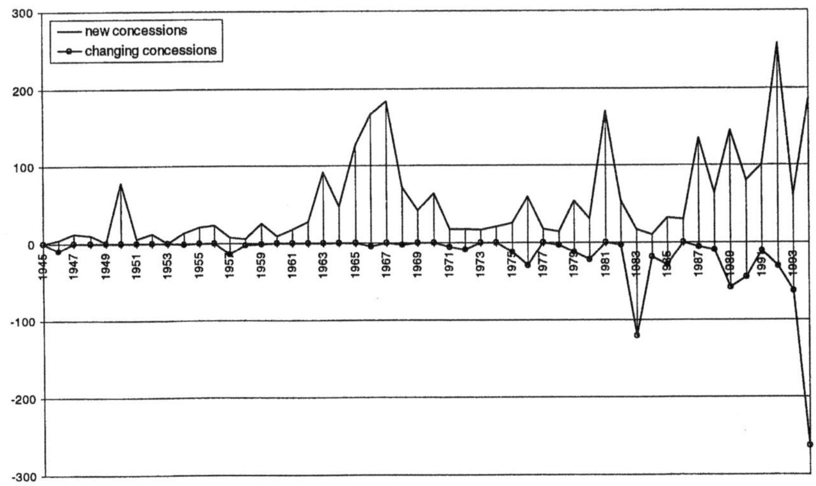

Source: City of Antwerp, *Municipal Journal.* (Note: sales of port territory not included.)

These conditions have since been changed in 1994 and in 1997. The "concession formula" provided the City with a powerful weapon. This became especially apparent in a recent case involving Katoen Natie, the third-largest cargo handler in the port. When it was unable to obtain a riverside terminal, this "victim" of the City's land policy started operations in the petrochemical and automotive industries at several locations in the world, thus becoming a global player.

Table 14.12. Net surface area by branch and sub branch (1994)

Sector	Right Bank (hectares)	Left Banks (hectares)	Total (hectares)	Proportion
Services	1.495	408	1.903	39 %
Containers	240	-	240	5 %
Other transhipment	621	330	951	19 %
Conventional	329	279	608	12 %
Dry bulk	194	35	229	4 %
Wet bulk (incl. tanks)	98	16	114	2 %
Distribution	361	73	434	9 %
Others	273	5	278	5 %
Industries	2.023	869	2.892	60 %
(Petro)Chemical	1.199	562	1.761	36 %
Others	824	307	1.131	23 %
Total	3.518	1.277	4.795	100 %

Source: Antwerp Port Authority

Fig. 14.6. Total surface in hectares of industrial and non-industrial companies in the port of Antwerp (1946-1994)

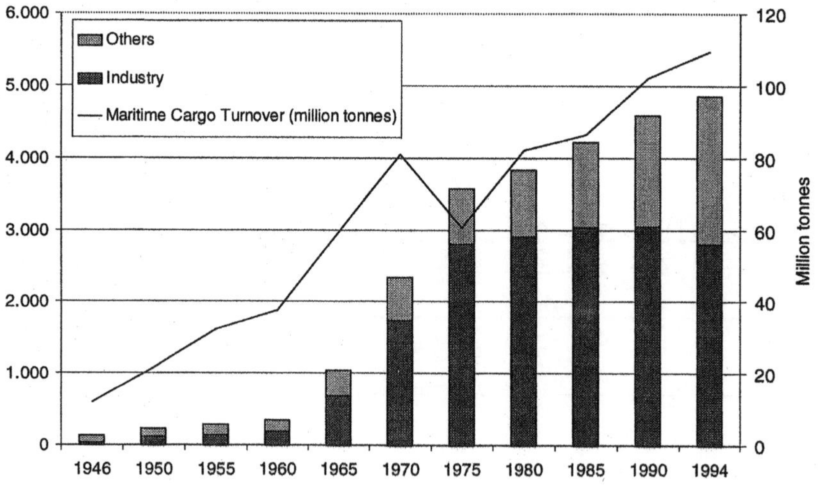

Source: City of Antwerp, *Municipal Journal.* (Note: sales of port territory not included)

In 1994, a total of 4.795 hectares of land on the Right and the Left Banks were conceded or sold for commercial and industrial purposes (Table 14.12). Over the past quarter of a century, more land has been conceded to port services (53 hectare/year) than to industry (44 hectare/year). Peaks were reached in periods when new docks were inaugurated (e.g. Churchill Dock in the late 1960s, Delwaide Dock in the early 1980s and Vrasene Dock at the beginning of the 1990s). Especially in the past ten years, the need for larger terminals has become greater in consequence of the emergence of new logistical concepts, scale increases in maritime traffic and the growing significance of the port's commercial function with the development of distribution zones. Between 1975 and 1994, long-term concessions were mostly granted to cargo handlers. The City never sold them plots of land.

From the 1960s, industry in the port has grown rapidly. Indeed, the majority of disposable land was leased or even sold to industry (Fig. 14.6). The petrochemical industry in particular developed quickly. Antwerp is now the second largest maritime centre for petrochemical processing in the world, after Houston[3], and this branch of industry occupies no less than 64 % (1994) of the industrial land in the port.

Table 14.13. Added value and employment per hectare on the Right and the Left Bank in 1997

	Added value/hectare	Employment/hectare
Right bank		
Industry	67.664	11,6
Petro-chemicals	65.605	8,1
Car assembly	89.867	38,4
Refining	84.246	5,0
Services	27.386	8,5
Services (incl city services)	34.307	10,7
Left bank		
Industry	31.745	5,1
Services	14.932	3,8
Services (incl city services)	18.172	4,8
Right and Left Bank		
Industry	54.178	9,1
Services	30.474	9,1
Services (incl city services)	35.390	11,8
Total	44.723	9,1
Total (incl city services)	46.684	10,21

Source: Antwerp Port Authority

[3] Recently this situation was stated by the Port Authority, although according to some, Antwerp occupies the third place after Houston and Singapore.

In a first phase, long-term concessions were granted on the basis of the financial strength of the applicant, the intended investments and the potential traffic generation. Subsequently, more attention was paid to the added value of port traffic. Antwerp is not a "stevedoring" port such as Rotterdam. The old "naties" still determine the face of the port with its impressive warehousing area. Indeed, Antwerp is the largest provider of storage space of all European ports. The port supplies 1.200 hectare (net) for maritime purposes, a third of which consists of covered storage space. Physical distribution, including preassembly, labelling, quality control, inventory management and after-sale services, generates the greater part of value-added. Nevertheless, relatively speaking, industrial activity creates more value-added. The type of industries and the surface area of conceded land mean that VA/ha ratio is higher on the Right Bank than on the Left Bank. As such, the value-added factor has more recently become a criterion in the port authority's land-use policy, which appears to have been quite successful. The port of Antwerp now accounts for two thirds of tonnage transhipped and between 70 % and 80 % of the value added and employment created in all Belgian ports.

Be that as it may, the commercial function of the port is becoming more significant. The recent trend of co-operation between container lines and large terminal operators underlines the importance of projected tidal docks on the Left Bank. The construction of additional capacity is absolutely necessary in order to keep up with the explosive growth that is unfolding in the container trade.

Fig. 14.7. Revenue of port duties and land concessions in real prices (Belgian Francs, 1945-1994)

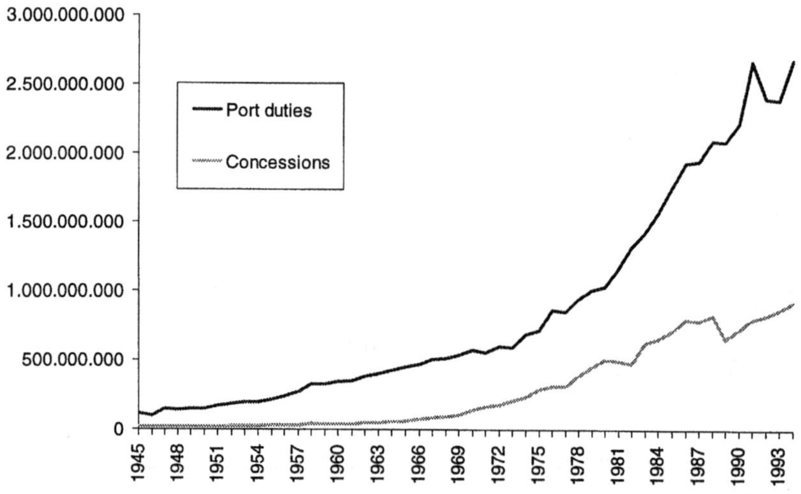

Source: City of Antwerp, Rekening over het Dienstjaar 1945-1987. Antwerp Port Authority, Financial Department (Note that the method of calculation was modified in 1988).

Especially after 1945 the City has endeavoured to balance income and expenditure. Port-users were charged by paying port duties or concession rates. The latter depended on the location of the plot, the quay equipment and the accessibility. Concession-rates evolved in line with the port-tariffs, although the cyclically sensitive port duties always surpassed the more stable revenues from the leasing of land (Fig. 14.7).

References

Devos G (1993) The Antwerp "nations" during the period 1815-1940. In: Asaert G (et al.) The naties in the port of Antwerp. Tielt

Devos G (1994) Moderniseringen in de haven van Antwerpen. De Compagnie des Docks-entrepôts et Magasins généraux d'Anvers. In: Maréchal G (ed) Een kompas met vele streken. Studie over Antwerpen, scheepvaart en archivistiek aangeboden aan G. Asaert. Antwerpen (VVBAD, Archiefkunde 5)

Devos G, Van Driel H (2000) De regulering van de overslag in de havens van Antwerpen en Rotterdam van 1870 tot 1950. NEHA-Jaarboek, LXIII: 151-152

Lemayeur B (1999) Het concessiebeleid en de maritieme sector te Antwerpen tussen traditie en vernieuwing (1918-1940). Antwerpen (Internal report).

Stad Antwerpen (1966) Uitbreiding van de haven op de Linker Scheldeoever. Antwerpen

Suykens F (1978) A few observations about productivity in seaports. European Transport Law. Journal of law and economics, 1978: 444-475

Suykens F (1979) A few observations about productivity in seaports. Hinterland, 1979: 435

Suykens F (1982) An example of the co-operation between the public and private sector in the port of Antwerp. Lloyd Anversois, 25-11-1982: 15

Suykens F (1991) The Major Breakthrough. In: Suykens F (et al.), Antwerp, The New Spring. Antwerp, pp 87-95

Toekomstproblemen (1942) voor Antwerpen als Handelscentrum en Haven Rapport sur l'équipement et l'outillage du port d'Anvers (Voorlichtingsdienst der Kamer van Koophandel van Antwerpen). Antwerpen

Van Tichelen J (1942) Le régime administratif et financier du port d'Anvers, rapport confidentiel (Chambre de Commerce d'Anvers). Anvers

Port of Rotterdam: land-use policy during the twentieth century

Ferry de Goey

Erasmus University Rotterdam, The Netherlands

Introduction

The transhipment of goods in the port of Rotterdam was able to grow by several per cent each year in the twentieth century, thanks to the renting of land to commercial firms specialising in the mechanized (sometimes even automated) handling of bulk goods. The selection of firms was connected with the way in which the port was organized and exploited. The main argument of this paper will be that there was a close causal link between the management and expansion of the port, policy on land use, and the increase in transhipment[1]. Figure 15.1. provides a basic outline of the complex economic relationship between port expenses and revenues. This relationship will be explored in this contribution.

In 1880 Rotterdam port's gross surface area was circa 200 hectares. By the year 2000 this area had grown to some 10.000 hectares, circa 4.800 of which were reserved for commercial purposes. There is still an option or reservation on part of the remaining available land (460 hectares). The area rented out to commercial companies was 4,208 hectares at the end of 1999. However, the area in effective use is smaller than the published extent of land in commercial use. At the present date, nearly 60% of the plots are being exploited by the petrochemical sector for transhipment and processing (see Table 15.1.) (RMPM 1999).

---

[1] Unless otherwise noted primarily based on de Goey 1990. For a recent survey of literature on maritime history in the Netherlands, see Broeze 1998.

Fig. 15.1. Port economics: expenditures and income

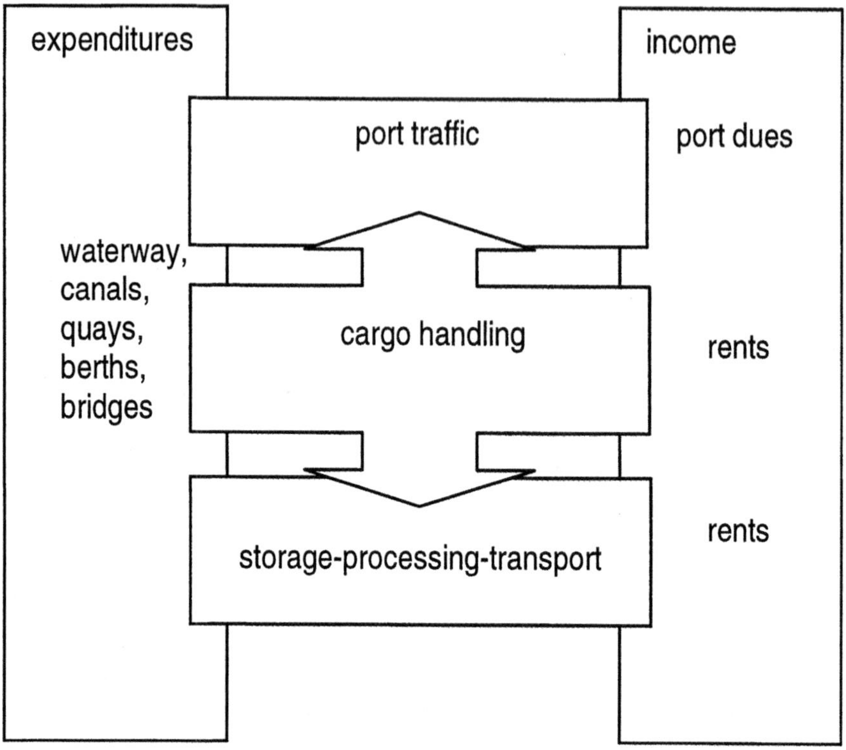

Table 15.1. Land rented in 1999

	Hectares
Liquid bulk	2394
Containers	998
Dry bulk	428
General cargo	388

Source: RMPM 1999

The following questions occupy central place here. What was the Municipality's point of departure for its policy on land use? What were the concrete effects of this policy? To what extent did the policy contribute to the increase in the transhipment of goods in the port? Here, "land-use policy" means the construction and exploitation of commercial land. First, a few general remarks have to be made about Rotterdam's port policy, the nature of the port, and the organization of port management (section 2). Next, the land policy itself is discussed in sections 3 (the period up to 1940) and 4 (the post-1940 period). These questions will be answered in the final section: Conclusion.

1. The management of the port in the twentieth century

Rotterdam is a municipal port, i.e. the Municipality is the port's formal owner. There is investment in the design, construction, maintenance and renovation of the infrastructure. In the period 1869-1939 this involved a total of 189 million guilders. A sum like this cannot be compared with the 2.058 million guilders invested in the port between the years 1995 and 2000 alone[2]. The Municipality recovers this money by taxing the port's users. The chief levy of this kind consists of harbour dues and the rents or leases on port land. Almost 70% of the income raised in 1980 came from harbour dues, while rather more than 20% came from rents (RMPM 1980). These sums are unlikely to be very different at the present date. The result is that, the greater the number of ships entering Rotterdam port, and the greater the volume of goods transhipped there, the greater the income earned by the Municipality.

Down the years the Municipality has endeavoured to balance income and expenditure. As far as possible, exploitation of the port must cover its own costs. Initial losses resulting from large-scale investment have always been accepted, but not structurally negative results.

In 1932 the Municipality decided to hand over the exploitation of the port to a separate Municipal service, the "Gemeentelijk Havenbedrijf Rotterdam" (Rotterdam Port Authority). This is now called the Rotterdam Municipal Port Management (RMPM). By instituting this body, Rotterdam Municipality hoped to improve the direction of the port's economic development. The new service was given three main tasks: port planning (design of new harbours), port exploitation (collecting harbour dues en rents) and port management (supervision of safety, and inspecting the compliance with rules and regulations).

In small countries like the Netherlands and Belgium land is considered a scarce resource. Claims on land for competing functions are normal. Discussions on how much land should be reserved for industrial activity, recreation, housing, roads, take a long time. Lengthy procedures on consultation and negotiation with all stakeholders are even required by law since the 1960s. The time lag between the first draft of a port plan and its final realization has steadily increased from a few months at the beginning of the twentieth century to almost two decades by the year 2000. This has made port planning a difficult task.

Ports usually occupy large tracts of space that rules out any other activity in the area nearby. A port infrastructure last for at least 100 years. Dedicating land to port development is thus a very important decision for any authority. Since the end of the nineteenth century the port of Rotterdam could only expand by enlarging the boundaries of the Municipality at the expense of neighbouring villages and

---

[2] Source for 1869-1939: van de Laar 1999. Source for 1995-2000 RMPM 1999.

towns[3]. These border corrections as they were called in the Netherlands, required two things: a port plan and the approval of the national government. The neighbouring municipalities and provincial governments were not always willing to comply to the wishes of Rotterdam and some put up a good fight, but in long run they were not able to prevent port expansion. As a result the port now stretches from the city centre into the North Sea, which is almost 30 kilometre.

Rotterdam is usually typified as a "landlord" port, i.e., the Municipality is responsible only for the port's infrastructure (van Klink 1995, Stevens 1999). This infrastructure can be divided into public facilities such as roads and bridges, and infrastructural provisions for the port itself. The latter can again be divided into "wet" and "dry" infrastructure: the waterways, harbour basins and quay walls, the land occupied by commercial enterprises, and so on. The Municipality does not interfere with "superstructural" matters such as cranes, storage sheds and warehouses, storage tanks, commercial premises, for example.

This characterization of Rotterdam port is not entirely accurate. After all, for nearly a century (1882 to circa 1970) the Municipality itself also owned a large number of cranes, storage sheds, warehouses and dry docks, facilities that were rented out to commercial firms in the port. However, the Municipal Port Authority always regarded these facilities as a non-municipal activity. In the 1960s they were sold or discontinued.

The Municipality, as owner of the land in the port and as financier for the infrastructure, has always had the ultimate voice in deciding which firms should be given access to port land. The Municipality can also decide the way in which the facilities can be used. For example, the Municipality requires guarantees concerning the quantities of goods each firm plans to tranship each year. This was always important in deciding whether or not to allot plots of land with access to deep-water moorings. The way in which commercial plots were awarded in the twentieth century, and the results achieved, is discussed in the subsequent two sections. Section 2 deals with the period up to 1940, while developments since 1940 are discussed in section 3.

2. Policy on land use before 1940: points of departure, and results

Before there can be any question of a land-use policy, the land for commercial use has to be made available. Rotterdam achieved this by constructing new harbours[4]. There were two phases of large-scale harbour expansion: 1880-1920, and 1950-1975 (see Figure 15.2.). Here, we will be discussing the first period. No historical scolary research has been done on port expansion and land-use policy covering the

---

[3] This concerns the following villages and towns: Charlois, Cool, Delfshaven, Hillegersberg, Hoogvliet, Katendrecht, Kralingen, Overschie, Schiebroek, Pernis, IJsselmonde.

[4] Since Rotterdam is a tidal port there are no locks. For this reason I prefer to use "harbour" and not the more conventional "dock".

period before 1940. The remarks below are based on secondary sources and a few case studies[5].

Fig. 15.2. Port of Rotterdam: expansion 1400s - 2000

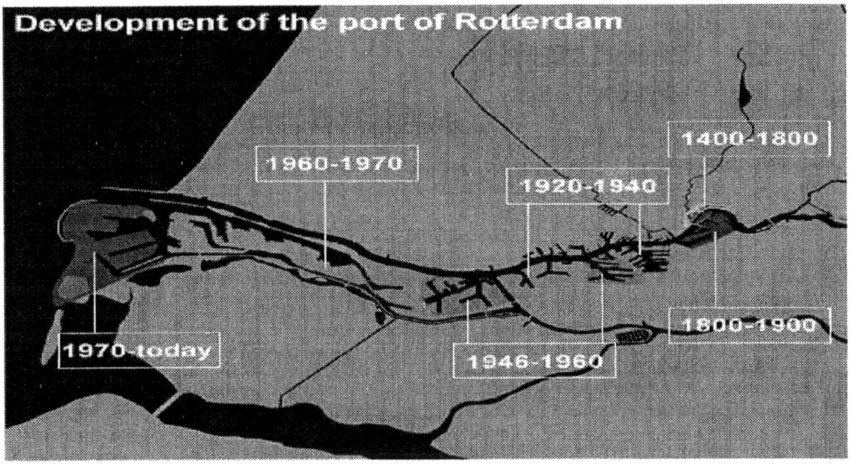

Between 1880 and 1914 the Municipality invested a total of eighty million guilders in the port (van de Laar 2000). Most of the money was spent on constructing harbours for handling bulk goods on the South bank, and general (mixed) cargoes on the North bank (see Table 15.2.). The result of constructing new harbours was an increase in the overall port area from circa 200 hectares in 1880, to some 1.800 hectares in 1940.

The harbours on the southern riverbank, especially the Rijnhaven, Maashaven and Waalhaven, were destined for the transhipment of bulk goods like coal, ores, grain and wood. These commodities were either coming from, or going to the German hinterland. Seagoing and inland shipping mingled in the harbours, which consequently required more room, a factor taken into account in the plans for the new harbours. The relationship between quaysides and water surface area favoured the water over quaysides.

The harbours on the northern bank (the Driehaven and Vierhaven plan) were planned with the transhipment of mixed cargoes in mind, and also the location for smaller seagoing liner traffic - for example, the Batavier Line to England. In contrast to the harbours on the South bank, these North-bank installations were still being designed according to old principles. In other words, they were narrow, with a large proportion of quaysides in relation to water surface. Inland shipping was of less importance here. The goods customarily carried by inland shipping were usually transported to market by rail, and later also by goods lorries. The construction of these mixed-cargo harbours was an attempt to reduce Rotterdam's existing ar-

---

[5] The well known Ph.D of (Backx 1929) has no information at all on land-use policy.

rears in comparison with Antwerp, where the transhipment of mixed cargoes was concerned (van de Laar 2000, 97-98).

Table 15.2. Port expansion Rotterdam (1870-1940)

North bank River Maas:
Dokhaven (1882, Municipal Dry Dock)
Parkhaven and Nassauhaven (1890)
Schiehaven (1904-1909)
St. Jobshaven (1906-1908)
Vierhavenplan (Four Harbour Plan) (Lekhaven, Keilehaven, IJsselhaven and Koushaven, 1911-1916)
Driehavenplan (Three Harbour Plan) (Merwehaven, 1923-1930)
South Bank River Maas:
Spoorweghaven, Entrepothaven, Binnenhaven, Koningshaven (formerly owned by RHV, 1872-1882),
Persoonshaven (1873-1897, owned by the government)
Eerste Katendrechtsehaven, Robbenoordsehaven, Kortenoordsehaven, Rijnhaven (1887-1894)
Maashaven (1898-1905)
Waalhaven (1906-1922)
(First) Petroleumhaven (Petrol Harbour) (1929)
Second Petroleumhaven (started 1939)

In the distribution of these new harbour lands, Rotterdam was guided by rather general criteria such as harbour exploitation (was it self-supporting?), competitive relations (what was going on in Antwerp and Hamburg?), and employment opportunities offered. For the few plots with their own quaysides giving on to deep water, the main criteria for allotting a site was the nature and quantity of the goods to be transhipped. Before 1940 Rotterdam Municipality had no fundamental policy on land use. In some parts of the city pieces of land were sold, while in other parts the land was only rented out. In general though, we can say that no land was sold in the newly constructed harbours on the South and North banks. It was only rented to business concerns. However, there could be exceptions to this general rule, as we can see from the case study of the Ford Motor Company.

When the Ford Motor Company decided in 1929 to build an assembly factory in the Netherlands, its first choice was Amsterdam. However, in 1918 that city had decided not to sell any more of its land, but only to rent it, in order to combat land speculation. Because this policy was firmly adhered to, Ford decided to try Rotterdam. According to the Municipality, a parcel of land on the Waalhaven (on the South bank) was most suited to the assembly of cars. Ford could have purchased this plot, had it so wished, but the Company felt among other things that the land was too far from the city centre. In the end, Ford built a factory on the edge of the city centre, on the North bank.

Ford would also have liked a plot with its own quayside giving on to deep water. The Municipality refused to countenance this request since there was too little traffic into, and out of the Ford factory. The Company had to be content with a wooden jetty on the Maas, where the car parts, packed in wooden chests, were unloaded and transported to the factory. In 1932, however, while the Rotterdam factory was almost finished, Ford decided to build a much larger factory in Amsterdam. The Rotterdam establishment was transformed into a showroom. In Amsterdam the Ford Company was after all able to buy land with direct access to water, because the local authorities decided to "postpone" their land policy just to accommodate Ford (de Goey 2000).

Table 15.3. Bulk import in Rotterdam (1910-1920 and 1925 in thousand tons)

Year	1910	1920	1925
Grain	3.991	1569	2.938
Ore	6.237	932	7.766
Coal	1.448	2.707	831
Wood	1.452	233	1.008
Subtotal	13128	5441	12543
Other	4.731	1.908	4.503
Total	17.859	7.349	17.046
Bulk (%)	74	74	74

Source: Herbig 1928, 15 and 65.

A consequence of the construction of harbours for handling bulk goods was that, even before 1940, Rotterdam became a major European bulk-goods port. In the first quarter of the twentieth century the proportion of bulk to general mixed cargoes was 75: 25 (see Table 15.3.). This table does not include the storage and transhipment of petroleum - facilities existing in Rotterdam from 1862 onwards. In 1880 some 230,000 barrels, each weighing 150 kg (circa 34,500 tonnes) were shipped into the port. By 1939 this figure had risen to 6.6 million tonnes. The transhipment of these bulk cargoes did indeed provide work, but the added value of this was extremely limited. Barely anything was done with the goods themselves in Rotterdam. Before 1940 some 70-75% of all goods were transit goods, coming from of going to Germany.

One result of this dominance of bulk goods was that tramp-steamer-shipping companies had greater importance in Rotterdam than the liner companies. However, from 1883 onwards the liner companies (for example, the Holland America Line - HAL - and the Rotterdam Lloyd line - RL) were given priority in renting berths from the Municipality. A factor that may well have played a major role here, is that in Rotterdam the liner traffic was less developed than it was in Antwerp. The choice in favour of liner companies was also certainly prompted by the fact that the very nature of these companies ensured a moderately secure income for the Municipality. Once these companies had guarantees for permanent berths for their expensive passenger ships, they also began to invest in buildings and installations on the lands behind the berths. In 1890 the Municipality entered into a contract for thirty years with HAL, and for twenty-five years with RL.

After 1890 independent stevedore enterprises were also granted the opportunity to rent lands fronting deep water, even though they were not involved in actual shipping-company business. These stevedore firms usually worked for foreign shipping companies regularly putting into Rotterdam port, which usually contracted out to local stevedore firms for the loading and unloading of their vessels.

Consequently stevedore companies began to place their own installations (cranes, weighing bridges and so on) on these lands, and to build storage sheds and warehouses. Since they were investing their own money in cranes, rather than depending on the Municipality for their use, they had a much sharper eye for technical and economic possibilities. As a result there was a rapid introduction of new transhipment techniques, and an increase in the volume of bulk goods handled in Rotterdam. One must ask whether these improvements and innovations would have been achieved, had the stevedore firms not been able to acquire their own plots of land in the port before 1940.

In this way the practice developed, circa 1900, in which Rotterdam Municipality confined its activities to the port's infrastructure, and in which private enterprises themselves invested in the superstructure. Land in the port was also rented out to business concerns in Rotterdam, for periods of twenty-five to ninety-nine years (Devos and van Driel 2000). In the long run the Municipality made no distinction between liner companies, stevedore concerns, or industries. Thus Royal Dutch Oil (De Koninklijke Olie company, after the merger with Shell in 1907: Royal Dutch/Shell) was given permission in 1902 to build a petrol processing plant on the location Charlois. The site fronted deep water. The deciding factor was no longer the kind of activity carried out, but rather the quantity of goods shipped in and out of the port or - to put it another way - the harbour dues paid to the Municipality.

The construction of harbours on the South bank (Rijnhaven, Maashaven and Waalhaven) had a major influence on the development of Rotterdam as a bulk-goods port. In the three harbours just named, seagoing ships were able to unload their cargoes directly onto inland-shipping vessels. The cargo no longer had to be transhipped via the quays, a technique that saved time and money. Seagoing ships were moored directly to mooring posts and chains in the harbour basins, while inland boats could lie alongside (van Driel and de Goey 2000). This was possible because the water surface area of these harbours was much greater than it was in the harbours built in an earlier period or on the North bank. Thanks to this factor, and to the use of floating cranes and elevators, the rate of transhipment in Rotterdam could at last match that in Antwerp, eventually surpassing it (Table 15.4.). Transhipment increased from one million tons in 1870 to nineteen million tons in 1939.

Table 15.4. Net Cargo Rotterdam and Antwerp (1970-1939 in thousand tons)

Year	Rotterdam	Antwerp
1870	1.026	1.317
1880	1.682	2.650
1890	2.939	3.840
1900	6.360	5.688
1910	10.877	10.756
1920	7.607	9.230
1930	20.536	19.242
1939	19.392	15.899

Source: Veraghtert 1978

3. Land-use policy after 1940: points of departure and results

In the second phase of large-scale port expansion, 1950 - 1975, even larger harbours were constructed than before 1940 (Table 15.5.). The Botlek Plan (1947) and the Plan Europort/Maasvlakte (1957) provided some seven hundred hectares and one thousand hectares respectively in commercial plots. The Eemhaven complex (constructed in the 1960s) added another 250 hectares to this total. From 1955 onwards, very large plots of ground were rented out to companies. In contrast to the period before 1940, a great many industries were involved here: refineries, petro-chemical and chemical plants. As we shall see, Rotterdam did in fact exercize a certain amount of selection in the case of land in Botlek and Europort. With the construction of these large harbour complexes the port area, measuring 1400 hectares gross in 1950, grew to some 7.600 hectares gross by 1975. This went hand in hand with large-scale investment. The value of the permanent assets involved, gives us a some impression of this. The acquisition value of these permanent assets increased from 210 million guilders in 1950, to 1.662 million guilders in 1970.

How did the Municipality distribute this vast amount of newly developed harbour land? What was its aims? One aim of the policy on land use has always been the Municipality's desire to make harbour exploitation at least self-supporting. Before 1940 this policy was reasonably successful, although the available figures are extremely unreliable (Serton 1919). However, after 1955 sharply increased outlay far exceeded income. Up to 1963 income and outlay still balanced each other, but from 1964 on, losses were much greater than gains. Such losses pressed hard on Municipal budgets. In 1972 the port related financial expenses were separated from the municipal accounts (Hazewinkel 1978, 23). Since the 1990s however, the port has (once again?) been making a profit. In 1999 the positive turnover amounted to 149 million guilders, of which ninety millions was deposited in the Municipal account. Remarkably enough, this development was more or less predicted as early as 1972 by a former Director of the Municipal Port Authority, ir. Frans Posthuma, who was the principal architect of the Europort/Maasvlakte (Posthuma 1972, 15-83).

Table 15.5. Port expansion, Rotterdam (1950-1975)

Botlek area: Chemiehaven, St. Laurenshaven and Derde Petroleumhaven (1947-1955)
Eemhaven: Eerste Eemhaven, Tweede Eemhaven, Prins Johan Frisohaven, Prinses Beatrixhaven, Prinses Margriethaven and Prins Willem Alexanderhaven (1955-1965) Europoort: Vierde, Vijfde, Zesde and Zevende Petroleumhaven, Beneluxhaven and Dintelhaven, Brittanniëhaven and Seinehaven (1955-1975)
Maasvlakte: Mississippihaven, Achtste Petroleumhaven (1968 -)

Rotterdam's land-use policy changed course several times after 1940. Perhaps its better to conclude that new criteria were added to older ones. Most important of all, the Municipality finally introduced a system of renting out lands in the port. The renting of lands in Rotterdam could, as before, be for periods of twenty-five years, with a maximum of 99 years. This system is called "erfpacht", or: long term lease. The user had some legal rights and obligations, but the land itself remained the property of the Municipality. The rent was revised every five years, in accordance with the current high rate of inflation in 1950s and 1960s. Before 1940, as we have seen, there had still been a mixed policy of renting and selling of land, and the Municipality pursued a pragmatic course in this. After 1940 the sale of land was ruled out. Requests from enterprises wishing to buy land in Botlek, Europort, and Maasvlakte, were refused. These request came mainly from capital-intensive businesses in the oil and chemical sector, which usually preferred to buy their land. This might have constituted a disadvantage in relation to the competitor Antwerp for example (as happened with the German company BASF in 1964. BASF choose to build their new plant in Antwerp and Rotterdam, partly for this reason). Nonetheless, the principal of renting land in fact entailed few disadvantageous results for Rotterdam, even though we cannot know how for sure how many enterprises moved to other ports for this reason alone. However, the ability to buy land was only one factor in deciding whether or not a company established itself in a particular place. In many cases Rotterdam obviously possessed so many other conditions attractive to investors that the purchase of land was one of the lesser importance.

After 1945 the employment factor played a major role in Municipal policy. This derived from the experience of mass unemployment in Rotterdam in the 1930s, and the population growth expected after 1945 ("baby boom"). Industrialization occupied a more important place in port policies than it had done before 1940. Rotterdam wanted to become independent of the German hinterland, so turned to the hope of attracting American companies, in particular. This aim was actively promoted by sending trade missions to the USA.

From circa 1960-1965 Rotterdam was to its own surprize confronted with a shortage of labour rather than a surplus. Moreover, this was now the beginning of a period in which the Municipality suffered large-scale budget deficits as the result of its investments in the new harbours. This gave new importance to the sound exploitation of these harbours. The Municipal Port Authority decided to introduce a system of selection. This system was known at the port authority as "klap-hek", roughly meaning: "turnpike". Enterprises generating large-scale transport of goods (and preferably of a labour-extensive kind) were given preference in the renting of port lands. This selection mechanism became widely known as the "tonnage system", in which the annual tonnage handled or attracted was the decisive factor in whether or not land was rented out to a business. In this way businesses transporting, transhipping or processing large quantities of goods found their way into the port, extensive lands being made available to them. Up to 1975 the port of Rotterdam was in the enviable position of finding that demand for port lands far exceeded supply, despite the enormous enlargement of the harbour after 1950. There were sometimes three or four applicants for the same plot of land. The Municipality opted for firms that fitted in with the "tonnage handled" system. Between 1963 and 1975 there were some 250 applications for commercial plots (Botlek and Europort/Maasvlakte area only). Out of these, some 109 (44%) were immediately rejected by the Municipality as being of little interest to port interests. Further consultations were held with the remaining applicants.

In circa 1975 port policy changed course once again. The establishment of new enterprises was subjected to much closer control. From that time on, such enterprises were obliged to conform with certain environmental demands. Rotterdam was confronted with large-scale anti-pollution protest and numerous pressure groups from Rotterdam and the surrounding cities (Boender 1985). The expansion of the port between 1950 and 1975 had taken place in such a rapid and according to critics uncontrolled manner that it could be said to constitute a serious pollution of the environment. The point of departure in policy, however, coincided with the economic recession after 1979 (the second oil crisis), resulting in a much reduced demand for plots of port land. Port expansion plans were cancelled[6]. After 1985 the number of new businesses to be established in the port once more began to increase, but this has involved a relatively small number of new investors. Most of the alterations made between 1975 and 1995 have resulted from mergers and takeovers, as well as expansion of those enterprises already existing. However, the port is running scarce on available sites. A Second Maasvlakte has already been proposed a few years ago (original plans dated form the 1970s!). In May 2001 the government in principal was in favour of the plan. Construction will take at least five to ten years.

Instead of trying to promote as much transhipment of goods as possible (tonnage), from 1985 onwards the Municipality's efforts lay in the direction of creating the maximum amount of added value. To this end the port had to direct greater attention to the processing of raw materials, the development of logistic chains in transport (for example, through the "Distriparks"), and - recently - the "network and knowledge harbour". In future added value has to come especially from the intelligent application of the computer tracking the movement of goods and the related flow of information and documents. This change in the point of departure was not an easy one to realize. The "tonnage system" was clear, and easily established, but the calculation and stimulation of added value presented greater difficulty.

A survey of the available commercial land, and the area leased out, shows that between 1950 and 1968 there was a great leap. From 1975, there was only limited growth (Table 15.6.).

Table 15.6. Land use (hectares) and throughput (million tons)

	1950	1958	1968	1975	1999
Gross	1.404	2.333	6.222	7.698	10.000
Available	780	1.530	3.530	4.790	4.800
Rented*	414	1.077	2.900	3.774	4.208
Throughput	30	74	160	273	303

Source: de Goey 1990. RMPM 1999. *Not recorded are reserved sites.

[6] The Second Maasvlakte plan was already drafted by engineers of the port authority in the early 1970s.

Between 1945 and 1975, fifty-six leasing contracts were made with enterprises, twenty-seven of which were industrial concerns and twenty-nine were transhipment firms. This still concerned only the Botlek and Europort/Maasvlakte. In the Eemhaven complex, especially meant for storage and transhipment activities, there was also a considerable number of enterprises already established. These included large-scale businesses such as Quickdispatch, W.M. Müller, KNSM (liner shipping), Burger, and after 1967 especially Europe Container Terminus (later called Europe Combined Terminals).

However, the rapid growth in transhipments from the port resulted from the advent of four refineries and a number of petro-chemical enterprises (Table 15.7.). Besides the Royal Dutch/Shell (1902/1931) installations, refineries were also built by Texaco, Esso, Gulf and BP. These companies also constructed large storage tanks. The presence of the refineries stimulated the establishment of related chemical enterprises handling the raw materials (oxygen for example), or processing byproducts obtained from the refineries.

Table 15.7. Oil and chemical industry in Rotterdam

	Number of sites	Site in square metres
Oil Refining	5	8.730.000
Chemical Production	40	7.280.000
Industrial Gases	7	254.000
Tank Storage	20	7.554.000
Total	72	23.818.000

Source: RMPM 1999.

The geographical expansion of the port, and the establishment of a large number of enterprises, was translated into an increase in the volume of transhipment. This rose from 29,7 million tons in 1950 to 273.2 million tons in 1975, and again to 303 million tons in 1999. The transhipment of bulk goods accounted for almost three-quarters of these figures (Table 15.8.).

Table 15.8. Throughput 1999 (million tons)

	Ton	%
Liquid bulk	139	46
Dry bulk	80	26
Containers	66	22
General cargo	18	6
Total	303	100

Source: RMPM 1999

Conclusion

The central questions are: what was the Municipality's point of departure for its policy on land use in the port? What were the results of this policy? To what extent did the land-use policy contribute to the growth in the transhipment of goods in the port?

In circa1900 the custom developed in Rotterdam whereby the Municipality took care of the infrastructure while the enterprises concerned themselves with the superstructure. This was a stimulus to investment in the most up-to-date storage and transhipment techniques.

The land-use policy is determined above all by the fact that the Municipality is, at the same time, the port's manager. The Municipality has to recover the costs of its investment in the port, which also constitutes a major source of employment (both direct and indirect) in both city and region. From 1940 onwards, the Municipality acknowledged only the obligation to rent out land, not to sell it outright. During the period 1955-1975 Rotterdam employed a system of selection in renting out commercial plots - the "tonnage system". In this, preference was given to enterprises which were engaged in a great deal of transhipment, and which, from the 1960s onwards, were not labour-intensive.

The results of this land-use policy could be measured by the increase in the volume of goods transhipped, from 2.1 million tons in 1884 to 303 million tons in 1999. It is also possible to calculate the increase from (for example) the number of ships putting into Rotterdam, or the growth in employment. Yet the conclusion must still be that the port of Rotterdam experienced a very striking growth in the twentieth century. The question now is, was there a positive causal relation with Rotterdam's land-use policy? In my view one can, indeed, talk of such a positive causal link. Granted, any enterprise ultimately decided for itself whether or not to invest in the port. Yet it was precisely at vital moments that Rotterdam Municipality was fortunate enough to find that the demand for land plots in the port was greater than the amount of land available. Because of this roles were reversed, and it was the Municipality that decided which enterprises were to be permitted access to port lands.

In my opinion the Municipality's land-use policy, and then the "tonnage system" in the period 1965-1975, had a great influence on the port's development. In fact, the result of this policy was that enterprises handling a very large volume of transhipment were allowed access to land in the port. This greatly increased the figures for transhipment of goods. Not only the volume of goods handled, but also the typical composition of the cargoes transhipped resulted directly from the selection criteria applied by the Municipal Port Authority. Goods of lower value but greater volume dominated the Rotterdam harbours. Large-scale mechanized firms handled their transhipment with relatively few workers. The classic, labour-intensive general mixed-cargo sector has for years been undergoing reorganization, and will ultimately disappear completely.

References

Boender K (1985) Milieuprotest in Rijnmond. Sociologische analyse van milieusolidariteit onder elites en publiek. Rijswijk

Broeze F (1998) The sea and ashore. A review of the historiography of modern shipping since the 1970s. NEHA-Bulletin XII- 1: 3-38

de Goey F (1990) Ruimte voor industrie. Rotterdam en de vestiging van industrie in de haven. Rotterdam

de Goey F (2000) De assemblagefabriek van Ford in Rotterdam (1924-1931). *NEHA-*Jaarboek voor economische, bedrijfs- en techniekgeschiedenis LIII: 166-195

Devos G, van Driel H (2000) De regulering van de overslag in de havens van Antwerpen en Rotterdam van 1870 tot 1950. NEHA-Jaarboek voor economische, bedrijfs- en techniekgeschiedenis LIII: 145-166.

Hazewinkel F (1978) Zeehavenbeleid van Rotterdam 1967-1975. Rotterdam

Herbig K (1928) Die Entwicklung der Häfen von Amsterdam und Rotterdam seit 1914. Leipzig

Posthuma F (1972) Het Havenbedrijf der Gemeente Rotterdam 1945-1965. In van Walsum GE (ed) Rotterdam Europoort 1945-1970. Rotterdam pp 15-83

RMPM (1980) Annual report. Rotterdam

RMPM (1999) Annual report. Rotterdam

Serton P (1919) Rotterdam als haven voor massagoederen. Nijmegen

Stevens H (1999) The institutional position of seaports. An international comparison. Dordrecht

van de Laar P (2000) Stad van formaat. Geschiedenis van Rotterdam in de negentiende en twintigste eeuw. Zwolle

van Driel H, de Goey F (2000) Rotterdam cargo handling technology 1870-2000. Eindhoven

van Klink A (1995) Towards the borderless mainport Rotterdam: an analysis of functional, spatial and administrative dynamics. Rotterdam

Veraghtert K (1974) Havens. In: Maritieme geschiedenis der Nederlanden. Bussum, part IV: 53-88

Commentary on the papers of Devos and de Goey

Sarah Palmer

Greenwich Maritime Institute, University of Greenwich, United Kingdom

In commenting on these two very good papers dealing with the construction and exploitation of facilities by these two municipal authorities, it is tempting, given the comparative focus of this volume, to dwell on the similarities and differences which emerge. Indeed in working out what I was going to say about the papers, I began with two columns headed ANTWERP and ROTTERDAM and noted down similarities and differences along a time line. This proved interesting but seemed in the end to be "forced" because arguably what is striking about these two policy histories are not the differences but the broad similarities.

We have here two ports both publicly owned, which to a greater or lesser degree at the beginning of the period and certainly at its end were not involved in day-to-day operations or the provision of working equipment, but chose instead a landlord function, leaving the provision of services to private enterprise. How, as public bodies, they related to their private sector partners provides the focus for both studies. One criticism one might make here is that neither paper perhaps explores sufficiently the process by which the land available was itself steadily expanded. Both take this context as given.

Looking then, not at these papers as parallel chronologies but in terms of common features, we can see that both authors have three aims:

- To answer the question, "*Who* was given access to this infrastructure and on what terms?"
- To answer the question "W*hy* was any particular group of service providers favoured?"
- To answer the question "What was the consequence of the 'who?' and the 'why?' for the port's development? What was the result?"

Reviewing Professor Devos' and Dr de Goey's papers, I would say that the "who?" is well answered and here we must acknowledge the enormous amount of meticulous research needed to establish such basic facts. I would say that the "why?" is partially answered. Finally, I would say that "with what results?" is less satisfactorily answered. This is not, it is fair to say, so much the fault of the authors as a reflection of the difficulty of establishing direct causal links.

Considering the question of who was given access to the infrastructure, we can see in the case of Rotterdam that liner companies, stevedore and other transhipment enterprises feature. In the case of Antwerp, the starting points are different; the Natie contribution gives a distinct flavour, industrial sectors particularly benefit and there is over time a shift of superstructure from public to private operators.

In the case of the question, "On what terms?" we can see in Antwerp a tendency to long term lets, with sale becoming more common by the 1960s. Rotterdam is different, with sale possible up to the Second World War, then renting out becomes the preferred option. It would have been good in the case of both papers to have more assessment of the significance of these shifts. If we turn to the "Why?" I would comment that the underlying financial imperatives come out more clearly in the Rotterdam paper than they do in the Antwerp paper. I would have liked to see in Professor Devos' paper some indication of the relative importance of rents, as against dues on shipping, in generating port authority income. In Dr De Goey's paper it is clear that taxes on users are by far the most important revenue source for Rotterdam.. This provides an explanation of the "tonnage system" as the dominant criterion for the award of land until the 1990s. In the case of both papers, it would, however, have been useful to have some explanation of the policy shift to a value-added approach in more recent years.

A weakness of both authors' contributions is that policy imperatives are treated as a "given". We do not get much sense of the interests and pressures which, for example, led to a preference for rent over sale. Where did the environmental concerns, which surfaced in Rotterdam in recent decades, come from? I accept, of course, that other papers in the volume explore these issues, but I think that some indication of an awareness that policy is itself constructed, that it does not develop *sui generis,* would strengthen the argument.

Finally, there is the question of the results of these landlord policies for the two ports. This is admittedly difficult because we have here two apparently successful ports so it is tempting to assume a causal link between policy choices and this outcome. We have to acknowledge that land policy is only one factor among many in traffic generation. These two well-researched and thoughtful papers do, however, demonstrate convincingly the way in which decisions on land use have shaped the characteristics of Antwerp and Rotterdam.

Evolution of the Rotterdam port authority's position

Henrik Stevens

Zeeland Seaports, The Netherlands

Introduction

This paper focuses on the past and current position of the port authority of Rotterdam. The general assumption laying behind the present volume is that the seaports of Rotterdam and Antwerp have reacted differently to more or less the same international economic developments and chances. To what extent this assumption can be justified is however the main theme and question of the volume itself. Before going into detail on the specific Rotterdam port authority's position some remarks on comparing seaports and seaport institutional structures have to be made.

The comparison of seaports has been a very interesting activity for various reasons. One reason has a commercial background. By comparing one discovers its own strong and weak elements which have to be put in perspective towards clients. Another reason is that port administrators like to know whether the port is performing well or that it can be organized in an other and even better way. In other words, ports are compared to compete as effectively as possible and to learn from each other. Finally a reason for comparing ports can be found in the fact that the port management is looking for agreement on topics like the uniforming of laws and legislation. This foremost European element is pushing for more than decades to establish a level playing field, which has to guarantee the fair competition between ports.

With respect to the starting point of the volume it is inevitable to say nothing about the competitive position of a seaport in general. Once one is talking about the competitive position of a seaport, which is the result of the combination of vision, strategies, chances, current developments and luck, one is comparing by definition. A port never takes an independent, stand-alone function. This position can only be made clear by comparing it with other ports. Therefor it is very important that in the art of comparing apples are not compared with pears. As soon as one realizes this fact together with the fact that ports have developed over centuries in different geographic, economic and societal circumstances, one has to admit that every seaport has its own advantages and disadvantages, its own chances and its own weaknesses.

If one is eager to make a port comparison then it is the question on what topics the ports will be compared. This certainly depends on the goal. In this respect the phrase "Where you stand depends on where you sit" says a lot. In other words, the way in which you compare, depends on how you are looking. When one as a port director wants to have information on the quality of the own location factors one makes comparisons on such items as nautical entrance, land prices, hinterland connections, environmental conditions, regional and local spatial plans, the amount of port dues in total, possibilities for subsidies, the quality and quantity of labour supply, possibilities for intermodal transport, etc. However as a port commissioner interested in the question of the own port records in comparison to other ports one is interested in elements like the quantity of land-leasing in the last ten years, the growth of the total and sector specific quantity of sea-borne cargo in the last five years, the added value for the region and the country, the modal split, the possibilities for new port developments and the implementation of approved plans, the growth of the port employment, the openness of the relations between port authority and port community, the ways in which legislation is executed, the ways in which other governments co-finance in port projects, etc. It may be clear that the way in which one compares ports will determine the result of that comparison.

Above all it is very clear that all comparisons are bound in time. Time does not end. New companies come, others go or are taken over or will expand in the port area; new infrastructure will be constructed, replaced or demolished. The port is always on the move. Some innovations or changes can be so highly influencing that the competitive position will be changed from one moment to another. Port comparisons have to be updated from time to time.

Finally it is important to know that a port comparison not only differs in time but also between different port activities. The handling of dry and wet bulk cargoes requires other location factors than the handling of containers or ro/ro-cargo. An oil refinery clearly has other requirements than a car producer. The first one desires deep water and an extensive pipesystem whereas the other is interested in large sites of land and congestion free hinterland connections.

The ways in which the Port of Rotterdam has found its solutions in different economic and societal times is to some extent unique and to some extent internationally structured. In the following sections the Rotterdam port authority's position will be treated along the lines of economic and societal changes.

1. The evolution of the Rotterdam port authority's position

To express and clear the evolution of the Rotterdam port authority's position three histories should be written: the evolution of the legal position, the evolution of port authority's position against the background of (inter)national economic, technological and societal developments and the evolution of the market position. This paper will handle the first two types of histories; the last one should be made as a result of the workshop because the market comparison combines the different insights of the other two for the question of business attractiveness.

1.1. The evolution of the legal position

The Rotterdam Municipal Port Management is the municipal department responsible for nautical management and the socio-economic development of the port. It functions as a spider in the web between various local, regional and national tiers of government and the national and international port business community. On the one hand it must promote the public interest in an accessible, safe and clean port and on the other it must ensure that the costs of port investments are recovered in a sound and responsible way. Balancing all these competing interests at once is the major, exciting yet frequently stressful challenge facing the Rotterdam port authority[1].

The Rotterdam Municipal Port Management (RMPM) was set up in 1932 and had sole responsibility for port management and port planning. The Public Works department was to be responsible for the actual construction and technical maintenance of the ports (van Walsum 1980). By integrating port management and port planning in one department, co-ordination was simplified and for the entrepreneurs it was clearer who they should tackle about port management (the modern "single counter" idea). "By establishing the Municipal Port Management department the Rotterdam city council acknowledged the port's great importance for the development of Rotterdam" (de Goey 1990, 253).

The RMPM is a municipal department whose Chief Executive Officer is appointed by the city council. The municipal executive at present has a separate port committee chairman. He and the port director meet formally once a fortnight at the "Port Coordination Meeting". Within the political regulatory framework, the port committee chairman is assisted by the port commission from the municipal council. He may ask for recommendations from this committee and other municipal council committees concerning port affairs, such as spatial planning and environment, traffic and transport. Each political party has a representative on the committees. The committee for the port consists of seven people and is headed by the port committee chairman. It convenes once a month. The opinion of the committee carries a good deal of weight as far as the decision making within the municipal council is concerned and their advice on how to vote is in practice always followed.

The director of the RMPM has been given a mandate for various tasks and powers through the Municipal Port Management Mandate Decree. Thus he is lim-

[1] The ex-director of the RMPM, Mr ir. H. Molenaar, once told me that the role of the RMPM could be clarified with the aid of the following anecdote. A man is travelling through the desert on a camel when he comes to a Bedouin camp where everyone is in mourning for their leader who has just died. The deceased has bequeathed seventeen camels to three children: half for his elder son, a third for the younger son and two camels for his daughter. The problem is, how do you divide seventeen camels into a half and a third? The visitor offers his own camel and the division can begin. The elder son gets nine camels, the younger gets six and the daughter two, which leaves one camel for the visitor to continue his journey on. The moral of the story is that when things are functioning well, the RMPM adds something to the system to help it carry on working, but without intervening directly in any further developments. The RMPM is the traveller and ties itself now to this party and now to that.

ited in his actions by the RMPM budget, the recommended prices for the long let of the sites and the maximum size laid down for a site, which is to be let. Furthermore he should take account of the limiting conditions which are laid down in consideration of spatial planning (local plan) and the environment. He is also responsible for the co-ordination of policy with the administrative department and other municipal agencies and companies. If the decisions or measures to be taken could involve political consequences, the director should provide feedback to the committee chairman or the committee at his own discretion. In an annual report he affirms accountability for the use of his powers. The previous mandate decree requires specific audits to be conducted by the municipal council but nowadays this is laid out in more general terms.

The RMPM is the only agency in Rotterdam with its own budget, which is uncoupled from the municipal budget. The reason for this uncoupling, which took place in 1970, lay in the political concern that the explosive development of the port would block the normal municipal facilities (van Walsum 1980, 151). Since 1964, the RMPM's revenue had no longer been sufficient to cover its investment costs and began to put too much pressure on the general municipal budget. Against the backdrop of the commercial operation of the port, the uncoupling also made the financial transactions more transparent for the port. Nowadays the port authority contributes annually directly for 66 million guilders to the municipal finances. It is formally expected of the RMPM in the long term that they run a closed commercial operation. In the last twenty-five years the turnover of the RMPM has more than quadrupled and its debt to the city has doubled. The net result varied over time and was only negative in the early seventies. This was due to the tremendous construction costs of the Europoort plan and the time lapse before the first ships could be accommodated.

Political direction of the RMPM

The director of the RMPM is formally accountable to the port committee chairman. He must also be available at the port committee meetings to answer any questions. Rotterdam council has a number of formal instruments for regulating the RMPM and adjusting it via consultation. These comprise the annual report, the corporate plan which remains in force for four years, the budget and the committee meetings. The political steering of the RMPM has changed a number of times over the years. Initially, the port came under the mayor of Rotterdam. Between 1946 and 1956 a committee chairman was responsible for the port and from 1956 until September 1970 it was once again a mayor. In 1970 it became once and for all the responsibility of a committee chairman. In the democratization period of the seventies, great importance was attached to the discussion on whether to place such a task under a politically elected person. There is not a lot of difference between the Port of Rotterdam being directed by a mayor or by a committee chairman, but for the function of mayor as an institution in Rotterdam it means a great deal. Within the framework of accountability, a committee chairman is a logical choice for this position since he can be held directly accountable by the city council whereas under the Dutch system of appointed mayors it is, formally speaking, far more awkward for a mayor to be held directly accountable[2].

From 1932 to 1970 the port committee consisted not only of elected representatives, as is now the case, but also of citizens from the business community (employers and employees). "The idea was to involve experts from various sectors of the port in the preparation of decisions, by showing the city council or mayor and committee chairmen around the port. This was intended to counterbalance the objections of people who felt that those with direct interests in the port had insufficient control over its management" (van Walsum 1980, 148). As a result of the wave of democratization and the desire to separate political and technical expertise, since 1971 the port committee has comprised only elected representatives in order to reinforce the position of the city council, to allow more scope for the consideration of others than those with direct interests in the port and to reduce the risk that port administrators could become the puppets of the business community.

Political control by non-elected representatives over specific questions is now exercized far more by the unions and interest groups and lobbies. They draw up a chair at the policy preparation table which is now less formally organized that it used to be. The Port of Rotterdam has a separate interest group for industry (the Europoort/Botlek Foundation; EBB) and an interest group for the stevedores and shipbrokers (Shipping Union South; SVZ) which also develop a number of joint initiatives. In addition, the Chamber of Commerce plays a role in representing the interests of the multiplicity of shippers. On balance, it is the RMPM and Rotterdam city council who give most consideration to the SVZ and EBB. The latter argue the case for their proposals to the council in shifting coalitions and occasionally in co-operation with the RMPM.

Formally speaking, the city council can of course implement emergency measures to discharge the chairman of the RMPM but a great deal of political clout is needed for this and it has never yet happened.

1.2. The port authority's position during economic and societal developments

The present port of Rotterdam developed in a number of phases. In his thesis, Van Klink talks of its evolution from "seaport to port network" (van Klink 1995). In a spatial sense the port of Rotterdam has undergone explosive growth. This was made possible by sound business sense on the part of both private investors and the city. They acted then and now as the developers and managers of this area. Against the backdrop of the massive expansion which the port of Rotterdam has undergone and continues to undergo, it is interesting to look at how the division of responsibilities between public and private parties is given shape. Furthermore, it is worthwhile analysing what steering capacity the port authority in the largest

[2] Nevertheless, the mayor of Rotterdam still can and does intervene in laying down conditions for the port. In the framework of the regionalization of the administration and the self-reliance of the RMPM, for example, the mayor plays an important political role. The mayor also steps in to fill the power vacuum during a period when there is no committee chairman.

port in the world has at its disposal in order to ensure that the port meets with the most up-to-date operational and political requirements.

The development of the port in the twentieth century is divided into two periods by the Second World War. Up until the Second World War the port still performed the transit function for the German Ruhr region whereas after the war an industrial port complex was developed. Early in the twentieth century the limits of port expansion on the right bank of the Maas were reached (border with Schiedam). On the left bank grain, coal, ore and petroleum were already being handled. In contrast to the older ports, the Rhine and Maashaven ports which were constructed early in the century were intended for larger ships with a greater draught.

During the period 1870–1880 the port of Rotterdam knew partial private port development in the construction of the harbour basins in the Feijenoord area. This private initiative stood up due to a waiting and doubting municipal attitude, given in by the feeling that a municipality should not lend any money to finance these basins by higher taxes. When the private basins were constructed they had to compete with the public docks near the city which could be cheaper by circumstances. Although the private port authority could have been successful without the large-scale fraud activities, the municipality developed the feeling that it was not recommendable to hand over the control of the berths and the spatial planning to private companies. The most important motives for this thinking were some undesired activities, which showed very clearly the not being in control of the complete port co-ordination. Due to fraud and financial mismanagement the private port authority failed in its job and went bankrupt in 1880. The municipality took over the harbour basins and from that time onwards the port of Rotterdam only has known a public port authority organization[3].

The annexation of the Pernis area made it possible for the city of Rotterdam to construct new petroleum ports and this occurred between 1934 and 1938. Whereas the older ports in the immediate vicinity of the city of Rotterdam principally handled mixed cargo, the ports in Rotterdam South were intended for bulk goods. A brilliant future was predicted for bulk goods and in Rotterdam South a new city grew around a fast-growing port area. After the war the largest dredged harbour basin in the world was constructed here: the Waalhaven.

The city of Rotterdam was badly hit in the Second World War, and it was many years before it was completely rebuilt. In the period after the war, the RMPM engineers were faced with a difficult task because the Germans had systematically destroyed the Rhinehaven and Maashaven docks in order to delay the Allies' landing. The period after the Second World War displayed an unprecedented economic growth, which did not slacken until the oil crises in the seventies. This growth can be broken down into four periods:

1. the period 1945-1950: rebuilding and modernising the port;
2. the period 1950-1960: constructing the Botlek plan and various facilities for the handling of bulk goods and mixed cargo in the old existing harbour area;

[3] For an extensive description: van den Noort 1990.

3. the period 1960-1970: the construction of the offshore development Europoort Maasvlakte, the dredging of a channel for the mouth of the Nieuwe Waterweg (the Eurogeul channel) and the advent of new mixed cargo ships, such as the container ships, roll-on/roll-off ships, LASH ships, etc. and
4. the period 1970 to date.

Two oil crises made the port of Rotterdam very aware of a number of facts: that it is entirely dependent on the developments in world trade; the almost total disappearance of general cargo in Rotterdam and the rapid growth of container transport; the steadily increasing need for space but also the hard confrontation between economy and ecology in this region. This was previously absent and implies that further expansion plans must follow completely different decision-making processes than during the first three periods.

In the second half of the twentieth century a tremendous industrial port complex has sprung up between the city of Rotterdam and the North Sea. Port planning and development are primarily the task of the RMPM as manager of the sites and also because the RMPM is judged by a growth in income (rents and ground lease) and freight (more wharves and sites mean more ships and yield more port dues). Opportunities for the port authority to interpret port planning and development at its own discretion have decreased over the decades as a result of spatial planning and environmental requirements. Moreover, the RMPM is less close to the market than to the commercial sector so that many initiatives for the improvement of its competitive position are given shape in concerted action with the business community.

General principles of port planning in Rotterdam

In the past there were clear agreements between central government and the city regarding the financing of maritime approaches to the sea and hinterland known as the respective "2/3-1/3 scheme". Nowadays, the approach tends to be project based and the division of costs is determined separately for each project. A similar approach is used for the region-specific port projects, such as the proposed construction of a second Maasvlakte. The forthcoming railway connection, the Betuwe Line, which is seen as a hinterland link, will be financed entirely by central government (including the section of the line which is located in the port area). The relationship between the RMPM and the business community has also always been clear. The RMPM is responsible for the construction and operation of adequate infrastructure. It finances the construction of new bays, sites, quay walls and so forth. Maintenance is also funded by the city, such as repairing quay walls and maintaining the appropriate draught in the harbour basins. Central government does not contribute to these costs. The business community is responsible for the construction and maintenance of the superstructure (cranes, sheds, warehouses, office space, loading and unloading gantries, trucks, etc.). This is not to say that the RMPM has no direct or indirect involvement with the superstructure. On the one hand, efficiency considerations may provide a reason for it to become indirectly involved with the deployment of superstructure. At the RMPM's insistence, various stevedore companies have merged to form the ECT (Europe Combined Terminals) and various petrochemical companies have established the Maasvlakte Oil Terminal which has reduced the need for the RMPM to build quay walls. On the other hand, the RMPM plays an increasingly facilitating role (see examples from the corporate plan 1996) in order to make a contribution to companies in constructing superstructure, starting up activities or expansion.

The port sites are rented or leased and never sold. The reason why Rotterdam only rents or leases its sites lies in the fact that the public interest requires that the city should retain as much control as possible over the use of the sites now and in the future. This policy also has its disadvantages, of course, for example in attracting major industries which can sometimes buy sites very cheaply in foreign ports. (..) Rotterdam has certainly encountered difficulties in attracting industry due to its leasing policy, although I can't think of a single industry which has rejected Rotterdam solely for this reason. The port authority has certainly benefited from it because it has always endeavoured to create the best possible facilities for the port users (Posthuma 1972, 34).

Different port planning phases and different port authority activity scope

In order to explore the various relationships between the RMPM and the external environment, port planning and expansion in Rotterdam has been broken down into four periods. The first runs up to the Second World War during which the expansion of the general cargo docks was continued. The period following the Second World War can be subdivided into three periods: from 1945 to 1970, from 1970 to 1990 and from 1990 to the present day. In the period between 1945 and 1970, the main success standard was growth and the RMPM had no need to demonstrate the necessity for expansion and received no criticism when carrying out the construction. After 1970 the situation changed drastically. Entirely different quality standards were applied to port planning so that the powerful position of the RMPM was relativized by the policy of other layers of government. After a "pure culture" period in the early eighties it appeared that industrial development would once more be permitted (de Goey 1990, 262). However, it was not until 1989 that the RMPM formally integrated its attention to industry, transport and distribution (RMPM 1996).

Until 1932, port planning and development mainly came under the former Municipal Commercial Premises Department (now Public Works) which had a predominantly civil engineering approach to port management. It constructed docks, which were specifically intended for the transport and transhipment of bulk goods. In the period prior to the Second World War, the city tried to reduce the distribution's sensitivity to economic fluctuations by attracting industry. It got no further than the planning stages, however. Initially, the call for industrialization appeared to be an arbitrary argument that vanished when trade picked up again. The period of economic decline turned out to be too short to initiate industrialization. Moreover, the Dutch pre-war entrepreneurs were not interested at all. The policy of the municipal authorities was passive and compliant rather than enterprising. It did not construct new docks until the demand for berths was overwhelming. The city council was only compelled to action by the massive unemployment: minimum prices, loans and the construction of a petroleum port in Pernis. Finally, the industrialization in Rotterdam itself was also slow getting underway due to a shortage of suitable industrial sites.

The implementation of the Botlek, Europoort and Maasvlakte I plans

Immediately after the war, efforts concentrated on the reconstruction of the port. Within only five years the port was made fully functional once more. In the early post-war years the city and the business community collaborated closely. The "Reconstruction Commission" was set up to "ensure the necessary contact between the city and the business community in order to make the best possible use of the overall port layout". This commission possessed considerable expertise, particularly in the technical field, but funds were lacking. These had to come from central government since the reconstruction of the port was in the national interest. The cost of the port reconstruction was estimated at around 40 million guilders. This government agency, the Rotterdam Reconstruction Agency, worked in productive co-operation with the RMPM and Public Works. Not only was the infrastructure restored, but a number of modernizations were introduced such as deepening the draught at the quays and increasing their permissible load plus a more efficient layout of sites.

During the Second World War, directors and civil servants from various municipal agencies gave talks and presentations on what should be done with the port after the war. The intention was to branch out in a different direction from in the thirties by making it less dependent on economic fluctuations, which had been the case with the transit trade to Germany. Rotterdam itself had to find a way to hold onto industry and the work flowing from it. The *Botlek* plan, which appeared in 1947, was a product of the war years and was wholly based on this vision. The business community, which insisted on upholding the old motto of the port, supported the RMPM in this plan: the ship must not wait at the quay, but the quay must wait on the ship. This turned out to be a good maxim but most entrepreneurs in the early fifties were biding their time. The RMPM was thus the lone driving force behind the development of the port. Although after the war there was a rush to repair the destruction wrought by the Germans and implement modernizations, it was another eight years before the first lessee was assigned his place in the Botlek.

There were a number of reasons for this. For a long time there had been an ongoing discussion on the issue of which ships this area should be able to serve. The compulsory purchase of the land was also a very slow business because the farmers held out for a good price for their land. Moreover, they had the backing of the Province of South Holland and the Ministry of Agriculture who approved the plan in 1950 and 1953 respectively. This was a new phenomenon for the RMPM because the expropriation of land had always been very easy in the past. It will be seen that this clash between the RMPM and the province was by no means the last. Posthuma, the RMPM's ex-Chief Executive Officer notes that: "The Province of South Holland provided little cooperation in this matter of compulsory purchase, which in fact was the case in nearly all matters relating to the development of the port between 1945 and 1970". Furthermore, the Botlek plan was being attacked from Dordrecht: it was opposing the construction of a Botlek bridge because this would mean less ships would be able to enter the port of Dordrecht. A third obstacle that was linked to the first was the requirement imposed by agriculture that in the plan use should be made of locks. This frightened off the business community (transhipment companies and petroleum companies) because the construction of locks would mean delays and an increased risk of collisions. It was only by remaining obstinate that RMPM were able to remove this point from the agenda. In 1955 the American Dow Chemical company was the first enterprise to be located in the Botlek area.

The second major plan to be developed after the war and which moved the port of Rotterdam a little nearer the North Sea was the "Europoort" plan. During the decision making pertaining to this plan, the Suez crisis (1956) flared up which ultimately led to the Suez Canal being closed for twenty years. Because ships could no longer use the Suez Canal they had to reach Europe via the Cape of Good Hope. This meant an unprecedented scale increase in shipping. Within a very short time, the tonnage of oil tankers shot up from 60.000 to 100.000 and 250.000 and there was even a ship built for Shell (though it was never put into service) with a 500.000 DWT. The scale expansion also entailed consequences for the lay-out of new ports (turning circles and depths) and by anticipating this (in so far as that was possible) Rotterdam ensured that this industry would choose this location.

In terms of area, the Europoort plan was three times larger than the Botlek (3.940 as opposed to 1.250 ha. gross area) and was implemented more quickly but preparations were entirely different than they had been for the Botlek plan. "Whereas these (previous Rotterdam port plans, HS) had been developed in a relatively small circle, in which only the Rotterdam agencies (...) and RWS had been involved, Europoort was the work of an extensive commission. Not extensive in the sense of size but rather as regards composition. It comprized civil servants from various departments, not only RWS. In the Europoort Plan, considerable account was also taken of planning aspects rather than just port construction" (de Goey, 1990, 92). The working party, entitled the Rijnmond Harbours Development Group, comprized 19 people of whom 7 were from Rotterdam. Rotterdam was thus in the minority. One point of contention between Rotterdam port opinion and national planning opinion was the issue of whether or not to relocate the village of Rozenburg: Rotterdam was in favour but it was refused for planning reasons. Ten years later Posthuma, the RMPM's Chief Executive Officer, was proved right by those same planners but by then it was too late. It was nonetheless the first successful attempt by central government to influence port development via formal channels, so in that sense the Europoort plan was not Rotterdam's plan.

The RMPM had learnt its lesson from the clashes that had occurred in implementing the Botlek plan and in 1958, after the foundation stone had been laid in Europoort, the first ship could be received in the port. In contrast to the approach used in the Botlek plan, this time the RMPM organized a comprehensive information campaign for the local residents and other parties involved. After all, the villages of Nieuwsluis and Blankenburg, and ultimately the De Beer nature conservation area, would have to be cleared to satisfy Rotterdam's hunger for land. It was also the spirit of the times in economic thinking, both at local and national level, whose flexibility ensured that the construction of Europoort entailed relatively few problems. The Port of Rotterdam was seen as a prime example of a macroeconomic instrument.

Due to economic growth and the increasing demand for industrial sites, political decision making regarding the first "Maasvlakte" was more or less bundled in with the Europoort plan. While the construction of Europoort progressed, plans had already been developed for the further expansion to the west. Financially, the two port plans were linked together because the first funding for the Maasvlakte came from the Europoort project budget. The Europoort plan that covered 3.940 ha. gross area (1.800 ha. net) ultimately cost 712 million guilders. In comparison with the Botlek project which involved 1250 ha. gross area (750 ha. net) and a cost price of 165 million guilders, this was a huge cost increase. It had already been foreseen in the early seventies that the first Maasvlakte would be an expensive project, but it was calculated that the costs could be recovered from the oil terminal and the power plan. The first Maasvlakte has a gross area of 2.690 ha. (1.270 net) and its construction ultimately cost the city 689 million guilders. In this context it is interesting to hear that for the projected construction of the Second Maasvlakte cost prices of 8 billion are being mentioned.

Closely related to the decision regarding the construction of the first Maasvlakte is the construction of the Eurogeul, which will offer accommodation of the largest tankers. In close consultation with nautical experts from Shell a decision has been taken to commence construction. In 1996, the estimated construction costs amounted to seventy million guilders with the annual maintenance costs being estimated at three million guilders.

Final remarks port planning

Port planning in Rotterdam during this century has developed both in a variety of institutional contexts and in various social environments. Port planning in Rotterdam before the war was a municipal affair. After the war the involvement of the province and central government steadily increased and the port authority's options for setting conditions became increasingly limited. The Europoort plan (in the fifties) was thus no longer called a Rotterdam plan because the government's town and country planners, to the great annoyance of the RMPM, were directly involved in it. This plan was able to be developed remarkably quickly, however, because there was complete agreement at national and local levels regarding the economic need to construct this industrial port area. After the realization of this plan and the ensuing wave of democratization, a change occurred both in the local political climate and in national involvement in the port area. The economic dispersion policy became an important national economic objective. In the early seventies, in addition to the spatial aspects, environmental interests arose and more stringent requirements were gradually imposed on (the location of) companies and the port's further development. There was to be no steel industry on the Maasvlakte and the demarcation line was a sign of the political limits to growth at that time. The relationship between politics and the business community made a u-turn and it was not until the eighties (high unemployment) that thinking was once more allowed to turn to commercial enterprise. Since the early nineties, the port of Rotterdam has again become an economic spearhead (mainport policy, seaport policy, major urban centres policy) and the local level appears once more to be able to interest the national level in the port (Betuwe Line and proposed second Maasvlakte), as was the case in the fifties and sixties. The considerable political attention devoted at present to national infrastructure is only temporary, however, as once the projects are completed Rotterdam will have to rely on itself again. Furthermore, Rotterdam remains dependent on the political climate at national level for the completion of these projects.

With regard to some sectors of industry (small-scale businesses, storage and container handling companies, stevedores) the RMPM has increasingly taken on the role of facilitator, creating a fusion of the RMPM with those companies. For the (petro)chemical industry, the situation remains largely unchanged in the sense that facilitation can occur to bring in such a company (e.g. by laying a pipeline) but that once the contract has been signed, the RMPM knows little about further developments. Joint projects with industry in the framework of environmental improvements have not yet been established.

In this context, the very limited options of the RMPM for regaining control over sites may also be mentioned. Port planning hardly exists in this sense; the RMPM is too dependent on the goals of the business community and there is no mechanism to ensure that land is managed carefully. The alliances which the RMPM has set up with other ports and transport centres appear to be the result of ad hoc opportunities and are not (as yet) underpinned by policy. Furthermore, the cooperation seems to have been a victim of its own success, such as the client who wanted to lease the entire lot belonging to the Exploitatiemaatschappij Schelde Maas (ESM; joint venture between Rotterdam and Vlissingen) which would have meant the cooperation would have achieved its aims in one fell swoop.

The redevelopment of old port areas requires a different approach from the RMPM than it is used to, since this does not immediately concern the expansion of the port area, as was the case with the Botlek, Europoort and the Maasvlakte. The immediate proximity of the city and the large number of small-scale businesses that were already located in the area also meant RMPM had to move very cautiously and tentatively in its search for options. The determining of its position vis-à-vis other municipal agencies also needed to be addressed. In direct contact with the business community a comprehensive vision was drafted and various projects were initiated. Just as in the construction of new sites, the initiative remains with the RMPM and the success of the project once again depends on the risks, which the business community is willing to take.

2. The question of the port authority's repositioning in Rotterdam

By means of a four-year corporate plan the RMPM makes it clear to the city council what it plans to do over the next four years and what the city council may expect of the RMPM. In the former corporate plan (1997-2000) the RMPM has brought up substantive arguments to make it clear that it cannot substantiate its future external expectations in the present institutional context. The present financial scope in particular is inadequate for this. Such issues and similar arguments have also played a role in the past. Van Walsum, ex-mayor of Rotterdam, wrote as long ago as 1972: "The value of an administrative structure depends to a great extent on the financial opportunities which it offers".

The corporate plan can be seen first of all as a plea to the city council to allow the RMPM a more independent position whereby the plan increasingly fulfils a political function. The external expectations are not immediately defined by the politicians, however, but follow an initial recommendation by the RMPM. The corporate plan sets the broad course which the RMPM intends to steer and contains few concrete indicators on the basis of which it is held accountable. The new corporate plan brings up the position of the RMPM for discussion and this is by definition a political discussion. The corporate plan is thus transformed from a primarily substantive touchstone into an overture to the political discussion about its position which has yet to take place.

Having specified the framework and the function of the corporate plan, in the light of the recently actualised privatization discussion it is interesting to look at the substance of the former corporate plan because this can be seen as the first formalized set up to get the topic on the agenda. Above all the essence of the arguments did not change in the new corporate plan. First of all a number of trends are distinguished which will influence the development options for the port in the future (RMPM 1996, 5-7). These involve a globalization of production and transport, increased flexibility regarding labour and capital, the sustainable development and use of land and energy, increasing difficulties in obtaining a wide support base in society, the increasing mutual dependence of organizations, the increasing economic expansion of the port, the growing arsenal of IT and the increasing competition between international governments and regions. The points on which the outside world may call the RMPM to account are also indicated. These comprise those factors relating to "the locational climate, logistics, distribution, industry and space."

As a municipal branch of service, the RMPM considers itself inadequately equipped for its task in view of the planned developments and the other demands which the rapidly changing environment makes of it, and thus feels that it should evolve "from port authority to director and facilitator of not only logistic but also industrial processes, in other words: the image of the RMPM will become more that of a business partner" (RMPM 1996, 9). This is the central reasoning underlying the Corporate Plan 1997-2000 and the details for the various policy areas are described in the following pages.

Returning to the statement made by ex-mayor Van Walsum, it is clear that financially speaking the RMPM has already been steering a different course in recent years and it is this course which is presented in the new corporate plan as strategically cohesive policy. A different course is already being steered within the existing institutional frameworks and this contextualizes the deliberations on repositioning through the corporate plan itself. Examples of financial innovations within the present institutional setting include: the joint financing, together with central government, of the infrastructure-plus in the Delta 2000-8 project; acting as intermediary in the purchase and resale of terminals (piers 6 and 7); and the establishment of a participation company in cooperation with a private actor in order to help set up small-scale businesses using venture capital.

In addition, in the field of acquisition and leasing the RMPM intends to implement "strategic acquisition" (linking companies, customer ties and public-private cooperation), "market-oriented facilitating" (see the already existing financial constructions and the tailoring of infrastructure to the wishes of the client), the "developing of products and concepts" (such as the planning of the Waal-/Eemhaven area and Maasvlakte II), "networking" (maintaining social contacts and arranging cooperation between companies) and finally "flanking" (influencing the decision making on spatial planning, environment, hinterland connections and IT through its own studies) (RMPM 1996, 10-11). In the field of nautical management, the RMPM wants control over the management of the nautical safety level, transport safety, environmental safety, crisis control and nautical service provision.

From the description a picture emerges of a port authority which wants to be in control as much as possible. There is something to be said for this on practical grounds because the RMPM is familiar with the day-to-day running of the port (expertise), but it remains to be seen whether the tight integration of public and private powers in a form other than the present one will be able to foster cross-fertilization in the long term. The RMPM already has its own budget and delegated/mandated powers at arm's length from everyday politics which leaves the practical interpretation of the success standards up to the RMPM itself. To whom will an even more independent RMPM be accountable for its actions and how is that institutionally organized? Which safeguards are in place in the other position for maintaining the care which is so essential to the public tasks?

It remains to be seen whether the range of necessary RMPM activities described in the corporate plan is essentially different from in the past. Plenty of examples could be provided of cases in which the port authority also took on the role of director and facilitator for unique issues which had arisen and for which a different institutional structure was not necessary. (Van Walsum 1972) concludes that the municipal structure of the port authority has never stood in the way of port development. Why should that suddenly be the case now? In developing new initiatives it was always the city council's confidence in the RMPM that ensured that the latter never had the slightest obstacle put in its way. Furthermore, the city council functioned as a financial safety net for the RMPM in less economically prosperous times (early seventies) and, as a municipal department, the RMPM pays less interest on its loans that it would if it were a company. Finally the question is whether, in a different institutional structure with different relations and expectations, the RMPM would accomplish its objectives more effectively than in the present familiar intermediary situation. Would the increasing self-reliance of RMPM not lead rather to unclear relations and the exclusion of the outside world in the long term?

Up to now, the city council has approved the erection of a separate private port body called "Mainport Holding Rotterdam" which covers the city council approved RMPM private participations. In this body which is under direct control of RMPM's Chief Executive Officer participations are managed in for example the private stevedoring company ECT and the joint venture with Zeeland Seaports (port authority of Vlissingen and Terneuzen). Next to this first step towards privatization another initiative took place namely the institutionalization of the direct interaction between the RMPM and the Ministry of Transport in a so called regularly administrative meeting. These two decisions can be seen as the institutional front doors of the discussion which was recently put on the Rotterdam political agenda for the complete privatization of RMPM. This discussion has also been fuelled again due to the financial discussions around the second Maasvlakte which in the eyes of the national government should be realized in a public private partnership way.

Conclusion

The port of Rotterdam plays an economic role which has (inter)national significance. In the national and local political arena, employment and added value are the most important assessment criteria for the success of the port, but an awareness exists that in other parts of the country unemployment is increasing. This is why local political parties are so insistent that the port should produce as much direct income as possible so that the RMPM's revenues can be used to provide "extra's" for the residents of Rotterdam. Due to the current national seaport policy and the port of Rotterdam achieving mainport status, over the next five years a relatively large amount of (political) attention will be devoted to the port and its infrastructural needs. After this national infrastructural stimulus, the city of Rotterdam and the business community will have to prove themselves.

As a municipal company that is responsible for the management and operation of the port, the RMPM has both public and private powers and enjoys a large degree of autonomy. There is back seat political control while a direct market mechanism is absent. After all, investments by companies are made for the longer term and companies cannot just pick up their superstructure and set it down elsewhere. Competition with other ports is mainly perceived when contracts are being renegotiated. All this means that the impact of strategic choices only becomes visible in the long term and that RMPM is not immediately confronted with its actions. In times of economic decline the city budget can serve as a safety net.

The RMPM, set up in the thirties as port authority to occupy an "independent position" between the authorities and the business community, considers it extremely important that the port should retain its competitive position vis-à-vis the surrounding ports. It judges the success of the port on the basis of price level, cargo tonnage handled and revenue acquired. The RMPM considers it unproductive to use the port as a direct employment instrument because, as a government company, it is too dependent on the enterprising spirit of the business community which in turn is dependent on trends in world trade. In the former Corporate Plan 1997-2000 both the city council and the RMPM have conformed to the general objective of optimising the port in a European context and not formally using it as an employment instrument.

In the past, for pragmatic reasons, (expertise, single counter principle, cohesive maritime policy, etc.) both public and private powers were integrated in the

RMPM. In the long term this hybrid position lays a heavy claim on the regulatory capacity of local politicians. They cannot actually live up to this because the distance between them and the RMPM is too great. This also holds for the national involvement in nautical management. "Checks and balances" will have to come more from other local and national public services, as increasingly seems to be the current practice (environment and spatial planning). If these divisions of responsibility take a more structural shape (clearer regulatory principles) there is much to be said for the RMPM's expertise motif.

The regulatory principles for port planning have changed over the years. Until the Second World War the city was expected to take the lead in the construction of sites. The business community in particular adopted a "wait and see" stance and did not develop an overall concept. After the war, port planning was no longer only a municipal concern but had now become a national interest as was made clear by the development of the Europoort plan and the acquisition of companies. In the sixties, the RMPM occupied a position of supremacy as the implementer of ambitious plans and due to the great interest shown by international companies. This position suddenly changed in the seventies when the national economic interest in the port waned and other quality standards were adopted by the Rotterdam city council. Due to the economic crises no further expansion plans were made and the RMPM concentrated instead on developing the existing area. They had to take increasing account of spatial planning criteria, environmental requirements and global locational criteria. In contrast to the sixties, they were now forced to develop the port area together with other layers of government and the business community. It is expected that contemporary port planning will take shape through the control relations of government conditioning and co-arrangements.

The current political attention devoted to infrastructure at a national level has ensured that the port of Rotterdam will be able to strengthen and possibly even expand its international competitive position. The construction of the Betuwe Line, to be financed by central government, will mean that the poor rail link to the hinterland will be phased out and Rotterdam could develop into a container hub. The spatial expansion of the port depends on the political discussion on a second Maasvlakte, the costs of which have been estimated at four to eight billion guilders. The question is, who will foot the bill in due course? Until now, port expansions have been financed by the city but the amounts were not particularly high. The current mainport policy has already accorded political goodwill to Rotterdam but the question remains of whether the construction costs will also be borne by the market and which financial role central government will play (full funding or partial hooking up with city initiatives). The main question which needs to be considered is how the land can be managed in a more innovative way in the future. What options does central government have to guarantee a balanced and innovative use of the land if it were to finance a second Maasvlakte?

All types of questions come together in the recently renewed debate on the port authority's position. The central theme in this discussion is the regulation of all kind of different relations and activities between the port authority and its economic, political and societal environment. Whether now is the time to renew the port community feeling and the institutional port structure at another scale and towards a privatized position will become clear in the coming year. When in the end there should be no commitment to such a privatized position the privatization discussion should be closed for at least ten years and to return to the real port management job.

References

de Goey FMM (1990) Ruimte voor groei: Rotterdam en de vestiging van industrie in de haven (1945 - 1975). Rotterdam

de Goey FMM and van Driel H (1993) De relatie tussen overheid en bedrijfsleven in de Rotterdamse haven. In: van Driel H (ed) Ontwikkeling van bedrijfskundig denken en doen: een Rotterdams perspectief. Rotterdam

Posthuma F (1972) Honderdjarig bestaan van de Nieuwe Waterweg. Rotterdam

RMPM (1996) Bedrijfsplan 1997 - 2000. Rotterdam

van den Noort JWPP (1990) Pion of pionier, Rotterdam - Gemeentelijke bedrijvigheid in de negentiende eeuw. Rotterdam

van Klink HA (1995) Towards the borderless mainport Rotterdam: an analysis of functional, spatial and administrative dynamics. Rotterdam

van Walsum GE (1980) Rotterdam Europoort 1945 - 1970. Rotterdam

Port user cluster

"Much ado about nothing?" Reorganising the hiring system and decasualization in the port of Antwerp during the 1960s: motives, obstacles, outcome

Stephan Vanfraechem

University of Gent, Belgium

Introduction

In the early 1960s, it became clearer all the time that the existing hiring system and the large extent to which dock labour in the port of Antwerp was still being done on a casual basis, gave rise to many abuses. Work refusal, temporary unemployment and job insecurity were phenomena which had always been linked to the dock industry, but which then kept on increasing. In 1963-1964 attempts were made under the impulse of the docker trade unions to reform the whole hiring and employment systems. The docker trade unions tried to find out how the singularities of the dock industry - with its varying arrival of goods, its varying labour demand and fluctuating unemployment figures - could be reconciled with the implementation of a form of permanent or casual/permanent employment which was affordable for the employers in general. With that idea of decasualization, the port of Antwerp jumped onto a train, which had been moving on an international basis for some time. In Great Britain and the Netherlands for instance, measures which went into that direction had already been taken before and after the Second World War. In the port of Antwerp, the switch over from a casual to a permanent or casual/permanent employment - indicated by the term "decasualization" - had not been firmly examined until then[1]. Against a background of work refusal, job insecurity, unemployment and other consequences of a labour organization which was largely oriented towards a casual basis, employers and employees tried to find solutions to give the occupation of dockworker some stability. In this paper I would like to touch lightly on the question which were the motives, reactions and objections of the different parties concerned and which were the ultimate results of the negotiations on "decasualization" carried on 1964.

[1] This paper reduces the meaning of the term "decasualization" to the switch over from a casual to a permanent employment Any preceding processes such as the compulsory registration of dockworkers, the reservation of work for registered dockworkers and the introduction of 'attendance money' will not be discussed in extenso.

1. Decasualization against a background of unemployment, work refusal and job insecurity

During their negotiations on a new long-term programming agreement for 1963-1964, it became clear to the docker trade unions and the port employers that the hiring system in the port of Antwerp was still an obstacle. The hiring of dockworkers had been a weak point in the labour organization in the port of Antwerp for years. Until the opening of the first hiring office in 1928, it was mainly a structural problem: the hiring of helpers for warehousing and stevedoring companies mainly took place on the street or at the warehouses of the warehousing companies. This historically grown abuse gave rise to all kinds of abuses and favoured favouritism. In order to centralize the hiring of dockworkers to some extent, the first hiring office was opened in 1928, which did, however, not have the effect, wished by the parties concerned. The hiring office did attract many employers and dockworkers, and the majority of the port population ignored it. One had to wait until 1937 when 8 hiring offices were opened under the control and management of the National Employment Office, before the hiring sessions could be centralized to some extent and be given a fixed place. When the structural problem had been solved for the greater part, another problem came to the surface. Both the employers' and the employees' mentality regarding hiring had to be changed drastically. The employers had to be convinced of the fact that the hiring of dockworkers should take place only in the hiring offices and that they could hire only dockworkers that presented themselves at such offices. The dockworkers, on their part, had to accept that apart from many rights they also had duties. One of their duties was that when they were offered a job, they had to accept it. The dockworkers had to be disciplined. The historically rooted tradition according to which dockworkers reserved the right to refuse work on certain days had to disappear from the port. In his "dockworker subculture", R. Miller put such refusal to work under the denominator "casual frame of mind" (Miller 1969). The central idea is that a dockworker defends his right to work in the sense that he decides himself whether he works and for whom he works. In a constellation in which an employer cannot give him his guarantee that he has work for him every day, the dockworker therefore claims the right to refuse to carry out certain jobs on certain days, as a form of compensation for job insecurity. The founding fathers Kerr and Siegel put it like this: "longshoremen do not aim to be no more considerate of the general community than they think the general community is of them" (Kerr and Siegel 1954). This work refusal became a real problem mainly after the introduction of subsistence allowance system in 1946. The acceptance by the dockworkers of the jobs offered to them was essential to keep the subsistence allowance system financially sound: work refusal resulted in higher expenses and brought the Subsistence Compensation Fund (out of which the subsistence allowances are paid) to the verge of bankruptcy a couple of times. It was impossible to get the situation in the hiring offices under control. The obstacles in the system were thus known. The dockworkers were not always hired through the official channels. The current hiring system gave all parties too much freedom. It also gave rise to abuses (work refusal was a real problem) and the unemployment statistics were alarming. The incessant payment of unemployment benefits in spite of a well-known deficit resulted in a misrepresentation of the actual situation.

The secretary of the largest docker trade union, viz the Belgian Socialist Transport Workers' Union, Georges Decrom, belled the cat in 1963. "Is it not crying that 2000 dockworkers regularly receive unemployment benefits and that we see at the same time that no one presents himself to work while there is work for 50 people"[2]. During informal talks with the President of the Cepa employers' organization ("Centrale des Employeurs du port d'Anvers"), Joseph Senders, he clarified his plans to drastically reform the hiring system. He was an advocate of the implementation of compulsory hiring. Together with severe sanctions, compulsory hiring would filter the so-called "professional recipient of unemployment benefits" out of the contingent. He also wanted to centralize the hiring of dockworkers in one big hiring hall, divided into different sections for the different categories of dockworkers. The main purpose of this "screening off" of the different categories was to prevent conflicts or small disturbances in one category from spreading very quickly over the whole hiring hall and from leading to a mass movement of all dockworkers.

Table 18.1. Daily average of unemployed

Date	Unemployed (daily average)	Deficit (daily average)
August 1963	1171	517
September 1963	1775	124
October 1963	1765	216
November 1963	1673	308
December 1963	1529	1031

Source: BTB 1966 Congress Report

It was, however, new that the whole was fitted in a broader project namely the decasualization of dock labour - compulsory hiring and the subdivision of the hiring hall were measures which had been lying on the table for discussion for some time.

When analysing the numerous problems in the hiring hall, the docker trade unions - a similar analysis was carried out by the Christian Transport Workers' Union - had not found only numerous abuses. They also found that job insecurity was still a real problem to a large part of the casual dockworkers. Until the early 1960s, the docker trade unions mainly tried to compensate such job insecurity with financial guarantees. The Subsistence Compensation Fund was set up in that context in 1946: it guaranteed dockworkers who presented themselves in vain for work, an additional premium on top of their unemployment benefits. Job insecurity did, however, not disappear. The subsistence allowance did, however, not guarantee that a dockworker would actually be hired. In essence, an Antwerp dockworker was still a casual day labourer, who had to look for a job every day anew. An Antwerp dockworker had no permanent employment agreement by which he was linked to one specific employer and by which job security was guaranteed to a certain extent. Only the warehousing companies had a number of peo-

[2] Cepa records, Contact Commission, Meeting of 15 October 1963.

ple who were employed on a permanent basis (Asaert 1993, 328). Most dockworkers were still employed on a "one-day basis". In the morning, the dockworkers presented themselves in the hiring hall where employers who came and recruited the manpower they needed possibly hired them. If a dockworker was not hired, he received his subsistence allowance plus his unemployment benefit. Until then the employment of dockworkers on a casual basis had actually not been questioned.

The employment of dockworkers on a casual basis had a number of advantages and disadvantages. The main advantage for the employer was undoubtedly that he had no permanent personnel costs. He had to pay a dockworker only for that one job the dockworker had been hired for. When the job was finished, the agreement between the employer and the employee terminated and the employer's financial responsibility ceased to exist. This small financial risk inherent to the employment of dockworkers on a casual basis had made the employers hold to as large a contingent as possible. The stevedoring companies in particular kept on giving preference to a large contingent from which they could freely chose and which enabled them to flexibly adapt to the evolving market and flow of goods. They found that the particular needs of the dock industry could never be exactly estimated and that therefore a surplus was necessary. Although not explicitly pronounced, the goods handling companies also seemed to want a large continent in order to keep the competition between the different dockworkers high and to increase their productivity by doing so. They were apparently convinced of the fact that the job insecurity aspect - which was especially the case in the event of a large (too large a) contingent - made the dockworkers' productivity increase considerably. In the event of an ample offer, the dockworkers had every interest in performing their jobs properly in order to guarantee their livelihood for the next day "In times of busyness, too small a contingent mostly results in delays, while in addition the work done leaves a lot to be desired both qualitatively and quantitatively. If the contingent is too large, laziness is encouraged" (Stouwerijbedrijf 1959, 6). The President of the Goods Handling Companies Association, Dierckx, summarized this as follows: "A reduction of the contingent still means a reduction of the gangs' productivity"[3]. The goods handling companies, however, still had other reasons to hold to a large continent. After all, practice also learned them that such a large contingent was necessary particularly because of the refusal by a part of the dockworkers to work. The stevedoring companies always wanted to have a kind of "surplus" of dockworkers to compensate those who refused to accept work. A reduction of the contingent was accepted only when it was clear that the contingent was entirely composed of willing workers. Another disadvantage of the employment of dockworkers on a casual basis was that the employer could not demand much from such dockworkers. This was made impossible by the short term of the agreement, viz. one job. He could demand more discipline from dockworkers employed on a permanent basis. As far as casual dockworkers are concerned, this was more difficult.

The main advantage for dockworkers within the current system was undoubtedly that he enjoyed very ample freedom. If they wanted to work on a specific

[3] Cepa records, Limited employers' delegation, Meeting of 26 June 1962.

day, they could go to an employer they wished to work for. A dockworker had little to lose, except a one-day job. This gave him a rather ample "freedom of movement". Particularly in times of a cyclical boom, his power was enormous. After all, in the event of a conflict, he could easily find a job with another employer the day after such conflict[4]. The disadvantage was that a dockworker also depended on the demand for his work. If there were no jobs available, he could not fall back on a permanent employment agreement guaranteeing a regular income (Baudez 1965, 402).

The Belgian docker trade unions now openly questioned the employment of dockworkers on a casual basis. They wondered whether the employment of dockworkers on a casual basis could not be replaced by another kind of employment (on a permanent or casual/permanent basis) making the ties between the employer and his employees within the dock industry closer. The replacement of the employment of dockworkers on a casual basis by one a casual/permanent basis was internationally known as decasualization. As far as the dockworkers are concerned, the advantage of this replacement was that they got a more regular job and that they had a greater financial security. As far as the employers are concerned, this meant that more could be demanded from a dockworker, who was now a regular employee, and that they could always count on the services performed by such dockworkers. The Belgian docker trade unions pinned much faith on such decasualization. In exchange for a "permanent" employment agreement (the form of such agreement had still to be determined), the employers would have more disciplined dockworkers at their disposal they could always count on and from whom they could demand more. Decasualization should lead to a properly working contingent of dockworkers willing to work. The contingent would always be at employers' disposal in the port of Antwerp[5].

The idea of decasualization was possibly based on foreign examples. In Great Britain - where dock labour was largely based on a "one-day basis" - studies had been carried out since the inter-war period in order to find out how the singularities of the dock industry - varying flows of goods and a varying demand for manpower - could be reconciled with a form of employment on a permanent basis. After the Second World War, the Netherlands also jumped onto that cart. However, the English and Dutch examples also clearly showed that a complete decasualization - namely a regular and direct agreement between the employer and the employee - was rather difficult. According to a trade union leader in the port of London, the chances to reach a complete decasualization were slim: "You cannot decasualize dock labour at all, you can relieve it but you cannot absolutely

4 The casual labourer had practically nothing to lose apart from a short-term job. If they were dismissed, they could find another employment, at least when the economy was running well (Weinhauer 1997, 229).

5 "The promotion of decasualization in the various ports if the world should result in an all-round improvement in conditions since it would help to ensure that the work is carried on by a contented body of workers with regular employment and steady earnings and thus produce the benefits accruing from good will and increased productivity." Decasualization of dock labour: third session of Inland Transport Committee - International Labour Organization, Geneva, 1949, 34.

decasualize" (Hill 1976, 15). In London, they opted for an intermediate form, which possibly also inspired Decrom.

2. "Pool" and guaranteed weekly wages as a variation on permanent employment

Georges Decrom introduced the idea of decasualization to the employers during an informal conversation with Joseph Senders. Instead of having the dockworkers employed on a permanent basis by the different employers in the port of Antwerp (warehousing and stevedoring companies), he opted for another way. He wanted to have all dockworkers employed by a paritary body (the so-called "pool") through which they would be at the disposal of the employers. Such pool would guarantee the dockworkers guaranteed weekly wages. If a dockworker had not earned such guaranteed wages by work actually done, his actually earned wages would be increased to such guaranteed wages with money from the Subsistence Compensation Fund[6]. A dockworker was free to carry out as many jobs per week as he wanted (not more than one per day) and to earn more than the guaranteed wages. The introduction of the pool and the guaranteed weekly wages were linked to the reform of the hiring sessions. Dockworkers forming part of the pool would be compelled to accept each job they were offered. Only if they accepted such jobs, they received their guaranteed wages. If they refused to accept certain jobs, their guaranteed wages were reduced accordingly and they risked being sanctioned. This system was thought to solve any problems arising at the hiring sessions immediately. It would no longer be possible for a dockworker to refuse to be hired and at the same to receive his unemployment benefit and a subsistence allowance.

Decrom also warned of the fact that if the pool and guaranteed weekly wages were introduced, the extent of the contingent would also have to be reconsidered. After all, the payment of guaranteed wages to too large a contingent would bring the Subsistence Compensation Fund (out of which such guaranteed wages were paid) once more into trouble.

With this proposal the "decasualization" idea was not carried through in its extreme consequence - a direct permanent employment agreement between the employer and the employee, but - exactly as in the Netherlands and in Great Britain - an intermediate form was opted for by Decrom. The employee signed a contract with such pool as through which he could be hired to the employer. The big advantage of this system was that the financial risks were being spread over different employers. In addition, it was easier to adapt more flexibly to real needs through such pool. It was no longer necessary that a specific employer was obliged to keep on employing dockworkers if he had no work, while another employer had too much work, but no dockworkers. The purpose of this system was that the pool would divide the available dockworkers efficiently among the different employers

[6] Cepa records, Limited employers' delegation, Meeting of 26 November 1963.

who asked for dockworkers. The main advantage for the dockworkers was undoubtedly that they received a guaranteed weekly income.

Prompted thereto by the ongoing problems in the hiring halls and the far from rosy situation of the Subsistence Compensation Fund, the employers and the employees decided to discuss the whole problem of the hiring system and the decasualization, if any, at an informal meeting. The "Reform of Terms and Conditions of Employment Commission" would meet from January to October 1964. The main employers' and employees' delegates were represented in this commission

3. Reform of the hiring system

As far as the reform of the hiring system is concerned, a lot of headwork had already be done mainly by the docker trade unions. They had been insisting on a radical reform for a long time. An important constant in their plans was that they wanted to reduce the enormous freedom of both parties - employers and dockworkers - during the whole procedure.

After the existing free hiring, a compulsory hiring would be introduced to counter the work refusal problem. In the event of shortages, those who were still in the hiring hall and who had not been hired, would be forced to accept a specific job. If they refused to do so, they did not receive an unemployment or subsistence allowance. In the event of repeated refusals, they would be excluded from the contingent[7]. Apart from the work refusal, the docker trade unions still had another motive to reform the hiring of dockworkers. The bringing together of all those dockworkers into one big hall had repeatedly proved to be the dreamed opportunity for anyone who wanted to start a protest action. Practice had shown that a small incident could develop into a massive protest action in which almost no one knew the exact cause of the polemics. In the immediate post-war period and also during the last big strike of December 1960-January 1961, the communist action committees gratefully made use of it. In the past the docker trade unions had had great difficulty in crushing such "wild" strikes. Therefore, they no longer wanted that during each hiring session all dockworkers met in one big hall. With such purpose in mind, they proposed to send each dockworker to one specific hiring session[8]. Each dockworker had to chose during which session he would have himself hired. By doing so, the big mass of dockworkers would be divided into 4 groups (day's work and three shifts. In order to counter such mass feeling in a big hall, the hiring hall had to be divided into different sections for the different categories. By doing so, the dockworkers would be hired in a separate part of the hall. Foremen, coopers, etc. were hired in the same way. This measure had to prevent conflicts from passing from one specific category to other categories.

---

7 Cepa records, Reform of Terms and Conditions of Employment Commission, Semi-official talks 28 January 1964.

8 Cepa records, Reform of Terms and Conditions of Employment Commission, Semi-official talks, 28 January 1964.

In such a system, dockworkers had to present themselves only once per day. The disadvantage was that they lost a part of their freedom. When they had been assigned to a specific hiring session, they could no longer chose freely, which hiring session they wanted to attend. It was therefore theoretically no longer possible for a dockworker to work the day shift and the night shift the next day. The introduction of the compulsory hiring system made it also impossible to wait to see which way the cat jumped and to come to the hiring hall only to receive a subsistence allowance. If shortages were found, dockworkers who had not been hired, were forced to accept the jobs offered on pain of suspension. It was no longer possible for a dockworker to have himself hired by preference by one employer and wait and see in the meantime[9]. The employers as well were forced into a tighter straitjacket. There were heavy fines on any hiring outside the hiring halls proper. During the different hiring sessions, they were obliged to hire in the first place those who had been assigned to those specific hiring sessions. Only if shortages were found - after the compulsory hiring - they were allowed to hire dockworkers who were normally assigned to another session. Therefore, a dockworker who normally worked a day shift, could be hired for an afternoon shift only if shortages had been found during the hiring session for the afternoon shift.

The employers were very critical on the compulsory hiring system. They thought that their free choice would considerably be reduced. Just like the dockworkers were entitled to determine for which employer they wanted to work, the employers wanted to reserve the right to refuse certain dockworkers. In a compulsory hiring system, this would become more difficult: in the event of shortages the employers would have to hire the dockworkers offered to them. The employers were of the opinion that at that moment they were entitled to give preference to a dockworker who had normally been assigned to another session. After all, they were afraid that in the event of compulsory hiring, only non-motivated dockworkers would remain. If such non-motivated dockworkers were included in a gang, the productivity of such gang would fall. In the past, the employers had already complaint about the fact that the contingent was partly composed of dockworkers who were unwilling to work. They were afraid that mainly those dockworkers would be hired obligatorily. The employers wanted to introduce the necessary flexibility in the first place in order to be able to hire "their" preferred dockworkers at all times, irrespective of the fact to which hiring session they belonged. Decrom countered that question. If they wanted to have specific dockworkers at their disposal at all times, they had to employ them on a permanent basis[10].

---

[9] On the proposal of a member of the board of the trade union to make such practice anyhow possible, Decrom answered resolutely: "The job offered must always be accepted. They are not at the service of one single person but of that of the community." BTB records, Executive Committee, meeting of the executive board of 13 January 1964.

[10] Cepa records, Reform of Terms and Conditions of Employment Commission, semi-official talks 28 January 1964.

4. "A bridge too far": permanent employment only for the executive staff

As from the start of the negotiations it became, however, clear that the employers did not easily accept the employment of dockworkers on a permanent basis. The fact that they would have to pay the dockworkers anyhow, whether they had work for them or not, deterred most of the employers. In their opinion, such construction would necessarily give rise to problems in such an environment as the dock industry with varying flows of goods and consequently a varying need of labour. The docker trade unions felt very soon that there was actually no space for negotiation. All employers' organizations pulled the same rope. An individual company could implement the employment of dockworkers on a permanent basis, but there was no question of a general measure[11]. Decrom's proposal to make all dockworkers sign a permanent employment agreement with a pool which would then spread the financial implications of such agreement over all employees in the port found no favour. The employment of ordinary dockworkers on a permanent basis was therefore dropped rather soon - after two meetings - still before real talks could be held. The employers' refusal to negotiate on this point did not really lead to a break. Both parties kept on negotiating and did reach an agreement on the other items. Besides, it is striking how easy this item was pushed aside

For the so-called "executive staff" - foremen and warehouse keepers - permanent employment was introduced anyhow. Pierre Van den Bergh who promoted the interests of this kind of executive staff within the Belgian Transport Workers' Union insisted on a guaranteed 5-day salary for this category. He was of the opinion that "those people have acquired such a position with their employer that the latter can do nothing else but guarantee a five-day salary. They are regarded as bosses and it is impossible to hire such people on a one-day basis"[12]. Van den Bergh's main objective was to have the important position held by the foremen within the current labour system in the port of Antwerp translated into a better statute. In the current system, a foreman worked mostly for the same company. When that company had to load or unload a ship, it ordered the foreman to compose a gang. The foreman was therefore in charge of hiring the dockworkers for his gang. When the dockworkers had been hired, he was in charge of the gang. Normally speaking he did carry out any jobs in the gang. Therefore, the foreman had a rather big responsibility. Just like the statute of the dockworkers hired by him, the foreman's statute was still that of a casual day labourer. Although he was working for the same company almost all the time, that company did not employ him on a permanent basis. Van den Bergh was of the opinion that the casual statute could no longer be reconciled with the managerial position held by the fore-

---

[11] "The problem of dockworkers employed on a permanent basis should certainly not be thrust on the employers". Cepa records, Reform of Terms and Conditions of Employment Commission, semi-official talks 5 February 1964.

[12] Cepa records, Reform of Terms and Conditions of Employment Commission, Semi-official talks 5 March 1964.

man[13]. He therefore suggested to employ the foremen on a permanent basis and guarantee them a 5-day salary. Because of their managerial position, the foremen should no longer be regarded as a part of the gang. After all, some companies were used to include a foreman in the gang to save a dockworker. This was no longer allowed. There should be a clearer separation between an ordinary dockworker and the executive staff, not only as far as its position but also as far as its statute is concerned.

Van den Bergh's proposals were initially rejected by the employers' delegation[14]. The employers accepted only a guaranteed 5-day salary for the warehouse keepers. As far as the foremen are concerned, they wanted to hold to the existing system: on top of the basic wages paid to dockworkers they received a 25% supplement. According to the new system they would receive a 25% supplement on the guaranteed weekly wages paid to dockworkers. In addition, it should remain possible to let foremen work in a gang. They did not wish such an explicit distinction between the executive staff and ordinary dockworkers.

In spite of these remarks, the negotiations showed that the employers were anyhow willing to make an effort. During a conversation with Senders, Van den Bergh made a counter-proposal, which was found acceptable by the employers: the warehouse keepers would be guaranteed 5 days, the foremen 4 days[15]. The employers accepted this proposal on 16 March. The explanation of this eventual implementation of a permanent employment of the executive staff is to be found in the tie, which already existed between the different companies and the executive staff. The general impression is that most companies had a permanent corps of warehouse keepers and foremen whose services they wanted to use by preference. A big labour turnover as that of ordinary dockworkers, was almost inexistent here. Such tie was now officialized in a statute by which they were also bound *de iure* to a specific company and by which a fixed salary was also guaranteed.

5. Guaranteed wages instead of a permanent employment agreement for dockworkers

Another statute for the casual day labourer - and the dockworkers were still casual day labourers - did not seem to be discussible. Therefore, the docker trade unions returned to the old trusted strategy, which had proved its soundness: the job insecurity inherent to this casual statute had to be compensated financially. This financial security was now guaranteed by the subsistence allowance. The docker trade unions suggested to abolish the subsistence allowance and to replace it by guaranteed weekly wages. Without regard to the number of days actually worked by the dockworkers, the docker trade unions wanted the dockworkers to receive guar-

---

[13] If they are regarded as holding a managerial position ,it is normal that all days are paid to them by their employer; this is a serious basis of departure. Cepa records, Reform of Terms and Conditions of Employment Commission, semi-official talks of 5 March 1964.

[14] Cepa records, Limited employers' delegation, Meeting of 9 March 1964.

[15] Cepa records, Limited employers' delegation, Meeting of 10 March 1964.

anteed wages on a weekly basis. The amount of BEF 1350 was taken as a basis for their guaranteed weekly income, both for day's work and shifts[16]. The amount of BEF 1350 corresponded with 60 % of 6 average daily wages in the port of Antwerp in the past year. If a dockworker had not earned the amount of BEF 1350 at the end of the week, the wages actually earned by him were increased to such amount. The money to make such payments would be taken out of the Social Security Fund. The subsistence allowance was abolished. If a dockworker could not work, he received only an unemployment benefit.

This construction protected the dockworkers better in times of poor offer. Dockworkers who presented themselves 6 days in vain were entitled to 6 x the unemployment benefit, plus the subsistence allowance. The total was BEF 1044[17]. Now BEF 1350 was guaranteed. The disadvantage within this structure was that he lost a part of his freedom. After all, the guaranteed wages were paid only if a dockworker had accepted every job offered to him. In the former system, he could refuse jobs and still receive his unemployment benefit and subsistence allowance (the so-called "continuous signing of the unemployment register").

The introduction of guaranteed wages found no favour in the eyes of the employers. They regarded such wages as an ideal tool to promote work refusal among dockworkers. How would it still be possible to stimulate dockworkers to effectively accept jobs offered to them, when they would received guarantee wages, whether they worked or not? The point of departure of this whole reform round was to dispose of certain abuses. Such measure would not do anything but perpetuate such abuses[18]. This system would financially favour the category to be excluded from the contingent - those who carried out only one to two jobs effectively and looked on the rest of the week without working[19]. From a purely financial point of view, the employers were right. Dockworkers who carried out only one to two jobs per week, were doing well from a financial point of view. In the current system with subsistence allowances their weekly income did not amount to BEF 1350.

This purely financial consideration of the employers was therefore correct but passed the fact that the docker trade unions had already agreed that before all reforms would be introduced, all dockworkers had to be screened[20]. A category which consequently carried out only one to two jobs per week - irrespective of the fact whether the offer of work was big or small - would already be excluded from the contingent in advance. Should jobs be refused in spite of this, dockworkers who refused to accept jobs would not received an unemployment benefit.

Apart from the fact that more work would be refused as a result of this system, the employers' delegation was also afraid that the dockworkers' general productivity would fall as a result of the guaranteed wages. The spokesman of the Goods

[16] Cepa records, Reform of Terms and Conditions of Employment Commission, semi-official talks of 20 April 1964.

[17] BTB records, Executive Committee's Reports, Meeting of 5 March 1964.

[18] Cepa records, Limited employers' delegation, Meeting of 21 January 1964.

[19] Cepa records, Limited employers' delegation, Meeting of 17 March 1964.

[20] Cepa records, Reform of Terms and Conditions of Employment Commission, semi-official talks of 28 January 1964.

Handling Companies, Dierckx, saw in the system "[...] a means to further reduce the labourers' productivity. It is an established fact that the labourers' productivity has been falling systematically for several years as a result of the introduction or the increase of the existing social benefits such as unemployment benefits, subsistence allowances and guaranteed weekly wages. As productivity will fall as a result of the introduction of guaranteed wages ..."[21]. Actually, this criticism came as a surprise. Until then the productivity of the dockworkers of the port of Antwerp had always been highly estimated, also by the employers. It had always been said that the port of Antwerp was able to compensate its high labour cost mainly by its high productivity (and flexible labour control). Actually, its high labour productivity was therefore never up for debate. Consequently, the productivity debate in the port of Antwerp drew attention mainly by its absence. Also after the introduction of the subsistence allowance system, the employers did not complain about the fact that productivity had fallen spectacularly. Therefore, the question was how low productivity would fall as a result of the guaranteed wages.

The balance of the talks held within the Reform of Terms and Conditions of Employment Commission from January to March 1964 was therefore rather poor. The employers and docker trade unions had not reached any agreement on the permanent employment of dockworkers or their guaranteed wages. Against all these failures, there was only the permanent employment of the executive staff. The dockworkers would push the negotiations into a new direction.

6. Trade unions called to order by their own members

Until then the members/dockworkers of the Belgian Transport Workers' Union had been left out in the cold. During the current negotiations they were never informed about the state of affairs and their opinion was never asked[22]. At last, on 22 March 1964, the Belgian Transport Workers' Union organized a general meeting at which the main lines of the talks were explained. The President of the dockworkers' union, Louis Major, addressed the mass of dockworkers: "I hope that there will be no demagogy during the interventions. Demagogy does not solve anything"[23]. The meeting was however "very constructive" and its members seemed to accept the main lines of the contents of the talks. They authorized their

[21] Cepa records, Limited employers' delegation, Meeting of 10 February 1964.

[22] This decision to involve the dockworkers as little as possible in the decision making process fitted in a general "tactic" of the board of the union (mainly its secretary, Georges Decrom, and the President of BTB, Louis Major). Decrom had always rejected any request to hold general meetings by stating that they only gave rise to slanging matches and conflicts, and that they were used by others - he probably referred to the communists - to provoke conflicts.

[23] BTB records, Executive Committee's Reports, Members' meeting held in accordance with the articles of association on 22 March 1964.

negotiators to further negotiate on the guaranteed wages and compulsory hiring[24]. At a Congress of the Dockworkers' Union, which was organized one month later on 26 April 1964, the atmosphere was totally different. At a very turbulent meeting, the resolution of the members' meeting of 22 March was rejected. Its members (no longer) appreciated the guaranteed wages[25].

As has already been shown, the introduction of guaranteed wages was very beneficial to the category of dockworkers that carried out only one to two jobs per week. Those who were used to carry out three to four jobs per week had to surrender part of their income. Dockworkers who carried out three jobs per week in the current subsistence allowance system, now earned BEF 1461 [BEF 313 day's work x 3) + BEF 174 subsistence allowance x 3)]. In the new guaranteed wages system, the three days of subsistence allowance (BEF 175 x 3) were replaced by three days of unemployment benefit (3 x BEF 121). Instead of earning BEF 1461, they would earn only BEF 1310. For those dockworkers, the new system meant a financial loss. Therefore, it was that category of dockworkers, which took the initiative in the protest. They rejected the guaranteed wages and gave preference to the maintenance of the subsistence allowance system.

In the meantime, the Christian Transport Workers' Union consulted its members[26]. The result was the same: its members rejected the guaranteed wages and opted for a subsistence allowance[27].

On 22 April, both the Belgian Transport Workers' Union and the Christian Transport Workers' Union announced that their members did not accept the proposal on the guaranteed wages.

7. Agreement on a guaranteed salary for the executive staff and a subsistence allowance: "much ado about nothing?"

The balance of the talks, which was already rather poor before this rejection, was now almost insufficient. The reform of the hiring system and the employment of the executive staff on a permanent basis were the only measures on which an agreement had been reached. By acting more repressively during the hiring sessions and by drawing the dockworkers' attention more to their duties, the unions hoped to be able to prevent dissipation such as work refusal, etc. As the employers themselves were, however, not immediately wild about this new measure, the

[24] "After the members' meeting of the dockworkers had been held in accordance with the articles of association" Transport. Orgaan van de Belgische Transportarbeidersbond, May 1964.

[25] BTB records, Congress of Dockworkers' Union and related trades, Antwerp, 5 June 1966.

[26] It was not mentioned when the meeting was held. In addition, it is also unclear whether the Christian Transport Workers' Union was used to consult its members regularly.

[27] Cepa records, Reform of Terms and Conditions of Employment Commission, Semi-official talks of 20 April 1964.

chances of success of this reform were, however, queried immediately. As far as "casual labour" and its inherent job insecurity are concerned, there was no fundamental change. The file containing the proposals on the introduction of a permanent employment in the form of a pool had hardly been circulating among the negotiators and it was already silently discarded. For most of the dockworkers casual labour remained their daily reality. The financial cost resulting from a permanent employment seemed to be an unbridgeable gulf for the port employers. This decision must also be situated within the specific context of the labour market in the port of Antwerp. The offer of labourers was always guaranteed in the port. Unlike the port of Rotterdam for instance where difficulty was found in (keeping on) motivating for the job of casual dockworker, the port of Antwerp had almost no problems attracting dockworkers (Ter Hoeven 1963, 454. Nijhof 1988, 492). If the contingent of dockworkers was insufficient in the past, occasional labourers or passport people could have been hired without any major problems[28]. The port of Antwerp succeeded in keeping on motivating labourers to do dock labour. The offer of manpower was therefore guaranteed all the time (whether through the contingent or not). The absence of a tie with the company and the lack of financial security/job security resulting from the casual labour system did not seem to play tricks on the port of Antwerp. In other words, at that moment the employers of the port of Antwerp had little reason to question this existing system and to exchange it for a new system which would demand more financial efforts and planning from them

In the mid 1960s it became however clear that Belgium's economic expansion also led to a number of awry situations (Mommen 1994, 266). The labour demand resulting from its economic growth could no longer be met. Unemployment was practically inexistent. Wages rose considerably not only as a result of the consumer price index mechanism by which the wages evolved in proportion to the increasing cost of living, but also because of all kinds of additional benefits granted to the employees. A tendency was nationally noticeable whereby the employers accepted all kinds of wage claims more easily to attract or keep qualified personnel (Vandeputte 1987, 99).

From the end of 1964 until the beginning of 1965, the same evolution was noticed in the port of Antwerp. In a cyclical boom with very high growth figures and yearly new records as far as the handled tonnage is concerned, the demand for good labour was high. In the second half of the 1960s, the employers' complaints about the shortages of manpower were sounding louder and louder. The extent of the contingent was apparently insufficient. In order to meet the shortage of manpower, the contingent was thrown open at the end of 1964. By means of the written press and radio, men aged 21 to 45 were called to apply for the job of dockworker[29]. After one year they could claim a subsistence allowance. Candidates could present themselves with recognized trade unions, which would recommend them. If someone wanted to be become a dockworker, he had to affiliate with a

[28] The first category were dockworkers who were temporarily recognized. The second category were employed labourers from several sectors who just produced their "passports" (hence "passport people") or identity cards.

[29] BTB records, National Committee of the Port of Antwerp, session of 17 December 1964.

trade union[30]. The first call did not have the hoped-for success: in January 1965, 265 new dockworkers were included in the contingent, but an average of 50 of them left the contingent every week[31]. The fact was that the port did not succeed in attracting a sufficiently high number of dockworkers. The contingent did not increase spectacularly: it rose from about 12.800 in October 1964 to 13.400 in October 1965[32]. From 1966 onwards the contingent started decreasing. At their wits' end, the employers even asked to include anew people in the contingent who had been excluded from the contingent because of having carried out to few jobs[33]. At the end of 1968, the contingent had fallen to about 12.000[34].

The trade unions and employers noticed that their calls to do dock-labour work did not have the same success as before. According to the legislators, the lack of success was due to the fact that nationally speaking there was a shortage of labour and the fact that advertising was insufficient. The trade unions interpreted this as a signal that the characteristics of the occupation of dockworker (casual labour, no tie with the company, job insecurity) made potential labourers drop out. Such a scarcity forced the employers to be creative if they wished to have a sufficiently large number of dockworkers at their disposal. A way to be able to count on the services of a sufficiently large number of dockworkers had to be found. The hiring of dockworkers outside a hiring hall fitted in this tactic: if a dockworker came directly to a warehouse, they had the first option to hire him. If he went to a hiring hall, another employer would possibly hire him. To be sure of the services of these dockworkers, the employers went apparently rather far: "the dockworkers are telephoned and transported from their homes to work for another shift than for the one they must normally be employed. They no longer go to the hiring hall"[35]. The names of dockworkers were phoned through. Even if the employers did not know whether they would need a dockworker the next day, they called him and asked him to come to work immediately[36].

When there was a shortage of labour, the employers were obliged to lure dockworkers by means of additional benefits. It was common practice to pay dockworkers some "black" money on top of their basic wages. Internally, employers talked openly about it. Mainly stevedoring companies are said to have made such "black" payments. Apart from such black payments, they were also offered free

[30] The Belgian nationality was apparently a requirement to be good dockworker. "We do not accept that Moroccans, Algerians, Turks, etc. form part of the contingent. We must see to it that the contingent is composed of people from here instead of foreigners. They are unsavoury individuals; here they earn high wages to which they are not used". Cepa records, Contact Commission, Meeting of 15 December 1964.

[31] "The wages are extremely high, labour is still very heavy, working hours are irregular [...] all these elements deter candidates from being a dockworker". BTB records, National Committee of the Port of Antwerp, Session of 25 January 1965.

[32] Cepa records, Annual Reports, 1965 and 1966 financial years: Labour statistics.

[33] BTB records, National Committee of the Port of Antwerp, Session of 7 November 1966.

[34] Cepa records, Annual Reports, 1968 financial year: Labour statistics.

[35] Cepa records, Contact Commission, Meeting of 17 October 1966.

[36] Cepa records, Limited employers' delegation, Meeting of 27 November 1967.

transport and free meals[37]. The leading man of ABAS, Sirtaine, defended such practices: "finds this normal [...]. He [Sirtaine] is of the opinion that almost 95 % of the goods handling companies of the port of Antwerp pay additional wages and compensations to their labourers"[38]. An examination by Cepa showed that the wage slips often contained payments by the companies concerned the dockworkers were, strictly speaking, not entitled to. Actually, there seemed to be a discrepancy between the basic wages the dockworkers were entitled to and the wages actually earned by them. According to Dierckx there was no other choice: "Mr Dierckx points out that, as far as his company is concerned, a third of the dockworkers receive an additional payment. If no such payments are made, he would have no one to work for him"[39]. The goods handling companies are said to have been under pressure of their foreign customers. They are said to have insisted on making "black" payments if necessary, if by doing so the ship was loaded or unloaded in time[40]. Such black payments also sharpened the race among the goods handling companies: they were apparently obliged to pay ever-increasing supplements if they wished to hire specific dockworkers[41]. Such "black payments" were nothing new of course. In the past, they had also been made from time to time, albeit on a less frequent basis. But according to what is said by the employers, such payments now seemed to be made rather massively.

Conclusion

When in the mid 1960s it became clear that the port of Antwerp started finding difficulty in motivating labourers to do dock labour, the docker trade unions tried to convince the employers that this was also due to the disadvantages of casual employment. They were hoping that this "new" issue would convince the employers introduce a form of permanent employment anyhow. However, the employers kept on searching in another direction. Numerous measures were taken. They all had one thing in common, namely they did want to link the dockworkers in one way or another to a company. The most striking fact is, however, that the employers as well keep themselves from taking on permanent financial obligations. All measures were clearly temporary. They were not established by any joint indus-

[37] Cepa records, Limited employers' delegation, Meeting of 12 July 1968.

[38] Cepa records, Limited employers' delegation, Meeting of 16 March 1965.

[39] Cepa records, Limited employers' delegation, Meeting of 23 March 1965.

[40] President Senders informs to have heard that a shipbroker told his goods handling company in writing to hire labourers at any price and that if it did not do so, he would be obliged to look form another goods handling company. Cepa records, Limited employers' delegation, Meeting of 27 April 1965.

[41] The labourers took advantage of this situation and made their own demands. If the employer did not want to pay the supplement asked by them, they did not let themselves be hired. He even mentioned the case of a marker who had himself assigned a supplement of BEF 50 by a company and who returned the hiring note a few moments later because another company offered him a supplement of BEF 100. Cepa records, Limited employers' delegation, Meeting of 12 July 1968.

trial committee and they could, therefore, be revoked without any problem. Besides, the reactions already formulated during the first few talks on permanent employment, make us think that this was not only a financial but perhaps also (or still more) a mental consideration. The employers in the port of Antwerp apparently remained convinced that casual employment should remain inextricably bound up with the port.

This discussion on decasualization also rises another interesting question. In a comparative aspect it would be interesting to analyse the difference in view on dock-labour by Antwerp and Rotterdam dockworkers. It is striking to see which efforts had to be made by the Rotterdam port employers to convince labourers to do dock-labour. They had to recruit their dockworkers in a far broader area than the Antwerp port-employers did. Special bus-services were established to bring the potential dockers to the port. In Rotterdam dock-work was also regarded - by outsiders as well as by dockworkers themselves- as being very low-status. In Antwerp we get a totally different picture. The port kept on attracting labourers from the city itself and the immediate surrounding villages and smaller cities. The supply of labour-force was mostly sufficient. Dockworkers worked at the port from a very young age until they retired. Dock-work was not seen as a temporary job. Why is there such a difference in appreciation on - at least to a great extent- a similar job? For the port of Rotterdam we can fall back on some older and more recent research by Ter Hoeven and Nijhof. For Antwerp, such research has never been done on the same scale. Maybe a interdisciplinary historical-sociological interview project would give us some answers to these and other questions.

References

Asaert G et al. (1993) De Antwerpse naties. 6 eeuwen actief in stad en haven. Tielt

Baudez L (1965) Naar algehele decasualisatie van de havenarbeid. Economisch en sociaal tijdschrift VI: 402

Hill S (1976) The dockers: class and tradition in London. London

Kerr C and Siegel A (1954) The interindustry propensity to strike - An international comparison. In Kornhauser A (ed) Industrial Conflict. New York, pp 189-212

Miller R (1969) The dockworker subculture and some problems in cross-cultural and cross-time generalizations. Comparative studies in society and history III: 302-314

Mommen A (1994) The Belgian economy in the twentieth century. London/New York

Ter Hoeven PJ (1963) Havenarbeiders van Rotterdam en Amsterdam: sociologische analyse van een arbeidsmarkt. Leiden

Nijhof E (1988) Gezien de dreigende onrust in de haven.... De ontwikkelingen van de arbeidsverhoudingen in de Rotterdamse haven 1945-1965. Amsterdam

Vandeputte R (1987) Sociale geschiedenis van België (1944-1985). Tielt

"Dock-work is a skilled profession". Decasualization and the Rotterdam labour market (1945-1970)[1]

Erik Nijhof

University of Utrecht, The Netherlands

1. Casual labour: employer or worker strategy?

It is a commonplace to identify dock-work with casual labour. The unpredictable supply of cargo to be handled and the omnipresent surplus of labour created a pattern of employment characterized by a minimal fringe of regular workers to meet the basic and guaranteed demand for labour, and a large, sharply fluctuating army of casual labour hired for one day according to the irregular supply of cargo (Weinhauer 2000, 580-581). Until 1950, this policy was common practice in nearly every port of the world. It seems obvious that employers were the initiators as well as the greatest beneficiaries of this casual labour system: if offered them the possibility to meet the requirements of the unstable cargo supply at minimal costs and responsibilities. For this reason port employers everywhere persisted in this policy. However, the history of labour relations has convincingly demonstrated that for many dockers (and other casual workers as well), casual labour was not only their inescapable fate imposed by the prevailing circumstances, but also their natural habit, imbedded in locally based communities ("isolated mass") and specific ways of life ("dock-workers subculture"); the mentality that was produced by this style of living was baptised "a casual frame of mind"[2]. They too defended casual labour, because of the relative autonomy this system seemed to offer to them; it was their way to resist to the growing dominance of disciplined wage-labour.

The weak point of the casual labour system was the assumption that there would be always plenty workers available to meet the peak demands in handling the cargo. When however, after 1895, under the influence of the upward swing of the business cycle, the west-European economies resumed their expansion, it became clear that many emerging industries would compete on the same labour market segment of unskilled labour: the building trade, metallurgy, food process-

[1] This contribution leans heavily on the research done for my doctoral thesis: (Nijhof, 1988) and also on (Nijhof 1997), 73-95.

[2] Classic statements of this mentality are formulated by Kerr and Siegel 1954, 195; Miller 1969, 305.

ing and allied industries. During the same period the new discourse on the social consequences of the Industrial Revolution (the "social question") put the problem of structural and chronic unemployment on the national political agenda. As a consequence of these two developments, some port employers started to reconsider their policy of casual labour. But unlike the kinds of industries that by their skilled and capital-intensive character provoked social provisions to attract or bind experienced workers, dock-work was a low-skilled and labour-intensive job dominated by the close interaction of the manual operations of a team inside and outside the ship.

In this contribution will be analysed, how and why decasualization developed so strongly in the port of Rotterdam after 1945. To do this, we need to say a few words on the evolution of casual labour in the pre-1945 period.

2. Casual labour in the port of Rotterdam before 1945

From 1870 on, Rotterdam developed as a port for mass scale transhipment of bulk goods with destination the rapidly industrialising Ruhr region. It was mainly a port for tramp ships and it had an abundant supply of labour originating from the rural surroundings hit by the agrarian depression of the 1880s. These factors strongly favoured an employers' policy of massive recruitment of casual labour and non-responsibility for the dockers. Nevertheless, in the port of Rotterdam at least three groups of actors resisted to the dominant system of casual labour.

For their part, the newly recruited dockers showed an atypical behaviour by not becoming an "isolated mass" with a specific sub-culture; they showed ambitions to become respectable, disciplined workers. Their agrarian roots and orthodox-protestant background are commonly mentioned as the decisive explanation of this attitude; in contrast, the autochthonous dockers of Rotterdam showed many similarities with the ascribed general characteristics (Nijhof 1988, 161-181).

The trade-unions were another force acting against casual labour: this type of work contradicted strongly the system of regulated labour relations advocated by the social-democratic, orthodox-protestant and roman-catholic trade-unions that, to be sure, had no adherence among the casual workers. Hence they stood for a kind of labour pool that should act as an employer for a fixed number of casual workers (that would become "semi-regulars"), and legislation to prevent the worst kinds of exploitation and dangerous work, which resulted in the 1914 Stevedoring Act.

As a third force emerged some enlightened employers, who were influenced by the ongoing discourse on the "social question" and who hoped to bridle the unlimited competition among and between the different sectors of the employers (shipowners, shipbrokers and stevedoring companies) by settling some rules for the labour and market conditions. In 1908, the port of Rotterdam had the first collective labour agreement in the Netherlands. Because of mutual distrust and competition among the employers this attempt shipwrecked. In 1918 the Labour Pool was established, that guaranteed work and income for a fringe of some thousands of dockers (it fluctuated with the business cycle, varying between 2000 and 6000).

This Labour Pool remained in operation until 1955 (Stakenburg 1957, 103-105 and 122-124). Another remarkable initiative was the "Wages Board" (1918-1921), founded to settle disputes between employers' and workers' organizations on labour conditions; it collapsed during the big port strike of 1920-21 (Stakenburg, 1957, 94-98).

Economic factors remained predominant, however, in preventing any further step towards decasualization: the recession of 1922-23 and the great depression of the 1930s put down all port traffic and incited the employers to restrict their regular labour force to the utmost.

3. The expansion of the port after 1945

The Second World War had heavily damaged Rotterdam. In 1940, Nazi bombing ruined its center, causing numerous casualties. And in 1945 the Germans devastated most of the immovable port facilities, after having dragged away many cranes in the preceding years. All traffic had come to a standstill in 1944 and 1945, so that it seemed that Rotterdam had completely lost its important pre-war position (Nijhof, 1988, 52-56).

However, the reconstruction of the port and the city proceeded with utmost speed; the port equipment was renewed according to modern standards, giving Rotterdam an ultimate advantage over non-destructed ports like Antwerp that could make a quicker start. Goods for the devastated zones of Germany went via Rotterdam, and the German economic miracle caused also a spectacular recovery of the port of Rotterdam. The rapid expansion of all kinds of traffic placed it at the lead in Europe in 1952, and in the whole world in 1962. Its tonnage raised from 8 mlns. in 1946 to 122 mlns. in 1965 for all goods, and from almost 6 mlns. in 1946 to 56 mlns. in 1965 for all goods except oil. As for comparison, in 1938 the latter tonnage had been 40 mlns. If we want to measure the consequences for employment, we certainly have to exclude mineral oil that is pumped practically without interference of human labour. The transhipment of general cargo, where constantly about 80% of the dockers worked, had preserved its share also after 1945, even raising to one-third of all goods except oil. A problem with these data was, however, that many goods, registered as general cargo, were transported in bulk and should have been labelled as bulk goods. Nevertheless, we may safely put its share on 20% of all goods except oil during the years 1945-1965 (Nijhof 1988, 49-56).

4. Labour productivity and technological innovations

As a consequence, the number of dockers rose steadily, from 5,913 in 1945 to 13,196 in 1950 (in 1938 there had been 9,300 registered workers). After minor oscillations this number began to rise again, amounting 16,706 in 1965 (Nijhof 1988, 423).

However, labour productivity told quite a different story. Whereas in 1938 a tonnage (minus oil) of 40 mlns. was handled by 9300 port-workers, i.e. 4308 tons pro worker, this average had sunk to 1218 tons for 6650 workers in 1946, and had with 3376 tons for 16,706 workers in 1965 still not reached the 1938 level[3]. This is a strong indication for the very slow technological development of cargo handling, that was only partially caused by the government policy of keeping wages low; technological bottle-necks played a far more decisive role. The average tonnage of sea-vessels was raised steadily though not in a very spectacular degree, but that of the Rhine barges remained remarkably constant. Quay equipment was modernized after its destruction during the war, and thereafter it was only modernized gradually in ore handling; the productivity in the transhipment of general cargo was raised by making cranes more versatile and by the introduction of the pallets. But all these innovations did not change the character of the work, dominated by physical interaction between the members of a team. The real break-through in productivity was caused by the sudden introduction of the containers in 1965 that was to change totally the system of labour relations in the port.

5. The labour market: searching for dockers

Already during the war, unemployed dockers were used to clear the ruins, and after liberation all dockers were mobilized to restore the traffic in the port and so to contribute to the economic recovery of the country. But many dockers from the pre-war period did not return, and in 1947 for the first time there was a shortage of labour. In the 1950s this problem became very urgent, but was acerbated by the dismissal of dockers during the recessions of 1950-1951 and 1957-1958: in the past these dockers had always returned when they were needed, but now they easily found employment in the building trade and the metallurgy and were lost for the harbour. From 1959 on there was a structural shortage of labour in the port, and the employers were forced to make expensive arrangements in order to attract commuters from the surroundings of Rotterdam; some people had to travel five hours a day for their work in the harbour. In the sixties they gave a bonus to persons who persuaded workers to become a docker (Nijhof 1988, 136-143). In 1961, they launched a huge sociological inquiry to the labour market position of the harbour to find out what their future chances would be, given the fact that the basic character of the work could not easily be changed (dirty, irregular and dangerous in comparison with other types of jobs competing on the urban labour market) (ter Hoeven 1963). One of the causes of their difficult position was the impossibility to pay wages high enough for competing on the Rotterdam labour-market: the "wage policy" of the post-war period forbade it by the force of law.

3 This difference may have been smaller, because this regards to all of the workers, irrespective of the numbers of workers engaged in the handling of oil, that were negligible in 1938 but became more significant as the quantity of imported oil expanded enormously after 1948; in absolute numbers, however, they must not have been too numerous.

6. Governmental intervention: the "wages policy"

The Dutch government in exile had already in 1944 expressed its intention to structure post-war industrial relations more actively by creating a system of institutionalized negotiations on labour conditions under government supervision. After liberation, this intention was materialized in what came to be called the "wages policy". This system was based upon two Extraordinary Decrees on Labour Relations (1944 and 1945) and made operative by creating provisions on two separate but related fields.

First of all, strict procedures of bargaining on wages and other labour conditions were formulated. The government determined the maximum wage-increase it wanted to allow, and this was the basis on which the parties could negotiate; the result had to be subjected for approval to the Board of Mediators. These negotiations were always on the level of national branches of industry, so on a very centralized scale. Crucial for the way this system functioned was the rule that all parties had to promise in advance that, in case of controversies, they would acquiesce in the final decision of the mediators. As an effect, the use of a strike as a means of enforcing workers' demands was practically reduced to zero and if a spontaneous strike nevertheless occurred, no allowances were to be made to the workers before they had called it off and had promised to await the decision of the mediator. Because especially the Rotterdam dockers had launched several strikes that were ascribed to the EVC (Unitarian Trade-Union Federation, founded in 1944 by the Dutch Communist Party), the latter organization was not admitted to the whole bargaining system and, therefore, could not sign collective labour contracts - a serious handicap in a system so strongly centralized and dominated by formal rules. Even after the strikers had pronounced their willingness to accept the rules of the wage-system, the EVC was kept out, mainly on instigation of its social-democratic rival CBT that needed the exclusion of the EVC to regain the influence in the port of Rotterdam that it had lost by its controversial attitude during the war. It had one year (May 1941-May 1942) co-operated with the trade-union policy of the German authorities (Coomans, de Jonge and Nijhof 1976, 19-20, 122-124).

Secondly, the wage policy had material aims: by keeping wages low, the export industries would regain their competitiveness and thus stimulate the recovery of the national economy. In exchange, the government, in which the social democrats held key positions, promised to control prices and house-rents and to create a system of social security. In short, the workers were guaranteed a minimal and decent subsistence level. This policy had some important and long-range consequences that were not foreseen nor intended. Low wages made labour relatively cheap and discouraged massive labour-saving investments. For dock-work another aspect turned out to be very decisive: the definition of a hierarchy of wages ranging from typically unskilled to skilled and highly specialized or responsable work. In 1945 officially determined wages were *f*35,- a week for unskilled urban workers, for semi-skilled *f*38,30 and for skilled *f*42,- creating a difference of 10% between each category (Pels 1955). This corresponded strictly with maximum wage-levels that could move upward all together with the economic expansion, but were extremely unflexible in their mutual relationship: the higher levels jeaulously watched the distance with the lower levels. Because ordinary dock-work was defined as unskilled, some types as semi-skilled, the official wages were necessarily not competitive with the wages paid in other branches on the local labour-market, that became every year more strained by the combination of rapid economic growth. This created an outburst of creativity at the side of employers' and workers' representatives to concoct all types of "grey" and semi-legal bonusses that could be admitted by the Board of Mediators. But also in this respect the ports were in an unfavorable position, because the way out of a system of tariffs for good working was not practicable here, because the diversity of the cargo was too great to propose a system that would not have the character of a lottery and thus would induce unfair results and even foster favouritism and endless disputes (Nijhof 1988, 339-346).

7. Labour conditions: decasualization as a forward flight

This situation was especially embarrassing for the more conservative employers, who were accustomed to an oversupplied labour market, authoritarian behaviour towards their subordinates and casualization. Now that this policy did not work anymore, a minority of more enlightened (though not necessarily less authoritarian) employers took the initiative for a policy of more institutionalized industrial relations. They pleaded for regular contacts with the trade unions, collective labour contracts and a moderate program of decasualization. This was, in short, the kind of policy that had become inevitable under the post-war wages policy, but they embraced it whole-heartedly. They had the sympathy of public opinion and the support of the key figures of the wage policy.

In the period 1945-1965 decasualization was realized in many forms. First and foremost, all dock companies raised their number of regulars at the expense of the casuals, and since 1952 the proportion of the regulars definitively exceeded that of the casuals and reached 80% in 1965. Of course the spectacular expansion of the port played a role, as well as the necessity to retain the trained workers on such a strained labour market (Nijhof 1988, 423).

The remaining casuals were offered a formal tenure in a Labour Pool that, for the first time, operated as a responsable employer, granting them for instance holiday benefits, formal rules of dismissal and labour disputes etc. Psychologically, this was felt to be a major accomplishment all over the port. In addition, also the humiliating way of reporting, where the dockers were physically picked out for a shift, referred to by all trade-unions and even by some employers as a "slave market" and considered completely outdated, disappeared step by step: most pool-workers were now engaged for a new shift before they had finished their old one and returned home; only a small minority had to report, but the ability and the willingness on the side of the employers to estimate their need of labour were growing every year (Nijhof 1988, 110-117).

Last, all parties tried to create schemes of employment with working weeks that were as normal as those in other branches: in the 1960s, most dock-workers now made a normal working-day from 07.30 a.m. till 16.15 p.m. and dockers who had to work an evening or a night-shift made even less working-hours, they knew a month before that they had to work in the evening or during the night and they worked at least one week on that time, thus creating better possibilities to adapt family life to these circumstances. Only a very small fringe of the dockers was kept mobile to ensure the quick dispatch of all incoming vessels, and such on a voluntary basis (Nijhof 1988, 324-330). Moreover, to show the willingness of the port to do away with the old casual frame of mind of the employers, the port was one of the first branches in the country to introduce the free Saturday (1961) (Nijhof 1988, 342-344).

8. Employers' policy: upgrading dock-work

Decasualization was, however, only a part of the employers' policy, though a crucial one. Important components were a policy to raise the social status and respectability of the docker and one to create a positive attachment to the employing companies, including the Labour Pool.

In 1949, an initiative was taken that was a world-wide innovation: the founding of a school for the vocational training of dock-workers (Haven Vakschool). Originally, it was a voluntary training for dockers in the age of 18-30, but later on it also trained crane-drivers, overseers and bosses, whereas it also tried to fill the gap for school-leavers between 14 and 18 year, who were forbidden to do dock-work by the 1916 Stevedoring Act: if they were trained as future dockers before they had to do their military service, they were more likely to return to the port afterwards. This training comprized much general education, which was in perfect harmony with the intention to use the school to raise the social status of the dockers. Because most employers wanted to keep the training of their regular personnel in their own hands, most trainees of the Haven Vakschool were casual workers. The collective labour-contract of 1962 recognized the function of stevedore (stuwer) as a skilled profession and was remunerated accordingly. Many officials from all countries visited the Haven Vakschool, thus enhancing its prestige, with an official visit of the Queen in 1954 as its apotheosis. It published also numerous reports and brochures, stressing the skill needed for dock-work (Peters 1951). There is some evidence that the school indeed did something to raise the status of dock-work (Ter Hoeven 1963, 46) and also had a positive impact on the level of accidents, although this effect was countered by the great turnover among the dockers, the trainees of the Haven Vakschool included (Nijhof 1988, 98).

The strained labour-market also induced the employers to formulate as a target a greater personal attachment of the dockers to the port and its companies - a quite astonishing ambition for a trade where traditionally the dockers had been treated as pack-mules, mutually interchangeable, of which there were always plenty supply; some employers even boasted they had never met any docker in their whole life. "I'd rather see three workers drop dead each day than that my machine breaks down, which costs me 25 guilders" another one should have said (Jansen 1979, 67). So this new policy must have been difficult to accept for the still numerous die-hards; nevertheless, the official employers' policy was carried out with conviction, varying from social funds for destitute dockers, family care for sick house-wives, holiday provisions and all kinds of hobby clubs: walking, acting, pottering, fishing, football, etc. EVC and OVB repeatedly warned against this new policy denunciating it as hypocrisy, to be replaced for the old habitudes as soon as the labour-market would change, but the workers involved did not take much heed to these warnings: the majority of the dockers joined one of these initiatives (Nijhof 1988, 130-132).

9. Mentality and life-style of the dockers

In the first post-war decade the mentality and life-style of the dockers did not change very much. An important cause was the continuity of the group of dockers: in 1947 66% was older than 39 years and 35% even older than 49 - for the whole of the male professional population these figures were 41% and 22%[4].

This older generation dockers was experienced and good in their job, but they resented the bad treatment by the employers in the days of casual labour. Many of them were (grand)sons of immigrants from the islands who had gained a position in the harbour by hard working and a sober style of living. Their wives did a good job in running the household as well as possible despite the irregular working-hours of her husbands. Their feelings of solidarity were based upon their common backgrounds and the co-operation in the port-team[5].

New cohorts of dockers entered the port with the expansion that started in 1947 and among them many younger ones in all categories of work. The vocational school (Haven Vakschool) produced a steady influx of trainees who became regulars, and the commuters (casuals) of the 1960s were also in majority young. These new generations of dockers had a different mentality and style of living. They moved to the newly built residential quarters at the outskirts of Rotterdam like Pendrecht, Hoogvliet, Barendrecht, that had no traditions of working-class solidarity. Their personal loyalties gradually shifted to their leisure activities, as was the case with all workers in general. They had a more instrumental attitude to their work and made use of the possibilities of the strained labour-market, which implied a much greater labour turn-over.

10. Strikes and dockers' organizations

The development of strikes and organizations in the port of Rotterdam is so closely interrelated that these can only be treated together.

---

[4] Nijhof 1988, 102-105. The Extraordinary Decree Labour Relations, promulgated by the Dutch government in exile in 1944, stipulated that all workers become unemployed on account of the war had the right to return to their pre-war jobs, but especially the younger ones had found other employment.

[5] Nijhof 1988, 177-181. This analysis of the family-life of the dockers is based on 30 interviews with dock-workers and their wives.

In 1945 and 1946, a chain of strikes paralysed the port for some crucial periods. The immediate causes were various, ranging from protests against frisking for stolen foodstuffs (June 1945) to material demands (August 1945), and from solidarity to a program of decasualization. As for the last two issues: solidarity was at stake, when the Rotterdam dockers refused to unload oranges from Franquist Spain (March 1946) and went on strike on behalf of the seamen who lost their war bonus (April-July 1946; this was the biggest strike in the port); decasualization became a continuous bone of contention between dockers and employers, with the prohibition of separated shifts in 1945 as one of the first successes of the Rotterdam dockers.

In these strikes the already mentioned EVC played a crucial role. Founded in 1944 but launched massively early in 1945, it immediately after liberation won wide adherence among workers of all tendencies, favoured by the failure of its greatest rival as "neutral" organization, the social-democratic NVV (Dutch Federation of Trade-Unions), that had collaborated just one year too long with the occupier (May 1941-May 1942) in the vain hope to become the all-embracing organization and thus was hopelessly discredited among a majority of the workers. As the old trade unions reappeared nevertheless and so tried to restore the pre-war union landscape, the EVC constituted itself as a fourth trade-union federation. This organization was to be neutral and open to all denominations, in accordance with the prevailing communist policy, but in reality communists were in command everywhere -except in Rotterdam.

During the first dock-strike in Rotterdam (June 1945) an organization was created that joined the EVC, despite its different ideological background: its leaders were radical socialistst who had always been critical to the communists, labelled by them as "stalinists". This coalition was rather fragile and during the 1946 strikes it almost broke down because the communists hoped to gain ministerial posts in exchange for their moderating influence on social conflicts. In March 1948 the Rotterdam branch broke away and established its own organization named OVB (Independent Federation of Industrial Organizations) with a syndicalist program, of which the dockers were (still) the most important component. Since that date, the battlefield of unionism was enriched with new front-lines, as the OVB waged war against the communists as well as against the social-democrats.

Especially during strikes these animosities became clear, with each organization developing its own strike policy that was opposed by the other ones.

The CBT did not strike at all, because it was loyal to the "wage-system" that granted the exclusion of its rivals OVB and EVC from bargaining on labour-contracts; during the negotiations it often invoked the menace of an OVB-led strike to exert pressure on the employers (Nijhof 1988, 318-319). There was one exception: the boycott of ships under "cheap flags" with inferior labour conditions, proclaimed by the ITF - the social-democratic unions, how moderate their own policy, seldom disregarded strike-calls of the ITF. In 1958 the NBV waged a symbolic struggle with ominous consequences: in 1960 the High Court of Justice principally labelled this strike as a non-fulfilment of contractual obligations which created jurisprudence to forbid future strikes (Nijhof 1988, 333-336).

The EVC, reduced after the 1948 secession to a marginal organization, never proclaimed a strike under its own name, but set up "independent strike committees" with some (mostly misled or simply naive) CBT or OVB members on the foreground but with their own members in command (Nijhof 1988, 272-286).

The OVB was at least until 1955 the most important organization. It principally concentrated upon labour disputes on the work-floor and rejected loyalties to political parties that always set different priorities: the EVC obeyed to the will of the communists and hence of USSR-policy, the CBT/NBV defended the "wage-system" and the position of the social-democrats in government. There were constantly minor conflicts on issues like the payment of bonusses for dirty cargo and on disciplinary measures against casual workers against which no appeal was possible. The latter point was connected with the tenure of the casuals and was also in discussion within the organization of the employers, the SVZ[6] as a part of its strategy of decasualization; the formal tenure for the casuals, introduced in 1955, was certainly stimulated by these OVB-actions, but the credits were given to the SVZ and the CBT. The same mechanism was in operation with the demand of the OVB that also the first two days of illness should be paid by the employers: after a lost strike this point was granted one month later (Nijhof 1988, 296-303 and 307-315).

These continuous struggles were not to foster unionization. In 1945 and 1946, the Rotterdam EVC-branch had organized more than 90% of all port-workers; as OVB this was already significantly less - perhaps still a majority - but in 1955 the revived social-democratic union NBV (Dutch Transport Union, successor to the CBT) equalled the OVB-adherence of 20% and in 1965 this NBV had 35% against 5% for the OVB. This dramatic turn should not conceal an almost greater change: the majority of the ordinary dockers was again not unionized (the NBV was strongest among crane-drivers, overseers etc.). This situation lasted until the 1980s, when the successor to the NBV became dominant.

11. Collapse of the "wage-system", collapse of EVC and OVB

An alarming labour turnover[7] constantly haunted the minds of the reforming employers, and when the national wage policy came under heavy pressure after 1959, it became clear that the policy of the port employers could not bring a lasting solution. A desparate recruiting campaign of commuters could only gain partial results: they were too few and costed too much. As a consequence, wage-increase

[6] The name "Scheepvaart Vereniging Zuid" (Southern Shipping Association) dated from 1919, when the already existing employers organizations in the ports of Amsterdam and Rotterdam tried to co-operate more closely; its Amsterdam counterpart was named "Scheepvaart Vereeniging Noord" (Northern Shipping Association); the SVN, organising many shipowners with regular lines, had already in 1945 created a regular tenure for its casual workers.

[7] On the basis of obligatory medical examinations of dockers a yearly turnover of 40-50% could be calculated for the 1954-1965 period, see Nijhof 1988, 130-134.

reappeared on the top of the agenda, causing much embarrassment among the officials of the wage policy, who silently admitted the problem that the port was structurally handicapped on the Rotterdam labour-market. When in 1963 the wage-system collapsed, official wages rocketed to the sky, with an increase of 15% in that year and 10% in the next (Nijhof 1988, 348-357).

The collapse of the wage-system created a tragic paradox for its opponents. The EVC split up in 1958 and collapsed in 1964, whereas the OVB had become marginal in the sixties and lost an important part of its remaining adherents in 1969 to its rival NBV.

The decline of the OVB manifested itself in different ways: new dockers were either not unionized or joined the NVB, and the existing membership grew older and greyer every year and the same happened with its leaders, who lamented bitterly: *The older generation, the real fighters, are pensioned or dead. The youth proves to be indifferent to class struggle, they do oppose themselves, sure, but everyone in his own way, unconsciously, not understanding how fatal this will be for their future* (Nijhof 1988, 362). The deeper reason for this decline was that the very existence of the wage-system that excluded its opponents from bargaining on labour-contracts, made their menace to this system indispensable: to enforce betterment that would have been far more difficult to realize along the official way. Unwillingly and unconsciously, they acted as the flexibilizing factors of an essentially rigid system. During the period of 1945-1955 it were the employers who carried out much of the program of decasualization of the radical EVC of the years 1945-1946, enhancing the status of the docker and creating more normal industrial relations, and in the period of 1955-1965 it was the re-emerged social-democratic union that could claim the unofficial wage increases. In all these cases the remembrance of the vehement strikes of 1945 and 1946 and the permanent menace of new (though smaller) ones, as was showed in 1950, 1953, 1954 and 1955, helped to overcome the institutional barriers of the wage-system and the conservatism of the die-hard employer wing. That was the reason that all parties, the employers, the official unions and also the OVB and EVC constantly referred to the image of the wild and rebellious docker of 1945 and 1946 that seemed in such a perfect accordance with the general image of this worker, pictured by so many social scientists, politicians and publicists. As long as this system prevailed, all parties, whether belonging to the establishment or to its radical opposition, for their own and different reasons, maintained this image of the militant and rebellious docker that had become in reality an anomaly of the past, when decasualization dominated all labour relations, inside and outside the port.

12. Respectable radicals

To understand this attitude, we must go back to the origins of the majority of the Rotterdam dockers, who were the second or the third generation of the immigrants from the southern islands. As stated before, their ambition for a better life as part of the respectable working class was permanently frustrated by the employers' policy of casual labour. This group proved to be very susceptive for all the explicit and implicit promises for a better existence after the war; these were made by enlightened stevedores like Backx (Thomsens Haven Bedrijf) and especially by the Dutch exil government as well as the first post-war government Drees-Schermerhorn. When these perspectives turned out to be unrealistic, at least in the short run[8], they reacted with bitterness and massively joined the newly founded EVC that pretended to be a militant and unitarian organization for all workers irrespective their religious or political backgrounds. As such, the Rotterdam EVC-branch became the vehicle of the emancipation of these dockers, the second and third generations of the former immigrants. This explains more than any other argument the perseverance and the militancy of the social struggles in the port of Rotterdam in these years: the felt this to be a crucial era in which many betterments so long desired for could be and should be realized. This explains too, why the bonds of solidarity in the proletarian quarters proved still to be so strong and vital: the strikers were backed by a massive support at the home-front, as in the days of the earliest port-strikes, and not unlike the attitude in the typical dockers' quarters in cities like London (Nijhof and Schrage 1988, 30-38). But in contrast to these foreign ports, this was no manifestation of a "dockworkers subculture" operating as an "isolated mass" but of their will to become, and to be treated as respectable workers[9].

And to return to our concept of identity groups: the common background and shared feelings of frustration of these second and third generation of immigrant dockers proved to be an alternative basis to unionization to the sectionalism of earlier decades. It created the EVC and paved the way for decasualization and other improvements, that in the longer run undermined the basis of this kind of unionism.

Conclusion: stages and shapes of decasualization

In this narrative, decasualization has passed through many stages and has assumed different shapes. If we look at the juridical shape of the tenure, we can distinguish several stages between the extremes of an exclusively casual labour force and its opposite of only regular labour contracts.

In the first stage there was a small fringe of regular workers - experienced stevedores working as overseers and bosses in the general cargo, most workers in the bulk sector - and a huge mass of casual workers hired by day on all possible spots: street-corners, pubs, entrance gates of harbour areas, etc. Apart from that, companies employing regular workers could sack them quite easily, if they wanted.

A second stage was entered when a labour pool guaranteed a small fringe of casual work and income. They were still hired by the day but were in fact a kind

[8] In Rotterdam, the 1938 collective labour contract was continued with some amendments, whereas in Amsterdam all casual workers were now employed by a Labour Pool that offered them a virtually regular tenure; this solution was reached in Rotterdam only in 1955.

[9] For this rejection of the theses of Miller and Kerr and Siegel with regard to Rotterdam, see Nijhof 1988, 161-181.

of "semi-regulars", positioned between the regulars and the flexible mass of real casuals.

When the labour pool acquired the monopoly for hiring casual workers, a new stage was reached: there were to be no casuals outside the pool, as was the case in Rotterdam after the founding of the Port Labour Pool in 1918. The pool was extended or diminished according to the needs of the port, and this need determined the distribution of the dockers over the companies. Only in exceptional situations and on a temporary basis, companies were allowed to hire workers from outside the pool.

The fourth stage was the regular tenure for the dockers of the pool, created in Rotterdam in 1955. The difference was the granting of the same rights as those of the regulars: holidays, the possibility to appeal against disciplinary measures, normal procedures for dismissal, the same social benefits, etc. The only differences were the varying places of work, which attracted especially the younger workers who loved some variation.

Apart from the juridical status of the tenure, changes took also place in the quantitative division of the different categories of dockers. First and foremost, after 1945 a steady absolute and relative enlargement of the regulars was the most visible manifestation of this kind of decasualization. Much more hidden were changes in the actual employment of the pool workers: they were increasingly hired by the same employers, they had not longer to report at the hiring office but were told at the end of the shift to return next day, and the stevedoring companies became more able to predict their long-term needs of labour, which resulted in monthly schemes of employment.

To return to our question on the evolution of casual labour in the port of Rotterdam, it was primarily the government policy of the post-war era, combined with the position of dockers on the Rotterdam labour market, that produced this remarkable tendency to ban casual labour and to upgrade dock-work as a "skilled profession". But this policy could only be effective to the extent that the dockers and their unions accepted the loss of relative autonomy and the adoption of a respectable life-style that were the inevitable consequences of decasualization.

In Rotterdam, overwhelming evidence shows that they were not simply accepting these changes, but that these changes mirrored their genuine aspirations, and that they fostered these ambitions long before the employers policy embraced decasualization. In international perspective, this lends the case of the Rotterdam dockers some uniqueness.

References

Coomans P, de Jonge T and Nijhof E (1976) De Eenheidsvakbeweging (EVC) 1943-1948. Groningen

Jansen T (1979) "De wil der bazen regelt het werk". Havenarbeiders rond 1900 in Amsterdam en Rotterdam. Jaarboek voor de geschiedenis van socialisme en arbeiderbewging in Nederland: 67

Kerr C and Siegel A (1954) The interindustry propensity to strike, an international comparison. In: A. Kornhauser et al., Industrial conflict. New York

Miller RC (1969) The dockworker subculture and some problems in cross-cultural generalization. Comparative studies in society and history XI: 305

Nijhof E (1988) "Gezien de dreigende onrust in de haven..." De ontwikkeling van de arbeidsverhoudingen in de Rotterdamse haven 1945-1965. Amsterdam

Nijhof E and Schrage P (1988), Behind the Picketline. The homefront of the Rotterdam dockers in times of social warfare. In: Heerma van Voss L (et al.), Industrial conflict, Amsterdam, pp 30-38

Nijhof E (1997) Les syndicats de dockers de Londres, du Havre, de Rotterdam et de Hambourg 1850-1914. In: Robert JL (et al.) L'invention des syndicalismes. Le syndicalisme en Europe occidentale à la fin du XIXe siècle (Série internationale, 53). Paris, pp 73-95

Pels PS (1955) De ontwikkeling van de loonvorming. Alphen aan de Rijn

Peters P jr. (1953) Havenarbeid is een vak, Mens en Onderneming, V

ter Hoeven PJA (1963) Havenarbeiders van Amsterdam en Rotterdam. Een sociologische analyse van een arbeidsmarkt. Rotterdam

Weinhauer K (2000) Power and control on the waterfront: casual labour and decasualization. In: Davies S (et al.), Dock Workers. International explorations in comparative labour history (1790-1970). Aldershot/Burlington, pp 580-581

Commentary on the papers of Vanfraechem and Nijhof

John Barzman

University of Le Havre, France

My comments on Mr. Nijhof's paper on Rotterdam, and Mr. Vanfraechem's on Antwerp come from the perspective of a specialist of labor in the port of Le Havre interested in the comparative method in history. They begin with a reminder of the long-standing interest in these two ports extant in Le Havre. I then briefly present some problems of comparative studies, summarize what appear to me to be the main findings of the papers of Mr. Vanfraechem and Mr. Nijhof, and conclude with some questions which arise from recent debates over the transition from a single regulated hiring pool to multiple private employers.

1. The French tradition of comparisons with Antwerp and Rotterdam

There is a long history of comparison of dock labor in Antwerp, Rotterdam and Le Havre, not only as three among several European or world ports, but also as three ports of the northern range. The reasons must be sought first in the comparability of the geographic sites. Like Hamburg and Bremen, all three ports are located in the estuary of major rivers, the Rhine, Maas, Scheldt and Seine, flowing from the center of the continent northwestward toward the busy waters of the Channel and North Sea. For dock labor, this means transshipment between river and maritime navigation, as well as similar tides, turn-around times, and silting and dredging problems.

In addition to these features of geography common to all northern range ports, the three ports dealt with here have attracted specific comparisons because of the competition between them: competition for a hinterland which overlaps substantially since it includes northern and eastern France, Switzerland and southern Germany, as well as competition for the "foreland" of oceanic freight moving through the Channel and North Sea lanes. This rivalry has led to numerous attempts at comparing the advantages and disadvantages of each harbour, among which the expense and speed of cargo handling, and therefore of dock labor, figured prominently.

In the French case, the anxious comparisons seem to date from the middle of the nineteenth century, perhaps because the arrival of canal and railroad networks into new areas, as well as the emergence of new borders between states (Belgian independence, Zollverein, annexation of Alsace), changed the conditions of the competition. In 1882, Senator Félix Faure, former head of the Le Havre Chamber of Commerce and future President of the Republic, commissioned a parliamentary investigation entitled: "Inquiry into the situation of French Channel ports with regard to the competition of foreign ports"; chief among which stood Antwerp, Rotterdam, London and Hamburg (France 1883). There is a long line of reports in the same vein after that time, one of the latest avatars being a parliamentary report in 1989, which examines four ports, two rivals of Marseille and two rivals of Le Havre. The latter two are Antwerp and Rotterdam (Beaufils 1990).

There is also a scholarly side to the rivalry. In 1950, the Chamber of Commerce of Le Havre helped to publish a review called "Porte Océane", which featured articles by Marcel Amphoux, a Havrais geographer who distinguished himself by taking issue with what he called the Netherlands school of maritime economic geography. The writings in question were those of J. Bouman, a Dutch scholar who had studied the port of Rotterdam and emphasized the importance of the hinterland for understanding the development of ports. Amphoux counterposed the notion that hinterlands mattered very little compared to the maritime foreland, giving examples such as Malta and Singapore[1]. Some thirty five years earlier, in 1986, when the Port Authority of Le Havre tried to introduce the notion of a "harbour community" and to promote friendlier working relations between labor and management, it asked two French sociologists, Thierry Baudouin and Michèle Collin, to produce a report on the community of spirit which, in its opinion, drove Antwerp forward (Baudouin and Collin 1986). The fixation of Havrais leaders on the operation of Antwerp is still alive and well, and was vividly expressed by the leader of the dockers union of Le Havre in a public meeting in 1998: "I heard just before that Antwerp was the competitor of Le Havre. I would like to say that beginning today, beginning this evening, we should say that Le Havre is the main competitor of Antwerp."[2]

Of course, the impulse to compare dock labor in these three ports did not come only from merchants' and shipowners' search for harbours with the most favorable labor conditions for their particular business, but also from public authorities worried about the consequences of poverty, alienation and social agitation on the waterfront. Some time ago, I conducted a study on the origins of such comparisons and found that the first is probably the work of a Belgian scholar familiar with Antwerp, Baron Charles Gillès de Pélichy, a social Christian, who published a book in 1899 comparing labor conditions in twelve great European ports, among which Antwerp, Rotterdam and Le Havre (de Pélichy 1899). One lesson of my survey is that the international comparisons appeared at a certain date and contained a definite agenda: they corresponded to the anxieties and projects of particular interest groups at a particular juncture in history (Barzman 1997). With the formation of international employers organizations, the International Federation of Transport Workers (ITF) and the International Labour Office in Geneva, there were more systematic attempts at comparison with a broader scope. Some of these

[1] A summary of the 1950 debate can be found in Vigarié 1984, 13-22 and in Charlier and Cabanne 1986, 12.

[2] The Havrais dockers' leader in 1998 was Patrick Mineau, whose words are reported in Brocard 1998, 42.

are listed in two recent articles[3]. The latest product of this vein is of course the book produced by the International Institute for Social History of Amsterdam, to which Erik Nijhof and myself have contributed (Davis 2000).

2. Problems of comparative research

One of the difficulties which was visible in the first attempts at comparisons of dock labour by Baron Charles Gillès de Pélichy in 1899, and which is still visible in the IISG book in the year 2000, is finding the equivalent of the terms used in each country or harbour. The issue often appears to the researcher as a problem of linguistic translation: finding the right word in English, French or Flemish. But one realizes rapidly that there is more to it: the words "dock" and "dockers" do not describe the same facility and occupation in different places and different epochs, not to mention its different emotional and cultural connotations. In French, the word "docker", borrowed from the English language, does not correspond exactly to the older word "portefaix" which was translated porter.

Even attempts to quantify the comparisons by using monetary units, tons of merchandise, meters of quay, deadweight tonnage, productivity of a crane, number of days worked in a year, number of dockers, active population in the travel-to-work area, run up against insoluble difficulties. The two French sociologists who reported on Antwerp asserted that a financial comparison of the performance of the port and workforce was impossible because items which appeared in another port as expenditures of a private company or of the port authority, were provided in Antwerp as a public service by municipal staff, whose pay is inextricably mixed into the general budget of the city, funded by taxes. Another frequent problem is comparing the purview or competence of different levels of government bodies and semi-public organizations, such as cities, provinces, super-regions, national states. The instructions and definitions given to census takers and other gatherers of economic and social information are different from one country to the next.

As a result one of the most instructive aspects of international comparisons is to look for important issues which may be hidden by the use of a universal term, and seek to clarify the exact difference. Quantification can only go so far. International comparisons must rely on qualitative evidence and analysis. The comparison between Antwerp and Rotterdam seems particularly useful because of the geographical proximity of the two harbours. Differences which have arisen must be attributed to human action, the legacy of pre-existing social and political situations. Sometimes the difference turns out to be only a matter of schedule: the same trend appears later in the second port, but it is then no longer a pioneering effort, but a painful effort to catch up with the pioneer.

It is to be expected that the work of historians of single ports will stress what is particular, while the view of other specialists, such as geographers, working on ports in general, will rely on the conventional wisdom of the academy at the time

[3] See footnotes 2, 3 and 4 in (Weinhauer 1997 pp 219-220) and the many references in Tunrbull 2001 and Domenichino 1999.

at which they write. The value of the two papers before us will perhaps be more apparent when set against the assertion of a generalist, writing in 1968. André Vigarié, from whose writings I have selected the following quote. Vigarié is a geographer with considerable knowledge of all aspects of the maritime world and a great sense for the history of ports. His description reflects the trend which he observed in the early 1960s, which are the focus of Mr. Vanfraechem's paper and an important turning point in Mr. Nijhof's paper:

"Dockers offer us one of the neatest cases of how maritime transportation has rendered an occupational group uniform: they display similar features beyond the races and ideological differentiations to which they are subjected... The longshoremen's occupation is organized in a way that is found across the entire world, even in the Communist countries such as Poland and is one of the most typical aspects of port internationalism... This labor system is less and less accepted by dockers who are demanding more security, and, under the influence of trade unions, we are witnessing a drive toward "decasualization" of the occupation of dockworker, which is already a fact in some countries, such as England since 1961, and Antwerp and the United States since 1966."[4]

In the face of this broad overall view, historians can uncover particularities, and this is often made easier by close comparisons. The first step of comparative work is to juxtapose accounts of the two situations to be compared. This is the framework of our panel on the history of dock labor in Antwerp and Rotterdam. The two papers represent an attempt to confront current knowledge of these ports' labor history in the light of current concerns of the discipline. They are somewhat asymmetrical in their presentation, but reveal some basic features of the labor forces of each port, which we can begin to put into comparable terms.

3. Vanfraechem's paper

Stephan Vanfraechem presents us with a detailed account of a discussion between employers and dockworkers about decasualization in the port of Antwerp in 1964. He draws on records of the employers association (the Centrale des employeurs du port d'Anvers [CEPA]) and, to a lesser extent, on those of the labor union (the Belgische Transportarbeidersbonde [BTB]), as well as on some economic histories of the harbour[5]. His account illustrates the fundamental issues involved in the history of all dock labor in the twentieth-century, as well as the specific evolution of the discussion in the port of Antwerp at a time of great economic expansion, the

[4] (Vigarié 1968, 432-434). The dates given by Vigarié do not seem to correspond to clearly identified major changes in practice (the United States had different rules in each port) and may refer to statements of intention.

[5] CEPA records include the Contact Commission (1963-64), the Limited Employers' Delegation (1962 to 1965 and 1968), the minutes of the 1964 Reform of the Terms and Conditions of Employment Commission, and Annual Reports (1964-1968). BTB records include Executive Committee reports (1964), National Committee of the Port of Antwerp (1964 to 1966) and the Congress of the Dockworkers' Union and Related Trades (1966), and some publications.

years from 1963 to 1965. The framing of the subject, dictated by the sources used, leaves outside its compass certain questions which may have a bearing on the issue of decasualization notably the human relations between gang members, possible divisions by origin, skill or orientation, the definition of exactly who were the "non-docker workers" hired by bosses in case of a labor shortage on the waterfront, as well as life outside the workplace (neighborhood, family status). The two main actors of his tale are the employers and the union leaders. Public authorities, either in the form of the central state or municipality, appear very little.

Vanfraechem illustrates, in a brief but crucial section entitled "Trade Unions Called to Order by their Own Members", the gap which sometimes existed between union leaders and a majority of the rank-and-file. Can we identify more precisely the rank-and-filers who dissented? Vanfraechem suggests that the dockers who customarily accepted three or four shifts per week (as opposed to those who took only one of two shifts), formed the backbone of the opposition. This pattern of division between union leaders inclined to seek binding decasualization and members trying to preserve their right to choose has been extensively studied in the case of England (Phillips and Whiteside 1985). Their research has shown a rather consistent reluctance of the rank-and-file to accept the proposals worked out by the trade union leaders and employers, because a substantial section of the dockers wanted to keep a degree of freedom to refuse unsafe jobs or choose the best ratio between effort, safety and pay.

Vanfraechem's main point is that casual work persisted for the vast majority of the 12.000 Antwerp dockers until the end of the 1960s because, on the one hand, employers believed they could still operate with the same small permanent staff that they had used in the past, and choose the exact number of additional casual relatively skilled workers which they needed, freely, on a daily basis. On the other hand, most dockers did not want "to surrender a part of their income" to the fund from which the "guaranteed weekly wage" would be drawn, as implied in the decasualization plan. In the end, that is, in the second half of the 1960s, after the agreement of 1964 went into effect, only warehouse keepers and foremen were decasualized. Employers obtained the number of extra workers which they needed by offering bonuses and incentives, and calling on occasional "non-docker" workers.

We may provide some additional context to Vanfraechem's story by referring to studies by other scholars. The period from 1960 to 1965, described by Vanfraechem, can be characterized from the point of view of the demand for labor by examining rough figures provided by (Baetens 1997). These five years are part of a decade and a half of rapid growth of a particular type: the total goods handled in the port of Antwerp increased of course, but not at the expense of labor intensive piece goods (general cargo or conventional merchandise). Port equipment was adapted, but chiefly by expanding the size of machines and multiplying their numbers, rather than by a drastic transformation of the technical system. The latter only began to change in 1965 with the gradual introduction of the container, much larger vessels, the roll-on roll-off ship, straddle carriers, expanded storage space in the harbour, data processing tools and integrated logistics. Therefore, in the 1950-1965 period, the expanded tonnage and multiplication of equipment of a well-known type meant that employers continued to need the same large number of dockers at unpredictable times, and expected them to possess more or less the same skills as in the previous decade. The figures given by Baetens include both the 1960-1965 period (which Vanfraechem has shown to be a period of relative labor scarcity) and the 1965-1970 period (which we can describe as that in which the technical transformation began). They reveal a slight decline in the total number of laborers: 1950: 14 329; 1960: 14 354; 1970: 12 090; 1975: 12 289; 1980: 9 530[6]. 1960-1970 is also the decade when the number of regular laborers (as opposed to candidate laborers) fell by over 2000 men (13 012 in 1960, to 10 937 in 1970). From Baetens' description, it is likely that the decline in regular laborers and total laborers occurred mainly after 1965, as technology began to change.

The picture can be complemented with some elements from (Baudouin and Collin 1986). They point out that in the middle of the 1950s, there were about 20.000 unemployed workers in the Antwerp district (p. 14), but that the following decade, 1956 to 1965, was one of rapid industrialization of the metropolitan area, in connection with the port. During this period, they claim, the city and port employers had the impression that manufacturing (and perhaps construction) competed with the harbour for members of the local workforce and drove wages up. With these two additional elements about technological evolution and urban labor market trends, we see that Vanfraechem's study is focused on the moment when the dockers' relative bargaining power had increased steadily for a decade but had not yet been undermined by the new technological system, centered on the container, introduced after 1965. The incident is characteristic of the apex of docker power.

4. Nijhof's paper

Erik Nijhof's paper covers a far longer period: 1880 to 1965, and deals with a far broader range of issues, including the general profile of Rotterdam's traffic and the regional origin, residential habits and political orientation of its dock workers. Nevertheless, for the sake of coherence in my comments on the two papers, I would like to focus on the comparable period and issues present in both papers. Nijhof's describes the contrast between the heyday of casual labor, 1880 to 1945, and the rise of decasualization, which occurred, between 1945 and 1965. After 1945, a growing section of port employers increased the number of regular workers, by which I understand the permanent employees or staff of a private company. By 1965, Nijhof reports, 80% of all dockers were regular workers. The remaining 20% were hired in a very civilized fashion by a Labor Pool. Nijhof uses the term "formal tenure" to describe the rights of these protected casual workers in the Labor Pool. Thus Rotterdam dock labor was decasualized far earlier than Antwerp dock labor.

Nijhof explains the particular form of decasualization, which came about in Rotterdam after 1945, by a combination of reasons:

---

[6] Baetens 1997, 15 cites: Annual Report CEPA, Harbour of Antwerp, Study and Prospection, WE, 5/10/1987.

- Great increase in the traffic, including bulk goods;
- Moderate pace of innovation;
- Competition for scarce labor with the urban construction and manufacturing sectors;
- Strict government control of wage increases;
- Unofficial strikes or strike threats by the outside unions (EVC and OVB);
- Good relations between moderate employers and labor leaders.

Nijhof presents the old casual labor regime of the pre-1945 period as humiliating for the workers and described "even by some employers, as a 'slave market'". The acquisition of permanent jobs and the upgrading of their social status and skill classification after 1945, were therefore welcome by the vast majority of dock workers. According to Nijhof, they had not been attached to a "casual dock workers subculture", but frustrated to be forced into the lowliest rungs of the proletariat, despite their hard honest work.

For Nijhof, many Rotterdam dockers' support for the more radical unions, the EVC and OVB, in the 1940s and 1950s, did not reflect a profound disagreement with the moderate union, the NBV, over the goals of the struggle. He argues that the NBV negotiated and obtained the type of decasualization which the EVC and OVB had demanded in 1945. Nevertheless, the dockers continued to support the EVC and OVB for a time because they sensed that the militant legend strengthened their hand in negotiations with employers. "The memory of the turbulent strikes of 1945 and 1946 and the permanent menace of new (but smaller) ones... helped to overcome the institutional barriers of the wages system and the conservatism of the die-hard employer wing." (Davies 2000, p. 424)

5. Questions

The presentation of these two papers is an opportunity to move toward some clarification on issues which often come up in twentieth-century dock labor history. Some concern the technological and economic context, others the various possible meanings of the term "decasualization".

A first series of questions has to do with differences over the traffic and equipment used in Rotterdam and Antwerp between 1945 and 1965, that is when Rotterdam moved rapidly toward decasualization, while Antwerp chose to postpone it:

1) Can one say that the greater percentage of bulk products in the traffic of Rotterdam in those years meant that loading and unloading operations were more regular and predictable than in Antwerp?

2) Did the low wages policy of Rotterdam (as a result of state pay guidelines) mean that less new machinery (forklifts and pallets) was introduced there than in Antwerp?

3) When did the new technology of containers become capable of handling a sufficient volume of cargo to reduce the number of dockers needed in the moments of most intense activity?

A second set of questions has to do with the urban environment and its effects on the marker for dock labor:

4) What evidence do we have of links between the market for dock workers and city-wide markets for general workers? How often, if at all, did casual dockers take jobs outside the harbour? In what circumstances did non-dockers have a chance to be hired by port employers? Was there much more reconstruction work in Rotterdam than in Antwerp until 1955?

The third main group of questions concerns the concept of decasualization. I admit to being influenced by the terms of the recent debate in Le Havre. In 1992, a reform law put an end to the obligation of employers to hire their workers in the general labor pool (Bureau Central de la Main-d'Oeuvre) created in 1945[7]. The dockers union, with the support of the rank-and-file, fiercely resisted this law for two years. The dockers finally accepted a deal which eliminated about one thousand dockers, transformed about one thousand others into permanent staff hired by a small number of large private cargo-handling companies, and left a few hundred others in a provisional status. The reform was presented by the employers as "decasualization", and as a measure to bring French ports into line with other European ports.

However, it is possible to consider the reforms introduced between 1928 and 1947, including the creation of the BCMO in 1945, as an earlier form of "decasualization", which was perceived by dockers as a protection of their rights. If we accepted this interpretation, we would be faced with two types of decasualization: one favored by the rank-and-file, the other by the employers. The choice would not always be "*either* permanent hiring by private firms *or* the slave market", but, at least in some instances, "*either* civilized, regulated, daily hiring with income maintenance in case of unemployment, for all, *or* permanent hiring for some and extreme precarity for others". The feelings of both employers and dockers may have changed somewhat with the trend towards unemployment and the evolution of cargo-handling technology.

Both Mr. Vanfraechem and Mr. Nijhof allude to the existence of these two forms of "decasualization" in their paper. Mr. Vanfraechem states in note 2:

"This paper reduces the meaning of the term "decasualization" to the switch from a casual to a permanent employment. Any preceding processes such as the compulsory registration of dockworkers, the reservation of work for registered dockworkers and the introduction of "attendance money" will not be discussed in extenso".

Mr. Nijhof, speaking of the casual workers in 1945, states:

"The remaining casuals were offered a formal tenure in a Labor Pool which, for the first time operated as a responsible employer, granting them for instance holiday benefits and formal rules over dismissal and the solving of labor disputes."

My question therefore is: Should we not distinguish "real decasualization", in French "permanentization", from "soft decasualization" also known as "formal tenure" or the "protected casual system" or the "attendance money system"? Is not

---

[7] For a summary of events leading to its establishment (Barzman 1997 and 2000); for the 1992 debate see chapter 2 "La résilience d'une culture de métier modale: les dockers du Havre et de l'ITF" (Barzman 2001).

the rejection of "real decasualization" by rank-and-file dockers the expression, not of a preference for true casualism and the "slave market", but for "formal tenure"?

A second question about decasualization concerns the outer borders of the "docker group". If we take a bird's eye view, it seems that in almost all ports at almost all times, three groups of workers contributed to cargo handling operations:

1) Public workers employed by the port authority, the city, or some other collective entity;

2) Permanent employees of private cargo-handling firms;

3) Casual workers ranging from very regular dockers to workers who were hired in the harbour only very occasionally.

The need for permanent employees of private firms derives from the 1) rarity of the skills needed to operate expensive machines, 2) foremen, 3) workers who can be trusted not to break or steal the merchandise, 4) a guarantee against shortage of manpower. It would seem that insofar as employers could rent public services such as cranes and equipment driven by public workers, the private companies' need for a permanent staff was reduced.

The question for Antwerp is: did the municipal harbour services contribute to make real decasualization less urgent, at least until very new large investments were needed for container handling, which municipal finances were reluctant to undertake alone?

References

Baetens R (1997) Harbour development and Dock Labour. The Case of Antwerp, 1945-1990. In: Port Reports prepared for the Conference Comparative International History of Dock Labour, 1790-1970, Amsterdam, 13-15 November 1997. Volume I. Amsterdam.

Barzman J (1997) Labour Relations in the Port of Le Havre 1928-1947. In: International Journal of Maritime History, IX-2: 83-106

Barzman J (1997) Origins of comparative studies of dock labor 1870-1914. Paper submitted to Session HO9: Comparative International History of Dock Labor 1790-1970, Twenty-Second Meeting of the Social Science History Association, October 16-19, 1997 - Washington D.C. (Publication forthcoming in a French version).

Barzman J (2000) Les dockers du Havre, de la brouette au portique (XIXe-XXe siècles)", Université de Paris I-Panthéon-Sorbonne. Habilitation à diriger des recherches

Barzman J (et al.) (2001), Transports, mutations des techniques, emploi et cultures professionnelles. Rapport au PREDIT/Lettre de commande DRAST 98 MT 12. Le Havre

Baudouin T, Collin M (1986) La notion de communauté portuaire. Le cas d'Anvers, Paris

Beaufils J (1990) Rapport d'information sur les ports autonomes en Europe. Assemblée nationale n° 1144, Annexe au procès-verbal de la séance du 20 décembre 1989. Paris

Brocard M, (et al.) (1998) "Port 2000" Contribution au débat public. Le Havre

Charlier J, Cabanne C (1986) Biobibliographie d'André Vigarié, géographe maritimiste, In: Ports et mers. Mélanges maritimistes offerts à Jean Vigarié. Caen

Davies S (et al.) (2000) Dock Workers: International Explorations in Comparative Labour History. Manchester. 2 volumes de Pélichy CG (1899) Le régime du travail dans les principaux ports de mer de l'Europe. Louvain

Domenichino J (1999) (et al.) Dockers de la Méditerrannée à la mer du Nord: des hommes et des quais. Aix-en-Provence

France. Ministère des Travaux publics. Comité consultatif des chemins de fer. Commission constituée par arrêté minstériel du 31 août 1882 sous la présidence de Félix Faure (1883) Enquête sur la situation des ports français de la Manche au point de vue de la concurrence avec les ports étrangers. Paris

Phillips G, Whiteside N (1985) Casual Labor. The Unemployment Question in the Port Transport Industry1880-1970. Oxford

Turnbull P (2001) Labour Regulation and Competitive Performance in the Port Transport Industry: The Changing Fortunes of Three Major European Seaports, In: Barzman J (et al) Environnements portuaires. Actes du colloque tenu au Havre du 24 au 26 mai 2001. Le Havre (forthcoming).

Vigarié A (1968) Géographie de la circulation. Tome II: La circulation maritime. Paris

Vigarie A (1986) Le Havre et l'évolution de la pensée méthodologique en économie portuaire et maritime. In: Etudes normandes, III (1984): 13-22.

Weinhauer K (1997) Labour Market, Work Mentality and Syndicalism: Dock Labour in the United States and Hamburg, 1900-1950. In: International Review of Social History, XLII (1997): 219-220.

The first mechanization wave in coal and ore handling as an example of patterns of technological innovation in the port of Rotterdam

Hugo van Driel

Erasmus University Rotterdam, The Netherlands

1. Introduction

Since 1885, a series of new cargo-handling techniques have been introduced in the port of Rotterdam. These technological innovations were not unique to Rotterdam. The strong increase of the volume of cargo flows and the scaling-up of the sea-going vessels have stimulated technological innovations in the European ports in general since the latter part of the nineteenth century. The development of the cargo-handling technology has, however, also been determined by the interference of deep-sea shipping with the modes of inland transport by barge, railway, truck, and pipeline. It is particularly in this respect, that ports differ from each other and that the cargo handling technology can get a specific local flavour. Furthermore, the specific needs of the shippers and receivers of cargo and the existing trade practices have influenced the method of cargo handling in the ports in different manners[1].

The technological innovations in cargo handling took the shape of mechanization. In Rotterdam (and other ports) this process has taken place in different waves (van Driel and de Goey 2000). At the end of the nineteenth century and in the beginning of the twentieth century the handling of liquid and dry bulk goods such as oil, coal, ore, and grain was mechanized. In break-bulk handling the mechanization process took place much more gradually. It was not until the middle of the 1960s that the container caused a revolution in the handling of break bulk.

This paper focuses on the first mechanization wave in the major dry bulk goods ore and coal in the period between circa 1885 and 1920. There are several reasons for this choice. First of all, ore and coal developed into the major categories of goods handled in the port of Rotterdam during this period. In particular these two

[1] A global comparison between the development of cargo handling technology in ports can be made with the help of several general overviews published in different periods: Zimmer 1905 and 1916, Haase 1913. Cunningham 1926, Wundram 1939, Oram 1965, Oram and Baker 1971. The volumes of the Jahrbuch der Hafenbautechnischen Gesellschaft (since 1918) and the Handbuch für Hafenbau und Umschlagtechnik (since 1953) are very informative too.

products shaped Rotterdam's character as a transit port of bulk goods. Second, eventually ore and coal handling became dominated by one and the same technology: the grab crane. In retrospect, we can say that the period 1885-1920 was formative for Rotterdam dry bulk handling technology. Third, Antwerp clearly lagged behind Rotterdam in the modernization of the handling of coal and ore in this period. This provides us with an interesting opportunity for comparison between both ports. Unfortunately, not much is known about initiatives for innovation in ore and coal handling in Antwerp in the period studied. As a consequence, the comparison is only very general and speculative; it can be found at the end of the paper.

Nevertheless, the interest in comparison has indirectly influenced the set-up of the paper. Attention is paid to self-evident questions, namely the characteristics of the innovations, and the bottlenecks and prospects to which they were related. Special to the paper, however, is the strong focus on the political and commercial context of the innovations. Innovation is an instrument firms use to gain profits or, more generally, to create a competitive advantage. Therefore, some authors consider a rather fragmented, competitive industry structure as the most conducive to innovation (Klein 1977). However, innovation also entails relatively high levels of risk and uncertainty. This feature of innovation has led the famous Joseph Schumpeter to argue that oligopolistic (and not fragmented) industry structures are the most innovative, because in this context large firms with secure market shares and considerable investment resources are able to risk uncertainty (Barras 1986, 164). Given this discussion, the paper particularly deals with the structure of the industries involved and the identity of the innovators, i.e. their positioning in the trade and transport chain. It is hoped that in this way a more focused comparison with the Antwerp case will become possible.

2. The first mechanization wave in Rotterdam coal and ore handling

In this empirical section, attention is paid to the major innovations in Rotterdam ore and coal handling between around 1885 and 1920. Before this analysis is presented, it is necessary to sketch the organization of cargo handling at the outset of the mechanization wave, in order to assess the context in which the innovations took place.

2.1. The organization of stevedoring in the port of Rotterdam before mechanization

Ore and coal were the main dry bulk products handled in Rotterdam in the period studied[2]. In the end, ore and coal handling became dominated by one and the same technology: the grab crane. However, the product characteristics within and between the categories of "coal" and "ore" differed considerably. First of all, the sizes of the pieces of coal and ore varied. Both coal and ore knew fine and coarse variants. The ore lumps were, however, considerably larger than the pieces of coal. Furthermore, coal could be vulnerable to loss of quality due to breakage during handling, whereas ore was not. In this respect, the differences in the characteristics of coal were relevant. Coal not only varied in the size of the pieces (fine or coarse), but also in the fat content.

Fig. 21.1. Volume of handling of ore and coal in the port of Rotterdam 1881-1913

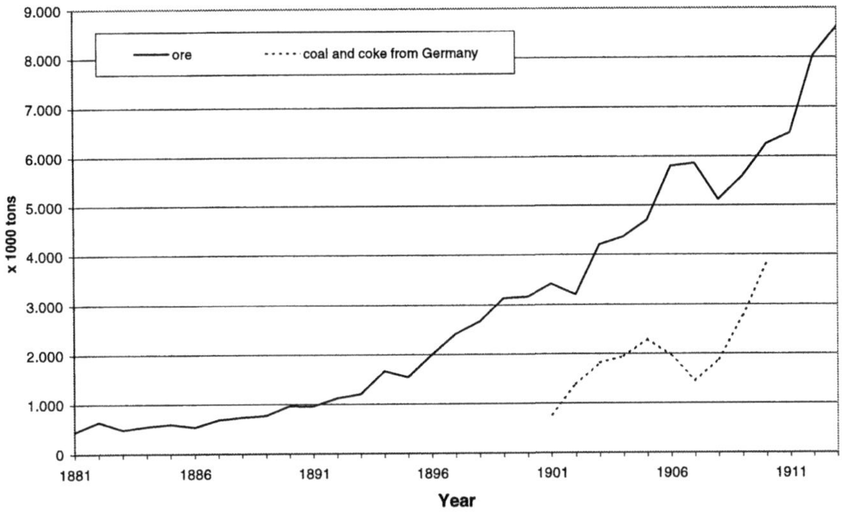

Source and note: *Jaarverslagen Kamer van Koophandel en Fabrieken van Rotterdam* (collected by P.T. van de Laar) coal and coke from Germany: addition of the transport by rail of coal and coke to Rotterdam, extracted from: van Rijckevorsel 1912 and the Rhine transport of coal and coke from Germany to Rotterdam, extracted from *Jahres-Berichte der Zentral-Kommission für die Rheinschiffahrt 1901-1913* (collected by H.P.H. Nustelling).

Not only the nature of the products was different, but also the direction in which they were transported. Until the Second World War coal was mainly an export product, transported from the German mines via the Rhine and railway to

[2] Another major category of dry bulk cargo was grain, but the handling of grain became dominated by a specific, separate type of equipment, i.e. pneumatic machines and therefore is not dealt with in this paper.

Rotterdam. Ore, on the other hand, was an import product that the German iron and steel industry had shipped in via the Rotterdam port (see Fig. 21.1). This difference is relevant because the unloading of sea-going vessels puts other demands on the functions of cargo-handling equipment than the loading of ships. The same holds true for the modes of inland transport involved, in particular in the case of rail wagons.

A third difference concerned the mode of inland transport used. From the start of ore imports through Rotterdam, Rhine shipping has had the largest share in the transport to the German hinterland. In contrast, Rhine shipping did not succeed in dominating the transport of coal from Germany to the Netherlands in the last quarter of the nineteenth century. At that time most coal was not meant for transit (export), but for use in the Netherlands. The railway network was better able to service the domestic destinations than Rhine and inland shipping. Moreover, the fragile coal had to be handled several times during its transport by barge from the German mines in the Ruhr area, which affected its quality.

The different sorts of coal and ore could be handled, in different settings, manually by using more or less the same equipment and techniques. The practice around 1880 was that dock workers in the ship's hold shovelled the cargo into buckets, which were subsequently lifted by winch or shore-based crane and then emptied by tipping them into a barge (in this case often by means of a spout) or rail wagon. In the case of export cargo, the buckets were filled in the barge hold or from the rail wagon and then transferred to the sea-going vessel. In other words, the vertical movement of the goods occurred with the help of machines (including hydraulic and steam cranes since the late 1870s), but the majority of the work was performed manually.

Several kinds of parties were involved in stevedoring before the mechanization process started. More or less reluctantly, the Rotterdam municipality became involved in the operation of stevedoring installations in 1882 (Devos and van Driel 2000). Ten years before, it had decided to grant the extension of the port by installations on the Feijenoord peninsula on the south side of the river to the Rotterdamsche Handelsvereeniging. This private company - controversial from the very beginning - got into serious financial problems when the complex was finished in 1879. Director Lodewijk Pincoffs had used funds from the Rotterdamsche Handelsvereeniging to cover losses in his other commercial enterprises. On 14 May 1879, when he could no longer hide his fraudulent actions, Pincoffs fled to the United States. The Feijenoord-complex at that time was the only one in Rotterdam equipped with hydraulic and steam cranes, sheds, a large bonded warehouse, and a railway directly linked to the quay installations. The municipality saw no other way than to take over the Feijenoord-complex in 1882. Subsequently, it was more or less natural for the municipal government to equip the new quay space on the south bank it created from the late 1880s on with sheds and cranes which could be hired by private firms that rented the wharves from the municipality. Initially, the municipality rented out quay space and sheds at Feijenoord for relatively short periods, ranging from one or a few days to four years at most. In this way, flexibility was maintained and monopolization of certain sites by private firms was avoided. This implied that private firms were strongly dependent on allocation decisions by the municipality for the operation of shore-based stevedoring activities (only the

Maatschappij tot Exploitatie van Staatsspoorwegen, hereafter called "Staatsspoorwegen", a private railway company, could continue its exclusive use of quay space at the western side of the Spoorweghaven (Feijenoord) after the Pincoffs crisis). However, from 1890 the newly created quay space at the south bank (and later also at the north bank) was normally rented to users for relatively long periods, in some cases even 25 years.

The municipality did not want to get involved in commercial activities, but nevertheless wanted to regulate them. To this end, the regulation on the *kadegeld* (wharfage) was introduced in 1883. It granted only liner shipowners or their agents the right to a fixed berth. The city executive wrote in the explanatory memorandum that independent middlemen should not get the chance to make money out of the right on fixed berths, because this would make the harbour less attractive to shipowners. It is clear that the experience with the Rotterdamsche Handelsvereeniging (which at one time had started to raise its own harbour dues in addition to the municipal ones) influenced the tenor of the regulation. The regulation implied that master stevedores were not able to operate a wharf. They could only load and unload ships at the quay when the liner shipping firm or the ship agents hired them as subcontractors. However, the loading and discharging of cargo in midstream, which represented a large part of dry bulk stevedoring, was not regulated. Shipowners, shippers and receivers could undertake such handling themselves, but more often than in the case of quay operations left it to the stevedores. These stevedores did not need to invest in machinery: the winches were part of the ship. Entry barriers were not high in this respect: around 1890 approx. 25 master stevedores, handling of all kind of goods, were operating in the port of Rotterdam. On balance, a variety of parties undertook stevedoring activities before the mechanization wave in mineral bulk handling started. Finally, from 1900, after extensive discussions, the right to a fixed berth along the quay became admissible for all kinds of firms.

There were two major, related trends underlying the mechanization of dry bulk handling in the port. Firstly, in the second half of the nineteenth century steam ships became dominant, not only in liner shipping but eventually also in tramp shipping. Steam ships were much more expensive than sailing ships and therefore their laytime in the ports had to be kept to a minimum. At the same time their loading capacity was much higher than that of sailing ships, which intensified the need for faster loading and unloading. Secondly, the incoming and outgoing flows of dry bulk cargo started to swell in Rotterdam from around 1870 on, when the industrialization of the German hinterland started its "take-off". This strong increase in cargo flows also stimulated the search for faster handling techniques. However, for innovation to occur conscious action by (several kinds of) actors was needed.

2.2. The first innovation: the coal tip

Given the predominance of transporting coal by rail, it was not very surprising that the first mechanization of coal handling in Rotterdam concerned the discharge of the contents of rail wagons into sea-going vessels. The German coal exporters were the ones to instigate this. Since 1877 the export of coal from Westphalia had been co-ordinated loosely by the Westfälischer Kohlen-Ausfuhr-Verein, a joint venture of 23 mines. This organization, which remained in existence until 1894, intended to stimulate the export of Westphalian coal through the North-Sea ports to compete with the English coal that had been dominant until then.[3] In these seaports the method of handling formed an impediment to the expansion of this export. The labourers were hired under contract and worked as fast as they could, so that the coal was not handled carefully enough and often broke into pieces.

For the mechanization of the handling of export coal from Germany in the port of Rotterdam a special-purpose machine was preferred. In January 1878 the Ausfuhr-Verein distributed a circular to the export ports urging them to bring coal tips into use, following the example of English ports. A coal tip was a device that could lift rail wagons and subsequently toppled them in order to discharge the coal at once into the sea-going vessels. The German coal exporters triggered innovation, but it left - or had to leave - the actual role of innovator to parties that controlled the quay space in the ports. "Staatsspoorwegen" reacted comparatively quickly and installed a "coal tip" at the Spoorweghaven in 1880. However, the exact character of this piece of equipment had remained obscure[4]. Only in 1884, it became clear that the idea of the Ausfuhr-Verein appealed to the Rotterdam municipal authority, because it saw the export of Ruhr coal as a possibility to make the port as a whole more attractive. [5] Increasingly, there was no return cargo for the incoming vessels (the share of outgoing ships that were in ballast increased from 26% to 39% between 1877 and 1882). German export coal was ideally suited to fill this gap. The director of the municipal port installations visited England in 1884 and came back enthusiastically: loading 1000 tons of coal, which took cranes with buckets seven days, required one day only by means of a coal tip. The coal tip was not only much faster, but - still according to the director - at least twice as cheap as the operation with cranes and buckets. Furthermore, the coal tip also met the third requirement formulated by the Ausfuhr-Verein: the quality of the coal would, by and large, remain intact during handling.

Finally, in 1886 the municipal coal tip, the first hydraulic one on the European continent, was put into operation in Rotterdam at the Binnenhaven (Feijenoord),

[3] Nusteling 1974, 283-284. Gemeentelijke Archiefdienst Rotterdam (GAR), Nieuw Stadsarchief/Algemene Zaken (NSA/AZ), inventory number (inv. no.) 2404, no. 370, Westfälischer Kohlen-Ausfuhr-Verein, Einladung zu einer Versammlung in Hamburg behufs Besprechung über Herstellung zweckdienlicher Kohlen-Verladungs-Vorrichtungen in den Hafenplätzen, Düsseldorf, Januar 1878.

[4] Verslag van de Maatschappij tot Exploitatie van Staatsspoorwegen over 1880, 77. On 12 February 1885, during the discussion on the proposal to install a municipal coal tip, several well-informed members of the city council even referred to rumours about a plan of "Staatsspoorwegen" to adopt a coal tip! (Handelingen van de Gemeenteraad van Rotterdam 1885, 15-16). This makes us wonder what kind of 'coal tip' the company was actually using at that time. Obviously, its "coal tip" did not serve as a model for later innovations in the port of Rotterdam.

[5] "Rapport van den directeur der Handelsinrichtingen. Uitvoer van Duitsche steenkolen", 29 november 1884, in: Verzameling gedrukte stukken aan de Gemeenteraad van Rotterdam 1885 (Gedrukte Stukken), nr. 3, litt. c, 21-28.

followed by a second one in 1895 and a third one at the Katendrechtse haven in 1900. When the municipality installed the first coal tip, it still rented out quay space only for short periods of up to around four years (as indicated, "Staatsspoorwegen" was an exception). Therefore, it was hard to imagine that private firms would even think of investing in an expensive shore-based piece of equipment like a coal tip (the purchase price of the first municipal coal tip was 60,000 guilders). Perhaps the municipality did not realize this when it used the lack of private initiative as an argument for the provision of the coal tip by the government. Nevertheless, without the risk-carrying role of the city of Rotterdam (functioning) coal tips would probably have appeared on the scene much later. The city openly indicated that the operation of the coal tip did not necessarily have to be profitable. In the words of the director of municipal port installations: the vicious circle of coal exporters complaining about insufficient cargo handling installations in the ports and the port authorities answering that the low levels of exports did not justify heavy investments in such equipment had been broken.

2.3. The introduction of shore-based slewing cranes for ore handling

Mechanization of the discharge of ore was more difficult than that of coal, because it was very heavy and awkward to handle due to the size of the lumps that could vary from tiny to very big. The structure of the ore heaps in the ship's hold differed from that of the coal heap; because coal tended to remain lying "high in the corners", trimming was less necessary. Therefore, in ore handling manual discharge by means of buckets and winches remained in use longer. This manual discharge was only defined as a bottleneck in 1893, when the Rotterdam Chamber of Commerce received complaints about a lack of berths for ore ships for direct discharge into rail wagons due to seasonal peaks[6]. The municipality blamed the lack of capacity largely to unusual low water levels of the Rhine, which temporarily had urged shippers to shift from barge to rail transport. Nevertheless, the city did not want to take the risk of disturbing the system of carrying coal by rail from Germany to Rotterdam and using the same wagons for the transit of ore in the opposite direction, which was vital for Rotterdam's continuous existence as a major bulk port.

To study the problem, the directors of public works and of port installations - just as for the coal tip - did some research in England. They concluded that the discharge of ore into rail wagons in England was up to twice as fast as in Rotterdam, where the operation was very time-consuming. In Rotterdam the ore was first taken from the hold by means of winches, subsequently weighed on deck, and

---

[6] Jaarverslag Kamer van Koophandel en Fabrieken van Rotterdam 1893 (Jaarverslag KvK Rotterdam), 77-79; Bijlage XXV, Rapport van de Commissie voor de Reederijen over de quaestie van ligplaatsen voor ertsbooten, oktober 1893, 71-76; Jaarverslag KvK Rotterdam 1894, 86, and "Het graven van eene 2e haven aan de Katendrechtse kade en het inrichten van drie ligplaatsen voor overlading van erts in de Katendrechtse haven" (2 augustus 1894) and Extract uit het Rapport van den Directeur der Handelsinrichtingen d.d. 22 juni 1894, in: Gedrukte stukken 1894, 228-230 and 237.

then put into wagons by quay cranes. This was necessary for two reasons. First, the Rotterdam cranes with their lifting capacity of 1,5 tons were not strong enough to drag the buckets along the ore in the ship's hold, as was necessary for filling the buckets without involving too much manual labour (dragging was a time and labour-saving method compared to the dock workers filling the buckets completely by means of shovels). Second, in Rotterdam there were no weighing bridges for weighing the loaded wagons, so that each bucket had to be weighed on deck separately. It sometimes also happened that the wagons had to be moved manually when no locomotive was available for shunting.

In September 1894 the city council agreed to the construction of a new basin west of the Katendrechtse haven, which was equipped with six electric cranes with a lifting capacity of 3 tons maximum. The cranes could cover three railway tracks along the quay, so that wagons could be replaced when one was loading on the other track. In this way, the cranes could operate continuously. Furthermore, electric capstans were installed, used for shunting the wagons, as was a weighing bridge. Compared to the coal tips, the new cranes were more versatile pieces of equipment. They could also be used for other cargo than ore. Furthermore, their use was not restricted to transfer of cargo in one direction.

Again the municipality - in the interest of the port as a whole - appeared to be willing to carry the risk of an investment, of which it was not sure in advance that it would be profitable. But contrary to the coal tip, most of the ore cranes were given in exclusive use to one private firm, Wm. H. Müller & Co (part of the capacity was reserved for irregular users, because the municipality was keen to avoid a private monopoly of unique equipment at a unique site). Müller was a Rotterdam company heavily involved in ore trading and shipping. It is plausible that, from the perspective of available sources and risk-taking, the concentrated structure of the ore trade was more conducive to innovations by private firms at this time than the fragmented coal trade had been at the time the first coal tip was installed. In ore trading, at both ends of the chain, relatively powerful parties were to be found (Serton 1919, 76). Mines often had a strong position. Their output and the quality of that output were normally stable. At the other end, the buyers - the steel industries - were small in number. Furthermore, they were particularly interested in an uninterrupted supply of raw materials because the furnaces had to be kept going. In other words, all the conditions for direct contact between producer and consumer seemed to be present. Faced with this danger, when the trade flows became denser, traders had to find ways to maintain their position. One strategy was to take control of mines, just as the steel industry did. Müller & Co., based in Rotterdam since 1869, was one of those trading firms that gained control of mines. The company not only traded in ore and had mines; it also transported it by its own ships, and was also an agent of "Staatsspoorwegen". In other words, Müller had a stake in several parts of the transport and trade chain. The company was assured of a certain employment of the cranes and therefore the risks of renting the new cranes were reduced.

2.4. Change of focus of the innovations and the identity of the innovators

I have now dealt with the first major innovations in the handling of coal and ore respectively. It was mainly the municipality that absorbed the risks of the innovation. The focus was on the transfer of cargo between vessel and train. Both characteristics of the innovation processes in mineral bulk handling changed around the turn of the century. Firstly, rail transport lost ground in mineral bulk transport; in the case of ore it had almost completely vanished in 1905 (Fig. 21.2). The scaling up of Rhine ships, the sizes of which increased to 2,000 to 3,000 tons, was mainly responsible for this; it made them much cheaper than the trains with a capacity of around 500 tons (Serton 1919, 85). The second change was that the municipality no longer involved itself in the innovations in bulk stevedoring equipment; private firms became the sole innovators. The municipality focused its innovative efforts on the stevedoring that took place at its own quays, but it left innovations in the floating stevedoring equipment to private initiative.

2.5. Innovations in coal handling with floating equipment

The change in focus of the mechanization of coal handling was initiated by the concentration among the German coal mines. In 1892, the P.W. Louwman company in Rotterdam was charged with the transfer of coal from rail wagons and Rhine barges for the Kokssyndikat, a combination of German coal mines aimed at the joint selling of coke (Sneller 1946, 210-211). Louwman originated from the coal trade, which it bought in the Ruhr area and then transported to Rotterdam.

Around 1885 Louwman started with the sale of bunker coal (the fuel needed for the sea-going vessels' own propulsion) in Rotterdam. Probably, Louwman used the coal tips for the unloading of the rail wagons. Comparable mechanical equipment for the handling of barges was missing, however. Although nothing is known about the backgrounds of Louwman's decision, it is plausible that its exclusive contract with the German coal exporters served as the basis for Louwman's innovation in barge-vessel transfer in 1898, when the Kokssyndikat had been replaced by a much larger combination, the famous Kohlensyndikat (see below). Louwman focussed on a specific kind of coal; the fine coal that at that time dominated German coal exports. "Fine coal, Louwman reasoned, may be handled like sand. So, it does not need to be hoisted - like large and fragile coal - ... but can be dredged and dumped in bulk"[7]. To this end, Louwman bought his first floating bucket elevators in 1898. These floating bucket elevators were, like the coal tips, special-purpose machines.

Louwman's innovation in the equipment for floating coal handling was followed by several other ones by the Steenkolen Handelsvereeniging (SHV), founded in 1896 in Utrecht. This association of Dutch coal traders based its innovative role on the exclusiveness in the trade of German coal in the Netherlands it was granted by the famous German coal cartel, the Rheinisch-Westfälische Koh-

[7] SHV Archives, Sneller, Geschiedenis van de SHV, 100 (unpublished manuscript).

lensyndikat. In the Kohlensyndikat, founded in 1893, a large part of the Westphalian mines were joined (Wilhelm 1966). The Kohlensyndikat took over the entire production from the shareholders and sold it on their behalf. The syndicate also determined the selling prices: its pricing policy was focused on stabilization. It divided the market into 37 districts: 29 German and 8 foreign ones. As a rule each of these districts was covered by one syndicate trader, but only for one type of coal. These traders, however, sometimes joined forces per district, with the syndicate's permission. This was also the case with the SHV that obtained the exclusive right for the sale of the Kohlensyndikat's coal brought in by rail into the Netherlands.

Fig. 21.2. Share of Rhine shipping in the transport of coal and ore to and from the Netherlands and Rotterdam 1884-1913

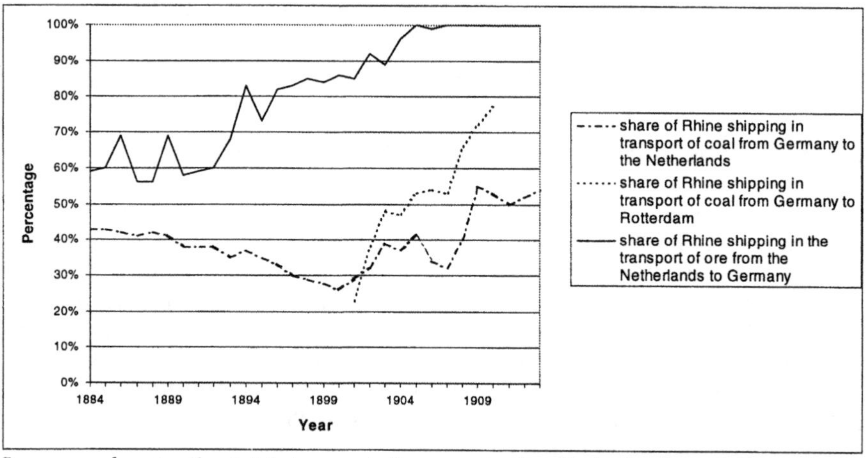

Source and note: the total transport from or to the Netherlands and Rotterdam was calculated by adding the transport along the Rhine (for sources: see Fig. 21.1) and the transport by rail (based on: Ministerie van Financien, *Statistiek van de in-, uit- en doorvoer 1884-1913* (collected by H.P.H. Nusteling). With the exemption of coal in the period between 1902 and 1910, in this figure the data for the Netherlands are shown and not those for Rotterdam, because accessible data for the volume of the rail transport of ore and coal from Rotterdam are not available. The share of Rotterdam in the Rhine transport of ore from the Netherlands to Germany varied from 71% to 82% between 1884 and 1892, and from 85% to 91% between 1893 and 1913 (*Jahresberichte der Zentral-Kommission für die Rheinschiffahrt 1884-1913*

From its foundation in 1893, the Kohlensyndikat strongly promoted coal transport by rail. The SHV's two main founders, the brothers-in-law H.A. van Beuningen and D.G. Bingham, were not only traders but also railway officials and the SHV was located at the railway junction of Utrecht. However, in 1902 and the following years the transport of coal via the Rhine to Rotterdam showed a very marked increase, so that inland shipping outstripped railway transport. As from 1 October 1903 the Kohlensyndikat extended to nearly all Westphalian mines. That year also saw the foundation of the Rheinische Kohlenhandel & Rhederei Gesellschaft, better known as the Kohlenkontor, in Mühlheim. It incorporated several large coal traders from the Ruhr. Besides the monopoly on direct shipments of coal by rail to Southern Germany and parts of Austria, Switzerland and France, the new enterprise also obtained the monopoly on the coal transported by barge to the Rhine ports from the Kohlensyndikat. In addition to the rail coal of the Kohlensyndikat, the SHV managed to obtain the Dutch sales monopoly on the Rhine-shipped coal as from 1 April 1904, partly in exchange for participation in the Utrecht company by the Kohlensyndikat and the Kohlenkontor.

The certainty offered by the sales monopoly on the Rhine-shipped coal was the basis for the SHV to undertake substantial innovations in coal handling in Rotterdam, particularly in bunker coal. However, before that the SHV had already started to show interest in port operations in Rotterdam: in October 1901 it decided to establish a branch there[8]. This was the result of the Kohlensyndikat's wish to compete more strongly with English coal, which then dominated parts of the coal trade in Rotterdam (Sneller 1946, 211). It is important to stress that the SHV was not involved in the export of German coal through the Dutch seaports to foreign destinations. But the SHV monopoly did include the trading of bunker coal in the Dutch seaports. It was in this respect that the extension of the exclusive sales right to Rhine coal made such a difference. D.G. van Beuningen, son of one of the SHV founders, who became in charge of the new Rotterdam branch, concentrated his attempts at modernization in the first place on the bunker coal, by floating equipment. The coal tip could be used to dump coal into the bunker holes of the ship, but this work was still largely done by manual labour[9]. The bunker coal was usually taken to the vessel by a lighter. Then the dockers climbed a ladder with a bag of coal on their backs in order to empty it into the bunker holes. Hard though the carriers worked, it happened frequently that bunkering was the cause for a ship's delay in port. Growing ship sizes made this bottleneck more pressing. In addition, and this was very important, speeding up bunkering would be a powerful weapon for the SHV in the competition with bunker coal shipped in from England, which the shipping companies usually preferred because of its better quality. In time the acquisition of the sales rights and the efforts to mechanize bunkering ran parallel. The minutes of the meeting of the SHV's Board of Directors on 23 December 1903 mention the establishment of the Kohlenkontor as well as a journey to America by one of the directors and Van Beuningen in order to study a floating coal transporter. Subsequently, on 2 March 1904, it was mentioned in a meeting of the Board of Directors that the exclusive selling rights of coal shipped via the Rhine were given to the SHV and that the Board agreed to the purchase of the floating coal transporter.

---

[8] SHV Archives (SHVA), Minutes of the meeting of the Raad van Beheer of 4 October 1901. All references given hereafter to the meetings of this governing body, which in 1905 was rechristened to "Raad van Commissarissen" (council of supervisory directors), have been extracted from the minute books. Most of the relevant minutes have also been literally reproduced in SHVA, OTC, 1900-1909 file, Ontwikkeling van het filiaal Rotterdam.

[9] This and the following information about the actions of D.G. van Beuningen is based on GAR, Handschrift 326, Memoires D.G. van Beuningen.

The floating coal transporter was a mechanical device that would create spectacular savings in time and manpower. At first Van Beuningen had tried unsuccessfully to design a coal transporter himself. "Without illusions" he then turned to shipbuilder A.F. Smulders (later named Gusto), a relation from his Utrecht period at the SHV. The Smulders engineer, J.D. Dresselhuys, remembered a magazine article about an invention by a French engineer. It probably concerned the "self trimmer" here, designed by M.J. Paul around the turn of the century (Buhle 1901, 44 and Zimmer 1905, 273). Such a vessel was provided with lockable openings at the bottom of the loading compartments in the hold. When the slides were opened, the goods automatically fell onto a belt conveyor, which then carried the load from the bottom of the ship upwards. Van Beuningen travelled to both England and America to study two of these malfunctioning vessels and, according to his own words, subsequently managed to redesign the machinery into a properly working piece of equipment.

The improvement in productivity was impressive: a coal transporter was able to load 250 tons of coal per hour into the ship. This required a crew of seven men. For completely manual handling of such a quantity in the same time about 250 people would have been necessary. It will be clear that it was virtually impossible to deploy such an army of coal carriers at the same time (Dresselhuijs 1911, 196).

The use of the coal transporter did not mean that coal could now be directly dumped from the barge into the bunker holes of the vessels. A separate device was necessary to load the coal transporter with coal from the barges. So, together with the coal transporter, the SHV ordered a floating grab crane from the Haarlem factory Figee. This was the first floating grab crane in the port of Rotterdam.

The coal transporter appeared not to be the end of the technological development in bunkering. As a modern liner needed 5,000 to 6,000 tons of bunker coal, the coal transporters still had to collect cargoes from the barge several times (Zimmer 1916, 481-82). It was not attractive to increase the capacity of a coal transporter from 600 to 700 tons to for instance 2000 to 3000 tons, because such a vessel could not easily manoeuvre in the port (Serton 1919, 116). In 1908 the SHV therefore put the "Holland" into use, a so-called floating coal elevator. This was able to bring the bunker coal directly from the barge into the vessel. To that end Dresselhuys from the Smulders company had invented a combination of the belt conveyor and the ladder of the coal transporter and a bucket elevator, which collected the coal from the barges and put it on the belt conveyor via a funnel. According to his memoirs, Van Beuningen once more gave the technical finishing touch to the "Holland".

The SHV's coal transporters and elevators became the dominant technology. They were responsible for the fact that the company could secure 90% of bunker coal handling around 1913 (Serton 1919, 114): the subordinate position of German coal in bunkering was reversed into a dominating position within a couple of years. Around 1910 the SHV's competitor, the Steenkolen- en Scheepvaartmaatschappij (SSM) trading in English coal, also brought into use a coal transporter. Shortly after, the SSM, founded by the American Petroleum Company, was secretly taken over by the SHV that from then on controlled the entire mechanized bunker coal handling.

All in all coal-handling technology more and more assumed a varied aspect in Rotterdam in the years around the turn of the century. Manual handling partly remained in existence, but an increasing part of the coal was handled by special-purpose machines: coal tips, floating bucket elevators, the slewing cranes at the quay originally installed for ore handling (from 1898 on), floating coal transporters and floating coal elevators. In other words, by 1905 every kind of coal had its own special purpose-handling device. However, more versatile mineral bulk handling equipment, the grab, appeared at the Rotterdam scene at that time.

2.6. Innovations by more versatile equipment: the grab cranes

The principle of the grab is age-old. Grabs were initially developed for excavation works. As early as 1703 a modern-looking grab is supposed to have been designed for this purpose in France (Zimmer 1916, 392). Around 1900 several grabs were already in use, also in ports. Grabs had as a major advantage over buckets that they could be filled and emptied automatically, without manual labour. The grabs firmly lodged themselves in the cargo by their own weight, after which the load could be transferred from the ship at one go. This method, of course, saved labour. The disadvantage of grabs in comparison to buckets was their higher weight (necessary to wedge themselves into the cargo). Compared to coal tips, bucket elevators and floating coal loaders, grab cranes were much more versatile. Coal, ore as well as other dry bulk cargo could be handled by a grab crane, just by replacing one type of grab by another (a simple, quick operation). For instance, coal grabs were larger and lighter than ore grabs. Similarly, the type of grab could be accustomed to the direction of the transfer of cargo: from sea-going vessel into barge, rail wagon or onto the shore, or the other way round.

The first grab cranes in Rotterdam were all applied to specific, relatively small niches, reacting to specific bottlenecks and prospects. The first grab crane was installed in Rotterdam in 1903 by the municipality for the handling of basalt at the Tweede Katendrechtse haven on behalf of the London Basalt Stone Company[10]. Just as in the case of the coal tip, the municipality considered this installation primarily as a way to make the port of Rotterdam more attractive to shipping companies by offering return cargo. It was, however, the private firm that took the initiative for the installation of the crane and selected the specific equipment to be used.

---

[10] For the following, see: Van IJsselsteyn, Haven van Rotterdam, 279; GAR, NSA/AZ, inv. no. 2960, no. 10708, letter from the Basalt Maatschappij (Rotterdam) to Burgomaster and Eldermen of Rotterdam of 24 November 1898; inv. no. 2995, no. 9236, letter of Johnston (Rotterdam) to Burgomaster and Eldermen of 21 October 1899; inv. no. 456, no. 1225, in particular letters from the London Basalt Stone Company to Burgomaster and Eldermen of Rotterdam of 25 March 1902 and 7 July 1902, and a letter from the management of public works to the subcommittee of the city council of public works of 1 April 1902 and 15 July 1902; and inv. no. 458, no. 1667, letter from the management of public works to the subcommittee of the city council of public works of 7 October 1902, and a letter from the managing director of the municipal port installations to the subcommittee of the city council of municipal port installation of 11 October 1902.

This slewing grab crane on a bridge could discharge the basalt from Rhine barges onto the shore as well as reclaim it and dump it onto a belt conveyor, after which the goods were loaded into the sea-going vessel via a sort of funnel. A rate of discharge of 125 to 150 tons per hour was possible; this was several times the hourly production of a normal slewing crane.

The Basalt Stone Company clearly based its innovation in Rotterdam bulk handling on the cargo it could supply to the installation as a shipper. It was the last time that the municipality financed the purchase of a specialized piece of equipment for bulk handling. In fact, it shared the financial risks with the private party involved because, in addition to the normal (reduced) crane hire, each year the Basalt Stone Company had to pay 5% of the purchase price of the crane to the municipality, with a minimum of 10 years, even when the company would not extend the rent of the site after the first contract period of five years. In this way the risk of the local government was significantly reduced. It expected that, in case the Basalt Stone Company would stop exploiting the crane before it had paid back the full price of the crane, the municipality would be able to deploy it for the handling of other heavy bulk loads.

As we have seen, the first floating grab crane in Rotterdam introduced by the SHV in 1905, was an auxiliary innovation triggered by the first floating bunker coal transporter. In 1905 the SHV extended the use of floating grab cranes to the handling of export coal. The sale of Rhine export coal, that is, coal exported to foreign destinations via the Dutch ports, was not included in the SHV's monopoly. At the foundation of the Kohlenkontor in 1903 Louwman was assigned all handling of this coal of the Kohlensyndikat in Rotterdam (very likely, this was a continuation of an existing agreement). Louwman thus was an attractive prey for the SHV, which took over the company in 1905. The assured supply of work the takeover provided the SHV with, stimulated further mechanization of the handling. As of 1 April 1905 Louwman and the Van Nievelt companies that were also taken over (Van Nievelt was one of the SHV's founders), became incorporated into the SHV Rotterdam. Shortly after, in June 1905, the SHV decided to increase its capacity, not by more bucket elevators (Louwman owned six bucket elevators at the time), but by two grab cranes. This decision resulted from the growing importance of the lump coal in German exports. The bucket elevators that dug into the coal and dropped it from a great height were only suitable for fine coal and slack. The floating cranes indeed affected the quality of the lump coal far less than the elevators[11]. How much the SHV could anticipate the Kohlensyndikat's policy and thus minimize the risk of the innovation, becomes clear from the words of the Kohlensyndikat representative at a meeting of the SHV Board of Directors on 19 June 1906, who: "... gave as his opinion that under the present conditions, that is, at the still persisting shortage of coal and coke, it cannot be in the interest of the Kohlensyndikat to extend the export and therefore he does not deem it advisable to purchase more material for the time being...".

In 1907 the SHV took a following step in the application of grabs to coal handling. In that year, it put into use a location on the Maashaven, equipped with, among other things, a shore-based grab crane with a lifting capacity of 5 tons,

[11] SHV Archives, Jaarverslag SHV, 1905/06.

where mainly coal was handled that was brought in by rail (Sneller 1946, 213). Just as the basalt crane mentioned earlier, the SHV-crane consisted of a slewing crane on a bridge (Inspectie 1913, 71). In that year, in the New Waterway area, the firm of De Poorter in Maassluis owned a gantry crane (Moderne kabelbanen 1907, 235). In contrast to the existing shore-based or floating slewing cranes, a gantry crane made a straight movement at discharging and loading of the cargo. In this way, a much higher handling speed was possible (Mills 1955, 115). Like Müller, De Poorter was an ore trading firm that used its own ships to transport the material to Rotterdam. At that time, ore could not be handled by grabs in a satisfactory way. When the ore consisted of large lumps, the grab could not close properly and the finer ore fell from the grab again. In working with the gantry crane De Poorter used buckets for ore and grabs for the coal it was also handling.

Again, a firm with a stake in several parts of the trade and transport chain of dry bulk cargo was responsible for a major innovation in Rotterdam stevedoring. However, it was a specialized stevedoring firm, Thomsen's Havenbedrijf, which became responsible for the major breakthrough of grab gantry cranes, or "loading bridges" as they were called, in Rotterdam. In 1912 the company installed four loading bridges with a lifting capacity of 8 tons each, built by the DEMAG factory in Duisburg. These DEMAG cranes differed from the ones built by Bleichert from Leipzig for De Poorter in several important respects. The De Poorter's crane had a fixed cab. In this case a long wire was used that ran along the entire length of the bridge. This was somewhat awkward because of the many pulleys and other parts across which the wires had to be guided. This made the energy consumption higher than that of the Thomsen cranes. In these loading bridges the trolley, with the grab suspended underneath, did not run along a wire, but along a rail under the bridge. The crane driver operated from a mobile cab, so that he "could keep abreast of" the grab and could also look into the ship's hold. Therefore, the crane driver had a better view of the cargo-handling operation here than from a fixed cab and could work faster (The loading bridges with mobile cabs, however, were more difficult to operate and had a higher purchase price (Zimmer 1916, 421, 423, 428-429)). The loading bridges installed by Thomsen were also equipped with a so-called slewing trolley. This enabled the grab to make a circle of 8.5 metres: large enough for covering an entire hold. During discharge the crane itself did not have to be moved: a considerable gain in time was the result (we may assume that at the same time, this also reduced the inflexibility of this type of crane in stacking and reclaiming on the shore). The DEMAG construction became the standard in the port of Rotterdam for the following decades.

In the period studied, the loading bridge is the only clear example of a major innovation in mineral bulk handling undertaken by a private stevedoring firm, which - to my knowledge - did not possess an exclusive contract or controlling stake in the mineral bulk trade. One - very well informed - observer argued that the fixed costs of a shore-based installation with several loading bridges were so high that only the few largest traders in mineral bulk would have been able to furnish this plant with enough work of their own (Serton 1946, 92). Therefore, stevedoring firms servicing several principals were the appropriate operators of these installations. The same author reasoned, however, that in coal trade the dominance of two large entities (SHV and SSM) made it logical that they would run stevedoring operations themselves (Serton, 1946, 111).

Why Thomsen decided to invest in loading bridges is not known. The purchase of the loading bridges was just one in a series of innovations Thomsen implemented in the port of Rotterdam in the twentieth century. After Jan Key - a former head of a post office who started to work at Thomsen in 1896 - had become one of the company's managing directors in 1903, the stevedoring firm again and again turned out to be a pioneer in technological innovation. It seems that the company since the arrival of Key in its management was trying to innovate wherever this was possible. In 1910, Thomsen was the first stevedoring firm to follow the example of SHV and put into use floating grab cranes for coal handling.

We do not know with certainty why the Thomsen-loading bridges were seen as a major breakthrough. A gain of 20% in the handling speed compared to floating grab cranes was impressive, but the difference in the rate of discharge between manual handling with buckets and floating grab cranes introduced before 1912 was certainly more than 20% (i.e., at least 100%) (Serton 1919, 90-91). Furthermore, discharge by floating cranes was cheaper, because for operations in midstream no use had to be made of the expensive quay infrastructure. On the other hand, the loading bridges were more versatile instruments than the floating grab cranes. They could easily discharge directly into barges as well as onto the shore, including bunkers from which rail wagons could be loaded. In addition, Thomsen introduced the loading bridges in a period that the technology had advanced so far that ore in general could also be discharged by means of grabs (in 1911 the first floating grab cranes for ore handling were introduced in Rotterdam by the Stuwadoors Maatschappij Victoria (nothing else is known about this company) and the Handels- en Transport Maatschappij "Vulcaan", a Rhine shipping company, founded in 1911 by the German mining-entrepreneur August Thyssen).

Judging from their reactions, it is clear that with the DEMAG loading bridges Thomsen took a huge lead on the other stevedoring companies, who felt forced to imitate the innovation. In 1913 Frans Swarttouw, until then the largest stand-alone dry bulk stevedoring firm, was convinced of the superiority of the shore-based gantry cranes over floating grab cranes and he ordered four loading bridges from DEMAG that, as it turned out, could not be delivered until 1922 because of the First World War (de Gast, Oosterwijk and de Regt 1987, 108-109). The investments raised the risks to such an extent that Thomsen was prepared to give up part of the advantages it had gained only shortly before, in order to reduce the competition by Frans Swarttouw to a significant degree[12]. In January 1915, both companies agreed that Thomsen would put part of its wharf at the Waalhaven at the disposal of Frans Swarttouw and even that Thomsen would lend its competitor money for the purpose of buying the loading bridges (in return Thomsen gained the right to appoint one supervisory director of Frans Swarttouw's firm, which

[12] For the following, see: ECT Archives, inv. no. 24766904, Bipartite contract between N.V. Thomsen's Havenbedrijf and N.V. Frans Swarttouw's Havenbedrijf and tripartite contract between the two companies and N.V. Corns Swarttouw's Stuwadoors- Mij., both dated 17 August 1922 and Contract between the Nederlandsche Havenbedrijf and the participants in the tripartite contract, June 1923 (unsigned).

was restructured into a public limited company at that time). Also the third large stevedoring firm, Cornelis Swarttouw's Stuwadoors Maatschappij, decided to order DEMAG loading bridges. On 17 August 1922 the financial alliance between Thomsen and Frans Swarttouw was extended to Cornelis Swarttouw. The three stevedoring firms then formed a profit-pooling agreement in bulk handling, called "The Combination". This was a major event, because since 1886, when the brothers Cornelis and Frans Swarttouw clashed about the continuation of the stevedoring activities of their deceased father, their firms had been fierce rivals. Because of Thomsen's move, the SHV for the first time was put in a subordinate position in the mechanical handling of coal: it had to recognize the superiority of Thomsen's loading bridges[13]. Apparently Thomsen did not only handle ore and import coal, but also infringed on the SHV's position in the handling of German export coal. Mid-1915 the SHV decided to purchase four of those loading bridges from DEMAG as well. Subsequently, as of 1 May 1923, the three partners in the Combination also made a market sharing agreement with the Nederlandsch Havenbedrijf, where the SHV's stevedoring interests were then placed. On balance, the loading bridges were innovations accompanied with risk reducing measures, in this case not before the first investments, but afterwards. In this way, the adoption of the new technology led to a strong concentration in the dry bulk stevedoring industry.

2.7. Conclusion

In the period between circa 1885 and 1920 a series of new techniques mechanized the handling of ore and coal in the port of Rotterdam. The culmination of all these innovations was the introduction of the most versatile technology imaginable, the floating and shore-based grab cranes. Direct transfer of cargo between sea-going vessel and barge became the common denominator of the techniques applied. In no other port this kind of direct transfer occurred on such a scale. The well-known image of Rotterdam as transit port emerges here. At several times, there was pressure from the German hinterland to innovate in cargo handling, in particular from the coal mines. However, local actors that were no passive followers of German initiatives or directives carried out the innovations. The main innovators were the municipality (until the turn of the century) and, in particular, private firms with a larger stake in transport and trading than cargo handling only. The innovative role of the municipality was more or less a consequence of its take-over of the Feijenoord installations in 1882, which was made necessary by the debacle of the original private owner. Nevertheless, by innovating in cargo handling itself, the city consciously absorbed the risks which private firms may have considered too high. When the focus in the innovations shifted to operations in midstream, private transportation and trading firms started to play a dominant role. They were the ones that directly benefited from the increase in speed. At the same time, as they supplied work to the cargo handling installations themselves, a certain utilization of the new expensive equipment was guaranteed in advance. In other words, the

[13] SHVA, Notulen Raad van Commissarissen van de SHV op 1 juli 1915.

Schumpeterian view of innovation was confirmed in the study: an oligopolistic structure of the trades involved promoted innovation in the handling of coal and ore. Contrary to the existing image, one has to conclude that in this important field Rotterdam was not a typical stevedores' port. Only at the end of the period studied, a major innovation by Thomsen started the advent of stevedoring companies in Rotterdam mineral bulk handling.

3. Comparison with Antwerp

It was remarkable how far Antwerp, Rotterdam's main competitor, lagged behind in the mechanization of coal and ore handling. In the 1896, a first coal tip was installed there (Decock 1978, 25-28). However, no grab cranes were introduced before the First World War. Manual handling remained dominant in the Antwerp mineral bulk sector until well into the twentieth century. In the year 1925 the discharge of about 2,000 tons of ore required six days in Antwerp versus two days in Rotterdam (Wäänänen 1930, 120).

One can only speculate about the reasons for this difference between Rotterdam and Antwerp. Maybe there was less need for innovation in mineral bulk handling in Antwerp, because in particular the coal trade was a "protected" trade after the First World War? Antwerp did not act as a large transit port for Germany, but mainly served its own national hinterland. However, this cannot explain why the speed and the costs of cargo handling should be of less interest to Antwerp shippers and receivers and why they should have taken a more passive attitude towards innovation than their Rotterdam counterparts (in fact, sometimes these actors were users of both ports). A possible explanation is that Antwerp deliberately left bulk handling to Rotterdam and focused itself on general cargo. In such an explanation, however, the Antwerp port is too much seen as an entity, as a "black box". It is certainly true that the Antwerp docks at least until 1907 - when an important expansion programme was agreed upon - were too narrow to permit the typical Rotterdam practice of direct transfer of bulk cargo between seagoing vessels and barges in midstream on a large scale. Nevertheless, fast handling by shore-based equipment was possible and the example of relatively quick adoption of the pneumatic grain elevators from 1910 onwards shows that there was room for the application of floating cargo-handling equipment in Antwerp.

It is clear that not much innovative activity was to be expected from incumbent cargo handling firms in Antwerp during this period. The relevant existing private companies, the "naties" (firms involved in cargo handling as well as local transport and distribution) and the stevedores, had little capital. The "naties", established as co-operatives, for example, each year still paid out their profits to the partners. As is suggested in the paper by Greta Devos in this volume, the municipality showed itself remarkably sensitive to the interests of these numerous existing small cargo-handling firms. On several occasions, initiatives for new large-scale cargo handling installations by financially strong outsiders were blocked by the city, formally because the government feared a monopoly, but also because it wished to protect vested interests. In addition, unlike Rotterdam, the city of Antwerp - with the exception of the floating grain elevators - did not invest in specialized dry bulk cargo-handling equipment, probably because it considered the financial burden of underutilization as too high. So, maybe differences in the financial position and the financial policy of both municipalities can help to explain the different paths of innovation followed in Rotterdam and Antwerp. Not until 1929 did the municipality of Antwerp decide to order two loading bridges, to be used by Stocatra, a joint venture of the two largest Belgian Rhine shipping firms (Lemayeur 1998, 261). The wish to strengthen its position in relation to Rotterdam played a major role in this decision.

4. Epilogue

A final word on the representativeness of the pattern of innovation in coal and ore handling in this paper for the technological development of the port of Rotterdam as a whole is due here. Around 1923, when the sector of mineral bulk stevedoring had been consolidated by several cartel and pool agreements, innovation by sector-wide collaboration could be considered a routine in the port of Rotterdam. In grain stevedoring, the Graan Elevator Maatschappij (Grain Elevator Company) was founded in 1908 as the outcome of the heavily contested innovation of the pneumatic grain elevators. This joint venture represented a very broad community of interests, including the major shipping agents and stevedores and several important traders, and it maintained a quasi-monopoly in Rotterdam grain handling until the 1980s. After the loading bridges of 1912, the port of Rotterdam had to wait for a new major innovation in stevedoring for decades. From the late 1950s, under the pressure of a spectacular increase in ship sizes, the Rotterdam practice of transferring dry bulk cargo directly between sea-going vessel and barge was replaced more and more by indirect transfer via the shore. A new kind of bulk terminal was built, characterized by belt conveyors, which until then were hardly used in Rotterdam. The pioneer was an end user: Hanna Mining Company, an American ore mining company and shipper, that became involved in Rotterdam stevedoring by a joint venture with its European agent, Müller & Co. Incumbent stevedoring firms and other trading companies and industrial users followed suit, in several cases in combination.

Finally, containerization revolutionized break bulk handling. In 1966, even before containerization had started, the five largest Rotterdam stevedores decided to allocate their entire container handling activities to a joint venture, the Europe Container Terminus. This company, which was renamed in Europe Combined Terminals in 1989, became responsible for a series of important innovations in container handling, culminating in the semi-automated terminals on the Maasvlakte. In recent years, more and more deep-sea shipping firms - and in the case of Antwerp even a railway company[14] - have indicated that they want to have their own "dedicated" terminals in ports like Rotterdam and Antwerp. This large involvement by shipping firms with general cargo handling is a new phenomenon

[14] See the paper by Theo Notteboom in this volume.

in both ports, although it partially resembles the situation in the late nineteenth and early twentieth century. However, thus far this growing interest of shipping companies in cargo handling has not resulted in major innovations, simply because the container still seems to be the superior technology for general cargo handling.

References

Barras R (1986) Towards a Theory of Innovation in Services. Research Policy XV: 161-173

Buhle M (1901) Technische Hülfsmittel zur Beförderung und Lagerung von Sammelkörpern (Massengütern). Berlin

Cunningham B (1926) Cargo handling at Ports. London

de Gast K, Oosterwijk B, de Regt W (1987) Wij pakken alles. Honderd jaar Frans Swarttouw (1887-1987). Rotterdam

Decock P (1978) De evolutie van de havenuitrusting voor goederenbehandeling. Deel 1: van de oudste tijden tot wereldoorlog II. Hinterland: 25-28

Devos G, van Driel H (2000) De regulering van de overslag in de havens van Antwerpen en Rotterdam tussen 1870 en 1950. NEHA-jaarboek voor de economische, bedrijfs- en techniekgeschiedenis, LXIII: 145-165

Dresselhuijs JD (1911) Inleiding tot het bezoek aan de steenkolen-transporteurs van de Steenkolen-Handelsvereeniging te Rotterdam op 22 October 1910. De Ingenieur XXVI-4: 196

Haase A (1913) Die modernen Lösch- und Ladeeinrichtungen und ihre Bedeutung für die Seeschiffahrtsbetriebe. Jena

Klein BH (1977) Dynamic Economics. Cambridge

Lemayeur B (1998) De geschiedenis van de Onderneming Plouvier (1896-1997). In: Baetens R (ed) Spiegels van Mercurius. Plouvier & Kreglinger. Tweehonderd Jaar Handel en Maritiem Transport te Antwerpen. Deurne

Mills HR (1955) Discharge of Iron Cargoes. Part 3. Cargo Handling: 115

Moderne (1907) kabelbanen en overlaadinrichtingen (deel 4), Holdert's Polytechnisch Weekblad I, no. 30 (14 augustus 1907), 235

Nusteling HPH (1974) De Rijnvaart in het tijdperk van stoom en steenkool 1831-1914. Amsterdam

Oram RB (1965) Cargo handling and the modern port. Oxford

Oram RB, Baker CCR (1971) The efficient port. Oxford

Serton P (1919) Rotterdam als haven voor massale goederen. Nijmegen

Sneller (1946) Geschiedenis van den steenkolenhandel van Rotterdam. Groningen

van Driel H, de Goey F (2000) Rotterdam Cargo-Handling Technology 1870-2000. Zutphen

van Rijckevorsel WFH (1912) Het spoorweggoederenvervoer te Rotterdam, De Ingenieur XXVII-10: 211 (5 maart 1912)

Wäänänen I (1930) Rotterdam als Seehafen unter besonderer Berücksichtigung des Konkurrenzkampfes mit Antwerpen. Weida in Thür

Wilhelm D (1966) Das Rheinisch-Westfälische Kohlensyndikat und die Oberschlesische Kohlenkonvention bis zum Jahre 1933. Erlangen
Wundram O (1939) Mechanische Hafenausrüstungen insbesondere für den Umschlag. Berlin
Zimmer GF (1905) The mechanical handling of material. London
Zimmer GF (1916) The mechanical handling and storing of material. London

Commentary on the paper of Van Driel

Gordon Jackson

University of Strathclyde, United Kingdom

Van Driel's fine paper is an important exploration of the circumstances surrounding the adoption of technical changes in the port of Rotterdam in which, having established a theoretical basis for innovation, he examines the details of mechanization there. These comments are not a criticism of his argument or facts, but rather a suggestion that the history of Rotterdam and Antwerp ports might be further illuminated by contextual and comparative study.

It is possible to view innovation in theoretical terms by examining the well-known inter-relationship of invention and innovation, seeing the "entrepreneur" as the innovator in search of profit in a risky market. While that may explain events within individual firms, it may not offer a total explanation of mechanization within very complex port systems, where individual firms may be of little account, and where competition between ports may alter views about the necessity of "risky" innovation. On the one hand new equipment was of no value if port and transport infrastructures were not concurrently available or coming on-stream. But, for ports as a whole, innovation was not an "optional extra" in the late nineteenth century period. They either mechanized, or failed to secure or develop what were, in many cases, *new* trades; and if that happened national economies would also fail to develop. In this regard the details of innovation in Rotterdam and Antwerp are clearly of importance, and their significance as part of both port and general economic development may be more clearly understood by a comparison with similar ports in Britain which, because of its early start in both trade and port infrastructures, was more experienced in the mechanization of transport. In the circumstances there is little wonder that German coal producers were anxious about conditions in Rotterdam, and one is surprized that they did not try more effectively to by-pass the Rhine.

The boom in Rotterdam trade and facilities from the 1880s to 1914 was in no way remarkable. It was but a minor part of the "Europeanization" of the world, drawing raw materials and foodstuffs to Europe and sending manufactures and migrants to vast new tracts of territory in America, Africa and the East. This is turn depended on the evolution of the large modern steamer in the 1880s, which in turn was an outcome of the boom in iron and steel production and of mechanical engineering in general. Thousands of inventions eased the way towards the modern world: the ship-test tank, for instance, rarely noted but without which large vessels could not have been constructed. Civil engineering enabled longer quays and deeper water. Moreover, since ports were "intermediaries" in the transport business, it is worth considering whether business initiatives and integration outlined by Van Driel played a greater or lesser role than the concurrent integration of all manner of inland and external transport mechanisms which raised the flow of goods for which the innovations were required.

It would be interesting to know to what extent stevedores were free agents in their innovations. They obviously played a part, but one suspects that the pace of change may have been determined by port, railway and local government authorities who created the physical context without which they "could not have modernized" and with which they "were forced to modernize". Rotterdam was certainly a strange mix of influences for a mineral port, and needs comparison with British ports to determine unique features and evaluate their application. Since minerals were the major consumers of shipping and dock space in Britain, there was less movement from "integrated" firms to stand-alone stevedoring firms (or vice-versa) than appears in Rotterdam. For instance, the first British steam railway - the Stockton-Darlington - was created to carry coal from Darlington to the company's own staithes at Port Darlington, in Stockton; and railway/dock/port integration was inherent in many subsequent developments in both coal ports and in general commercial ports, where minerals were often the principal trades by volume[1]. But comparison also raises another issue. The apparent muddle and inefficiencies in Rotterdam's early mineral handling were perhaps of financial benefit, but perhaps also they were only possible because Rotterdam's mineral traffic was small in comparison with even a medium-sized British mineral port. Whoever would have thought of a major port unloading coal wagons by grab crane? The relative importance of Rotterdam's coal and iron-ore trades would be worth assessing, especially in relation to the investment in equipment. It might also be worth considering that mechanization can be seen as a function of the price of dock labour, which presumably depended on the general wage levels in a country less developed industrially than Britain or Germany. However this only works up to a point. The labour-saving machinery described by van Driel was essential anyway if larger volumes were to be handled without causing unacceptable - and expensive! - congestion. As far as the stevedores were concerned, the reasonable assumption that uncertain innovation involved high risk may result from this relatively low through-put in minerals at a time when the insistence on competition may well have prevented profits from reaching a level which would have supported investment in (locally) untried innovations. This raises serious questions about the function of stevedores. If it was their job to handle cargoes using their own equipment, one might guess that they would not be enthusiastic about investing. New trade in its early stages may shift between competing ports or agents or shipowners, thus reducing the certainty of stevedores who will put off investment until they are reasonably sure of their customers' loyalty. As trade improves they will gradually invest, which in turn will produce more trade, which will exceed the capacity of facilities, which will mean that further custom will be lost unless more facilities are laid on, and so "ad infinitum". It may be that the problem in Rotterdam was aggravated by the relatively small amount of throughput

[1] For early integration in Britain see Jackson 1983, 83-9 and chapter 5 for the impact of the coal trade on ports, 1870-1914. The importance of coal and the physical structure of the trade is described briefly in Hoole 1972; and in great detail in Newham 1908. For Grimsby, see Anon 1913.

and the reliance on barge transport. Where trades were established, profits reasonably assured and volumes very large, as in the major British coal ports, the ownership of expensive facilities (of which dedicated coal docks and mineral quays were the chief) was from the start in the hands of dock and/or railway companies, and mechanization as and where appropriate was a necessary part of the whole process. On the other hand, the partial monopoly of "their" coalfield enjoyed by British ports was mirrored in the monopoly of the German coal owners and their move into stevedoring.

There is another issue here. In order to save costs, many British mineral harbours were custom-built outside existing ports, where innovation was easier, while other major ports or railways tried to poach coal traffic to intensify the use of their rails, or provide export cargoes for ships that would otherwise leave in ballast, thus raising the costs of using the ports[2]. By what process of business or legal privileges did Rotterdam retain control of German coal and iron-ore traffic, and why was handling equipment introduced in Rotterdam rather than at dedicated quays elsewhere? Was it simply the lack of alternative waterways plus that famous link to the sea? Or was the coal cartel happy enough with a single outlet over which it had at least some control? If, as suggested, coal was a desired return cargo (alternative to ballasting) that may largely answer this question. Many British commercial ports sought to attract coal to their quays.

Comparisons also raise questions about the over-all background to innovation. Simple bulk-handling methods were centuries old, and only changed when trade expanded rapidly with steam transport and hydraulic power. In Britain coal, steel, ships, mechanical engineering, civil and dock engineering and inland transport systems all developed together in a highly integrated manner. By comparison the Dutch economy was under-developed, and one would appreciate a more detailed examination of the sources of inspiration behind entrepreneurial decisions. How far were they German in origin? It looks as if Rotterdam's problems had arisen because its early manual handling system could not cope with relatively fast trade expansion, and this surely indicates that there was a structural flaw in a port where there was no obvious financial or decision-making connection between the private stevedores, the port authority and the private inland transport system. Is there any justification for *not* believing that Van Driel is right to emphasize that the only options were for the German industrialists to enter the port industry, or, when serious investment was required, for the port authority to interfere when the operations of handling systems produced a bottle-neck threatening the competence of the port. So far as the actions of individual stevedoring firms are concerned, in demanding or inventing handling systems, or applying those developed elsewhere, this outside observer would appreciate a little more detail, since the actual direction of influences in mechanization are notoriously difficult to determine.

---

[2] The Hull & Barnsley Railway and Dock Company was formed to draw Yorkshire coal to Hull in the 1880s, while the North Eastern Railway had earlier tried to divert expanding coal traffic from Hull (because it would mean increasing the number of its lines) to its own port at West Hartlepool which was underused, largely because it was an unwise speculation.

The fact that Rotterdam did not build enclosed docks in the British fashion may also have affected the role of the entrepreneurial stevedore in the application of machinery, since it was long the custom in Britain that docks and their equipment were designed by Consulting Engineers (or, in the case of major ports, by their Chief Engineer), who also introduced the most modern cranes, coal handling equipment, and so on, as part of the design. In fact mechanization was not beneficial only to its *user*. Since its object was to permit or increase the flow of goods, a faster turn-round of shipping reduced pressure on harbour and quay space and was therefore of interest to both port authorities and shipowners, who also put pressure on stevedores.

One major difference between Rotterdam and most British mineral ports was the degree of over-side handling which offers a chance to assess the relative demand for mechanization from rail and barge systems and its value to port operators in the different systems. There is, perhaps, a paradox here. Rhine transport was inherently cheaper than land carriage, and capital costs were obviously cheaper than building railways. But the handling of coal (more than iron-ore) over-side appears primitive compared with high level delivery systems employed in major British ports (even more so the emptying of railway wagons by grab cranes!) The question is: how far was the cheapness of barge transport offset by the time-penalty of increased demurrage and inventory costs, and handling costs in Rotterdam harbour? It would be interesting to know if anyone in Rotterdam experimented with possible variants of the elevators installed in Goole by the Aire & Calder Navigation Company in 1868 to raise and tip small barges into ship's holds (designed, incidentally, by the company's own chief engineer). Were conveyor delivery systems as efficient as coal hoists?

The motives of innovative entrepreneurs - and the obstacles to easy decision-making - are fairly clear. But in many areas of port activity the investment costs are inevitably huge and, as van Driel points out, such matters are better dealt with outside the vagaries of competitive capitalism. It may be important to note that the "Staatspoorwegen" introduced the first Rotterdam coal tips in their own harbour at the instigation of the Westphalian coal-owners. (This may have been a tacit admission that the most sensible way to transport coal is by railway!) Most attempts at vertical integration were basically attempts to carry into transport operations the monopoly that ensured the profitability of the coal and steel companies. How far, then, was modernization in Rotterdam hampered or delayed by the insistence of the port authority that competition between stevedores should be maximized? And would the mineral sector of port activity have benefited from further integration of stevedoring and other transport operations? One thing seems clear: when mechanization became really expensive it was undertaken not by competitive capitalism but by either the port authority or the coal companies themselves. So perhaps the era of encouraging competitive stevedoring was a passing phase in the early development of a port which by necessity or design had chosen a different system of mineral transportation system from that which had evolved, with much trial, error and success, in nineteenth century Britain.

Collaboration makes sense, and was the traditional system for maintaining the physical structure of ports and regulating trade within the legal confines of their privileged, self-governing, burghs. Their leading citizens built and maintained quays and cranes, dredged silt and regulated trade, financed by taxes on usage. For various practical, financial and misguided doctrinaire reasons, this system did not survive the British industrial revolution. Towns lost control over their ports.

There seems to have been no doubt in Holland or Belgium about waterways, harbour and quays, which were provided by local or national governments, with the result that facilities in the twentieth century were far superior to those affordable in Britain. This is worth some elaboration, since the system was not followed successfully in Britain. Was it because the emerging industrial/trading nations were too poor, or because they lacked the effective railway industry that built or bought its own ports in Britain? In any event the contribution of Dutch government funding is of great importance in assessing the success or failure of the British and Dutch ports, especially in recent times. The downside of this was a determination at all levels to prevent monopoly *within* ports. In Britain, on the other hand, the chief concern among manufacturers appears to have been the prevention of monopoly *by* ports, a policy which led to wasteful duplication of facilities, encouraged not least by competing railway companies, who themselves were often regarded as monopolists disregarding the interest of the port community[3].

Although a single, sensible authority may control a port, the creation of particular facilities is still a finely-balanced response to the needs of vastly differing interests. When and where should water be deepened, oil jetties built, cranes for ship's engines and boilers provided, electricity installed, larger cranes, conveyors, grabs and hoists erected? The demands of liners were completely different from those of coal exporters and corn importers and ports had to decide which interest group, which size of ship or type of quay, should receive a ration of limited funds. Clearly much depended on the quality of the port authority; and that meant the people in charge, whose biographies might be worth examining to elucidate the experience they brought to the higher levels of port management on which mechanization ultimately depended. Was there a chief port engineer in Rotterdam in this period? Who led the pressure for port modernization or mechanization, and by what networking of personalities and organizations were ideas (and complaints) transmitted round the port? The local newspapers were a common medium in Britain. Was the same true of Rotterdam?

The physical structure of ports commonly impinges on the merchant quarter and the "sailor town" and here, too, there are interests to be balanced. Above all, what goes on in a port at the highest level of innovation, namely the building of new quays, the extension of timber yards, the doubling, trebling, quadrupling of rails, or the introduction of noxious chemicals, is determined not least by the value of land and the structure of land-ownership within the port. In some of the British cases local landowners were a driving force in development: the Marquis of Bute in Cardiff; the Earl of Yarborough in Grimsby; the Earl of Eglington in Ayrshire; and the Dukes of Devonshire and Buccleuch in Cumbria.

Anywhere in Britain serious mechanization usually involved acquiring very expensive urban land for docks or quays, and required an Act of Parliament (which was itself expensive), so some brief mention of the legal and financial background to innovation might reveal the comparative underlying costs in European ports. So

[3] For the most obvious example, see Jackson 1989.

too, would a consideration of the political influence of Rotterdam. In major British ports it was taken for granted that one of the leading merchants or shipowners would enter Parliament. The Wilson brothers in Hull debated at length which of them should enter Parliament and which should run Thomas Wilson & Sons, with the world's largest private fleet; it was a necessary sacrifice. By what process was Rotterdam's influence exercized?

Above all, to the integrated innovations essential to port growth - transport systems, harbours and quays, abundant land and appropriate warehouses - the attitudes of central government are crucial. Ports in Britain competed with each other to handle goods brought and sent by rail, and so could be created wherever there was a suitable coastal situation. But the Rhine was a one-off feature. Rotterdam had little to fear for the port infrastructure, and short of building very extensive railways there was no alternative to improving its seaward connection. That was so important that it was regarded as essential to the State's well-being. No British port, not even London was in such a favourable position. While Rotterdam with its privileged monopoly role became a world-class port, London began its slide into the deep because competing dock companies over-invested in what was essentially an out-of-date place.

Finally, in all things to do with ports it was the inter-play of people that got things done. Unfortunately the understandable modern interest in "theory" explaining economic growth or business functions tends to underestimate the role of people, and the same thing happens in many port histories which, sometimes for lack of sources, treat physical structures in the abstract, as lumps of concrete and iron, rather than the designed facilitators of the business of ports: shifting goods and ships with maximum speed. The recent work which has been done on dock engineers (especially in Liverpool; Jarvis 1996) helps to set port innovation in perspective. Now that we have an increasing knowledge of what went on inside ports it might be time to work outwards from what actually happened to a general theory, rather than starting with an abstract theory based on a slight (and sometimes curiously manipulated) data source and work inwards to explain how ports worked. There might then emerge a clearer understanding of the differences between, and the relative advantages and disadvantages of, "extended river ports" such as Rotterdam compared with "concentrated docks ports" of the usual British sort. One thing is clear: in the history of ports something as hidden away by historians as mechanization (and its motivation) is actually at the very heart of port operations, and Van Driel is to be congratulated in drawing it so ably to our notice.

References

Anon. (1913) Per Rail (Privately printed for Great Central Railway Co)
Hoole K (ed.) (1972) The Hull & Barnsley Railway. Hull. vol. 1
Jackson G (1983) The History and Archaeology of Ports. Tadworth
Jackson G (1989) Shipowners and Private Dock Companies. In: Akveld LM, Bruijn JR (eds.) Shipping Companies and Authorities in the 19th and 20th Centuries: Their Common Interest in the Development of Port Facilities. Den Haag, pp 47-61
Jarvis A (1996) The Liverpool Dock Engineers. Liverpool
Newham HEC (ed.) (1908) Hull as a Coal Port. Hull

Research agenda

Opportunities in comparative Antwerp-Rotterdam port history

Erik Buyst, Reginald Loyen

University of Leuven, Belgium

The main theme of this volume is the evolution of the seaports of Antwerp and Rotterdam over the last century and a half. The papers presented here have emphasized micro- and macro-economic as well as institutional, social and political factors to explain the spectacular growth of both ports. The volume illustrates once again that, for seaports, history does matter. Decisions taken decades ago still determine to a considerable degree the functioning of both ports today. Therefore, a long-term view of seaport development not only enhances our understanding of the current situation, but also and more importantly helps us to distinguish promising new developments from lingering old ones.

After fifteen papers and several lively discussions, let me return to the general concept of this volume. The first aim was to present the major conclusions of our research project on "functional shifts" in the port of Antwerp. After four years of hard work, it was time to present our findings to an international audience of maritime economic historians. The second goal was to give a boost to the just started comparative project on Antwerp-Rotterdam port history. The many useful comments and suggestions made during the conference will certainly be taken on board and will improve the quality of the projects' outcome in a significant way.

In this context, the emphasis on the comparative element is of decisive importance. For several decades, maritime economic historians, economists and geographers alike have investigated the development of Rotterdam and Antwerp extensively, but separately. So far, only few attempts have been made to analyse both ports from a comparative perspective. As a rule, papers in the field of port history tend to be single-port studies. Therefore we have coupled a scholar on Antwerp, to one on Rotterdam.

As conference organizers, we have explicitly asked for problem oriented papers and we have been well served indeed. In so doing we attempted to find out why and how the two ports reacted so differently to virtually the same economic, social and political trends. Consequently, we were not so much interested in describing, but in explaining each port's core-business, i.e. throughput.

The problem-oriented approach implies however that the reader will look in vain for a broad survey of seaport development. In emphasizing the comparative dimension, many other important aspects of port development have been left for future research. Let me name only but a few of them. We have only sporadically touched upon the important manufacturing plants in both ports. Thus business history largely remained out of the picture. A far-reaching spatial analysis of the ports' development was also left for the geographers to complete. The recent waterfront redevelopment and the urban dimension, which is invariable part of every major port-city, was hardly discussed. Contrary to many maritime economic conferences and notwithstanding its importance, innovations in shipping were only marginally touched upon. On the land-side, technological progress in trains and trucks was ignored as well, despite its importance for port development.

As indicated before, the volume does not intend to exhaustively cover the development of both seaports. Besides the emphasis on throughput, we have concentrated on the pivotal role of local players, namely port authority and port users. The interaction between the port authority and the port users after all determines the economic fate of the ports of Rotterdam and Antwerp. Since both ports are largely subject to the same international social and economic trends and share virtually the same hinterland, the actions of these local players account to a substantial degree for the two separate paths of development experienced.

Now that new databases and hypotheses have been launched, it is time to take some distance and to evaluate the new research opportunities for port history in the Low Countries. The many research questions, which appeared in the margin of the "functional shift project", encouraged us to set up a new, more comparative research project together with our colleagues and friends of the Erasmus University Rotterdam. The Dutch-Flemish research council (VNC) generously honoured our proposal.

The basic point of departure of our analysis is the following stylised fact. Although the ports of Rotterdam and Antwerp were confronted throughout history with the same exogenous factors and the same hinterland, they became entirely different ports: Antwerp focused on general cargo and Rotterdam on bulk trade. How did this division of labour come about? Are these ports complementary? To what extent did transport prices and port transit costs (port dues, pilotage fees, cargo handling costs etc.) determine the development of both ports? Using a long term comparative perspective the project intends to disentangle the many but often hidden interactions between both ports.

By estimating the value added related to those activities we hope to break new ground in historical port research. Value added is indeed a crucial variable to evaluate the economic performance of a port. We hope that this quantitative framework will serve as a basis for further research. We also hope that the Rotterdam-Antwerp comparative effort in the longer run will be extended to the other ports in the Le Havre-Hamburg range and the British ports. Only in this way we will get insight into the mechanisms of port choice and port development.

Annex

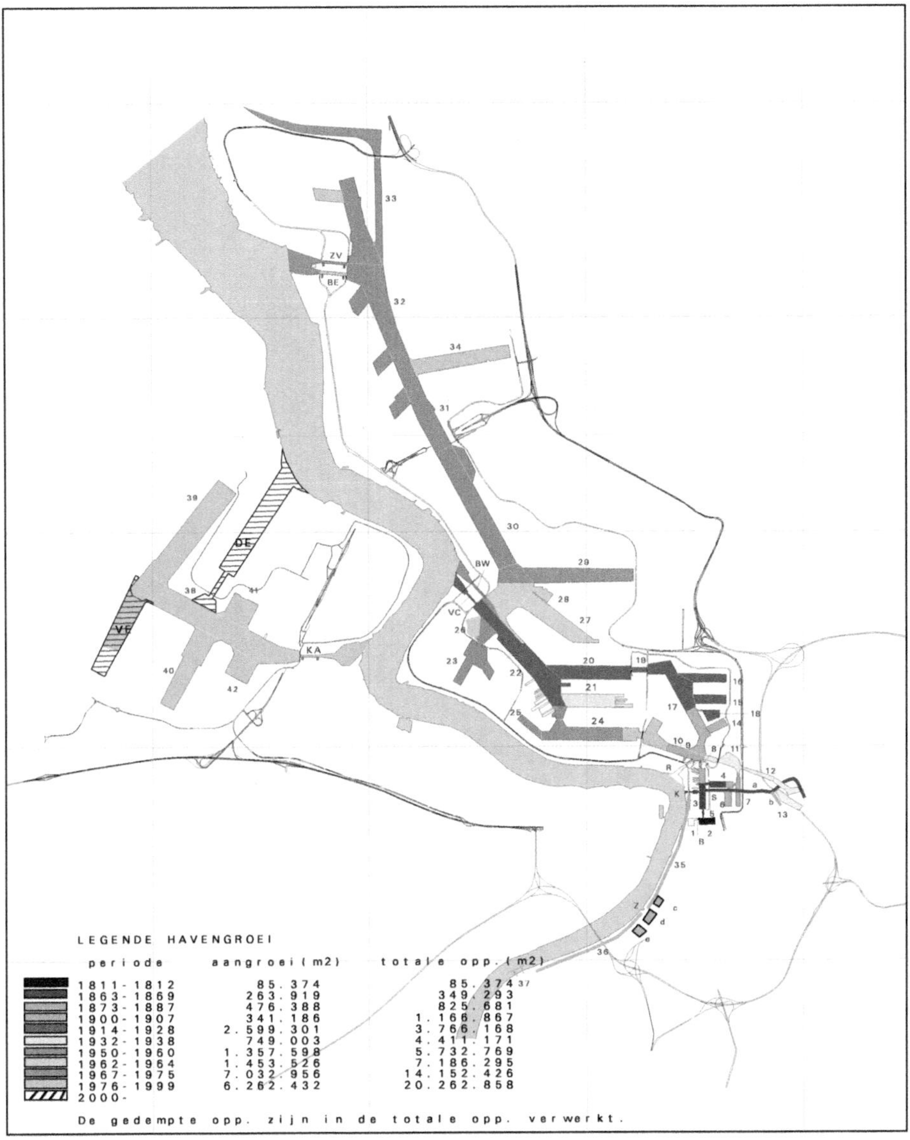

LEGENDE HAVENGROEI

periode	aangroei (m2)	totale opp. (m2)
1811-1812	85.374	85.374
1863-1869	263.919	349.293
1873-1887	476.388	825.681
1900-1907	341.186	1.166.867
1914-1928	2.599.301	3.766.168
1932-1938	749.003	4.411.171
1950-1960	1.357.598	5.732.769
1962-1964	1.453.526	7.186.295
1967-1975	7.032.956	14.152.426
1976-1999	6.262.432	20.262.858
2000-		

De gedempte opp. zijn in de totale opp. verwerkt.

SCHAAL 1/75000

meter

0 750 1500 2250 3000

N

LAMBERT 72

GX 136608 GY 205985
GX 157384 GY 232235

Raster 5000m

PORT OF ANTWERP

GIS

UITGAVE 22-MAY-2002

Referentienr. 29713

Evolutie Antwerpse Haven

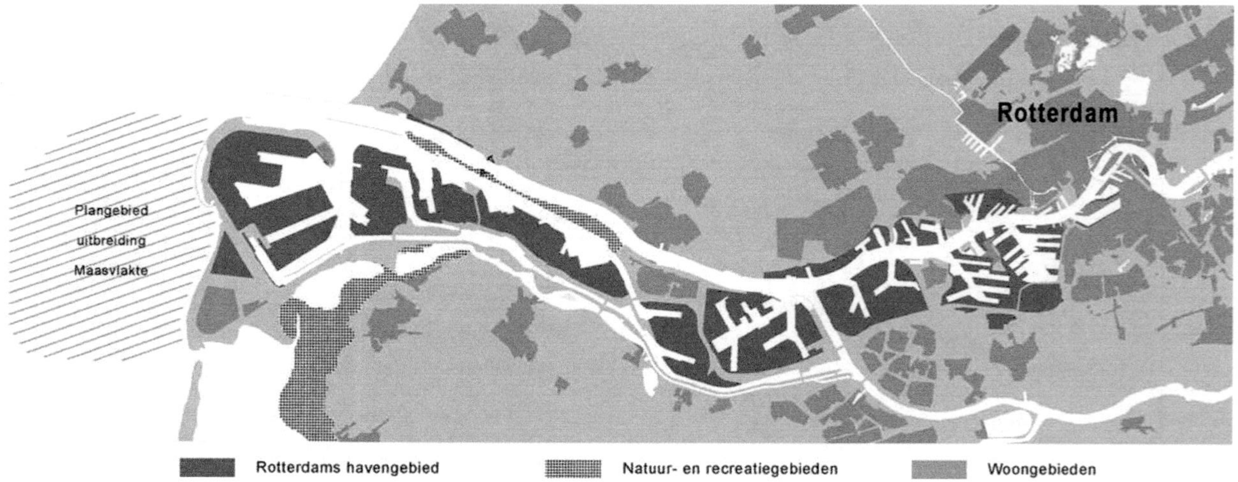
Rotterdam
Plangebied
uitbreiding
Maasvlakte
Rotterdams havengebied
Natuur- en recreatiegebieden
Woongebieden

Contributions to Economics

Nikolaus Thumm
Intellectual Property Rights
2000. ISBN 3-7908-1329-X

Max Keilbach
Spatial Knowledge Spillovers and the Dynamics of Agglomeration and Regional Growth
2000. ISBN 3-7908-1321-4

Alexander Karmann (Ed.)
Financial Structure and Stability
2000. ISBN 3-7908-1332-X

Joos P.A. van Vugt/Jan M. Peet (Eds.)
Social Security and Solidarity in the European Union
2000. ISBN 3-7908-1334-6

Johannes Bröcker/Hayo Herrmann (Eds.)
Spatial Change and Interregional Flows in the Integrating Europe
2001. ISBN 3-7908-1344-3

Kirstin Hubrich
Cointegration Analysis in a German Monetary System
2001. ISBN 3-7908-1352-4

Nico Heerink et al. (Eds.)
Economic Policy and Sustainable Land Use
2001. ISBN 3-7908-1351-6

Friedel Bolle/Michael Carlberg (Eds.)
Advances in Behavioral Economics
2001. ISBN 3-7908-1358-3

Volker Grossmann
Inequality, Economic Growth, and Technological Change
2001. ISBN 3-7908-1364-8

Thomas Riechmann
Learning in Economics
2001. ISBN 3-7908-1384-2

Miriam Beblo
Bargaining over Time Allocation
2001. ISBN 3-7908-1391-5

Peter Meusburger/Heike Jöns (Eds.)
Transformations in Hungary
2001. ISBN 3-7908-1412-1

Claus Brand
Money Stock Control and Inflation Targeting in Germany
2001. ISBN 3-7908-1393-1

Erik Lüth
Private Intergenerational Transfers and Population Aging
2001. ISBN 3-7908-1402-4

Nicole Pohl
Mobility in Space and Time
2001. ISBN 3-7908-1380-X

Pablo Coto-Millán (Ed.)
Essays on Microeconomics and Industrial Organisation
2002. ISBN 3-7908-1390-7

Mario A. Maggioni
Clustering Dynamics and the Locations of High-Tech-Firms
2002. ISBN 3-7908-1431-8

Ludwig Schätzl/Javier Revilla Diez (Eds.)
Technological Change and Regional Development in Europe
2002. ISBN 3-7908-1460-1

Alberto Quadrio Curzio/Marco Fortis (Eds.)
Complexity and Industrial Clusters
2002. ISBN 3-7908-1471-7

Friedel Bolle/Marco Lehmann-Waffenschmidt (Eds.)
Surveys in Experimental Economics
2002. ISBN 3-7908-1472-5

Pablo Coto-Millán
General Equilibrium and Welfare
2002. ISBN 7908-1491-1

Wojciech W. Charemza/Krystyna Srzala (Eds.)
East European Transition and EU Enlargement
2002. ISBN 3-7908-1501-2

Natalja von Westernhagen
Systemic Transformation, Trade and Economic Growth
2002. ISBN 3-7908-1521-7

Josef Falkinger
A Theory of Employment in Firms
2002. ISBN 3-7908-1520-9

Engelbert Plassmann
Econometric Modelling of European Money Demand
2003. ISBN 3-7908-1522-5